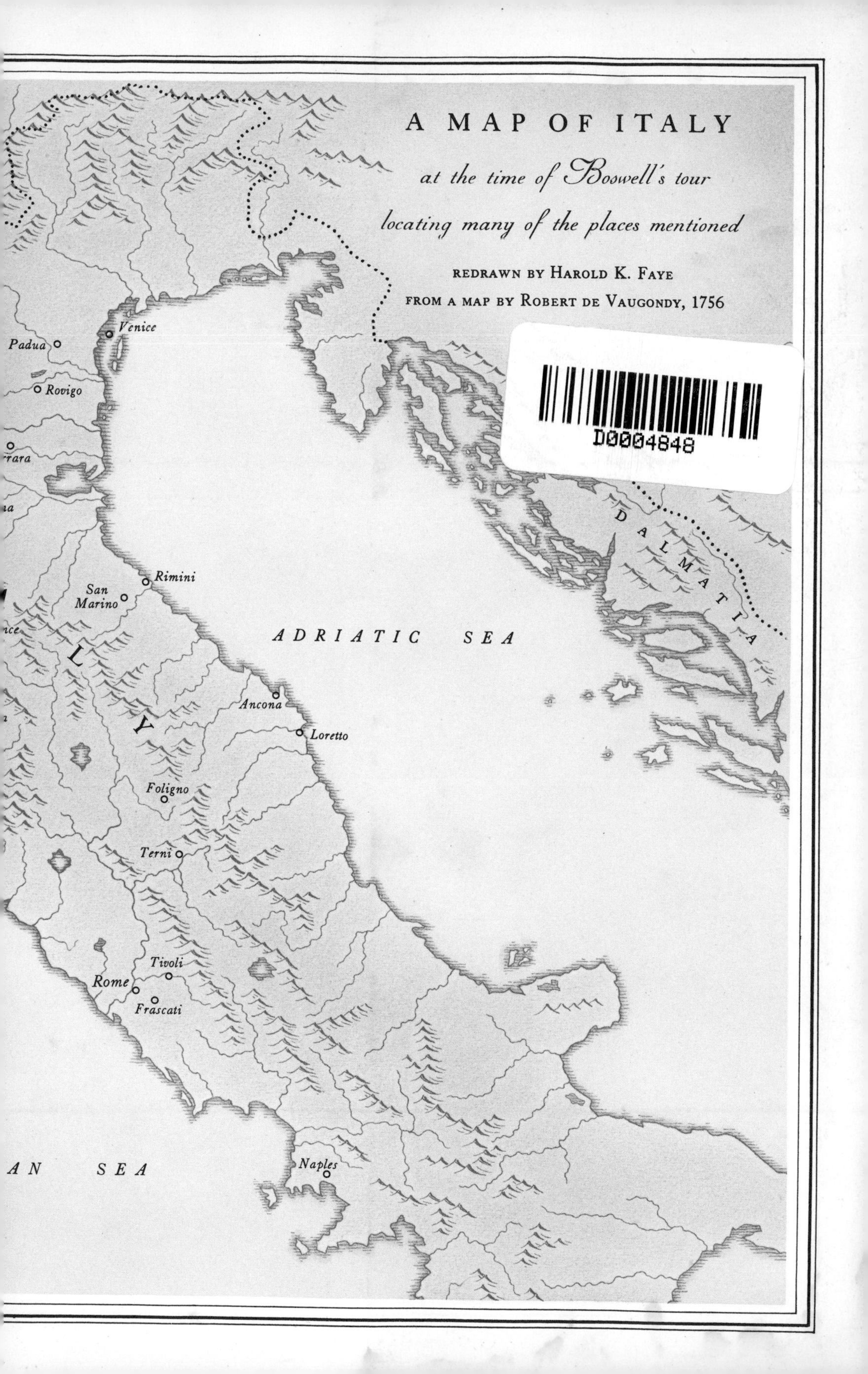
A MAP OF ITALY
at the time of Boswell's tour
locating many of the places mentioned
REDRAWN BY HAROLD K. FAYE
FROM A MAP BY ROBERT DE VAUGONDY, 1756
Venice
Padua
Rovigo
Rimini
San Marino
ADRIATIC SEA
DALMATIA
Ancona
Loretto
Foligno
Terni
Tivoli
Rome
Frascati
Naples
SEA
D0004848

THE YALE EDITIONS OF

*The Private Papers of James Boswell*

*Boswell's London Journal*, 1762–1763

*Boswell in Holland*, 1763–1764

*Portraits*, BY SIR JOSHUA REYNOLDS

*Boswell on the Grand Tour: Germany and Switzerland*, 1764

*Boswell on the Grand Tour: Italy, Corsica, and France*, 1765–1766

The Campo Vaccino, or Forum, engraved by Giovanni Battista Piranesi; from a print in the collection of Warren H. Lowenhaupt.

# ON THE GRAND TOUR

## ITALY, CORSICA, AND FRANCE

## 1765 - 1766

EDITED BY FRANK BRADY, INSTRUCTOR IN ENGLISH
AND FREDERICK A. POTTLE, STERLING PROFESSOR OF ENGLISH
YALE UNIVERSITY

McGRAW-HILL BOOK COMPANY, INC.

NEW YORK TORONTO LONDON

 Library of Congress Catalogue Card Number: 55-7270

FIRST EDITION

## EDITORIAL COMMITTEE



## ADVISORY COMMITTEE

*The Yale Editions of the Private Papers of James Boswell will consist of two independent but parallel series planned and executed for different types of readers. One, the "research" edition, will give a complete text of Boswell's journals, diaries, and memoranda; of his correspondence; and of "The Life of Johnson," from the original manuscript: the whole running to at least thirty volumes. It will preserve the spelling and capitalization of the original documents, and will be provided with extensive scholarly annotation. A large group of editors and a permanent office staff are engaged in this comprehensive undertaking, the first volume of which may appear by 1956. The other, the reading or "trade" edition, will select from the total mass of papers those portions that appear likely to interest the general reading public, and will present them in modern spelling and with annotation of a popular cast. The publishers may also issue limited de luxe printings of the trade volumes, with extra illustrations and special editorial matter, but in no case will the trade volumes or the de luxe printings include matter from Boswell's archives that will not also appear in the research edition.*

*The present volume is the fifth of the trade edition.*

## CONTENTS



## LIST OF ILLUSTRATIONS



Boswell's journal for 1776 shows that he had seen and admired a portrait of Mountstuart "by Mr. Hoare," and that Mountstuart made him a

# INTRODUCTION

## § I

James Boswell's main concerns during the period of his life covered by this volume were sex, religion, and politics — the three subjects of conversation forbidden in polite society. To be sure, these essential interests occupied his mind a great deal throughout his life, as they do most men's; where he differed from others was in the determination with which he explored them both in words and in action, and in the frankness and relish for detail with which he set down not only conversations, but also his feelings and his experiences in general. This is not a polite book, because Boswell insisted on asking fundamental questions both of himself and of others — a trait that some have found indelicate, but which accounts in part for the warm response he evoked from such varied and distinguished men as Rousseau, Paoli, and Dr. Johnson.

Boswell's personal writings also reflect the intense concern with which he searched for a balance between the claims of principle and desire in the major areas of experience. In writing down what he thought, felt, and did, he fixed in relative clarity his impressions of a confused existence; momentarily he arrested the onrush of daily life in a search for its direction and significance. At this point in his life he wanted to discover whether he was fundamentally a libertine, a faithful lover, or would be satisfied with the respectable permanence of marriage. He wanted to decide whether the comforting deism of Rousseau, the solid support of an historic church either Roman Catholic or Anglican, or the stern worship of his Presbyterian ancestors provided a true and enduring faith. Finally, he hoped to find in politics both an acceptable escape from, and reconciliation with, his projected destiny as a Scottish lawyer. Perhaps as a foreign envoy, or as Ayrshire's representative in the House of Commons, he could pursue a respected and profitable career which would not limit him to the provincial round of Auchinleck and Edinburgh. Boswell knew that the grand tour was his father's last concession; it was a final and glorious opportunity to explore his own character and capacities, and to enjoy himself, before he assumed the dull duties which awaited him in Scotland. Just how deeply the tour was to affect him did not become apparent until after his trip to Corsica and his meeting with Pascal Paoli, an event which was to colour his entire life.[1]

## §II

By the time Boswell crossed the Alps into Italy, he was already set apart from the average young Englishman on his travels, since he came straight from a triumphal survey of Voltaire and Rousseau.[2] Of the two, Rousseau had affected him far more strongly: his emphasis on self-expression had led Boswell to choose him as his mentor for life in general and for his conduct in Italy in particular. Under his influence Boswell resolved to behave well, to spend his time profitably, and to return to Scotland a wiser and more cultivated man. Yet like poor Jack Falstaff, Boswell felt also that if Adam fell in days of innocency, what could he do in days of villainy? Italy was not simply a great religious and cultural center; it was noted for the beauty and reputed availability of its women, and he headed for Turin, in Geoffrey Scott's phrase, "with mingled feelings of awe and adulterous anticipation."

The opening Italian love scene is one of the great comic interludes in Boswell's life, a pendant in its shining hopes and drab results to his later affair with Rousseau's mistress, Thérèse Le Vasseur.[3] He saw himself as a leading tenor in the land of opera, Don Giovanni among the great ladies and their *cicisbei*. In rapid succession he approached three countesses, interpreting any casual response they made as calculated, and moving impatiently from one to the next at the first signs of resistance. His letters reflect his technique with some accu-

[1] This Introduction deals with Boswell's life until his departure for Corsica in October 1765. Subsequent events are covered in separate introductions, pp. 143 and 207.

[2] A number of ideas and phrases in this section are taken from Geoffrey Scott's perceptive Introduction to the fifth volume of Colonel Isham's privately printed *Private Papers of James Boswell*.

[3] For Boswell's affair with Thérèse, see p. 277.

racy: he is twenty-four and impetuous, his heart is at their mercy, and time is short. Over all lies the pervasive hint that any favours granted are not solely on one side, since women of fifty, like Mme. de St. Gilles, cannot be choosers. The results of these efforts could easily have been predicted. Women who were perhaps attracted at first to this singular stranger found his precipitate behaviour uncomplimentary, even in a country where love was often taken lightly; they repulsed him with laughter and contempt, and Boswell was reduced to more quickly procurable game.

These simple conquests, ranging from "charming girls" to "monsters," provided the staple of Boswell's sexual experience throughout Italy, although he pursued an opera singer in Naples and a Mme. Michieli, a woman of some social standing, in Venice. But such affairs failed to satisfy him, for they lacked the aura of true though easy passion which Boswell felt was indispensable to a successful fulfillment of the role of gallant he had ordained for himself. It was with a feeling of urgency, then, that he arrived at Siena, near the end of his Italian trip, with a letter of introduction to Porzia Sansedoni, once mistress of his friend, Lord Mountstuart. This letter was complemented by the odd and characteristic "romantic idea" that an affair with Porzia would unite the three of them in an enduring if puzzling relationship. His object was thirty-five, wife of a prominent Sienese official of the Holy Roman Emperor, and the mother of three children. Porzia's personality does not emerge very distinctly from Boswell's records, but as well as can be determined she was clever, well-bred, flirtatious, and never seriously interested in his proposal.

To reduce Porzia to acquiescence, Boswell threatened her with a rival, Girolama Piccolomini, or Moma for short. Moma was two years older than Porzia; at twenty she had married a man thirteen years her senior, and now had four children. Her husband, Orazio Piccolomini, was Capitano di Popolo of Siena, a position roughly equivalent to mayor. Though Boswell, in his concentration on Porzia, had done no more, he thought, than to allot Moma his ordinary casual though pressing compliments, he soon became involved in an affair of serious proportions. He intended no more than a brief and essentially unsentimental interlude conducted according to the ground rules of gallantry, but he discovered that Moma played for keeps. Her passionate devotion touched him; he regarded her folly with complacent fondness, but a permanent relationship was out of the question. His father was angrily demanding that he return to Scotland, and would not long be satisfied with the explanation that Siena, as the seat of the purest Tuscan, was the best place to study Italian, though Boswell had avoided the embarrassment of a peremptory recall by failing to provide his address. The real reason, however, for the uneasiness Boswell exhibited in this situation may have lain deeper. Though one can hardly more than guess at his feelings, his numerous matrimonial speculations, delays, and flights, as well as his extensive promiscuity, suggest that Boswell found it difficult to adjust to any enduring sexual relationship. Though he parted from Moma with genuine regret, it is hard to imagine that he really believed in the possibility of the "eternal friendship" which he swore. Her response as he recorded it seems far more sincere: "You go to greater and greater happiness, but you leave me here to go continually from bad to worse; for after a few years my youth will be gone, &c., and I am among people for whom I care nothing."

Moma's character, mainly revealed through the letters she wrote to him after his departure, is striking in the candour and freedom of its expression. In turn passionate, angry, scornful, and sad, she never permitted Boswell to forget that he meant more to her than any one she had ever known, that their love was the most intense experience of her life. Love did not make her judgment of him more kind, however; she called him inconstant, hypocritical, petty, and selfish. And, for all that, he was possessed of "all the qualities necessary for being loved and to make another's happiness." "The good in you," she remarked over two years after his departure, "amazes me as much as the bad." Measured by this standard of love, Boswell's reaction seems explicable but trivial; he could fully admire his "Italian angel" only from the safety of Scotland. He had indeed found love in Italy, but he could not or dared not permit himself to love in return.

## § III

Confused, contradictory, and almost as spectacular if of less immediate interest than his amatory wanderings, Boswell's search for a solid religious foundation was of fundamental importance in his development. In violent reaction to his Presbyterian background, he had turned Roman Catholic and sceptic in quick succession, and in Holland had settled on the Church of England. But since he was further affected by the "agreeable ideas" of Christianity with which Rousseau's "Creed of a Savoyard Vicar" had furnished him, his views could scarcely have reached equilibrium. Italy impressed him spiritually in two different ways. Catholic worship stimulated his love for devotion and ritual, while Cicero's Tusculum inspired him to view Christianity as only one of the "three or four great systems said to be sent from heaven," all of which, he felt, were true to some extent.

It would be pleasant to report that Boswell found spiritual certainty in Italy, but his constant formulations and reformulations of religious and moral attitudes suggest that he had reached no satisfactory conclusions. To set himself rather liberal limits in theory was one thing; to justify his conduct to his uneasy conscience was another. Anxiety for Boswell, as for many others in the eighteenth century, often defined itself in the form of metaphysical problems: he fought a foreboding that he was helpless and damned. Rousseau saw Boswell's situation clearly, and for this reason advised his friend in Italy, Alexandre Deleyre, "to present him with moral objects only under such aspects as are consoling and tender. He is a convalescent whom the least relapse will infallibly destroy."

## § IV

Boswell's political relationships were as diverse as his religious interests, but in this field his goal was far more concrete. He wished to acquire a position of influence, which meant that he needed to meet and impress the great and near-great in England. No prudent considerations of interest, however, could prevent him from associating with interesting people, whatever their political connections, and he actually delighted in the social versatility these friendships sometimes involved.

His most dangerous political friend was John Wilkes, fifteen years his senior, who had been elected in 1757 to the House of Commons from Aylesbury. At first a quiet and neglected follower of Pitt,

Wilkes began to make himself known when the Earl of Bute, George III's favourite, came to power in May 1762. In collaboration with the poet, Charles Churchill, Wilkes founded a periodical, *The North Briton*, in which he not only attacked Bute's political policies but also insinuated that the King's mother was Bute's mistress. The King's natural resentment at this aspersion grew to fury when Wilkes, in the famous No. 45 of *The North Briton*, declared that the Speech from the Throne which had opened Parliament four days previously was "the most abandoned instance of ministerial effrontery ever attempted to be imposed on mankind," and that "the honour of the Crown" was "sunk even to prostitution." Jailed in the Tower on charges of seditious libel, Wilkes quickly gained his freedom when the general warrant on which he had been arrested was declared illegal, and on his release was greeted with cries of "Wilkes and Liberty" by the London mob, who saw in general warrants an infringement of their civil rights.

The House of Commons agreed with the King, however, that Wilkes deserved punishment. In November 1763 it voted the No. 45 "a false, scandalous, and seditious" libel, and deprived Wilkes of his Parliamentary immunity from prosecution in the courts. At the same time, the House of Lords condemned an obscene poem called "An Essay on Woman," whose printing Wilkes had arranged for, and of which he was probably co-author. Characterized by Pitt as "the blasphemer of his God and the libeller of his King," and in general lacking respectable support, Wilkes crossed over to Paris. Pleading a real illness, he refused to return in January 1764 to take his seat in the Commons, and was expelled. He was convicted of libel on both of the charges raised against him in Parliament, and when he failed to return for sentence was declared an outlaw on 1 November 1764. Another blow fell three days later, when Churchill, whom he had gone to meet in Boulogne, died there of fever, leaving Wilkes as his literary executor. Shortly thereafter, Wilkes followed his mistress, Gertrude Maria Corradini, to Italy, arriving in Turin at the same time as Boswell.

Certainly here was a man whom any respectable and ambitious young Scot should have avoided. Wilkes was not only an outlaw, he was notorious for his abuse of the Scots; and as a member of the monks of Medmenham Abbey, a club devoted to the celebration of the black mass and associated orgies, he had acquired the reputation of being one of the most licentious men of his age. But Boswell, who had met him casually in London in 1763, was fascinated by the wit and spirit of a man who in addition to his other traits was a fine classical scholar and a devoted father. Though he carefully defended his warm Tory soul against Wilkes's irreverent attitude towards monarchy, Boswell found his admiration for him growing rather than lessening in Italy as he observed Wilkes's serene gaiety in the face of extraordinary difficulties.

By coincidence, Boswell's other great political friend in Italy was John, Lord Mountstuart, eldest son of Wilkes's bitter opponent, Lord Bute. Mountstuart was also making the grand tour, although in a somewhat more elegant manner than Boswell, when the two met in Rome. At twenty, he was handsome, conventional, and indolent, proud of his royal Stuart blood and his father's eminence. Mountstuart, as the son of a man of wealth and power, falls into a category recognizable in any century. The grand tour was of little importance to him; it was merely an optional part of his preparation for an outstanding career. Alexander Pope harshly anticipated him in his description of the young Grand Tourist in *The Dunciad*. Led by his governor

> . . . he sauntered Europe round,
> And gathered every vice on Christian ground . . .
> The stews and palace equally explored,
> Intrigued with glory, and with spirit whored.

Highly conscious of his unassailable social position, Mountstuart was certain that all his mistakes would be readily excused — they always had been. With few problems of his own, he minimized or avoided the difficulties of others. Mountstuart would never face a final reckoning, though he might be caught in middle age by the feeling that some especially great future, once confidently foreseen, had somehow never materialized. He lived, in the fullest sense, on the initiative and accomplishments of his ancestors. Yet in his youth he was a charming person, with a self-confidence alternately attractive and offensive.

Dazzled by Mountstuart's prestige and ministerial interest, and envisioning him as a future political Maecenas, Boswell quickly accepted his invitation to join him and his entourage for the rest of their tour of Italy. The two other members of the party were men of distinct character. Col. James Edmondstone, Mountstuart's "governor" or overseer for the trip, was a veteran soldier who was content to give Mountstuart his way most of the time, but who asserted himself firmly when the occasion demanded; he treated Boswell, to whom he was vaguely related, with a coarse familiarity that Boswell found characteristic of his countrymen and detested. Paul Henri Mallet, Mountstuart's tutor, was a Genevan who achieved eminence as an historian. He had been preceptor to the heir to the Danish throne, and had turned down an offer to supervise the education of the future Czar Paul I in order to accompany Mountstuart in the pleasanter climate of Italy. Mallet was a conscious intellectual, hypersensitive, melancholy, exacerbated by his position and mode of life; he considered himself Boswell's social equal and intellectual superior, to Boswell's open annoyance.

A third political faction with which Boswell mingled during his stay in Italy was the small and pathetic band of Jacobites which clustered about the Roman court of the Old Pretender (James III to his adherents). Though the possibility of a Jacobite uprising had vanished, the Hanoverians through Sir Horace Mann, the British Envoy in Florence, still watched their rivals carefully. Boswell knew that it was not wise to become identified with this group, but so long as he kept his distance from the Old Pretender himself, and was discreet about his friends in his letters home, he ran little real danger of compromising himself. Among the Jacobites, Andrew Lumisden, secretary to the Pretender, became his closest friend. Lumisden's position was unpleasant: his master was no longer mentally capable of transacting business; the demands of the poverty-stricken Jacobites were incessant; and, above all, the cause was hopeless. Yet he remained faithfully at his post, and Boswell found his loyalty and "old-fashioned principles" as admirable as his cheerful and friendly attitude towards all well-intentioned visiting countrymen. Principally through Lumisden, Boswell was introduced into the hospitable Jacobite circle, which included such people as the Pretender's physician

Dr. James Murray, and Abbé Peter Grant of the Scots College at Rome. His Roman friends in turn arranged for him to meet other Jacobites in France: the Earl of Dunbar in Avignon, Boswell's relative John Nairne in Sens, and various members of the colony of exiles grouped around the Scots College and its Principal, John Gordon, in Paris. After meeting Mountstuart, Boswell saw less of his Jacobite friends in Rome, but he disclaimed neither them nor Wilkes. Acquiring a patron did not mean to Boswell that he must give up his independence, and it was this firm opinion to a large extent which was to prevent him from ever making effectual use of Mountstuart and his connections.[4]

## § V

The effect of new surroundings and new acquaintances must be considered in the delineation of any traveller, and especially of Boswell. Italy and Rome attracted the eighteenth-century Englishman as France and Paris drew the American traveller between the two World Wars, and for some of the same reasons: it offered a release from the conventions of his own society, and a chance to become acquainted with a culture certainly older and supposedly more profound than his own. Two great traditions, classical and Christian, mingled here to fascinate the English traveller who had learned his Horace and Virgil by heart as a schoolboy (Boswell knew forty Horatian odes), and whose sturdy Protestant mistrust of the Pope was soothed by the magnificence of St. Peter's. Italy, corrupt and mean as it seemed to many of its visitors, was still the mother of civilization and the greatest repository of its visible monuments. If Boswell's response to its wonders seems occasionally the product of exaggerated sensibility, it may be compared to the reaction of Edward Gibbon, who had visited Rome for the first time the previous year. Gibbon, a man whose dislike for enthusiasm was itself almost immoderate, later wrote: "At the distance of twenty-five years I can neither forget nor express the strong emotions which agitated my mind as I first approached and entered the Eternal City. After a

[4] Paoli was to affect Boswell's political life and thought enormously, but a discussion of this influence belongs to a subsequent volume.

sleepless night, I trod with a lofty step the ruins of the Forum; each memorable spot where Romulus stood, or Tully spoke, or Caesar fell, was at once present to my eye; and several days of intoxication were lost or enjoyed before I could descend to a cool and minute investigation."[5]

The Italy that Boswell visited was divided into petty states and dominated by foreign powers. The Kingdom of Naples and the Duchy of Parma were governed by branches of the Spanish Bourbons; the Grand Duchy of Tuscany was a direct fief of the Holy Roman Emperor Francis I, and the Duchy of Milan part of the Austrian dominions of his wife, Maria Theresa. The republics of Venice, Genoa, and Lucca, the Duchy of Modena, and the Papal States were in various stages of decline, and only the King of Sardinia, the ruler of Savoy and Piedmont, was strong enough to act as an independent power.

Boswell was well suited to the role of tourist: he was adaptable, he loved to travel and to meet people. As a gentleman of position, he was presented at the courts of Italy's rulers, and at Parma introduced into the fine literary group that Duke Philip had gathered to instruct his son. Otherwise Italy offered few famous men, although he met Batoni the painter, Winckelmann the great art critic, and a number of minor scholars and artists in his travels. He had two main sources of introduction, the Dominicans who handed him from monastery to monastery, and England's diplomatic representatives. And his English and Scottish compatriots were everywhere, some having settled permanently and others being in transit.

Nor did he neglect Italy's monuments. Boswell toured the art galleries, the churches, and the classical shrines, stood lost in admiration before the falls at Terni, scrambled up Vesuvius and over the ruins of Pompeii. Much of the journal and memoranda of the period are devoted, not surprisingly, to conscientious note-taking on these expeditions, most of which the present volume omits. Boswell's remarks on the arts are ordinarily conventional, although when he allowed himself to perceive directly and not through the eyes of the guide-book, his comments are amusing and sometimes shrewd. But it is the glimpses of the manners and conversations of his acquaint-

[5] *Autobiographies*, ed. John Murray, 1896, p. 267.

ances that provide probably the most immediately engaging sections of this volume.

§ VI

The appeal to the modern reader of Boswell's personal writings has been partly prepared for by developments in contemporary literature. In his work, as in that of a novelist like Joyce, the major figures are delineated by a mass of apparently unselected detail, although the selection is actually controlled by Boswell's own range of perception and characteristic reactions. Also, the vast quantity of modern autobiographical analysis has prepared the contemporary reader to understand Boswell's self-exploration, and to appreciate how his treatment of himself is heightened by his own awareness of his dual role as observer and participant.

This volume is unique so far among the present series in presenting Boswell's work in its three major stages of selectivity and arrangement: the rough notes or memoranda, the letters and fully written journals, and part of his book on Corsica published in 1768. Of these three stages the memoranda are in many ways the most interesting, though the most difficult to follow. They are a catch-all: conversations, sight-seeing notes, observations on love and politics, religion and melancholy are jumbled together. Though an indiscreet detail or two was inked out later and a few pages are missing, they remain largely as Boswell wrote them, unrevised and unexpurgated. Boswell could not describe everything that happened to him, of course, but what he did jot down in the memoranda has the freshness and impact of immediate observation.

The letters and journals clarify and expand the rough notes at the expense of a necessary suppression of detail; they also order events to bring out their essential significance. Boswell had the courage not to hide what he was like from himself, but like every man he had an image of his own character and position which coloured his version of experience. Yet the journals are remarkable for the extent to which he kept this manipulation, unavoidable in any connected account, to a minimum.[6]

[6] Boswell's fashioning of the *Journal of a Tour to Corsica* is discussed briefly on p. 145.

## § VII

The principal manuscripts from which this book has been compiled are the following:

1. Journal in Switzerland and Italy, 1–30 January 1765: 50 quarto pages, numbered by Boswell 857–906, continuous and complete; roughly 8 by 7½ inches, unbound. Some of this journal is written in French.

2. Memoranda and Notes for Journal in Switzerland and Italy, 1 January to 11 October 1765: 90 unpaged octavo leaves, nearly all written on both sides; ranging in size from 8 by 5⅝ to 7⅛ by 4½ inches, unbound. The entries until 30 January are expanded in the full journal (see item 1 above); thereafter they constitute our main record of Boswell's tour of Italy. They contain many passages in French, Italian, and Latin, and a few English words transcribed in Greek characters. Some leaves are missing, particularly for August where the entries fail after the 25th, and September which has entries only for the 9th, 10th, 29th, and 30th.

3. "Course of Antiquities and Arts at Rome," 25–30 March 1765: 4 quarto leaves, written on both sides, numbered by Boswell 1–8, continuous; ending in the middle of a sentence but perhaps carried no further; roughly 10 by 7¾ inches, unbound. In French.

4. Journal with Lord Mountstuart, 14–22 June 1765: 4 unpaged quarto leaves, written on 4 sides; roughly 8⅞ by 7⅜ inches, unbound. In Italian.

5. "Reflections Written in Siena, 1765": 12 unpaged quarto leaves, written on both sides; roughly 9 by 7⅜ inches, unbound. In Italian.

6. Memoranda and Notes for Journal in Capraja and Genoa, 22 November to 10 December 1765; 8 unpaged octavo leaves, all but the last written on both sides; ranging in size from 7⅞ by 5⅛ to 7¼ by 5⅛ inches, unbound.

7. Journal in Italy and France, 10 December 1765 to 6 January 1766: 48 unpaged quarto leaves, all written on both sides; ranging in size from 8¼ by 6⅛ to 7¾ by 5⅞ inches, unbound. This journal is enclosed in a wrapper which Boswell endorsed, "Tour in France."

8. Memoranda from Paris and England, 12 January to 23 Febru-

ary 1766: 37 unpaged octavo leaves, nearly all written on both sides; ranging in size from $7\frac{1}{16}$ by $4\frac{9}{16}$ to $6\frac{3}{16}$ by $3\frac{3}{4}$ inches, unbound. The leaves containing the entries for 1–11 February are missing. These memoranda are enclosed in a wrapper endorsed by Boswell, "Mems. From Paris, and so forth. Some of Dr. Johnson after my return from abroad in 1766."

9. Ten-Lines-a-Day Verses. Dated from 22 January to 10 March, 11–13 April 1765: 9 unpaged quarto leaves, all but the last written on both sides; roughly $9\frac{1}{8}$ by $7\frac{1}{2}$ inches, unbound. The verses for 13 February, 2, 5, and 6 March are unfinished; those for 11–13 April are placed in this series conjecturally.

10. Expense Accounts: "Expenses after Geneva," 7 January to 9 February 1765; "Expenses in Italy," 15 February to 26 July 1765; "Expenses at Siena," 1–27 September 1765. 7 quarto and 2 folio unpaged leaves, written on both sides; ranging in size from $7\frac{1}{2}$ by 9 to $7\frac{1}{2}$ by $12\frac{1}{4}$ inches, unbound. In French and Italian.

11. Upwards of 210 letters sent or received by Boswell between 1 January 1765 and 23 February 1766, and 5 letters of later date to or from Girolama Piccolomini. All but 21 of these letters are at Yale, and of these 21, 13 are represented at Yale by drafts. The letters to Boswell in the Yale collection are originals, as are Boswell's letters to John Johnston and W. J. Temple. (He retrieved his letters to Johnston after the latter's death from his executor, and Temple returned Boswell's letters written to him from the Continent because Boswell intended to use them for a book of travels.) Almost all the other letters by Boswell at Yale are drafts. Many of these letters are in French or Italian. Boswell's Register of Letters, now at Yale, covers this period: while neither complete nor entirely accurate, it is often useful for fixing dates and for proving the existence of lost letters.

12. Miscellaneous Documents, 1 January 1765 to 23 February 1766. These include such items as isolated journal entries for 1 August and 11 October 1765, travel notes, detached essays, and lists of various sorts.

The Journal of a Tour to Corsica is taken from the third edition (1769) of Boswell's *An Account of Corsica; The Journal of a Tour to that Island, and Memoirs of Pascal Paoli*, which was originally published the previous year. The journal for 1–30 January 1765, 11 October 1765, and 10 December 1765–23 February 1766 was published in 1928–1930 by the late Geoffrey Scott and Frederick A. Pottle in *Private Papers of James Boswell from Malahide Castle, in the Collection of Lt.-Colonel Ralph Heyward Isham*, an expensive limited edition of which only 570 copies were printed. Some forty of the seventy-five letters included in the present volume have also previously appeared, most of them in the *Private Papers* or in Professor Chauncey B. Tinker's *Letters of James Boswell*, Clarendon Press, 1924. A group of newspaper paragraphs composed by Boswell, describing in mysterious terms his activities in Corsica and events there, has been collected from *The London Chronicle*, 1766. This leaves much that now appears in print for the first time, notably the extracts from Boswell's Italian diary, the letters from Wilkes and Girolama Piccolomini, and the long and brilliant letter from Boswell to Rousseau with which the volume opens. The fully written journal is printed without cuts, but other documents have been abridged whenever it has seemed desirable. Notes saying that certain letters have not been recovered should not be taken as indicating a policy of including all the letters we have for the period, or even all the letters we have that are mentioned in the journal. Such notes are intended to explain why letters that sound important enough to be included in this edition do not appear here.

The spelling, capitalization, and punctuation of both manuscripts and previously printed material have been reduced to accepted modern norms, and abbreviations and contractions have been expanded at will. All quotations have been standardized in the same fashion. The standard of spelling for all but proper names is *The Concise Oxford Dictionary* (1951). For place names the English editions of Baedeker's *Italy* (1928), *Southern France* (1914), and *Paris* (1932) have been followed. Personal names, when the persons are certainly identified, are spelled as in the standard biographical dictionaries, or as they appear in authoritative documents in the local archives. Typographical errors in the Journal of a Tour to Corsica have been silently corrected by collation with the first edition. The texts have been broken into paragraphs where such breaks make for easier reading. Where names of speakers are supplied in conversations cast dramatically, they are put in small capitals. A few clear inadvertencies have been put right without notice. Square brackets indicate words added where the manuscript shows no defect, and where there is no reason to suspect a slip on the part of the writer; angular brackets indicate reconstructions of words lost through defects in the manuscript, where the reconstruction is not entirely certain.

Documents in foreign languages have generally been given in English translation only. Boswell wrote his journal for the most part in English, but he often used French for names of officials, buildings, and the like. Much of his conversation was conducted in French and Italian, and he recorded it in the original language. Most of this has been put into English, but certain occasional detached words and phrases have been left in the original to suggest as much as possible the foreign flavour of the manuscripts. The French and Italian retained has been standardized and modernized, and when written in contracted or abbreviated form has been silently expanded in some places in translation.

Those who wish to examine the unnormalized and unmodified text of the journal are reminded that it is available in Colonel Isham's *Private Papers*. The French of Boswell's letters to Rousseau can be consulted in Professor Tinker's *Letters of James Boswell*. The projected research edition of the Boswell papers will, of course, give all these documents in the language in which they are written.

The annotation and editorial notes to this volume have been designed for the general reader, though it is never easy to estimate how much the general reader knows or wants to know. We have attempted to provide essential information when it is available, and occasionally sidelights which are intended to characterize a person or event more firmly, but complete annotation — such as the name of Paoli's cook — has been reserved for the research edition. The indexes of this series are not mere finding tools, but supplement the annotation. In particular, we usually reserve for the index the function of supplying Christian names of persons mentioned.

An edition such as the present one is based very heavily on previous published and unpublished work; it is, in fact, a highly collective and cooperative enterprise, which draws on the minute and multiple accumulations of facts, inferences, and guesses of at least a generation of scholarship. As has been mentioned above, the late Geoffrey Scott and F. A. Pottle published a text of Boswell's Italian, French, and English journals for this period in the fourth, fifth, and seventh volumes of Colonel Isham's privately printed *Private Papers of James Boswell.* In the fifth volume, Mr. Scott provided texts and translations of Boswell's letters to the Countesses Burgaretta and Skarnavis, and Porzia Sansedoni. We have made grateful use of his translations and portions of his introduction.

The basic annotation for this volume has been furnished by the following sources. The Italian memoranda were edited by Professor Robert Warnock in his unpublished Yale dissertation, "Boswell in Italy, 1765" (1933). Professor Warnock has published an instructive survey of this material in his article, "Boswell on the Grand Tour," *Studies in Philology*, xxxix (1942). 650–661. Boswell's *Corsica* was edited by Professor Joseph Foladare in his unpublished Yale dissertation, "James Boswell and Corsica" (2 vols., 1936). The text of the Italian journal from 1–30 January 1765 was reviewed and annotated by Dean Helen S. Randall as a class exercise in the Yale Graduate School, and a similar service was performed for the journal for 10 December 1765 to 23 February 1766 by Professor Sylvester H. Bingham. Dr. Charles H. Bennett reviewed the text of the journal and memoranda for the period, and made additions to the annotation, especially for the journal from 22 November 1765 to 23 February 1766. He also translated the French dialogue in the journal, and drafted annotation for a trade or reading edition. Using these materials and others resulting from his own researches, Professor Pottle completed a text for a trade edition over fifteen years ago. The subsequent recovery from Malahide Castle of Boswell's European correspondence and of other papers of the first importance necessitated the planning of a quite different volume and extensive revisions of and additions to the annotation. In this project we have extracted much useful information from the work of Professor Warnock, who has traversed the libraries and archives of Italy, Corsica, and France in preparation for the forthcoming research edition of Boswell's journal.

The general plan of this volume, worked out by the editors, has benefited considerably from the advice of the Editorial Committee. As well, Mr. Liebert provided the artist with materials for the maps, and Dr. Metzdorf, who has been of assistance at every stage, assumed responsibility for collecting the illustrations. Both they and Professor Hilles read the proofs. Of the larger Advisory Committee, Dr. Chapman, Mr. Hyde, Mr. Lewis, and Professor Peyre read the proofs and provided corrections and suggestions for the notes. Dr. Bennett, Professor Curt von Faber du Faur, Professor Konstantin Reichardt, and Professor Warnock were also kind enough to perform these services. We are further indebted to Professor Bergin for assistance with the Italian sections of this volume, and to Professor Edmund T. Silk for his aid with classical references and Boswell's own Latin. Professor A. Guelfo Frulla transcribed the difficult originals of the Piccolomini letters for us.

In addition to the persons mentioned specifically in the notes, we gratefully acknowledge the assistance of the following: Frederick B. Adams, Jr., Jean Boorsch, Philip Daghlian, Sergio Dolfi, Sir James Fergusson, Robert L. Haig, Robert Halsband, Mrs. Donald F. Hyde, Robert S. Lopez, Albert K. Ludy, Miss Sibyl Marcuse, Sir Owen Morshead, Paul Pickrel, Miss Barbara D. Simison, Miss Annemarie Spahn, Domenico Vittorini, Marshall Waingrow, Ralph S. Walker, A. Dayle Wallace, and Miss Lydia H. Wentworth. Our next-door neighbours in the Walpole Office, George L. Lam and Warren H. Smith, have often taken time from their own pursuits to help with one of our problems. Finally we heartily thank all members of the office staff of the Yale Editions of the Private Papers of James Boswell during the last two years: Mrs. Jane H. Carroll, Miss Harriet Chidester, Mrs. Dorothy B. Moravcik, and Mrs. Marion S. Pottle. Mrs. Hope G. Waingrow is mainly responsible for the index.

F.B.

Yale University, New Haven
1 January 1955

# BOSWELL IN ITALY

*1765*

*I swear to you that I seriously think it my truest philosophy to be content with the powers which my Maker has assigned me, and not to torment myself by ineffectual struggles to change my nature. I find myself an amiable, pretty man of moderate abilities, but a soul truly noble, a soul which in reality sets me higher in the scale of being than if I had attained to the first honours which superior talents procure and been without such a soul.* [BOSWELL TO JOHN JOHNSTON, *11* MAY *1765*]

# Boswell in Italy, 1765

Sketch of Boswell's Life to January, 1765. James Boswell was born in Edinburgh on 29 October 1740, the eldest son of Alexander Boswell, whose title, Lord Auchinleck, indicated his position as a judge of the supreme courts of Scotland. Of an old family and an important landowner in his home county, Ayrshire, Lord Auchinleck imparted his strong sense of tradition and family pride to his son. Boswell studied law at the Universities of Edinburgh and Glasgow, frequenting the theatre in his spare time, until in the spring of 1760 he ran away to London and became a Roman Catholic for a brief period. From this dangerous lapse (in a practical sense), he was reclaimed by his father's Ayrshire neighbour, the Earl of Eglinton, who introduced him "into the circles of the great, the gay, and the ingenious." Loving everything about London, Boswell tried to persuade his father to secure a commission in the Foot Guards there for him, but Lord Auchinleck kept him in Edinburgh, and at least nominally at his studies, until he passed the examination in civil law in June 1762. Then, although refusing to purchase a commission in the Guards, his father permitted him to return to London to see if he could obtain one through influence.

Boswell's following year in London had two solid results: he wrote the first long stretch of his great journal,[1] and near the end of his stay he met Samuel Johnson. The journal records the wide range of his activities from parties at Northumberland House to his affair with the actress Louisa and encounters with street walkers in the Strand. Johnson was to become a permanent stabilizing influence on his life. Having failed to secure a commission, Boswell agreed to be-

[1] The journal for this year was discovered by Professor C. Colleer Abbott at Fettercairn House in 1930, and published in 1950 under the title of *Boswell's London Journal, 1762–1763*, by the McGraw-Hill Book Company, Inc. (New York) and William Heinemann, Ltd. (London).

come a lawyer as his father wished, and crossed over to Holland in August 1763 to continue his study of civil law at Utrecht. His year in Holland was not a happy one: he was lonely in this strange country whose inhabitants he found gross and stodgy. As well, he worked very hard at a subject he detested, and remained uncustomarily chaste. The result of his efforts to reform was a profound depression which centered on gloomy thoughts of predestination. These were partly relieved towards the end of this year by a relaxation of his religious and moral standards, and by his attraction to Belle de Zuylen (Zélide), a Dutch girl of noble family.[2]

In June 1764 Boswell started off on a tour of the German courts with revived spirits. In Berlin and Potsdam he saw but failed to meet Frederick the Great; in Brunswick he danced a minuet with the Princess Augusta, sister to George III; in Karlsruhe he became close friends with the Margrave of Baden-Durlach. But his greatest successes were reserved for Switzerland. First, having prepared himself by reading Rousseau's works, he approached the "wild philosopher" at his refuge in Môtiers with a mingling of enthusiasm, naïveté, and persistence which Rousseau was unable to resist, though he was ill and disliked visitors. Boswell wanted a father-confessor and guide, someone to tell him how to deal with hypochondria, Zélide, the problems of metaphysics, his father, and his desire for a harem. Rousseau was naturally unwilling to assume total responsibility for Boswell's career, but he did encourage and reassure him. Next, Boswell visited Voltaire at Ferney, and wangled an invitation to spend a couple of days with him in which he tried to ascertain Voltaire's true religious sentiments.[3] Having made the two great, antithetical spirits of the age conscious of his existence, Boswell headed happily from Geneva for Italy, where he had his father's permission to spend four months.

---

[2] See *Boswell in Holland, 1763–1764*, 1952, McGraw-Hill Book Company, Inc. (New York) and William Heinemann, Ltd. (London).

[3] See *Boswell on the Grand Tour: Germany and Switzerland, 1764*, 1953, McGraw-Hill Book Company, Inc. (New York) and William Heinemann, Ltd. (London).

[EDITORIAL NOTE: Boswell wrote the following résumé of his tour of Italy in the form of a letter to Rousseau which was apparently never sent. It is placed at the beginning of this volume so that, as Boswell's own summary of his tour, it may serve as an over-all sketch of and guide to the events which are detailed in chronological order hereafter. The letter exists in three states: remnants of a first draft, which Boswell preserved because they comprise material which he may have decided not to include, or had not finished copying into the letter in its final state; and a first and second fair copy. The second fair copy, a very slight revision of the first, is, so far as it goes, the basis of the printed text. The first fair copy is followed thereafter, and finally the draft to its conclusion. Annotation has been supplied only when matters are not explained elsewhere in this volume. For further remarks on this letter, see p. 5 *n.* 4 and p. 140.]

[Boswell to Jean Jacques Rousseau. Original in French]

Lucca, 3 October 1765

IF IT WERE POSSIBLE, ILLUSTRIOUS PHILOSOPHER! to write to you without that respect which hinders the imagination by introducing a degree of fear, I should flatter myself that I could entertain you with an account of my tour of Italy. I shall do my best; and if I am not successful you will know what to ascribe my failure to.

You were indeed right to congratulate me when my father gave me permission to travel in Italy. Nine months in this delicious country have done more for me than all the sage lessons which books, or men formed by books, could have taught me. It was my imagination that needed correction, and nothing but travel could have produced this effect.

I carried over the Alps ideas of the most rigorous morality. I thought of myself as a penitent who must expiate the sins which he had confessed to you in your sacred retreat; I felt like a hero of austerity in a dissolute age. But the ladies of Turin were very beautiful, and I thought that I might allow myself *one* intrigue in Italy, in order to increase my knowledge of the world and give me a contempt for shameless women. So I made myself into a gallant; but I was too modest a gallant to succeed with ladies who scorned the detours of delicacy, and who thought anyone a peasant or an imbecile who did not head straight for the main chance. Moreover, I had a heart. I was seized by passion, I could not hide it; and that was not reconcilable with the decorum which had to be maintained in public. In short, I had no success at all with the ladies of Piedmont. A French officer who was my instructor in gallantry, mortified by finding me *so young*, consoled me by procuring willing girls.

Thus, Sir, did I carry out the good resolutions I had made at Môtiers. I wrote on a piece of paper, "O Rousseau! How am I fallen since I left you!" Yet my principles remained firm. I considered that I had done wrong. I summoned my inclinations back to virtue, and at Parma M. Deleyre strengthened me in my resolutions. I was charmed by the fine mind and the finer soul of that amiable Frenchman; and the sincere evidence which he gave of his attachment to me brought me back again to the opinion that I was something above the crowd of mankind. You told me when I was about to leave you, "Sir, all you lack is a knowledge of your own worth." Believe me, illustrious philosopher! there is a great deal in that remark. I know my worth sometimes, and I think and act nobly. But then melancholy attacks me, I despise myself, and it seems to me a waste of time to try to improve so petty a thing.

I was well enough on my trip from Turin to Rome. I interrupted it often to stop in places where there was something to see. I was very curious, and because I moved from one scene to another, melancholy never had time to weigh me down greatly. I was struck with everything. I had the agreeable sensation that derives from a half-knowledge of things — to many minds perhaps as great a pleasure as knowing them thoroughly.

I had recommendations to the Dominican fathers, and under their protection I covered the whole of Italy. I visited many monasteries, including those of the strictest orders. I shall never forget an hour that I spent in conversation with the Prior and other reverend fathers of a Carthusian convent near Bologna. I encouraged in myself a sceptical but reverent superstition, which by a mysterious — an inexplicable — mixture of feelings, calmed my uneasy mind.

I entered Rome with full classical enthusiasm, but when I arrived at my inn and found myself surrounded by the landlord, by *valets de place*, by scoundrels, my fantastic sensibility was wounded, and at first I was in a bad humour. I had an odd thought which now makes me laugh heartily. As I was walking along the streets of Rome, which are very little different from those of any other city, I said to myself, "Was the Epistle of St. Paul to the Romans written to the inhabitants of this city? And did I use to be so terrified by it?" At once the Epistle of St. Paul seemed to me to be just an ancient writing by some ecclesiastical zealot. The word of God was no longer in it. Great chemist of human nature! you see how a mind can be changed. Ah, we must analyse with the most delicate nicety.[4]

Within a few days I set out for Naples, where I was richly entertained with the variety of interesting things to be seen there, especially in the environs. I found the famous Mr. Wilkes in his exile, and despite his sharp attacks on the Scots, we got along very well together. All theories of human nature are confounded by the resilient spirit of that singular factionary, who has experienced all the vicissitudes of pleasure and politics without ever having suffered a moment of uneasiness. He is a man who has thought much without being gloomy, a man who has done much evil without being a scoundrel. His lively and energetic sallies on moral questions gave to my spirit a not unpleasant agitation, and enlarged the scope of my views by convincing me that God could create a soul completely serene and gay notwithstanding the alarming reflection that we all must die. Wilkes pretended to be angry with you for having referred to him in so uncompromising a style in a note to one of your *Letters from the Mountain*.[5] He even said boldly that he would write a public letter to you on this subject, which would be entitled, *A Letter from the Other Man of the Mountain*.

I went little into company at Naples, and remember solely that the Neapolitan ladies resembled country chamber-maids. I was there during Lent when there are no public entertainments. During my

[4] At this point the draft contains three pages which are not reproduced in the fair copies. These pages are printed in Appendix C.

[5] In the ninth of his *Lettres écrites de la montagne*, Rousseau cited Wilkes's acquittal after his arrest for printing No. 45 of *The North Briton* as an example of the just government of laws in England, in contrast to the autocratic government of Geneva.

stay at Naples I was truly libertine. I ran after girls without restraint. My blood was inflamed by the burning climate, and my passions were violent. I indulged them; my mind had almost nothing to do with it. I found some very pretty girls. I escaped all danger. I have nothing to say about this period; I merely describe it for you as it occurred.

I returned to Rome for Holy Week. I grew calm. The solemn services of the Roman Catholic Church made a serious impression on me. I began to be a little melancholy and I recalled with religious regret how I had once been, like you, in the bosom of the faithful. But your Savoyard doctrines came to my aid and made me see a church even more catholic than that which I revered: the entire Universe, all souls being emanations of the Eternal Being. On Easter I was in St. Peter's, and in that superb temple I saw noble and mystical adorations offered to the Supreme Being. I was penetrated with devotion. I was sure that the revelation given by Jesus was true; and when I saw the Christian High Priest with venerable magnificence elevate before the Eternal Justice a Sacrifice for the sins of the whole world, I fell to my knees among the throng of my fellow men who remained fixed in respectful silence; I struck my breast, and with all the ardour of which my soul was capable, I prostrated myself at the feet of my Father "who is in Heaven," convinced that, by varied ways of which we know nothing clearly, he would one day lead all his creatures to happiness. Let cold beings sneer; I was never more nobly happy than on that day.

The study of antiquities, of pictures, of architecture, and of the other arts which are found in such great perfection at Rome occupied me in a wise and elegant manner. You must know that I have a great taste for *virtù*. It entertains me agreeably during many hours when without it my mind would be a prey to ennui. I shall say no more on that head, because I do not know whether you like *virtù* or not. Moreover, you have a more sublime taste, and it is more sensible to acquaint you with traits of character from which you can derive some philosophical reflections useful to him who has supplied them, and perhaps to others.

I must admit that in the midst of my Roman studies I indulged in sensual relaxations. I sallied forth of an evening like an imperious lion, and I had a little French painter, a young academician, always vain, always alert, always gay, who served as my jackal.[6] I remembered the rakish deeds of Horace and other amorous Roman poets, and I thought that one might well allow one's self a little indulgence in a city where there are prostitutes licensed by the Cardinal Vicar. Thus does an ill-regulated mind assemble scattered ideas and compose from them a principle for action. I was, however, brought to a halt by an unpleasant occurrence which all libertines have to reckon with. When we walked in your room, disputing about the commerce of the sexes, you said to me with a smile, "Watch out for Italian girls — for several reasons." I discovered at Rome that your advice was very sound.

In all the vicissitudes that I experienced, and which you are well qualified to imagine from what you have just read, I always preserved a certain external decency of character. But I suffered cruelly from hypochondria, whose pains are unimaginable to those who have not felt them. It is a certain truth, Sir, that I am afflicted by a malady which can make me see all things as either insipid or sad, which can take away all desire for enjoyment, which can make me lose taste even for virtue; and what is the darkest and the most inexplicable of all, it is a malady which can so destroy my spirit that I scarcely even wish to be cured. The variations of this malady are infinite. I write to you now when I am completely healthy, clear, happy. I am sure that to find myself existing after death will not be a more powerful sensation than that which I have in feeling myself the man I now am, after the state of prostration and despair in which I have been plunged. Can you believe that there are moments in my life when M. Rousseau appears to me a poor wretch who had tried to distinguish himself a little among his unfortunate fellows, and who will soon be lost like them in the darkness of the [grave]?[7] In such moments it is impossible to enjoy those feelings of admiration for your genius and your character which give me such great pleasure when I am well. But what can be done about it? My judgment tries in vain to free me

[6] "Jackal" is in English in the original. Boswell annotated it in French: "So we call in English the animal who runs before the lion to find him his prey. I have no French dictionary to consult at the moment." The memoranda show that the painter was named Martin, but he has not been further identified.

[7] Boswell left a blank here for "grave" in both copies.

from the grasp of a troubled imagination. It is hard to suffer so much. Kindly philosopher! keep me in your thoughts. I sustain myself by a firm trust in God.

Until Holy Week, I had seen little of my countrymen in Italy. I was looked upon as an odd creature who studied a great deal and was very proud. I was presented to the Pope. I went to *conversazioni* in the palaces of Roman nobles, where there was a great deal of formality and also a certain air of pleasing richness and grandeur. At Rome everything is external. They have scarcely any real society. A prince makes a point of having his dinner sent in for half a crown, and does not know the number of his carriages or of his servants. The parties are also formal, being generally given their tone by two or three cardinals. I went to the levee of Cardinal Orsini, the present Protector of France. I had been highly recommended to him, but he did not once invite me to dine with him. I had opportunity there to see the gross flattery, the obvious scheming, the discontents, and the universal ambition of ecclesiastical politicians.

I do not know that I did well in avoiding my compatriots so completely. I had good reason — to devote myself entirely to learning the language, studying the genius, and absorbing the thought of the Italian people. But in doing this I almost isolated myself. I formed exaggerated ideas of myself, and when I fell in with Englishmen was raw and irritable, and by too great a sensitivity I was inferior in social life to mediocre young men who were accustomed to live in general society.

I could not think of placing myself so soon on the footing of a philosopher who wishes to retire from the world. I had to accustom myself to being with my equals. I had to think of establishing some political connection.

I found all these advantages happily combined. I formed a close connection with Lord Mountstuart, eldest son of the worthy Lord Bute, intimate friend of our King. My Lord Mountstuart is a young nobleman who merits his being of the blood of the ancient kings of Scotland. He deserves my drawing his portrait for you. He is handsome, has elegant manners, and a tempestuously noble soul. He has never applied himself earnestly to anything, but he is not without knowledge and has an excellent mind. He has, though to a lesser degree, the same defect that I have, weak nerves; but he does not suffer from them, for although he is no metaphysician, he is a practical philosopher. He finds himself placed in an elevated rank. He enjoys his real advantages without worrying about imaginary ills. His money is for him in civilized society what physical strength is to a savage. His servants are his arms, his horses his legs, and he can count as surely on them as the savage on the parts of his body — more, even, for he can replace them when they fail, which savages cannot do. He calmly follows his inclinations: when he wishes to study, he reads; when he is indolent, he lies on a sofa. Sometimes he speaks in company, sometimes he says nothing. Sometimes his passion for women is very strong, and he pursues them with the greatest liveliness. He has even had several affairs, although rather from vanity than from genuine feeling. Sometimes he cares nothing for any kind of love; then he enjoys talking about his adventures, and wonders most gravely how he could have been so carried away by his inclinations. He is never out of sorts with himself, because he never disputes with himself. He made me a great deal more sociable. He often said to me, "Boswell, I will teach you how to live," and really he did me good. When I saw my countrymen, I became more and more composed, and the good side of my mind was made better. My social affections had an opportunity to expand. I did not disquiet myself so much by thinking of myself, when I was also thinking of others. From each character of our nation of originals, I always drew something which I could turn to profit, and I formed friendships with one or two worthy men that will last for the rest of my life.

My Lord Mountstuart insisted that I accompany him on the remainder of his tour of Italy, and I consented. He was already accompanied by a Scottish colonel, a very worthy man, and by M. Mallet, sometime professor from Geneva, who had been given a good pension in return for giving my Lord lessons in history. It would have been impossible to conceive of a more prudent or more agreeable project than ours. My Lord and I counted on profiting together from M. Mallet's instructions. The Colonel was the discreet governor, and I had the honour to be regarded by my Lord as a friend who would be very useful to him, since I should prevent him from being tempted by bad company to renew his dissipations. But matters did not go well. I found myself in my Lord's suite, and when I heard him hold forth on the pleasures of grandeur I began to wish for employment at Court. I thought of his great interest. Insensibly I tried to please him and was afraid of offending him. He soon noticed it, and could not keep from profiting a little from it. I realized it too. I was highly shocked by it. What! Boswell, *the man of singular merit!* The friend of Rousseau! Is Boswell so far overcome by vile interest as to depend on the moods of a young Lord? I recollected myself. I made my Lord realize that I was as proud as ever. I did it too emphatically. We began to dispute about our characters, and each stated bluntly all the other's defects and all his own merits. You can imagine that between two young men, both of whom have a good deal of temperamental warmth, such a dispute, so conducted, could not but occasion many disagreeable moments. Finally our spirits subsided, and we were sometimes on a basis of puerile familiarity, and sometimes in the vilest humour possible, even to the point of not speaking to each other. I always had a great advantage, for I was four years older than my Lord, and was possessed of a little philosophy. The Colonel and Mallet suffered from the fatigues of the trip, and were vexed to see the differences between my Lord and me. The worthy Colonel rallied us roughly through mere clumsiness. Mallet, from whom we had taken hardly any lessons since we left Rome, became irritated with me because I never ceased attacking his opinions and discovering his tricks; and to tell you the truth, there were never four men who travelled so ill together. It was indeed ridiculous, and my Lord and I in our hours of good humour were sometimes ready to burst with laughing.

We went to Venice. For the first week I was charmed by the novelty and beauty of so singular a city, but I soon wearied of travelling continually by water, shut up in those lugubrious gondolas. Almost all the nobility was at Padua, where we had seen them for several days in passing through. There were buildings and paintings to see at Venice.

I paid court to a noble lady, a little advanced in years. She told me that she would not wish to take on a good cook that she could keep only a fortnight, for fear of suffering too much when she lost him. It was an affair of pure vanity, so I gave myself little concern over it.

My fancy was stirred by the brilliant stories I had heard of Venetian courtesans. I went to see them, *et militavi non sine gloria*,[8] but the wounds of my Roman wars were scarcely healed before I received fresh ones in Venice. What is worse, my Lord Mountstuart was of the party. He saw that I was agitated, and demanded to know what I was intending to do. I told him I was going out to look for girls, to taste the pleasures of Venice and learn the fashion; but I begged him not to go. You can well imagine that we went together. A pretty dancer was our common flame, and my Lord was taken in as I was. A fine piece of thoughtlessness. M. Mallet had fine sport with me then; the Colonel took me seriously to task. When a man is in any way the cause of a misfortune, even though it is entirely unintentional, he is nevertheless always regarded as guilty. Thus I felt on this occasion, and was mortified by it. Behold now your philosopher, the steady young man who was to help Lord Mountstuart to improve himself!

We were staying at Venice with General Graeme, Commander-in-Chief of the forces of the Republic, a worthy Scotsman, an old friend of Lord Bute. Sometimes he was angered and sometimes amused by our quarrels. We went to his country-house to take a quiet cure. M. Mallet and I quarrelled more than ever. He discovered how little I had studied either of science or of history, and he said to me, "If I were as ignorant as you are, I should be ashamed to show my face." The truth is that because of the hypochondria I told you of, and which I inherit from my mother, my mind has been so restless and so distracted that I have never been capable of genuine application. I have studied languages and *belles lettres*, and because of the strength and vivacity of my mind in its lucid moments I have picked up enough philosophy to make me appear much better instructed than I really am. I maintained against M. Mallet that I had as many ideas as he had, and I give you my word that during the greater part of the time that we were together, I felt myself his superior. It is the soul, Sir, it is the celestial fire that gives a man his worth. One idea possessed by me has more value than a throng of ideas possessed by the majority of men. Yet M. Mallet is intelligent, and he is a fellow hypochondriac.

[8] "And I fought, not without glory" (Horace, *Odes*, III. xxvi. 2).

During that period I felt more discontented than I had been since I began my travels. In my black moments when I judged myself by the opinions of others, I was a libertine and an ignoramus. I was bashful, and distrustful of my ability to distinguish myself in my own country. I foresaw differences of opinion between me and my father. I needed relief, and according to the state of my circulation, I was servile or proud with Lord Mountstuart. I experienced a fluctuation of conduct which was very disagreeable for a man who has an idea of uniform dignity of character. Here, Sir, are very subtle shades of character.

During my stay with General Graeme, my Lord Mountstuart was recalled to England. We took time, however, to see the Venetian states. On this last tour, my Lord and I got on better together. We admitted each other's virtues. My Lord said to me, "I have great esteem for you. I shall always be your friend in London. But you have a terrible disposition." I accompanied him as far as Milan. There the Colonel, M. Mallet, and I drank good burgundy and resolved to forget our little misunderstandings. My Lord and I grew somewhat tender when we finally had to part. I felt an enthusiastic attachment for his ancient family. I loved him from my heart, and I said to him as we embraced, "My Lord, if you do not have a lasting affection for me, you will never have it for anybody." I was very sorry to lose him. Our inclinations often agreed, and he helped me greatly to understand the people we saw on our travels, for he has a singular talent for understanding character — up to a certain point.

So there I was back in my old state of solitude. I reflected on my conduct, and although I did not think I had done any great wrong, I saw myself fallen into a vile state of brutishness. I was completely discouraged. I hardly dared think of virtue. I had written to M. Deleyre that I should be again at Parma. I went there as to a consolatory refuge. Our friend received me with the same warmth that he had shown me the first time I had visited him. He was pleased to discover that my mind had been so much strengthened by travel. He declared his philosophic tenets to me without evasion. I was confounded by them. It was, however, in some way agreeable to be with the most amiable of men and to realize that he was at the same time a pure *atheist*. I considered his ideas. I admitted them momentarily as real, and caught from them a certain astonishing delirium which gave me pleasure. But I immediately returned with adoration to the Source of all spirit, and defended my exalted faith warmly, while admitting my deviations in practice. M. Deleyre said to me with his gentle and serious air, "It would be well, Sir, if you had my habits with your principles, and I your principles with my habits." I spent a week at Parma. M. Deleyre had me continually in his home. We spoke of you more than you could believe. That week did me appreciable good.

From Parma I went to Florence, where I remained a fortnight, to see the curiosities and a little of the society, which I did not find very agreeable. The Florentines (especially the Florentine women) are very proud and very mercenary. I shall not give you a detailed report on all the cities where I passed some time and in which I saw the nobility. I found in Florence one of the best teachers of the flute in Europe, Dothel, a Lorrainer. He gave me several lessons, and started me on a good plan of study.

From Florence I went to Siena, where I passed a portion of my existence in perfect felicity. The nobility there form a society of the most amiable sort. They have a simplicity, an openness, a gaiety which you cannot imagine without having been there. They have no society manners, none of that affected air which to the philosopher betrays artificial beings. You, Sir, as delicate as you are, could live in the society of Siena. Since there is no Court there and the nobles think only of living within their moderate incomes, you never see in Siena those gentlemen with great interest who spoil every company in a city where it is thought that something may be gained by paying court. The Sienese are independent, equal, and content to be so, and when a great prince comes among them he is politely received, but they do not put themselves out for him. While I was at Siena, the Constable Colonna spent several days there, and I, with my monarchical ideas, was scandalized to see him treated in so easy a fashion. "Come! Il Conestabile Colonna!" They laughingly replied to me, "Ma che fa a noi il Conestabile Colonna?"[9] Never have I seen so much of what I should call true humanity as at Siena. People there do not embarrass a stranger by giving him a studied reception. He

[9] "What! Constable Colonna!" . . . "But what's Constable Colonna to us?" Lorenzo Colonna was Great Constable of the Kingdom of Naples. His brother, Marcantonio Colonna, was the Cardinal Vicar of Rome mentioned on p. 7.

comes recommended by some person of distinction, as I was by my Lord Mountstuart. They greet him naturally. An easy conversation immediately ensues. He forgets that he is a stranger, and no longer is one.

I had excellent apartments at Siena. I ate well. The wine of the district was very good, and on holidays I regaled myself with delicious Montepulciano. The air is fresh, and the weather is always fine. My health was very quickly restored. An Abbé of talent and obliging disposition dined with me every day, and accommodated himself perfectly to the little variations of my temperament. He helped me as teacher in Italian. Every morning for two hours I read the divine Ariosto, and you can imagine the effect which that produced on my romantic soul. I also wrote in Italian with equal regularity, and as I used no other language in conversation, I made rapid progress. The Sienese dialect is the most agreeable in all of Italy. For me it was a continual melody. I had lively sensations of pleasure when I heard people merely discussing the good weather. A "professor" of music, who had very fine taste, came to me every afternoon, and we sang and played fine airs on the flute. Little by little I shall come to know something of music. I can already amuse myself with it tolerably. I lack application, but that will come. I have not forgotten you in a land where I have heard six different operas.[1] I am sorry not to have some of your music with me. I remember only "Quand on sait aimer et plaire"[2] and a little air with which you amused a lady of Neuchâtel:

> Nous habitons une maison,
> Où les biens pleuvent à foison . . . [3]

[1] Rousseau was well known for his operetta, *Le Devin du village*, and had suggested to Boswell that he send him a few operatic tunes from Italy (*Boswell on the Grand Tour: Germany and Switzerland*, 15 December 1764).

[2] "When one knows how to love and please" (*Le Devin du village*, scene 5).

[3] The song continues in another manuscript of Boswell's:

> Bonbon sucré, mets délicats,
> Propos charmants, jeunes appas,
> Et la maîtresse avec un mot
> De tout billet fait un bon lot.

It may be translated: "We live in a house where good things are found in

Ariosto, music, and pleasant company occupied my days at Siena. The circumstances were most precious to my imagination. I was in a provincial city in the heart of beautiful Tuscany; a city completely at peace where not a single soldier was to be seen, not even a pensioner. I was the only foreigner there. I was as though in the most remote of countries, the most hidden of retreats. My mind was healthy, easy, and joyful. Neither past nor future entered my thoughts. I thanked God for my present existence. It is an extraordinary mind which can do so.

But, Sir, I must tell you of more interesting things. Your Scot was very attentive to the ladies at Siena. I found that people lived there in a completely natural fashion, making love as their inclinations suggested. It was the custom of the society in which I lived. I yielded to custom. I allowed myself to become all sensation and immediate feeling. I did not wish to extend my mind to encompass a series of prudent considerations. I did not wish to be more profound than the others. To enjoy was the thing. Intoxicated by that sweet delirium, I gave myself up, without self-reproach and in complete serenity, to the charms of irregular love.

I paid court to a lady who had lived much in Florence, and whose noble manners incited my vanity; and through vanity I so heated my imagination with a desire to obtain that lady that I thought myself madly in love with her. As a matter of fact, I *did* suffer from her severity. She saw me frequently, showed a genteel esteem for me, called me her friend, wrote me tender letters, but assured me that she had really loved my Lord Mountstuart, and that he would be her last

---

plenty: a sugared *bon-bon,* delicate food, delightful talk, and alluring young feminine charms. And the hostess with a word makes every lottery ticket a winning one." On a visit to Mme. de Luze at Bied, near Neuchâtel, 3–5 July 1764, Rousseau said he would like to play at lottery, meaning presumably the card game so called. Mme. de Luze replied that she did not play for money, but that she would provide a lottery. Various trifles were set out for all those present and lots were drawn. Mme. de Luze so arranged matters that Rousseau drew a snuff-box in which was a slip of paper bearing certain of her verses praising him. When asked to do so, he read them out to the company, but substituted the name of another guest for his own. He then sang his reply to Mme. de Luze. Another and probably earlier version of this song is printed in the *Annales de la société J.-J. Rousseau,* v (1909). 241–242.

lover. I wrote her the most curious of letters on that subject. It was a delicate question whether to try the constancy of a friend's mistress, but as my Lord had given me permission to adore a goddess whom he scarcely gave a thought to any more, and as I was quite sure that Signora ——[4] had considerable inclination to be persuaded to change her mind, I continued to press her with great eagerness.

I was wicked enough to wait at the same time on a very amiable little woman to whom I made declarations of the most sincere passion, as can be easily done when one feels only a slight inclination. I fancied that she had no heart, and as I believed everything fair in the war of gallantry, I lied to her certainly no fewer than a hundred times a day. Behold me, then, very busy indeed, with two affairs going at the same time. It required an unparalleled dexterity, and I had it. Then nothing was difficult for me. I drifted pleasantly between my two loves, and my *valet de place*, a lout who could neither read nor write, was dispatched with his face turned towards the east to carry a letter for Signora A. in his right-hand pocket and a letter for Signora B. in his left.

In a fortnight Signora B., who was the most trusting of persons, and with whom I had used the full force of my reasoning powers to prove that in me she would have the most faithful of lovers, but that my sufferings were so excruciating that if she did not soon assure me of her affection, I feared so much the sad effects of a strong passion on a melancholy mind that I was determined to set out at once — and what a pity it would be to miss in this short life so fine an occasion for mutual happiness.[5] This amiable person, whose heart was already touched, listened to me kindly and granted me all, saying, "Ebbene, mi fido a voi com' a un galantuomo."[6] My conscience reproached me. It happened that Signora A. revealed her character to me. I saw that she conducted intrigues strictly according to the rules, without being touched by love. I abandoned my design upon her. I attached myself completely to my dear little mistress, through a principle of true gratitude.

[4] Dash in manuscript. Signora A. is Porzia Sansedoni, and Signora B. is Moma (Girolama Piccolomini). See Introduction, p. xi.

[5] The translation of this sentence reproduces the confused construction of the original.

[6] "Good enough, I trust myself with you as a man of honour."

I studied her character. I found many good qualities in her. I even found charms in her which the dissipation of my spirit had caused me to overlook previously; and with extraordinary joy I found myself truly in love with her. I opened my heart to her, made a full confession of the deceit I had practiced on her, while assuring her that she had gained my love. I enjoyed with her the exquisite pleasure of Italian gallantry, whose enchantments I had heard so much of; and I swear to you that experiencing them measured up to my ideas. She was struck with what I had told her. She reproached me tenderly for my treachery. But from that time on she had complete confidence in me. I was utterly happy and I risked nothing.

The times, Sir, are much changed in Italy. No longer does one have to fear the stiletto of a jealous husband. But as the dispositions of a people always persist under one form or another, and as the lively wit of the loose-living Romans is displayed in sonnets, in songs, and in ecclesiastical intrigues, so Italian jealousy survives feebly in the hearts of *cavalieri serventi*, of whom every lady has one or two. A *cavaliere servente* is a being whom I regard as illustrating the last stage of human degradation. A lover without love, a soldier without pay,[7] a being who is more a drudge[8] than is a *valet de chambre*, who does continual duty, and enjoys only appearances! Since Signora B. had to keep some of these gentlemen in her train, we had to manage them, and we were sometimes a little embarrassed how to do it.

I loved her more and more. She had a natural *allegria* which never changed and which so alleviated my sombre humour that it buoyed me up until I was quite free of melancholy. I found her a woman made for a life of virtue. When I explained to her the sweet and durable bonds of the conjugal union, she was enchanted and regretted infinitely that she could not experience them, insisting strongly on the advantage which a virtuous mother of a family must enjoy in old age. But said she, "They took me out of the convent and married me at sixteen, when I did not have the slightest idea what marriage meant. Ero totalmente senza malizia. Quando ero messa in letto col mio marito, trovava roba intorno di me, e pensava ch'era una bestia."[9]

[7] The French "un soldat sans solde" has a verbal parallelism which cannot be preserved in English. [8] The second fair copy ends here.

[9] Because *roba* (approximately "stuff") is a vague word, and three of the verb forms are ambiguous as to person, the precise meaning is uncertain. Perhaps, "I

The naïveté with which she made that remark and the laughable word *roba* diverted me infinitely. "I am married," she continued, "to a man considerably older than myself; a man whom I not only cannot love but whom I cannot even respect, for to tell the truth he has no liveliness of mind at all, and he is very coarse."

Hear me, illustrious philosopher! I dare ask you to tell me honestly without prejudice whether that woman was really married, whether she had made a true contract, whether she was obliged to remain faithful to a man to whom her parents had bound her; whether it was her duty to sacrifice her finest inclinations to the hard circumstances in which she found herself. I could not answer her arguments, but in my moments of virtue and piety I warmly repeated to her the common sentiments against adultery. She was very fond of your works. I read to her with a grave and serious air the beautiful and affecting words of Julie[1] on that terrible vice. I was so moved by them that she could not but feel something. But an onrush of passion overcame me. I embraced her with a kind of frenzy and repeated our criminal ecstasies. She said, "Voi siete precisamente quel Rousseau. Tale quale. Parlate moltissimo della virtù, e però fate il male."[2] I was stirred by a pride of sentiment.[3] She confessed to me all the love affairs in which she had engaged. She told me the names of her lovers, one of whom was always at our *conversazioni*. I wished him dead many and many a time. My extreme jealousy was tormented even by what no longer existed.

My Signora was sorry that I felt so. She assured me that I was the first for whom she had felt a true passion, because it was the first time that love had made her uneasy. The same thing, indeed, has happened to women of intrigue many times. I wished to believe her. But I could not endure the thought that she had been the mistress of others. Ah, I groaned from the heart. Signora B. made a rather subtle observation on that. She told me that a man is wrong to boast

---

was entirely innocent. When I was put to bed with my husband, I found *things* around me, and thought it was an animal." The first fair copy ends with *intorno*.

[1] The heroine of Rousseau's *La Nouvelle Héloïse*.

[2] "You are yourself precisely that Rousseau. Just like him. You talk a great deal about virtue, and yet you do wrong."

[3] Boswell deleted this sentence.

that he possesses the affections of a girl, because the poor ignorant being knows no better, never having had opportunity to know the merits of lovers. But when a woman has had a little experience and knows men, then her attachment is truly flattering. I believed that also. But do not call me a dupe. Do not say that I fell into very good hands. Have no suspicions of the sincerity of my charming Signora. No, Sir, although not from the richest of families, she was completely generous, completely disinterested. Although she could not doubt that I would lay everything at her feet that she might demand from me, she never made me play,[4] never told me that she wanted the least thing; and, take my word for it, such a character is very rare among the ladies of Italy, especially those of Tuscany where they make a regular business of English "milords," as they call us British gentlemen in general. She was a careful manager and advised me how to bargain so as not to be taken in, so as to spend my money wisely. I felt as though I were really married, so well did she play the part of an excellent wife. Never was vice so sanctified by virtue. She made me go to mass with her, and I dare say that while we were there we were as pious as if our conduct had been completely innocent.

Thus my life slipped away in a delicious dream, while my principles of systematic morality were melted down by the fire of a heated imagination. But time was fleeing. My father was in momentary expectation of news of my arrival in France, and before going there I had secretly resolved to make a tour of Corsica. How was I to decide? My inclination, and, according to the principles of true gallantry, my duty — for vice, when it is social, has its principles also[5] — demanded that I remain with a woman who had made me happy and to whom I owed so much. I thought also that a being who has had so sad an existence as mine would do badly not to profit as much as possible from happiness which he had finally found — if he did not drink from the stream of pleasure as long as Heaven caused it to flow. I was utterly happy. Everything seemed agreeable to me. Even God took on for me the most agreeable aspect, as he will appear to us when at the end our souls will be all purified and exalted into the divine

[4] That is, never made him lose money to her at cards.

[5] The draft here is confused by interlinear corrections which need some adjustment to make sense.

perfection. O dear St. Preux![6] Yes, my soul is bound to yours. I have loved like you, I am pious like you. If we have committed crimes, we have also expiated them.

I resolved to leave Siena, and I told Signora —— a week beforehand. I was firm though sad. Her good sense was such that she admitted that my reasons for leaving were irrefutable. But she could not but complain of her lot, which had made her taste real happiness only to feel its loss. When we enjoyed those delicious murmurs which your divine delicacy prefers to the moment of ecstasy itself, she said, "Ah, io piangerò questi momenti."[7] Her sighs pierced my heart. I was gentle in moments of. . . .[8]

O love, passionate fever of the soul, meteor of joy whose essence it is to be brief, how dearly we buy your transports! I tried to console us both for the sadness of parting by depicting the beautiful prospect of an eternal friendship. But the Signora insisted absolutely that she must see me again . . . [9]

---

TUESDAY 1 JANUARY 1765 [Geneva]. . . . I set out at eleven in a chaise mounted so high before that I was thrown back like a bishop in his studying-chair. All the chaises for passing the Alps are hung in this way. I jogged on, mighty deliberate.

WEDNESDAY 2 JANUARY. I was very drowsy and slept almost all day.[1]

THURSDAY 3 JANUARY. I can record nothing but that Jacob,[2] who observes me writing much, said, "Sir, I think you are making books like M. Rousseau."

FRIDAY 4 JANUARY. I now began to be really among the Alps.

[6] Rousseau himself, of course, is equated with the hero of *La Nouvelle Héloïse.*
[7] "Ah, I shall lament these moments."
[8] Boswell has deleted the next line of the manuscript with repeated scribblings.
[9] The draft breaks off here, ending Boswell's résumé. The journal follows.
[1] The memoranda show that Boswell stopped that night at Marignier.
[2] Jacob Hänni, a Swiss from Berne, was Boswell's faithful and sarcastic servant. His remark, as well as much of the conversation in this volume, is in French in the original. For an explanation of the editorial method used, see p. xxiii.

Jacob said, "If one were to transport these mountains to Holland, they wouldn't stay there. The watery earth could not support them. They would sink at once." I was now amused to see the Savoyards, whose minuet I have so often danced. I had this night for my companion at supper the Marquis d'Ais of Turin, a young Sardinian officer.[3]

SATURDAY 5 JANUARY. A poor *piémontais*, or Italian of some kind, who had been a Spanish officer (as he said) and was now going to see his friends, had lost his money upon the road by gaming, and was obliged to walk to Turin. He begged leave to put his cloak-bag behind my chaise, which I granted, although this might have been a trick of some rogue who wanted a snug opportunity to rob me. He trudged along till he was quite knocked up, although I now and then walked and let him into the chaise. Today I gave him a horse till the stage of dinner.

This morning, as the maid was lighting me to my chaise, the candle went out. I gravely said, "Bring it along just as it is," as if its going out had made little odds. She did so for some time and would have continued had not I burst out a-laughing at her amazing simplicity.

I find in Savoy the windows in the villages of oiled paper. I must not forget to remark a strong instance of the gloomy sentiments annexed to a church, which Christians endeavour to render as hideous as may be. I met with a church in Savoy which had the outside of its walls adorned with real dead skulls.

This evening I was a good way advanced on the Alps, and lay at Landau (I think)[4] by the foot of Mount Cenis. I was in firm frame and wrote a good letter to Mr. Love.[5]

[3] According to the memoranda the Marquis told Boswell that Mme. de St. Gilles, whom he was to meet at Turin, had had various lovers. Boswell notes: "Resolve to be firm and have dignity of Rousseau, nor yield to a creature whom many have had, if not very charming. Be grave and swear run no risk. Be master of self in Italy."

[4] Boswell was mistaken in this name, as he suspected. Possibly he meant Lanslebourg.

[5] James Dance, actor, playwright, and manager of the theatre at Edinburgh, performed professionally under the name of Love. An early friend of Boswell's, he figures prominently in Boswell's London journal of 1762–1763.

SUNDAY 6 JANUARY. I was this day to cross Mount Cenis and wished to set out betimes. Last night the men who were to carry me sent me word that as it was *le jour de la fête des trois rois*[6] they could not go till they had heard a mass. But if I would send to the *curé* and buy them an early mass, they would go when I pleased. I sent accordingly (my *voiturier*[7] being the messenger, and calling me an officer in the French service) and agreed for about two and twenty pence British. And this morning away I went at four o'clock most decently with my men to mass. For several nights I have been very late up; and, being rendered weak and sickly, I grew bad during service, and endeavouring to get away, I fell fairly down in a faint at the church door. A good peasant helped me up and brought me to my inn, where Jacob did not fail to scold me for irregular living. I went to bed an hour, sipped a little brandy, and was well enough.

At six I mounted the Alps machine, which consisted of two trees between which were twisted some cords on which I sat. There was also a kind of back and arms, and a board hung before on which I put my feet. In this machine did four fellows (six I should say), changing two and two, carry me over the *saevas Alpes.*[8] I drank some of the snow, that I might say, "I have climbed the rudest heigths — and drunk the Alpine snow."[9] The prospect was horridly grand. The snow was sometimes six foot deep, but the road had been well hardened by passengers. I saw the chamois at a distance, of whose skins is made the shambo or shammy leather. I then came to the plain which is upon the mountain, and to the Hôpital de Pèlerins,[1] which the worthy King of Sardinia maintains. There is here a church with a good bold bell, and a priest, who lives as a kind of hermit, takes care of the pilgrims and says mass. I heard part of the service with a good

[6] Three Kings' Day, the popular designation of the Feast of the Epiphany on the Continent.

[7] Carrier. The *voiturier,* or *vetturino,* to give him his Italian name, provided a chaise and paid for most of the expenses on the road in return for a fixed sum. Travelling by *vetturino* was cheaper but slower than travelling post.

[8] Juvenal, *Satires,* x. 166: "I demens et saevas curre per Alpes" (On, madman, and cross the savage Alps). The reference is to Hannibal.

[9] Boswell here seems to echo Virgil's *Eclogues,* x. 47–49, and Dryden's translation: "And climb the frozen Alps, and tread the eternal snow."

[1] The Pilgrims' Hostel.

deal of devotion. After which the priest and I went and sat down in his kitchen, where I found a very comfortable fire and a no less comfortable pot a-boiling. My reverend father had a kind of resemblance of my old friend Johnston.[2] He gave me a glass of excellent wine, good bread, cold capon, and pie made of white partridges which are found on the Alps. I gave the maid something. I afterwards was told that the priest would not have been displeased had I made him an offering. He was immensely ignorant. I loved the idea of crossing this immense mountain of a Sunday.

MONDAY 7 JANUARY. I arrived in the evening at Turin, which made me think of Lord Eglinton, who passed some time here and advised me to do the same.[3] I put up at the Bonne Femme, a most magnificent *auberge*.[4] I went dirty to the opera. The superb theatre struck me much, and the boxes full of ladies and gallants talking to each other, quite Italy. So fatigued was I that I fell asleep. When I got home and tumbled into a fine bed, it was most luxurious.

TUESDAY 8 JANUARY. I got up very fretful, but drove off the fiend. I got my coach and *valet de louage*[5] and went to M. Torraz, my banker, a good, brisk, civil fellow. I received a letter from my dear mother, which gave me great comfort, for I had not heard from her since I left England and had formed to myself dreary ideas of her being dead, or sick, or offended with me, which it had been thought

[2] John Johnston of Grange was an obscure "writer" (that is, solicitor or attorney) in Edinburgh. His mild, melancholy, affectionate nature made him very sympathetic to Boswell, whose closest Scottish friend he was.

[3] For Alexander Montgomerie, tenth Earl of Eglinton, see p. 1. He had made the foreign tour a little over twenty years before.

[4] A Dr. McKinlay had sent Boswell, through Lord Auchinleck, an extensive set of directions for a five or six months' tour of Italy. He begins with the following prudent comments: "Upon your arrival at Turin from Geneva, put up at the sign of the Bonne Femme. You must begin here to make strict bargains for everything in respect to diet, lodging, &c., before you fix in your quarters, and observe this caution through all Italy."

[5] As was customary, Boswell hired a local servant in each town in which he spent any time. Dr. McKinlay remarks in connection with these valets: "Let me recommend it to you to trust nothing to them, I mean of your linen, wearing apparel, &c. Some honest fellows you may meet with, but in general they are rogues. You give here and over all Italy to your servant three paolis (eighteen pence sterling) a day without eating or anything else."

prudent to conceal from me. I had also an exceedingly good letter from my brother David, in which he very sensibly and genteelly reproved me for yielding so much to the attacks of melancholy.[6]

I sent a letter of recommendation from Colonel Chaillet to the Comtesse de St. Gilles.[7] She received me at four o'clock. She was past fifty and had long been *hackneyed in the ways of men*,[8] but, being strong, was still well enough. She talked of Duke Hamilton who had been a great gallant of hers.[9] She had animal spirits and talked incessantly. She carried me out in her coach to take the air. I was already then quite in the Italian mode. We returned to her house, where was a stupid *conversazione*, all men. After this we all went to a public ball at the Théâtre de Carignan. It was very handsome and gay. I danced a minuet with the Spanish Ambassadress. There was here many fine women. The counts and other pretty gentlemen told me whenever I admired a lady, "Sir, you can have her. It would not be difficult." I thought at first they were joking and waggishly amusing themselves with a stranger. But I at last discovered that they were really in earnest and that the manners here were so openly debauched that adultery was carried on without the least disguise. I asked them, "But why then do you marry?" "Oh, it's the custom; it perpetuates families." I met here a Capitaine Billon to whom I had

[6] Brother David was a serious young man of sixteen apprenticed to a banking-house in Edinburgh. Their mother, Euphemia, was devoted to her children, but she was absorbed in her household duties and her devotions, and almost never wrote to them or to anyone else.

[7] Caterina Maria Theresa di San Gillio (Boswell used the French equivalents of Italian names where French was the medium of communication, as here) occupied a commanding position in the society of Turin, partly through her husband, who was a natural son of the late King of Sardinia, Victor Amadeus II, partly through her own considerable social gifts. She figures largely in the records of travellers to Turin for many years. Casanova says that she superintended all the intrigues in town. Dutens (whom Boswell met the next day) says that she had "a great predilection for young Englishmen, and when she was almost fifty inspired a violent passion in Lord Charles Spencer [same age as Boswell] and Mr. [that is, Sir Brooke] Boothby" (*Mémoires d'un voyageur qui se repose*, 1806, i. 154). This makes Boswell's pretended passion seem somewhat less grotesque. Boswell had met Colonel Jean Frédéric Chaillet at Neuchâtel.

[8] *1 Henry IV*, III. ii. 40 ("ways" for "eyes").

[9] James, the sixth Duke, who died in 1758 at the age of thirty-three.

a letter from M. de Froment. He was a blunt Frenchman, very obliging. I also met here young Gray, son to my Lord, a good, brisk little fellow.

WEDNESDAY 9 JANUARY. There was at present no minister here from our Court. But M. Dutens, who acted in his place, carried me to wait on the Comte de Viry, the Prime Minister.[1] The Court was in mourning, so I could not be presented till I had a black coat.[2] I trifled away the morning. I heard Wilkes was come.[3] I was very curious to see him in his misfortunes. I sent him this note:[4]

Turin, 9 January 1765

SIR: — I am told that Mr. Wilkes is now in Turin. As a politician, my monarchical soul abhors him. As a Scotsman I smile at him. As a friend I know him not. As a companion I love him. I believe it is not decent for me to wait upon him. Yet I wish much to see him. I shall be alone and have a tolerable dinner upon my table at one o'clock. If Mr. Wilkes chooses to be my guest, I shall by no means oppose it. I may venture to say he shall be very welcome, and do promise him a feast of most singular and choice conversation.

BOSWELL.

He was not at home, but in the afternoon when I was abroad he left a card for me: "Monsieur Wilkes pour Monsieur Boswell."

[1] Louis Dutens, a Frenchman, served under three English envoys at Turin, including Lord Mountstuart in later years. Tutor, secretary, and dramatist, he is best remembered for his anecdotal autobiography, *Mémoires d'un voyageur qui se repose.* — As Sardinian Ambassador to Great Britain a few years earlier, the Comte de Viry had established an enviable reputation for himself as a go-between in British politics. Sir Lewis Namier has described him as "a peculiar intriguer, an ample talker, assiduous, inscrutable, secretive, and yet plausible, who carried information or tales from Newcastle to Pitt, from Pitt to Bute, from Bute to Newcastle . . . " (*England in the Age of the American Revolution*, Macmillan & Company, Ltd., London, 1930, p. 91).

[2] The mourning had been ordered for the Princess Hedwig Sophia of Holstein, sister of the King of Sweden.

[3] For John Wilkes, see Introduction, p. xiii. Professor Chauncey B. Tinker has a charming and illuminating chapter on Boswell's relations with Wilkes in his *Young Boswell* (1922).

[4] The original of this letter, preserved among the Wilkes papers in the British Museum, is actually dated 10 January.

At three Billon went with me and saw some of the Turin churches. At the Bernardines' is a little place railed in like a particular burying-place, on the floor of which is recorded a miracle, which, as it is the first I have met with in Italy, I shall here relate. Some sacrilegious villains had broken into a church and stolen away the sacred calix with the Body of Jesus Christ. As he[5] was driving his beast laden with his impious spoils, it fell down of a sudden, and the holy transubstantiated wafer rose into the air and hovered there in the sight of thousands. The Archbishop of Turin came out with a train of his clergy and kneeled in solemn adoration holding the calix in his hands, when lo! the host gently descended into the calix. In commemoration of this miracle an annual feast is observed at Turin in this church which was erected upon the spot. The inscription is as follows: "Hic Divini Corporis Avector Jumentum Procubuit. Hic Sacra Sese Hostia Sarcinis Emancipata in Auras Extulit. Hic Supplices in Taurinensium Manus Clemens Descendit. Hic Ergo Sanctum Prodigio Locum, Memor, Supplex, Pronus, Venerare aut Verere. Die VI Junii, Anno Dni 1453."[6] This is a very remarkable story. It is said to be supported by very strong proofs.

I went at five to Mme. de St. Gilles', where I tired to death. Her husband was an old shrewd fellow, who had killed his man in Poland.[7] The room was full of young rakes, mighty stupid, and old worn-out miscreants in whom impotence and stupidity were united. I attended her to the opera, as one of her cicisbays.[8] She had two of us.

[5] Boswell apparently forgot that he spoke of several "villains."

[6] "Here fell the mule that was carrying off the Divine Body. Here the sacred host freed itself from the pack and rose into the air. Here it descended compassionately into the suppliant hands of the people of Turin. Here, therefore, mindful, suppliant, prostrate, venerate in awe a place made holy by a miracle. 6 June, A.D. 1453."

[7] In 1726 Vittorio Francesco, ninth Comte de St. Gilles, while in the military service of Augustus the Strong, King of Poland and Elector of Saxony, quarrelled at gambling with Count Vitzthum von Eckstädt, a man much older than himself, and as a consequence was condemned to three months' imprisonment in the fortress at Leipzig. He escaped to Poland and sent a challenge to Vitzthum. The duel was fought at Warsaw on horseback, Vitzthum being killed at the first stroke. St. Gilles took refuge in a monastery at Warsaw, which the King's troops burned; however, he escaped to France.

[8] That is, *cicisbei*. It was the privilege of the *cicisbeo* to accompany a married woman to evening entertainments, paying her small attentions with assiduity,

One held her gloves or her muff, and another her fan. After being heartily wearied in her box, I went down to the parterre, from whence I saw, in a high box, Mr. Wilkes. To see a man whom I have so often thought of since I left England, filled me with romantic agitation. I considered he might have been dead as well as Churchill,[9] and methought I viewed him in the Elysian fields. When I got home I sent him another note:[1]

I AM SORRY you could not dine with me. I find you have taken my card as I intended it. I would wait upon you, were I not an old laird and a steady royalist. Since Churchill's death, I have had a serious sympathy with you. Has it not made you pause and reflect a little? Might we not have an interview, and continue the conversation on the immateriality of the soul which you had with my countryman Baxter many years ago at Brussels?[2] To men of philosophical minds there are surely moments when they set aside their nation, their rank, their character, all that they have done and all that they have suffered in this jumbling world. Such moments may be most philosophical, as they are clear of all prejudices, good as well as bad. John Wilkes, the fiery Whig, would despise this sentiment. John Wilkes, the gay profligate, would laugh at it. But John Wilkes, the philosopher, will feel it, and will love it. You have no objection to sitting up a little late. Perhaps you may come to me tonight. I hope at any rate you will dine with me tomorrow.

He was gone to bed.

THURSDAY 10 JANUARY. I tried to write this morning, but could do nothing. I drove about in the environs. At three I called on M.

---

and returning her to her husband at the end of the evening. The word originally meant "whisperer." Smollett wrote: "For my part, I would rather be condemned for life to the galleys than exercise the office of a *cicisbeo,* exposed to the intolerable caprices and dangerous resentment of an Italian virago" (*Travels through France and Italy,* 2nd ed., 1766, ii. 55).

[9] For Charles Churchill, see Introduction, p. xiv.

[1] The original is preserved among the Wilkes papers in the British Museum.

[2] Andrew Baxter, a Scottish philosopher who died in 1750, dedicated one of his works to Wilkes, describing it as the substance of a conversation they had held at Spa in 1745. Baxter's proof for the existence of God is based on the supposed inertness of matter, which thus implied the constant action of an immaterial principle.

Bartoli, the King's Antiquary, whom M. Schmidt at Karlsruhe had advised me to see. I was courteously received. I found him confusedly learned and lively. He improved the more I talked with him. I gave him anecdotes of Voltaire and Rousseau. He did not approve of the writings of either of the two, for he was a man attached to the Catholic religion. I told him that Rousseau said, "I live in a world of chimeras." He replied, "Then let him keep his books there, and not be sending them out into the real world." He offered me his services while I remained at Turin.

I then went to Mme. St. Gilles'. The whim seized me of having an intrigue with an Italian countess, and, as I had resolved to stay very little time here, I thought an oldish lady most proper, as I should have an easy attack. I began throwing out hints at the opera. I sat vis-à-vis to her and pressed her legs with mine, which she took very graciously. I began to lose command of myself. I became quite imprudent. I said, "Surely there will be another world, if only for getting the King of Prussia flogged"; against whom I raged while the Imperial Minister sat by us.[3] Billon carried me to the box of the Countess Burgaretta, and introduced me to her. She was a most beautiful woman.[4] Billon told me I might have her. My mind was now quite in fermentation. I was a sceptic, but my devotion and love of decency remained. My desire to know the world made me resolve to intrigue a little while in Italy, where the women are so debauched that they are hardly to be considered as moral agents, but as inferior beings. I shall just mark little sketches of my attempts in that way. This night (the third of our acquaintance) I made plain addresses to Mme. St. Gilles, who refused me like one who wished to have me. But thinking me more simple than I really was, feared to trust me. I was too easy about the matter to take any pains.

FRIDAY 11 JANUARY. I had now my black clothes. My *valet de louage* told me my hair must be dressed "in a horse-tail." I was in droll bad humour and abused the fellow, saying, "Then you must get me shod too. Have you a good blacksmith at Turin? Send for him."

[3] Boswell had been annoyed by his failure to secure a presentation to Frederick the Great. The Imperial Minister was Johann Sigismund, Count of Khevenhüller-Metsch. An Austrian and consequently the subject of Frederick's bitterest enemy, Maria Theresa, he would not have been displeased by such attacks.

[4] Vittoria Enrichetta, wife of Pietro Giuseppe Bistorti, Count of Borgaretto. They had been married in 1755.

However, I did comply with the courtly mode. I waited on Dutens, who was about publishing a complete edition of the works of Leibnitz with notes and I know not what more. *Opus magnum et ponderosum.* Will men still be plodding in this manner? Let them alone. It is as good as playing at cards.[5] I was presented to the King of Sardinia, who, after all his Italian wars, was just a little quiet man. He only asked me whence? and whither? I looked at him as a kind of heir to the British Crown.[6] There was a numerous Court, mostly military. I went to mass in the King's chapel, which he attends regularly every day.

This morning I was quite in love with Mme. Burgaretta. Billon certainly officiated for me as a genteel pimp. To show how corruption may prevail without shame, thus in gross flattery did I write to him this morning:

My dear Sir, — If you are a man worthy of respect, an obliging man whom one must love; in short, if you have any noble virtue in your soul, arrange for me to see Mme. B—— today. You told me yesterday that it will be possible for me to enjoy the favours of that goddess in a very little time. Oh, how adorable she is! I beg of you to be at the coffee-house after the Court. I shall have the honour of finding you there.[7]

Was not this real rascality to prostitute the praises of merit in such a manner? But when a man gives himself up to gross gallantry he must lose much of his delicacy of principle. Billon told me with great simplicity, "It's a low game." I shall only talk in general of my Turin deviations. I had Billon to dine with me, after which Bartoli and I went and saw a church. I was madly in love with Mme. B——. I called on her thrice this afternoon, but did not find admittance.

At four Dutens presented me at the French Ambassador's to his

[5] This hardly sounds like the Boswell who a few months earlier was planning to produce both a Scots dictionary and a Latin translation of a book of law. But as Geoffrey Scott said, Boswell was "pedantic in Holland, princely in Germany, philosophic in Switzerland, and amorous in Italy."

[6] Charles Emmanuel III, who took his title from Sardinia but whose principal domain was Savoy, was a great-grandson of Charles I of England, and, in the Jacobite succession, next heir to the British throne after Prince Charles Edward and Cardinal York.

[7] Original in French.

Excellency's lady. I had the honour to hand her to her coach. About the middle of the stair we were met by a marquise, who of course was to turn back. But the great question was, who should be led first to her coach? *Madame la marquise! Madame l'ambassadrice!*[8] I was simple enough to be tossed from the one to the other, as I did just what I was bid; while the rogue Dutens enjoyed my perplexity and probably studied from it something to insert among his notes on Leibnitz on determining motives. At last her Excellency of France took the *pas*. I was deeply hipped,[9] and knew not what to make of myself. I went and lounged some time at Mme. St. Gilles'; then I returned to the drawing-room of the French Ambassadress, where I was presented to M. Chauvelin himself. I was quite loaded with gloom and stood at the back of the chairs of those who were playing, to whom I hardly gave any attention but was fixed in proud and sullen silence. This was a most sad evening.

SATURDAY 12 JANUARY. I called this morning on Gray, who lived at the Academy. I found there Mr. Needham of the Royal Society, whose acquaintance I much wished for.[1] When I hear of such a man's being in a place where I arrive at, I go immediately and make him the first visit, although I stand upon the very pinnacle of punctilios with the British in general. I found him a learned, accurate, easy man. He said he followed just the study which pleased him at the time, and went on calm and moderate, finding every part of knowledge add to the general stock. We talked of vanity, which I defended, and owned I felt a good deal. "Yes," said he, smiling, "you never hear of a great man but you would wish to be him. I am not so, for I have observed the condition of such men. I love fame only as an ingredient in happiness." This idea pleased me much. I then went to the King's museum where Signor Bartoli showed me a very curious collection of antiquities and natural curiosities. He then showed me His Majesty's library, which is truly noble.

[8] Agnès Thérèse de Chauvelin, later a marquise herself.

[9] Or "hyp'd" as Boswell often spells it, a contraction of "hypochondriacal."

[1] John Turberville Needham, Roman Catholic priest and man of science, was at this time serving as governor to the eldest son of Viscount Dillon. He propounded a theory of spontaneous generation, and his microscopic observations of animalcula roused great excitement at the time. He was a friend of Buffon, who described his work in the *Natural History*.

I dined with Billon at the Auberge d'Angleterre. My landlord at the Bonne Femme had endeavoured to impose upon me. I was enraged at the rogue, and determined to change him. I called up the landlord of this inn, who hates the other fellow. "Sir, are you a friend or relative of the landlord of the Bonne Femme?" "No, Sir." "Dare I speak ill of him to you?" "Yes, Sir," "Well, then, he's a rascal, and I should like to come to your house." The fellow was confounded and pleased, and having been lectured by Billon, he made a reasonable price with me.[2] We had another French officer with us, a lively young fellow. We were mighty gay. But I was in feverish spirits.

At night I sat a long time in the box of Mme. B., of whom I was now violently enamoured. I made my declarations, and was amazed to find such a proposal received with the most pleasing politeness. She however told me, "It is impossible. I have a lover" (showing him), "and I do not wish to deceive him." Her lover was the Neapolitan Minister, Comte Pignatelli, in whose box she sat. He was a genteel, amiable man. He went away, and then I pursued my purpose. Never did I see such dissimulation, for she talked aloud that I should think no more of my passion, and the *piémontais* around us heard this and said without the least delicacy, "A traveller expects to accomplish in ten days as much as another will do in a year." I was quite gone. She then said to me, "Whisper in my ear," and told me, "We must make arrangements," assuring me that she had talked severely to persuade people that there was nothing between us. She bid me call upon her next day at three. This was advancing with rapidity. I saw she was no very wise personage, so flattered her finely. "Ah, Madame, I understand you well. This country is not worthy of you. That is true" (like a mere fool). "You are not loved here as you ought to be." Billon came and repeated gross bawdy. This was disgusting. When I got home I was so full of my next day's bliss that I sat up all night.

SUNDAY 13 JANUARY. By want of sleep and agitation of mind, I was quite feverish. At seven I received a letter from Mme. —— telling me that people talked of us, and forbidding me to come to her or to think more of the "plus malheureuse de femmes." This tore my

[2] Boswell's Accounts show that six days' food and lodging at the Bonne Femme cost him about £3, and nine days at the Auberge d'Angleterre about £3.6.

very heart. I wrote to her like a madman, conjuring her to pity me. Billon came and went out with me in my coach. He told me I had lost her merely by being an *imprudent* and discovering my attachment to all the world. I had wrought myself up to a passion which I was not master of. I saw he looked upon me as a very simple young man; for amongst the thorough-bred libertines of Turin to have sentiment is to be a child. I changed my lodgings. She wrote to me again. I wrote to her an answer more mad than my former one. I was quite gone. At night I saw her at the opera. We were reserved. But I told her my misery. She said, "C'est impossible." I was distracted. I forgot to mention that I have paid her one visit.

[Boswell to the Countess Burgaretta. Original in French][3]

[Turin] Sunday [13 January 1765]

I HAVE NO WORDS, MADAME, to tell you how your letter has pierced my heart. I have been so agitated by that passion you have inspired in me that I have not slept half an hour all night. The thought never left me of the happiness which was to be mine today at "*a quarter past three.*" And now comes your cruel letter, forbidding me to come today to your house.

Madame, I am wholly yours. You may dispose of me as it shall please you, but consider that a worthy man's happiness should be a matter of consequence to a woman such as I have the honour to conceive you to be. Your conduct has roused hopes which it will cost me the bitterest regret to abandon. O Madame, you are generous! Think, I entreat you, of your unhappy lover who is tortured by his passion for you and dares to ask your pity as his due.

Madame, with your brilliance, with your knowledge of the world, you can find means to console this lacerated heart. Grant me, I entreat you, an assignation this evening at any hour when you can be alone. Reflect. Let your humanity speak. I am unwilling to see you in company: I cannot do so without confusion and torment. Dear Madame, adieu. Answer me unless you wish to kill me.

[3] This and the following letters to Mme. Burgaretta and Mme. Skarnavis were first printed, together with Geoffrey Scott's translations, in the fifth volume of Colonel Isham's privately printed *Private Papers of James Boswell*. Scott's versions are used here with slight changes. The letters to these two ladies are printed from Boswell's copies.

[Boswell to the Countess Burgaretta. Original in French]

[Turin, 13 January 1765]

FORGIVE ME, MADAME, if the pain and stupefaction caused by the blow of your first letter prevented me from paying attention to your commands for its return. Here are both your letters.[4] I have kissed them a thousand times, laden though they are with so much cruelty. They come from you: that is enough. Torments, from your hand, are to me precious. Baneful and delicious madness! O Love! Most adorable of women, my heart and my soul exist but for you.

You call yourself unhappy. Great Heavens! What can I do? Command me, Madame: you will see whether I am attached to you or not.

Yesterday evening we came to an explanation. I made you an unreserved avowal of my passion for you. You were good enough to tell me that your situation is a delicate one and that "the most careful arrangements would be necessary." I can be blamed for nothing but an excess of passion which almost deprives me of power to conceal it; and I believe, Madame, that this is why you hesitate to display your generosity to an unhappy foreigner who throws himself at your feet and pleads for pity.

But, Madame, if the utmost deference and discretion of conduct may yet earn some reward of gratitude, I shall not cease to flatter myself with hopes of your favour. My happiness, my life, depend on you. Persist in your cruelty, and I cannot answer for the consequences of the most violent passion man ever felt. You do not refuse me your friendship. O Madame! Dear and kind Countess! Give me a proof of your compassion. In granting that, you will grant all that my unhappy stars permit me to obtain. I shall do what I can to calm myself. I shall leave Turin full of sadness, but also full of gratitude. We shall correspond; and I, wherever I am, shall remain yours. Once more, my dear Madame, I beseech you think seriously. Write me a word or two before the opera; calm me as much as you can. I shall have the honour to be in your opera box for as brief a time as you command. I shall be all obedience; and always, always yours.

MONDAY 14 JANUARY. Night before last I plainly proposed matters to Mme. St. Gilles. "I am young, strong, vigorous. I offer my services as a duty, and I think that the Comtesse de St. Gilles will do

[4] Boswell does not seem to have kept copies of them.

very well to accept them." "But I am not that kind of woman." "Very well, Madame, I shall believe you." I thought to take her *en passant*. But she was cunning and saw my passion for Mme. B——, so would not hazard with me.

This morning I waited on Mr. Needham, who read me a defence of the Trinity which was most ingenious and really silenced me. I said, "Sir, this defence is very good; but pray what did you do before you thought of it?" He replied that he submitted to it as a mystery. He said the Catholic religion was proved as a general system, like the Newtonian philosophy, and, although we may be perplexed with partial difficulties, they are not to shake our general belief. He said the world would very soon be divided into Catholics and Deists. He threw my ideas into the orthodox channel. But still I recalled Rousseau's liberal views of the benevolent Divinity, and so was more free. Needham said that a man whose melancholy hurt his rational powers could hardly be accountable for his moral conduct. He consoled me.

After dinner I called on Norton and Heath, two English gentlemen. I did not know what to say to them. I liked the opera much tonight, and my passion was already gone. Honest Billon said, "If you want to make love, I can find you a girl." I agreed to this by way of cooling my raging disposition to fall in love. At night Mme. St. Gilles seemed piqued that I pursued her no longer, and, suspecting that I was enchained by Mme. B——, she said, "Really, you are a little mad. You get notions, and your head turns. I'll tell you: I think you have studied a great deal. You ought to go back to your books. You should not follow the profession of gallant or you will be terribly taken in. Be careful of your health and of your purse. For you don't know the world." Although my former love-adventures are proof enough that it is not impossible for me to succeed with the ladies, yet this abominable woman spoke very true upon the whole. I have too much warmth ever to have the cunning necessary for a general commerce with the corrupted human race.

[Boswell to the Countess Burgaretta. Original in French]

[Turin] Monday [14 January 1765]

I ENTREAT YOU, MADAME, to return me the two letters which I have had the honour to write you. Act towards me with the same generosity that I have shown you. Today I feel better. My passion abates; and for that reason I still have hopes that you will make the *arrangements* of which you spoke.

TUESDAY 15 JANUARY. Wrote all the morning. After dinner saw the King's palace, where are a number of very excellent pictures. I was shown the King's own apartment. I took up his hat and cane, but found them neither lighter than silk nor heavier than gold. In short, they could not be distinguished from the hat and stick of uncrowned mortals. I was much pleased with his closet, where he had a *prie-dieu* and a good many books of devotion. His Majesty is truly pious.

I then went to Billon's, who had a very pretty girl for me with whom I amused myself. I then went to another ball at the Théâtre de Carignan. I tired much. Billon had promised to have a girl to sleep with me all night at his lodgings. I went there at eleven but did not find her. I was vexed and angry.

WEDNESDAY 16 JANUARY. Billon and another French officer dined with me. We were well. I then called on Needham, who explained his philosophical opinion of transubstantiation, by which I was convinced that it was not absurd. He and I then went and waited on the French Ambassadress. After which I went to Mme. St. Gilles', where I was quite disgusted. I went home very dull. What a strange day have I had of it![5]

THURSDAY 17 JANUARY. All the forenoon I wrote. After dinner I took Bartoli to air in my coach. We went and saw the Bernardines' library. I was gloomy but patient. At night I was again at a ball. I was calm, pensive, and virtuous. Sabbati,[6] Secretary to the French Ambassador, talked a good deal with me, and said, "You are a man from

[5] The memorandum covering this day adds: "This day pause; swear solemn behaviour. Madness is no excuse, as you can restrain it. No girls or you're poxed. Swear this, and no more imaginary enjoying; it weakens. Be calm."

[6] Honoré Auguste Sabatier de Cabre.

another century." I had eyed a singular lady some time. She was very debauched. But I took a fancy to her. Sabbati presented me to her. I said, "Mme. S——,[7] this is the fifth evening that I have tried to make your acquaintance." She seemed gay and pleased.[8]

FRIDAY 18 JANUARY. I passed the morning at home, but was so sadly dissipated that I could do no good. While I was at dinner, an Augustine monk came and asked charity. He said he had been twenty-seven years *religiosus et semper contentus.*

I then went to Billon's, where I had a pretty girl. I was disgusted with low pleasure. Billon talked of women in the most indelicate manner. I then went to Mme. Burgaretta's, where I found two more swains. She grumbled and complained of a headache; and she dressed before us, changing even her shirt. We indeed saw no harm; but this scene entirely cured my passion for her. Her *femme de chambre* was very clever, and when the Countess was dressed, carried away her morning clothes in a little barrel. At the opera I sat in the box of Mme. S——, who was soft and gentle, and seemed to like my compliments. I was at Mme. St. Gilles' in good spirits, and went home pretty much content.

[Boswell to the Countess Burgaretta. Original in French]

[Turin, 18 January 1765][9]

PRAY, MADAME, allow me to tell how grateful I am to you for all the kindnesses you have extended to a stranger. You have, I trust, no fault to find with my conduct ever since I pledged myself to the strictest discretion. You do not know the value of your Scotsman. There is no suffering he will not endure for the lady he worships.

[7] Maria Anna Theresa Skarnavis (Boswell's spelling of Scarnafis, the Piedmontese version of the name) was the wife of Filippo Ottone Ponte, Count of Scarnafigi, who was appointed on 27 January Minister to Portugal from Sardinia. He was later Ambassador to France. Mme. Skarnavis was about seven years older than Boswell.

[8] The memorandum elaborates a little here: "Gave her arm going out. Asked you, 'Do you live close by?' 'Auberge d'Angleterre.' Perhaps she'll send."

[9] Scott dated this letter 12 January 1765 and placed it first in the series. However, the memorandum covering this day reads: "Short card to Burgaretta; thank and say it *injuste* to Pignatelli."

Madame, you will forgive me if my sincere passion compels me to ask you, with all deference, to tell me, yes or no, whether you will be able to receive me before I leave.

I will confess, Madame, that I find myself so much indebted to M. P—— that I should have scruples against doing him an offence. But I believe, Madame, that you have no ties with him which preclude generosity to another. If that is indeed so, I entreat you to make me the happiest of mortals, and I shall cherish an undying memory of the goodness of your heart. Of my discretion you have already made proof. Reflect on this, and answer me.

Your brother is my friend.[1]

SATURDAY 19 JANUARY. Here have I stayed a week longer than I intended, partly from love, partly to see a grand opera which is to be performed tomorrow. After dinner I sat some time with Needham, who told me he was in orders as a Catholic priest and had always lived with conscientious strictness. He said he had many severe struggles to preserve his chastity, but had done so, and was now quite serene and happy. He had also been distressed with a lowness of spirits which impedes devotion. Thomas à Kempis complains of a *siccitas animi*.[2] I was amazed to find a man who had such parts and had seen so much of the world, and yet so strict as worthy Needham. I talked of the eternity of hell's torments, which he defended as the continual shade which must be in the universe, which wicked beings ought justly to form. He said too that the pains would be in proportion to the offences, and that perhaps to exist with a certain degree of pain was better than to be annihilated.

At the opera I sat in Mme. S——' box, and fairly told her my love, saying that I could not leave Turin, being entirely captivated by her. She seemed propitious.[3] Mme. St. Gilles, deservedly balked of my services, was not a little angry. She was impudent enough to tell

[1] Mme. Burgaretta's brother has not been identified.

[2] A dryness of the soul.

[3] In the memoranda Boswell records the conversation (in French): "BOSWELL. 'I cannot go away. Why leave what is most dear to me?' MME. SKARNAVIS. 'I cannot make up my mind.' BOSWELL. 'I shall tell you without flattery, the women here have neither taste nor sentiment. I saw you. I tried to make your acquaintance, &c. Will you allow me a visit?' MME. SKARNAVIS. 'Yes. You may command me,' &c. She was truly *kind*."

about that I had made a bold attack upon her. I did not like to hear this joke.

SUNDAY 20 JANUARY. The Comte Pignatelli, Envoy from Naples, had given me some letters of recommendation for different places. I was struck with this piece of politeness, and waited upon him this morning. He was indisposed, and abed, where he had a neat little desk on which he wrote. We chatted very agreeably, and agreed in abusing the *piémontais*, who are indeed a good-for-nothing mongrel race, ignorant and trifling. I said a man of genius made such a figure here as Voltaire would do in a society of people that valued themselves upon cutting pens, and despised those who cut worse than they did. At the opera I again sat by Mme. S——. She advised me to go, and rather to think of such a scheme when I should return. She would not allow me any the least liberty.

Last night the new opera was played, called *The Conquest of Mexico*. The decorations were superb, and some of the music very good, but not so well as the last opera, which was by old Sassone.[4]

Sabbati and I talked again tonight. He said everything great and spirited was carried on by prejudices early implanted. He said a jealous man was most easily deceived. Last night I had taken *congé* of Mme. St. Gilles, so went no more near her. This evening I went to a ball given by some bourgeois at my inn. I danced one or two minuets, and thought to do them honour. But the good bourgeois gave me broad hints not to keep them from the floor.

MONDAY 21 JANUARY. Never was mind so formed as that of him who now recordeth his own transactions. I was now in a fever of love for an abandoned being whom multitudes had often treated like a very woman of the town. I hesitated if I should not pass the winter here and gravely write to my father that really a melancholy man like myself so seldom found anything to attach him that he might be indulged in snatching a transient pleasure, and thus would I inform him that an Italian Countess made me remain at Turin. Was there ever such madness? O Rousseau, how am I fallen since I was with thee! I wrote a long letter to Mme. S——, entreating her pity

[4] The "new opera," *Montezuma*, was composed by Francesco di Majo; the "last opera," probably *L'Olimpiade*, by Johann Adolph Hasse, generally known as *Il Sassone* (the Saxon).

and all that.[5] Her answer was that if she had known my letter was of such a nature, she would not have opened it. She had told me plainly her mind at the opera. Pedro, my stupid *valet de place*,[6] brought me this shocking word-of-mouth message. I saw that amongst profligate wretches a man of sentiment could only expose himself.

After dinner I went to Needham, and was consoled with learned and solid conversation. We went to the opera together, and sat in the middle of the parterre, from whence I never stirred but was quite independent. I enjoyed fully the entertainment. Needham talked of the religious orders, particularly of the Trappe, and explained them in so philosophical a manner that I had much solemn satisfaction.

After the opera Norton and Heath insisted I should go home with them and sup. I went, like a simpleton. They carried me into a low room of their inn, where they romped with two girls and gave me a most pitiful supper. This, now, was true English. I had now and then looked from the parterre to Mme. S——, but did not go to her box. I determined to set out next morning for Milan.

[Boswell to the Countess Skarnavis. Original in French]

[Turin] Auberge d'Angleterre, 21 January 1765

Permit me, Madame, to write to you, for it is thus that I can best express to you the nature of my feelings towards you. I shall express them very briefly, without timidity and without restraint.

You are already aware that I feel for you the strongest of passions. I glory in it, and make no complaint of all I suffer. I shall not again repeat my ardent professions. You have no doubts on that head; if you have, it is from an excess of suspicion. I have heard many tales of you. I believe none. I am determined to believe none. No, Madame, I adore you, and nothing could avail to weaken that adoration.

Yesterday evening I told you I was consoling myself with hopes of your goodness. Your answer, both tender and cruel, was, "It is far better to go away." You gave me the most cautious advice. But you

[5] One of the stock phrases of Bayes in the Duke of Buckingham's *Rehearsal*.

[6] In a descriptive list which Boswell kept of his *valets de place*, he characterizes Pedro as "old, small, and feeble."

refrained from telling me it would be impossible to win your favour. I implore you, Madame, to reflect seriously, and to use no evasions with a romantic lover who deserves quite other consideration than one gives to the kind who may be had any day. Madame, I venture to affirm that never have your charms been more worthily felt than by me. If you accord me the supreme happiness, you will be showing yourself generous to an excellent man who would be attached by gratitude to you for the rest of his life. You are in perfect safety with me. You can rely on my honour in every respect. Our characters, Madame, are alike. Yes, I am sure of it. We have the liveliest ideas, which we express only by our glances. We have a modesty which nothing can destroy. Assuredly we are not novices in love. Nevertheless, with exquisite delicacy you prevent my touching your hand; and I, if I hear mention of Mme. Skarnavis, find myself blushing. Ah! when we abandon ourselves to pleasures under the veil of darkness, what transports, what ecstasy will be ours! Pardon me, Madame, I am greatly agitated. I place myself under your protection: dispose of me as you see fit. If you tell me, "Sir, think no more of that happiness; 'tis impossible," — if you say that, I shall hear you with distress, I shall tear myself away from Turin, I shall leave on the instant.

But if I am not disagreeable to you, if your generous heart prompts you to say, "Stay: I am one who can value a true passion at its worth," you cannot conceive, Madame, how keenly I shall be touched. O love! baneful and delicious madness,[7] I feel you, and am your slave.

I well know, Madame, that I ought to remain long here to earn the great boon which I entreat. But just now I am not my own master. For the rest of my stay, I shall be entirely yours. I shall mix no more with the world. For all save you I shall have left Turin. I have tried to explain myself, Madame; it is for you to reflect and decide. It is a singular case. Have a care. Dear and amiable Countess, let your humanity speak. Let us see if you can rise superior to low prejudices and tell your true thoughts.

[7] "O Amour! Folie funeste et délicieuse!" Boswell was thrifty of his fine phrases: he had used this a week before in his second letter to Mme. Burgaretta. Seven months later he used the thought expressed in the opening sentences of this letter to Mme. Skarnavis to begin one to Mme. Sansedoni.

It shall be between ourselves. Oh, you have nothing to fear!

Reflect — and in a few hours' time give me your reply. I shall send to get it. You have told me what you would do in my case; I well know what I should do in yours. Have a care, Madame, there is here something important at stake. I tremble, but I have hopes. Heaven bless you.

TUESDAY 22 JANUARY. Needham and Gray breakfasted with me. I was quite easy and genteel. I sent to Mme. S—— and begged she would return me my letter. She bid the valet say that she had thrown it in the fire. Here was the extreme of mortification for me. I was quite sunk. Worthy Needham bid me continue to lay up knowledge, and took an affectionate leave of me, hoping we should meet again.

I set out at eleven. As I went out at one of the ports, I saw a crowd running to the execution of a thief. I jumped out of my chaise and went close to the gallows. The criminal stood on a ladder, and a priest held a crucifix before his face. He was tossed over, and hung with his face uncovered, which was hideous. I stood fixed in attention to this spectacle, thinking that the feelings of horror might destroy those of chagrin. But so thoroughly was my mind possessed by the feverish agitation that I did not feel in the smallest degree from the execution. The hangman put his feet on the criminal's head and neck and had him strangled in a minute. I then went into a church and kneeled with great devotion before an altar splendidly lighted up. Here then I felt three successive scenes: raging love — gloomy horror — grand devotion. The horror indeed I only *should* have felt. I jogged on slowly with my *vetturino*, and had a grievous inn at night.

WEDNESDAY 23 JANUARY. I set out by four o'clock. It was cold and wet. I slept all day. My blood stagnated and I was a deplorable being. My inn was again wretched.

THURSDAY 24 JANUARY. Still bad weather. I was much out of humour. I had only my servant to talk to. It was just living in a kitchen. My ideas were all mean. I despised myself. This is sad work, upon my honour.

FRIDAY 25 JANUARY. I arrived this morning at Milan. I drank chocolate, and got into spirits. This was the first town I saw mentioned by a classic. Often did I repeat, "Et Mediolani mira omnia, copia rerum,"[8] &c. I got a *valet de louage* and went to the famous great church. It is debased by little shops like the Cathedral at Strasbourg. I saw a vast number of people still at work preparing marble ornaments for it. It is disputed whether the administrators of the fund for building this church keep it back designedly to have the money longer in their hands, or if they really advance so slowly by reason of the immense work. On entering this church I felt the most solemn admiration. The statue of St. Bartholomew and the rich shrine of St. Charles Borromeo have been enough described by others. I mounted up to the top of the church by the inside stair so far, and then got out upon part of the roof, and from thence mounted by different stairs till I got to the highest part of this immense edifice. The number of the statues with which it is adorned is almost incredible. Many of them are very small, and many "entirely out of sight," and "therefore well placed on account of their deformity" (says Needham, who has been kind enough to give me a paper of directions for my journey through Italy). I went and saw a good many churches and convents.[9] At the Bernardines' I saw a spacious convent, and had the full ideas of such a sacred and studious retirement in Italy as I have often imagined to myself. I walked here peaceful and solemn, and thought perhaps I saw the lodging of my age. My hypochondria was quite removed. Over the door of the refectory of this convent is the following inscription, "Caenaculum Hoc Solertia Completum et Ornatum Anno 1712, Elizabetha Christiana Imperatrix Augusta Majestas Sua Presentia Illustrius Reddidit, Anno Insequente Kalendis Maii."[1] The reverend fathers seem not a little proud of having had an imperial guest. Their library is guarded by a tremendous anathema of the Pope: "Utere Hic Libris. Nam Abstrahere Anathemate Ferit Clementis Noni Diploma, MDCLXVIII."[2] So is the inscription above the door of it.

[8] The first line of the stanza on Milan in Ausonius' *Ordo nobilium urbium:* "At Milan also are all things remarkable, abundant wealth."

[9] In the memoranda Boswell mentions seeing Leonardo da Vinci's Last Supper in the refectory of the church of Santa Maria delle Grazie.

[1] "This refectory, which was skilfully completed and adorned in the year 1712, was rendered more illustrious by a visit of Her August Majesty the Empress Elizabeth Christine on the first of May of the year following."

[2] "Use the books here. For an edict of Clement IX, 1668, puts a curse on anyone who carries them off."

SATURDAY 26 JANUARY. I walked out a league to where is the famous echo. It is at a palace which was not finished on account of the dampness of the soil. It has three tier of pillars in front, and would have made a noble thing. I fired a pistol from the window of an upper story opposite to a wall; the sound was repeated fifty-eight times.[3] I then returned and saw the Ambrosian Library. I shall not be particular in describing it, after what Mr. Addison has said. Of English heads, besides that of Fisher, there are those of Sir Thomas More and Cardinal Pole.[4] I saw some of the volumes of the famous drawings by Leonardo da Vinci. The following inscription with regard to them is curious. "Leonardi Vincii Manu et Ingenio Celeberrimi Lucubrationum Volumina XII Habes, O Civis. Galeaz. Arconatus Inter Optimates Tuos Bonarum Artium Cultor Optimus, Repudiatis Regio Animo Quos Angliae Rex pro Uno [Tantum] Offerebat Aureis Ter Mille Hispanicis, ne Tibi Tanti Viri Deesset Ornamentum, Bibliothecae Ambrosianae Consecravit. Ne Tanti Largitoris Deesset Memoria, Quem Sanguis, Quem Mores, Magno Federico Fundatori Adstringunt, Bibliothecae Conservatores Posuere Anno MDCXXXVII."[5] I saw several more churches.

After dinner I waited on Padre Allegranza, a Dominican friar, to

[3] Boswell, in making this trip, was following in the footsteps of Addison, whose book he used as a guide throughout Italy. Addison says, "At two miles distance from Milan there stands a building that would have been a masterpiece in its kind, had the architect designed it for an artificial echo. We discharged a pistol, and had the sound returned upon us above fifty-six times, though the air was very foggy" (*Remarks on Several Parts of Italy*, 1711, p. 36).

[4] Addison had said that Bishop Fisher was the only Englishman represented.

[5] "You have here, citizen, twelve volumes of notes by the ingenious hand of the famous Leonardo da Vinci. Galeazzo Arconati, the best patron of the fine arts among your nobles, having with regal spirit refused the three thousand Spanish gold-pieces which the King of England offered for but one volume, gave them to the Ambrosian Library, so that you might not lose the distinguished work of so great a man. And lest so generous a donor be forgotten — a donor allied in blood and virtues to the great Federico [Borromeo] our Founder — the Trustees of the Library have put up this inscription in the year 1637." John Evelyn, who saw the inscription in 1646 and thought it "glorious" (that is, boasting) says that the Earl of Arundel had tried to buy the volumes for himself. Napoleon carried them off in 1796; in 1815 the largest and most important (the famous *Codice Atlantico*) was restored, but the smaller still remain at the Institut de France.

whom I had a letter from M. Bartoli at Turin. The convent was large and agreeable. My reverend Father received me very politely. He was quite a man of the world, decent and composed. He said he knew a Scots gentleman at Malta. This set me a-thinking. In short, by one question and another I found out that I was now sitting with the very man who had converted Sir Alexander Jardine, of whom I have thought so very much.[6] M. Allegranza told me, "That conversion occurred after a dispute lasting ten months and a half. He was a Calvinist, he was a Lutheran, he was a philosopher, he was nothing. He said, 'I am determined to find the truth.' He found it. He leads a very holy life." Padre à Porta, another friar, was with us. He had got an English letter from Mr. Kennicott at Oxford.[7] I translated it to him. I disputed a little with these two reverend fathers, but found myself too philosophical to feel the force of ecclesiastical reasoning. I told them, "Niger haereticus sum. 'Hic niger est, hunc tu, Romane, caveto.' "[8] Both of them made me presents of books which they had written. Padre Allegranza recommended me by a letter to a father of his order at Bologna.

I then went to the opera. The house was very large; the audience so-so. Rough dogs often roared out "Brava." The singers seemed slovenly. Blackguard boys held the sweeping female trains and often let them go to scratch their head or blow their nose with their finger. I wished to have had gingerbread or liquorice to give them.

SUNDAY 27 JANUARY. I left Milan betimes. I heard mass by an aged priest at a little village. The church I suppose was dedicated to the Virgin. Over the altar was "Nullum Donum Deus Dat Nisi Matris Intercessione."[9] I was drowsy all day. At night I was baddish.

MONDAY 28 JANUARY. I arrived at noon at Placentia.[1] In cross-

[6] Sir Alexander Jardine of Applegarth had not only become a convert to Roman Catholicism, but had also joined the Knights of Malta, a celibate order. His example may have been in Boswell's mind at the time that he himself thought of retiring to a monastery.

[7] Enrico à Porta, a distinguished Orientalist, was assisting Kennicott in the preparation of his critical text of the Old Testament.

[8] "I am a black heretic. 'He is a dangerous man. Therefore, Roman, watch him.' " Boswell is applying very loosely a line from Horace (*Satires*, I. iv. 85) to his own religious position.

[9] "God grants no gift without the intercession of his Mother."

[1] That is, Piacenza.

ing the river here I got my trunk sadly wet, so that I was stopped some time to get my things that had suffered dried. I resolved to stay all night. I saw in the market-place two equestrian statues of dukes of Parma. On the fiercest of them some sparrows sat and chirped. It had a singular effect. I saw one fine street, a new elegant church by Vignola, and the Cathedral, in which I found many good pictures. I wished to get to Parma next day, so I sent to the commander of the town begging a permission to have the gates opened at three in the morning. He was obliging enough to order that I might get out at any hour I pleased. I went at night to the *opéra bouffon*, which was really not very bad. I sent my respects to the commander, and begged leave to wait upon him in his box. He received me very politely. They had told me he was *un hollandais*. After I had made my bows and thanked him for his civility, I said, "You are Dutch, Sir?" He gave me a broad look and replied, "God forbid, Sir, that I should be of that tribe." (Poor Dutch, is your heavy race so despised?) "I am Irish." Upon this I spoke English to him, and very happy we were. He had been an officer in the Spanish service and had known my Lord Marischal.[2] His name was Griffith, a good, jolly, sensible man. He was quite a prince here. The performers of the opera came and paid him their duty, and the fair singers kissed his Excellency's hand. He introduced me to a Spaniard, an officer here. I promised to wait upon his Excellency as I returned to Genoa.

TUESDAY 29 JANUARY. After sitting up all night I set out drowsy and slumbered along. I got to Parma at night. I sent to M. Deleyre, *bibliothécaire du jeune prince*,[3] a letter which M. Rousseau

[2] George Keith, tenth Earl Marischal of Scotland, an old Jacobite hero and friend of Frederick the Great, was Boswell's travelling-companion from Utrecht to Berlin, and furnished him with letters of introduction to various people in Neuchâtel, including Rousseau. He wrote Rousseau on 18 January 1765 that Boswell was "a very worthy man, very full of hypochondriacal and visionary ideas; he has often seen ghosts" (*Correspondance générale de J.-J. Rousseau*, ed. Théophile Dufour, 1924–1934, xii. 228). For a summary of Lord Marischal's life and character, see the opening remarks to *Boswell on the Grand Tour: Germany and Switzerland.*

[3] Ferdinand, son of Philip, Duke of Parma, was grandson both to Louis XV of France and Philip V of Spain. His librarian, Alexandre Deleyre, was a French *philosophe* and a loyal and enthusiastic disciple of Rousseau. Boswell was very much attracted by his bland and serene personality, and Deleyre's comparative

had given me for him, in which the illustrious philosopher praised me and at the same time painted my melancholy disposition.[4] M. Deleyre came to me immediately. I found him a genteel amiable Frenchman with a simplicity of manners that charmed me. We were at once acquainted, and talked with unreserved gaiety. He said M. Rousseau was ever the same in private life that he professes himself in his writings. He said he hardly slept any, for he had passed part of a summer with him and heard him almost every hour in the night give signs of being awake. Perhaps I have taken up this anecdote wrong, for Deleyre must have slept as ill as Rousseau to have heard him awake. M. Deleyre said that M. Rousseau had now and then an inclination to reassemble the Jews, and make a flourishing people of them. What a vigorous mind must he have, and how much ambition!

WEDNESDAY 30 JANUARY. M. Deleyre came and drank chocolate with me. I presented him a genteel copy of English verses, which pleased him.[5] I was hipped and lazy, which vexed me. But his agreeable company revived me. He carried me to wait on the Abbé de Condillac, preceptor to the young prince. He was a composed, sensible Frenchman, which is perhaps the character that pleases the most of any; for the vivacity of the nation has still a certain effect in every character. A Frenchman may be grave, but is never sulky. Condillac is a second Mr. Locke. His books on sensations and the origin of human knowledge are much esteemed.[6] After talking a little metaphysically, I joked and said, "If I have gloomy chimeras, I also have agree-

---

intellectual mediocrity created a much more comfortable atmosphere for him than Rousseau's demanding brilliance.

[4] This letter is printed in the original French and in translation in *Boswell on the Grand Tour: Germany and Switzerland*, 22 December 1764 and Appendix II. Boswell, finding the letter open, supposed that Rousseau was taking him into his confidence. But in a later letter to Deleyre, Rousseau explained that it had been an accident, and Deleyre, probably to deflate Boswell's vanity, told him so.

[5] These couplets, Boswell's ten-line verses for 29 January, were later enclosed in a letter to Rousseau. See p. 54 *n.* 2 and p. 80.

[6] The Duke of Parma had gathered together a remarkable group of men, of whom Condillac was the most famous, to provide the best possible education for his son Ferdinand, then a boy of fourteen. Condillac wrote his comprehensive *Cours d'études* in thirteen volumes for the young prince.

able ones. When I lie down at night I think that perhaps I shall wake up a Locke. You cannot demonstrate the contrary to me." M. Deleyre then carried me to see young Ravenet, son to Ravenet in London. He is engraver to Don Philip, works well, and is a good-humoured, obliging man, a composition of French and English. We then went and saw the sculptor, M. Boudard, a Frenchman who is extremely ingenious in his art. He was then doing the story of Silenus with the boys and the nymph Aegle. He showed me the bust and the medal done for Dr. Tronchin,[7] and one or two French medals. I observed that the French struck many medals on their successes and the British very seldom. Boudard, whose tongue was ingenious as his chisel, replied, "You remember, Sir, the story of the man. . . . "

[EDITORIAL NOTE: The manuscript of the journal ends here. The memoranda show that the "story" was the old fable of the sculptor and the lion: the sculptor represented the lion being vanquished by a man; the lion replied, "But if lions could make statues!"

On 18 February Deleyre wrote to Rousseau: "I thank you for having introduced me to Mr. Boswell. . . . We spent two days together talking about you and looking at the few curiosities of Parma. I saw him go with the more regret because he has only himself for company: his oddness, his youth, and his melancholy being likely to keep him from gathering from his tour the fruits which he promises himself and which he badly needs. I am afraid that on his journey he will fall in with people who will set him a bad example or give him pernicious views on religion. He has already experienced many changes under that head, because he is seeking for the truth — a thing extremely difficult to discover in that heap of error in which the sects have buried it. Yet I ventured to promise him that at the age of thirty he would no longer be uneasy on that score, provided that in the five- or six-year interval he lead such a life as to keep himself free from remorse. . . .

"It is not hard to discern the source of a part of the troubles and

[7] On the occasion of the successful inoculation of Prince Ferdinand, the previous October. Théodore Tronchin, an eminent physician of Geneva, knew both Rousseau and Voltaire well. He had furnished Boswell with startling information about Rousseau just before Boswell crossed the Alps. See *Boswell on the Grand Tour: Germany and Switzerland,* 1 January 1765.

vacillations of our Scots patient. He told me enough so that I could see the physical and moral causes of the painful state in which his soul now is. But I hope that as the heat of youth subsides, the tumult of his blood will subside too. Then, if he will make up his mind to do all the good deeds which fall in his way, I have hopes that his English humour will evaporate by degrees, that he will form a virtuous attachment, and that as its bonds strengthen, he will acquire a taste for life. I hope so sincerely, for I conceived for him an immediate and lasting affection."[8]

From this time until he embarked for Corsica, we are mainly dependent on Boswell's memoranda to carry his story. It is unlikely that he kept up his journal during this period, though he mentioned it several times. He wrote his memoranda either early in the morning of the day of their date, or, more probably, late the previous night. They review the events of the day before, and outline a course of action for the day to come. Since these memoranda are extremely condensed and require a forbidding amount of annotation to make them intelligible, in this edition only the most central are printed, mainly those which deal with Boswell's impressions of himself or of other people. The selection therefore is somewhat misleading, since it omits most of Boswell's dutiful but uninspired notes on the visible wonders of Italy, its art and architecture. More representative specimens of this sort of record are provided in extended form in his "Course in Antiquities and Arts" in Rome, and in his journal from Genoa to Lyons. The memoranda are supplemented by letters, especially a series of fifty-one which he addressed (but did not post) to John Johnston, keeping them to deliver on his return to Scotland. Since his rule was to write to Johnston from each new town he visited, these letters form a valuable connected account of his tour. Separate short journals, miscellaneous documents, and editorial notes are used to complete the picture.

From Parma, Boswell started for Rome, travelling by way of Reggio, Modena, Bologna, Rimini, and Ancona. The memoranda

[8] A transcript of the portion concerning Boswell, in Deleyre's hand, is preserved among the Boswell papers at Yale, and is the basis for the translation given above. The original letter is published in the *Correspondance générale de J.-J. Rousseau*, xiii. 18–24.

record a number of brave resolutions to avoid risks with women so that he might preserve his health for the sake of his future family. He allows himself "one a month."[9] But his mind had higher reaches; impressed by the shrine at Loretto, he wrote to Johnston on 10 February: ". . . I am in a most pleasing solemn frame, and upon my soul I cannot refuse some devotion to this miraculous habitation without giving up my faith in human testimony. Such is the cloud of evidences for this history of the holy house. Who knoweth the ways of God: or who can say what may be the interposition of his supreme power. I am a sceptic. But a devout one. The grandeur of the high mass, the crowd of pilgrims, and the various sacred appearances now around me have made a strong impression upon my mind and fill me with a serious awe — which I greatly prefer to all the levity of mirth."[1]]

THURSDAY 14 FEBRUARY. Yesterday came to Terni. Took horses and rode to Cascade of Velino. Prodigious wild. Read Virgil's description thrice; was quite in *Aeneid*. . . .[2]

[9] So he wrote on 4 February, but his resolutions varied from day to day. On a separate undated piece of paper, he wrote: "No *sheets* till Rome, and then one a week girl — if not fine Roman. . . . Prepare mind by discipline for Scotland so as to fill the post Providence gives you at Auchinleck. Be patient; try this." "Sheets" seems to be a metaphor for intercourse. Compare *Hamlet:* "Post with such dexterity to incestuous sheets" (I. ii. 156–157).

[1] No. 20 of the series to John Johnston.

[2] Dr. McKinlay advised Boswell to "spend half a day here in viewing this stupendous natural curiosity. Be sure to view it from its fall above, and likewise from the opposite side. It will afford you wonder and astonishment." The passage from Virgil is *Aeneid*, vii. 563–571:

> In midst of Italy, well known to fame,
> There lies a lake (Amsanctus is the name)
> Below the lofty mounts: on either side
> Thick forests the forbidden entrance hide.
> Full in the center of the sacred wood,
> An arm arises from the Stygian flood,
> Which, breaking from beneath with bellowing sound,
> Whirls the black waves and rattling stones around.
> Here Pluto pants for breath from out his cell,
> And opens wide the grinning jaws of hell.
>
> Dryden.

SATURDAY 16 FEBRUARY. Yesterday rose fine, but sunk soon. Campagna charming. Approached Rome; not such feelings as [when approaching] London. Entered; some enthusiasm. At *douane*, Wilkes. Seized him; embraced. . . . Gloomy café; Wilkes lively. WILKES. "Write so well in such a cause. Christian religion — not Giant two toes, but *is* giant."[3] . . . You resemble Johnson; imitate him. Swear this, and read *Rambler*.

SUNDAY 17 FEBRUARY. Yesterday Dance came and breakfasted,[4] and then you went to St. Peter's. Approached grand area, piazza, &c. Not struck enough, but increased. Entered church; warm. Ah! noble, immense; quite rapt. Dance pleased to see you [so]. Walked around. At last, kneeled and adored. . . . This day, clear up. . . . Learn Italian. Lose not a day in Italy. . . .

MONDAY 18 FEBRUARY. Yesterday awaked vastly bad. Indulged hypochondria. Lay till eleven. Then up, dressed and walked. Dance dined. Good conversation. Then Mlle. Kauffmann: paintress, singer; modest, amiable. Quite in love.[5] Home, bad. Asked to visit Wilkes. He came. WILKES. "Want *your* letters at Naples. You must go on. Publish what you have by you. *You* could have best written for Scots, but would not trouble with politics." *Such* compliments.[6] . . .

[3] As the rest of the memorandum indicates, Wilkes and Boswell, after meeting at the customs, agreed to meet later in the day at a café. Boswell apparently mentioned Needham and his defense of the Athanasian Creed, and evoked this obscure remark of Wilkes about Giant two toes. Many of Boswell's conversations with Wilkes, which are difficult to reconstruct accurately, are well put together in Robert Warnock's "Boswell and Wilkes in Italy," *ELH*, iii (1936). 257–269.

[4] Nathaniel Dance (later Sir Nathaniel Dance-Holland), brother of James Dance. Nathaniel Dance became one of the better-known portrait painters of his day.

[5] Angelica Kauffmann, the famous Swiss painter, commemorated her divided ambitions by her picture, "A Female Figure Allured by Music and Painting." A year younger than Boswell, she was completing her art studies in Italy. The following year she went to London where she was much admired by Reynolds, and was elected one of the original members of the Royal Academy on its foundation in 1769. In her later years at Rome, she numbered Goethe and Klopstock among her friends. The high contemporary opinion of her painting may well have been influenced by her beauty. Dance was apparently in love with her.

[6] Wilkes, on his way to Naples, urges Boswell to write to him, and to continue with his journal, which Boswell thought of making into a book. Wilkes also

BOSWELL. "But is he[7] not a worthy man?" WILKES. "He has all the private virtues, all the Christian virtues, but he wants to encroach on our liberties. He is laying the foundation of the ruin of his family." BOSWELL. "Do you think he is really a Stuart?" WILKES. "Ay, every bit of him." BOSWELL. "Then I fall down and worship the image that he has set up. I reason not. 'Tis my taste." ...

WEDNESDAY 20 FEBRUARY. Yesterday morning called on Hamilton. Saw some fine pieces: Hector dragging. Superb.[8] Got into humour, but grew too lively.... Then to girl near Cardinal Protector of France; charming.[9] Sister, a nun. Mother, who sells daughters, talked of "vocation." Much enjoyment. Home. This day resolve clear [up] money. Nothing debases mind like narrowness. See Cardinal. Be Spaniard: girl every day.[1]

MONDAY 25 FEBRUARY. Yesterday in lazy humour. In bed twelve hours. Rose at ten.... Morison with you.[2] Saw he relished stories. Then Colonel Edmondstone came, and you three walked to San [Pietro] in Monte and saw famous "Transfiguration" of Raphael: quite rich. Then Lord Mountstuart's. He in bed. Quite English-

---

flatters him by saying that Boswell could best have defended the Scots and Scotland against his attacks in *The North Briton.*

[7] George III.

[8] Gavin Hamilton, a Scottish painter and excavator of antiquities, spent most of his life in Rome. His "Achilles Dragging the Body of Hector at His Chariot Wheels" was painted for the fourth Duke of Bedford, who later sold it because it reminded him too forcibly that his own son, the Marquis of Tavistock, had been dragged to death at his horse's stirrup.

[9] The Cardinal Protector of France was Prospero Cardinal Colonna, who died in April of this year, and was succeeded in the post by Domenico Cardinal Orsini (see p. 8). The girl is listed in Boswell's Accounts as "fille charmante," and cost him about seven shillings.

[1] Boswell was fascinated by his own conception of the typical Spanish gentleman, whom he imagined as proud, gloomy, and passionate. "Des filles" in the next three days ran to thirteen shillings.

[2] Colin Morison, a Jacobite refugee, was an antiquary and guide. Boswell described him in a letter to Gavin Hamilton (15 December 1765) as an "honest Aberdeenshire man" who had "such a prodigious quantity of body that it would require at least two souls to animate it; and therefore instead of saying, 'Such a man has more spirit than Mr. Morison,' we ought to say he has less matter." Morison had been recommended to Boswell by Dr. McKinlay.

man. O Stuart! Old race, where art thou? Well, no Jacobitism.[3] . . . Old woman; few words, business done. Quite brutish. . . .[4]

[EDITORIAL NOTE: Boswell set out on 25 February for Naples as he had originally planned, and also in pursuit of Wilkes. The trip over the Appian Way, which took five days, was disagreeably rough, but he was pleased by "swarming, intense" Naples. He called on William Hamilton, British Envoy to the Court of Naples (later the husband of Emma Hamilton, Nelson's mistress), who was a scholar and collector of art objects. Boswell, eager to learn, reminds himself to "cultivate great Hamilton's acquaintance" while guarding against too great a taste for "expensive *virtù*." He spent much of his three weeks' stay in Naples visiting various points of interest in the environs: the Royal Palace at Portici with its porcelain-panelled room, a grotto that passed for Virgil's tomb, the ruins at Herculaneum and Pompeii, where very little was yet excavated, and the usual churches. But the high light of his trip was his growing friendship with Wilkes, to whom on his arrival he had written in Latin, in deference to Wilkes's strong classical interests.]

[Boswell to Wilkes][5]

[Naples] Die 2° Martii, Anno 1765

CAESARIS ULTOR BRUTUM IN EXILIO SALUTAT. Hesterna nocte Parthenopen hanc attigi, membra fere fractus dura ista Appia, quamvis

[3] For Edmondstone and Mountstuart, see Introduction, p. xv. Mountstuart was a descendant of Robert II of Scotland, but his mother was English, daughter of the famous Lady Mary Wortley Montagu and grand-daughter of the first Duke of Kingston. Boswell's warning to himself not to show any Jacobite sympathies was dictated, of course, by a realization of the close ties between Bute (Mountstuart's father) and George III.

[4] The old woman is itemized in the Accounts simply as *monstre* costing about five shillings.

[5] This letter to Wilkes and all those quoted hereafter to him, unless otherwise stated, are reprinted from the *Letters of James Boswell*, 2 vols., 1924, with the kind permission of the editor, Professor Chauncey B. Tinker, and of the Clarendon Press. The originals are in the British Museum. The text of the present one is corrected in two places from Boswell's draft, now at Yale. A translation follows:

"The avenger of Caesar greets Brutus in exile. Last night I reached Naples,

John Wilkes (1725–1797), from an original pencil sketch by Richard Earlom, in the National Portrait Gallery, London.

tardissimus et etiam quodammodo serpens processus sum.[6]

Egregium sane tempus invenio Baiis; caelum luridum, procellam fortem, pluvium continuum. Tali tempore non mirandum si *Anglus Antiquus* fune se suspenderet; sed pauper Scotus, si victum tantum habet, omni tempore contentus vivit.

Precor mihi scire facias quando consortio tuo frui possim. Non interest quo praebente domum, nam apud te vel apud me vinum et hilaritas erunt. Ne obliviscaris promissi quod mihi Romae dedisti, nos multum simul fore Napoli. Summam spero voluptatem legendo notas tuas acres in poemata acria Churchilli, qui nunc cum Juvenale est. Musis amicus politica jurgia tradam ventis. Latinam linguam scribere haud assuetus, tamen in hac regione classica experiri volui. Excuses et valeas.

WEDNESDAY 6 MARCH. Yesterday ... visits of English and Wilkes. WILKES. "I wish I could write in any language as well as you."[7] BOSWELL. "[Such complaisance is] not in character." WILKES. "Yes. [I] always tell truth — for which I'm here." BOSWELL. "Had

my bones almost broken by that rough Appian Way, although I travelled at the slowest of rates, in almost snake-like fashion.

"The weather at Baiae is certainly fine: a lurid sky, a violent wind, and continuous rain. In weather like this it would not be surprising if an *old Englishman* should hang himself; but a poor Scot, so long as he eats, lives happy in all kinds of weather.

"I beg you to let me know when I can enjoy your company. It makes no difference at whose lodging we meet, for either at yours or mine we shall have wine and laughter. Do not forget the promise you made me at Rome, that we should be much together at Naples. I hope for the very great pleasure of reading your biting notes on the biting poems of Churchill, who is now with Juvenal. As a friend to the Muses, I shall throw political quarrels to the winds. Though little accustomed to writing in Latin, I still wished to make the attempt in this classical region. Pardon me, and farewell."

Wilkes was engaged in preparing an edition of Churchill's poems which he subsequently abandoned, and in writing a *History of England* of which only the introduction was completed.

[6] Boswell here seems to recall Horace's advice in *Satires,* I. v. 6: "Minus est gravis Appia tardis" (the Appian way is less rough for those who travel slowly over it).

[7] A short word here remains undeciphered. The division of speeches in the entire conversation is conjectural.

you told such [flattering] truths to Government, [you] had not been here." . . . WILKES. "I make it a rule to abuse him who is against me or any of my friends point-blank. If I find two or three faults, he's good for nothing." BOSWELL. "But Johnson, a respectable character in the world of literature." WILKES. "Oh, I abuse Johnson as an impudent pretender to literature, which I don't think, but 'tis all one. So is my plan.[8] . . . At school and college [I] never read; always among women at Leyden.[9] My father gave me as much money as I pleased. Three or four whores; drunk every night. Sore head morning, then read. I'm capable to sit thirty hours over a table to study. Plan for *North Briton:* grave revolutionary paper seasoned each time with a character from the Court list." . . .[1]

THURSDAY 7 MARCH[2]

> Why curse fair Naples, strangers, wherefore swear
> That all the human race are worthless there?
> Henceforth no more of this, unless your plan
> Be ordered so that I must kill my man
> Or fall myself, for if you still pretend
> That you say true, death must the quarrel end.
> At Naples lives the woman I adore,
> Oh, had I seen her ere she turned a whore!
> But whore or not I love her with my soul,
> And to her health will drink a brimming bowl.[3]

[8] Johnson and Wilkes differed violently not only in politics but in their basic views of life. Wilkes had attacked Johnson in *The North Briton* for accepting a pension, and Johnson replied in *The False Alarm* (1770) by calling him a "retailer of sedition and obscenity" (p. 35).

[9] Wilkes had studied at the University of Leyden in 1744–1746.

[1] Wilkes goes on to explain, in a passage too confused to reproduce, that he hated his wife but had been a civil husband to her. He loved his present mistress Gertrude Corradini, so he was "not hurt by her follies" or her stupidity. However, he could not stand her relatives whom she had brought to live with them: his eyes were open to them and his pockets shut.

[2] One of Boswell's Ten-Lines-a-Day verses, an exercise in self-improvement which he had begun at Utrecht. His object was to write ten lines of heroic verse as rapidly as possible on the first topic that came into his head. They are poor poetry, but sometimes, as here, supply interesting biographical details.

[3] This woman is perhaps the opera singer (*chanteuse*) mentioned in the entries

WEDNESDAY 13 MARCH. Yesterday morning at home, and wrote a little. Wilkes came, gay, and excused himself for tomorrow, and asked *you*. You agreed, as he's an *extraordinary*. He said he did not mind if his friends don't like his wife, as 'tis not for them he has her, but for self. WILKES. "After Lord Talbot's duel, Mother talked grave: 'Rush into presence of Maker.' 'I've been always in it.' 'And into eternity.' 'Where have I been all this time?'[4] — Never think on futurity, as not data enough." . . . This day Vesuvius. . . .

THURSDAY 14 MARCH. Yesterday morning in chaise to Portici. Then on foot to Vesuvius. Monstrous mounting. Smoke; saw hardly anything.[5] Dined Wilkes, gay. WILKES. "Never a moment in my life low-spirited." BOSWELL. "What shall I do to get life over?" WILKES. "While there's all ancient and modern learning and all arts and sciences, enough for life if three thousand years." BOSWELL. "Fate and free will?" WILKES. "Let 'em alone." . . . BOSWELL. "Why keep company with me?" WILKES. "[You're an] original genius. But they'll spoil you [in] Paris; lop luxuriances from you. Talked to Baxter of soul; two quarto volumes and never since." . . .[6]

FRIDAY 15 MARCH. Yesterday early, fine morn. Wilkes at door.

---

for 17 and 18 March.

[4] Wilkes had fought a duel with Earl Talbot in 1762 after Talbot had been offended by an article in which Wilkes satirized his horsemanship. By the time the duel took place, their feelings had cooled; no one was hurt, and a reconciliation followed immediately.

[5] Wilkes describes an ascent of Vesuvius to his daughter Polly, which he says took place on March 16, possibly again in the company of Boswell: "I had five men to get me up: two before, whose girdles I laid hold of; and three behind, who pushed me by the back. I approached quite to the opening from whence issues the sulphureous smoke; I guess it to be about a mile in circumference. I lay on my belly against the side on the edge and looked down, but could see very little; only now and then when the wind blew the smoke much on one side, I could see several ragged mountains of yellow (sulphur, I suppose). I endeavoured to go quite round, but was almost suffocated by the smoke, and obliged hastily to retire. You descend with great difficulty, sometimes almost up to the knees in ashes" (*Correspondence of John Wilkes*; ed. John Almon, 1805, ii. 146–147).

[6] Wilkes adds that he always took the sacrament, however. He also mentions that dissipation and profligacy renew the mind, citing as an example that he wrote his best *North Briton* in bed with Betsy Green.

. . . Asses, Wilkes so mounted, excellent. Men to help; sad fatigue; oft rested.[7] WILKES. "I'm always happy. I thank God for good health, good spirits, and the love of books. I'll live here retired, not go down to Naples; 'tis hell. 'He descended into hell' shall not be said of me. *Imitatio Christi* there; I'll not be a Thomas à Kempis. Quin said of Francis: 'Damn the fellow; he's but a curate in Norfolk and he has all the vices of a cardinal.'[8] When I was colonel of militia, wrote epitaphs on all my officers. Some [were] engraved at Winchester. Gardener died: 'Here lies ——, gardener, &c. *Hunc etiam flebant lauri,*' &c. Minister angry at Virgil's being in churchyard, a heathen poet. But I said he prophesied of Christ and made all easy."[9] BOSWELL. "If we were to die here, how they'd write of us!" WILKES. "If I died and you lived, by the L—d a Middlesex jury would bring you in guilty of my murder."[1] . . . A man who has not money to gratify passions [does] right to govern [them]. He who can indulge, better. Thank heaven for having given me the love of women. To many she gives not the noble passion of lust." . . .[2]

SUNDAY 17 MARCH. Yesterday hipped, but drove about and saw several churches (*vide* Cochin).[3] Called Colonel Edmondstone.[4] . . . Talked of Scots families and love of younger brothers to elder. One of his kept account of all his father had given him, with a firm resolution to restore it to the family. Noble, great affection; great spirit. Had Wilkes to dine. WILKES. "After *Rambler*, liked Johnson more,

[7] Boswell and Wilkes were going to inspect the Villa Pietracatella at Vomero, where Wilkes was to settle the next month. See p. 72.

[8] A remark of James Quin, the actor and wit. The Rev. Philip Francis preferred the social life of London to his parish in Norfolk, and supported himself by political hack-writing for Henry Fox. He had recently attacked Wilkes.

[9] Wilkes had quoted from Virgil, *Eclogues,* x. 13: "Illum etiam lauri, etiam flevere myricae" (the laurel and the myrtle wept for him). In the Middle Ages, Virgil's Fourth Eclogue was believed to prophesy the coming of Christ.

[1] Since Boswell was a monarchical Scot, and Wilkes a hero to the London mob.

[2] One of Wilkes's favorite thoughts, to judge from what he later said about Corradini: "She possessed the divine gift of lewdness, but nature had not given her strength adequate to the force of her desires" (*John Wilkes, Patriot: An Unfinished Autobiography*, ed. R. des Habits, 1888, p. 15).

[3] Boswell was using C. N. Cochin's *Voyage d'Italie*, 1758, as a guide-book.

[4] Edmondstone and Mountstuart were staying at an inn on the shore called Stephano's, as was Wilkes, but the two parties never spoke.

but not abuse by halves. — Churchill kissed Flexney's wife, and he did it cheaper for him."[5] . . . Read some Zélide [to him].[6] WILKES. "[You've] been topped. Go home by Holland and roger her. You might be in her." . . . BOSWELL. "A Presbyterian kirk makes me tremble." WILKES. "That's the strength of your imagination. Dr. Hayes, when hipped, said cross things; Armstrong only held his tongue. Lord Eglinton a good-humoured, laughing fellow, but never suspected him of parts. Nature would not have given him that lank yellow hair. An advantage to be in this fine climate; after thirty, though your mind strong, your body may be easily hurt. By the Lord, a fever makes you a Johnnie Home, and what will you do then?"[7] . . . Then opera singer,[8] &c.

[Boswell to Wilkes]

[Naples] Saturday [16 March 1765]

IF YOU DINE at home tomorrow, I hope you'll let me come to "your genial board," &c., as Armstrong says.[9] I would *carpe diem* as

[5] William Flexney was Churchill's publisher.

[6] Belle de Zuylen, or "Zélide," was the attractive, intelligent, and unconventional daughter of a noble Dutch family with which Boswell had become friendly in Holland. Alternately fascinated and repelled by her, he was corresponding with both her and her father, and evidently read some of her letters to Wilkes. His Register of Letters shows that he had received her most recent letter on 15 March. On 19 March he wrote to Temple that Zélide "has more genius than any woman I ever saw, and more acquired perfections. I shall correspond with her as a *bel esprit*, but I think it would be madness to marry her. She has weak nerves. I know the misery of that distemper, and will therefore choose a wife of a sound constitution that my children may at least inherit health."

[7] The Rev. John Home, Scottish author of the currently esteemed neo-classical tragedy, *Douglas*, had been Lord Bute's private secretary. Wilkes in an ironical dedication to Bute of Mountfort's *Fall of Mortimer*, referred to Home as a preacher who "was at the beginning looked upon as a prodigy of genius and learning merely from being thought to have, at an early age, produced one tolerable piece. He went on, and it was soon seen how mean and contemptible his talents were" (*Correspondence of John Wilkes*, i. 76 *n.*).

[8] Perhaps the woman mentioned by Boswell in his verses of 7 March.

[9] John Armstrong, Scottish physician and poet, had complimented Wilkes in *A Day: An Epistle to John Wilkes:*

much as I can while you and I are near each other. I go for certain on Wednesday. Pray don't grudge a little paper and ink and wax upon an *old* Scotsman who loves you as much as any Englishman whatever.

MONDAY 18 MARCH. Yesterday . . . dined Wilkes. . . . Then *chanteuse;* ventured. Swore no more here. . . . Wilkes talked of wife; Tierney, surprised: "Have you a wife?" WILKES. "Yes, Sir; very much at your service."

[Boswell to Wilkes]

[Naples] Tuesday [19 March 1765]

DEAR SIR: — I shall certainly go tomorrow morning. I have a favour to ask of you. Pray come to me between eight and nine and let us pass this evening together. Perhaps it may be our last. I don't like to think so. Order your supper. I shall value highly some years hence the hours which we have enjoyed at Naples. Your Addison shall not be *lifted.* Pray don't refuse me, for I wish much to take leave of you on friendly terms. You say you have two or three souls. May that which I have found so congenial to mine live for ever, while the spirit of the Whig goeth downwards. Yours very much,

BOSWELL.

WEDNESDAY 20 MARCH. Yesterday . . . Wilkes lowish: disliked his poor girl.[1] Said he'd pay you compliment: "I shall never forget your civilities to me. You are engraved on my heart." Up all night, &c.

---

When dinner comes, amid the various feast
That crowns your genial board, where every guest,
Or grave or gay, is happy and at home,
And none e'er sighed for the mind's elbow-room . . .

Armstrong and Wilkes quarreled in 1763 over which had been responsible for the publication of this poem, and over Wilkes's attacks on the Scots and Scotland.

[1] Wilkes later described Corradini as "a perfect Grecian figure, cast in the mould of the Florentine Venus, excepting that she was rather taller, and more flat about the breasts. . . . Impartial heaven had not bestowed on her a common share of understanding or wit, and of consequence her whole life had been sacrificed to the interests of others. . . . Her two prevailing passions were jealousy and a fondness of being admired. By these she tormented herself and all about her" (*John Wilkes: Patriot,* pp. 15–16).

[Boswell to John Johnston]

Naples, 19 March 1765

My dear Johnston, — If a man's mind never failed to catch the spirit of the climate in which he breathes, I ought now to write you a most delicious letter, for Naples is indeed a delicious spot; *praeter omnes ridet.*[2] I have been near three weeks here and have been constantly employed in seeing the classical places all around. Is it possible to conceive a richer scene than the finest bay diversified with islands and bordered by fields where Virgil's Muses charmed the creation, where the renowned of ancient Rome enjoyed the luxury of glorious retreat and the true flow of soul[3] which they valued as much as triumphs? But, my dear friend, modern Naples has nothing of the ancient Parthenope except its heat and its idleness. The people are the most shocking race: eaters of garlic and catchers of vermin, an exercise which they scruple not to perform on the public streets. . . .

The warmth of the air here has extracted the vicious humours from my blood and covered my chin and neck with a prodigious scurvy which plagues me much. But as it probably has saved me a fever, I do not complain, though almost certain that no woman under fifty would give me a kiss without being paid for it, as you have been paid for being the *doer* of some old lady. Go on and prosper. Ever yours,

James Boswell.

[Editorial Note: Boswell arrived back in Rome on 24 March, and immediately started on a six-day "Course in Antiquities and Arts," that McKinlay had recommended and which was customary for tourists. He kept a separate journal in French of this tour, which is given in part below.]

[2] "Which smiles beyond all others" (Horace, *Odes*, II. vi. 13–14).

[3] "The feast of reason and the flow of soul" (Pope, *The First Satire of the Second Book of Horace Imitated*, l. 128).

[Course in Antiquities and Arts in Rome, 1765.
Original in French]

MONDAY 25 MARCH.[4] Mr. Morison, a Scottish antiquary, began to show me the most remarkable sights of Rome. We went out in the morning, as we intended to do every day. We saw the Pope go by in procession through one of the principal streets on his way to the Minerva.[5] It was thus I saw for the first time a dignitary who was so important in former times, and who still remains a prince of extra ordinary power. We saw the ceremony at the Minerva, where his Holiness was carried on a magnificent chair decorated with a figure of the Holy Ghost. He made the round of the church and gave his blessing to the whole congregation, who knelt before his Holiness Then he took his place on a sort of throne, where, after he had per formed certain sacred rites of which I understood nothing, people kissed his slipper. After this there was a procession of Roman girls who had received dowries from a public foundation, some to be mar ried and others to become nuns. They marched in separate groups, the nuns coming last and wearing crowns. Only a few of them were pretty, and most of the pretty ones were nuns. It was a curious enough function.

Then we went to the Capitoline hill. We climbed on the roof o the modern Senate, from which Mr. Morison pointed out ancien Rome on its seven hills. He showed me a little map of it, and read me a clear summary of the growth of this famous city to its present extent

TUESDAY 26 MARCH. We viewed the celebrated Forum. I experi enced sublime and melancholy emotions as I thought of all the grea affairs which had taken place there, and saw the place now all in ruins, with the wretched huts of carpenters and other artisans occupy ing the site of that rostrum from which Cicero had flung forth hi stunning eloquence. I saw there the remains of the magnificent por tico that once adorned the Forum, whose three remaining column give us a superb idea of what it was.[6] . . . We entered the famou

[4] Events now belong to the date under which they are entered.

[5] Santa Maria sopra Minerva. Its feast day is 25 March, the Annunciation of th Blessed Virgin Mary. The Pope was Clement XIII.

[6] The area of the Forum, which has been extensively restored since the eight

Colosseum, which certainly presents a vast and sublime idea of the grandeur of the ancient Romans. It is hard to tell whether the astonishing massiveness or the exquisite taste of this superb building should be more admired. A hermit has a little apartment inside. We passed through his hermitage to climb to where the seats and corridors of the theatre once were; Mr. Morison gave me a clear picture of all this. It was shocking to discover several portions of this theatre full of dung. It is rented to people who use it in this fashion.[7]

WEDNESDAY 27 MARCH. We went out in the afternoon. . . . We climbed the Palatine hill, where the magnificent Palace of the emperors stood. Since it has suffered many changes, we must believe that the ruins we now see date from the time of Domitian.[8] . . . We

---

enth century, was then known as the Campo Vaccino, or beast market. In the omitted passage Boswell describes various other classical remains, such as the Arch of Titus.

That is, as sheds or pens for their animals. The memorandum for 27 March adds: "Yesterday wanted to find subject in Robertson's *History* for Hamilton. Morison proposed Lumisden. In palace. Not treason. *No.* Up stairs solemn. He overjoyed quite. True worthy Scotsman; genteel man, too. No politics. . . ." That is, earlier in this same day, Boswell, who was looking for a suitable subject for a large historical painting which he had commissioned from Gavin Hamilton, had gone to the Palazzo Muti-Papazzurri, the residence of the Old Pretender, to seek help from Andrew Lumisden, the Pretender's secretary. (See Introduction, p. xvi.) The memorandum reveals his fear that his act might be construed as treason, and shows him assuring himself that no treason was involved so long as he did not talk politics and did not meet the Pretender himself. He encountered no difficulties whatever. The titular James III, who was old and suffered from convulsions, saw very few people in any case. Lumisden was the soul of tact. He never mentioned current politics, and he and Boswell soon became firm friends. For a study of their relationship, see Robert Warnock, "Boswell and Andrew Lumisden," *Modern Language Quarterly*, ii. (1941). 601–07.

Actually a group of palaces built by various emperors from Augustus to Septimius Severus. The striking effect of the Palatine ruins was commemorated fifty years later by Byron in *Childe Harold:*

> Cypress and ivy, weed and wallflower grown
> Matted and massed together, hillocks heaped
> On what were chambers, arch crushed, column strown
> In fragments, choked up vaults, and frescos steeped
> In subterranean damps, where the owl peeped,

saw a superb hall from which one can judge the grandeur of this imperial mansion, and we went down to see the baths, where one can yet see on the ceiling fragments of stucco-work painted and gilded in a very elegant manner. We walked to where the house of Cicero had stood. A statue there resembles him a great deal. Struck by these famous places, I was seized with enthusiasm. I began to speak Latin Mr. Morison replied. He laughed a bit at the beginning. But we made a resolution to speak Latin continually during this course of antiquities. We have persisted, and every day we speak with greater facility, so that we have harangued on Roman antiquities in the language of the Romans themselves.

THURSDAY 28 MARCH. We climbed to the Palace again, where the cypresses seem to mourn for the ruin of the grandeur of the Roman emperors. The view from here is magnificent. . . . We went to the Capitoline hill. We saw a fragment of the temple of Jupiter Tonans, which was architecturally very handsome. We saw in a church the famous Tullia prison, of which Sallust gives so hideous a picture and where Paul and Silas were imprisoned.[9] Catholics say Peter and Paul. They show a stone against which the head of the Prince of the Apostles was dashed. The mark remains very distinct We saw the hole down which criminals were thrown, the stone to which the two apostles were chained, a well which sprang up by miracle to furnish them with water to baptize the ——.[1] The water ha a taste like milk. It's only a little [impregnated with] sulphur. . . .[2]

SATURDAY 30 MARCH. We saw the Baths of Diocletian, whos

---

> Deeming it midnight: — temples, baths, or halls?
> Pronounce who can; for all that learning reaped
> From her research hath been, that these are walls —
> Behold the Imperial Mount! 'tis thus the mighty falls.
> (Canto IV, stanza 107.)

[9] San Pietro in Carcere is built over the Carcer Mamertinus where Jugurth and Vercingetorix were imprisoned. Sallust records the execution there of Catiline's confederates.

[1] Blank in manuscript. Boswell probably forgot the French word for "jailer."

[2] Various legends were attached to this prison, but Boswell seems to have compounded the confusion by his recollection of the imprisonment of Paul and Silas at Philippi (Acts 16). — Boswell remarks in the memorandum that he had spoken nothing but Latin for four and a half hours. He also mentions comment by Dance, that the English said he spent all his time with Wilkes and despised his own countrymen.

ılan was explained to me by my antiquary. In the Carthusian church ve saw also a fresco by Pompeo Batoni depicting Simon Magus :arried in the air by demons to show that he could perform miracles ıs well as Peter.[3] The Saint worships God, and points with his finger o the place where Simon Magus will fall. A group watches this event. Che composition of this painting is excellent. But Peter appears too ıneasy, as if he were afraid that his prayers would not be effective. Che colouring is false and unnatural, as if Peter had not only caused ›imon to fall but had discoloured the flesh of all those around him. n Santa Maria Maggiore we saw some fine columns of oriental narble. I must not forget to add in passing that we saw a strange ellow sitting in the sun reading Tasso to a group of others in rags ike himself. . . .

MONDAY 1 APRIL.[4] Yesterday morning saw in Pope's chapel unction of palms given. . . . Disputed on religion with Morison. Low, his; no more.[5] — This day swear *retenue* with Jacob, and not a word about] religion with Morison, but antiquities. See to be somewhat Aarischal. Home at one and dress, blue and silver. Only burgundy. ʒe calm and make Lumisden speak. . . . Swear again behaviour. . . .

WEDNESDAY 3 APRIL. Yesterday saw . . . "Moses" by Michel-ngelo. Beard too long; horns, though sacred, yet ludicrous as like atyr; rest of the figure superb. . . . Night, Hamilton with you. Read ʒueen Mary; seized it fully. . . .[6]

THURSDAY 4 APRIL. Yesterday called on Lumisden, who romised miniature of Queen Mary. Saw him with English and 'rench gazettes; quite a Secretary of State. Then antiquities of Cam-us Martius. After dinner, at Hamilton's. Sketch of the picture done; t first confused, but by explanation understood it clearly and ap-roved it much. HAMILTON. "But are you really to have this picture?" OSWELL. "Indeed, am I. Am I to have it?" (taking him by the hand). ıAMILTON. "Yes, if you please." BOSWELL. "Make it full size and

The Carthusian church is Santa Maria degli Angeli, into which part of the aths had been converted by Michelangelo. Pompeo Batoni was one of the most ımous of contemporary Italian painters.

The text now returns to the memoranda. 30 March was Palm Sunday.

Presumably Morison was a Roman Catholic.

Boswell refers to a passage in William Robertson's *History of Scotland* i. 375) which describes the abdication of Mary Queen of Scots. This was to be ıe subject of the picture he had commissioned from Hamilton.

neglect nothing. As I'm to have a picture, don't mind price. I shal
not stand for £100 more or less." HAMILTON. "Don't talk of price.
don't intend to make you pay much money for this picture. I shal
make a great deal by the print. I like your spirit in bespeaking a pic
ture. In our country it is only men of the greatest fortunes, as Lor
Hopetoun, who do so." BOSWELL. "No, Sir, I could not be satisfied i
you did it a farthing cheaper for me than for another. Were I in
certain rank of life, I would ask you to make me a present of it. Bu
I am rich enough." HAMILTON. "I shall do it for £150." BOSWELL. "No
£200." HAMILTON. "You may pay me as you can, by degrees." BOS
WELL. "In Scotland they'll talk against me: 'What, is he bespeakin
history pictures?'[7] . . . " Letter from Father: somewhat disagreeable.
Ideas jumbled. Night, wrote much.

FRIDAY 5 APRIL. Yesterday morning went with Colonel Gordo
to St. Peter's; Abbé Grant, conductor.[9] Gordon said, though as hereti
[he was] sure to be damned, was glad to see so many other peopl
going to heaven. Chapel of Vatican. High mass; quite solemn. The
procession. Then Pope from window, malediction and benedictio
&c. The whole atrium filled with people on knees. Then saw cere
mony of washing feet of twelve priests of various nations. Did it wit
great decency. Then table. Pope said grace; served on knee with
dish, and presented it to each priest. Mingled grandeur and modesty
Peter and *Servus Servorum;* looked [like] jolly landlord, and smile
when he gave to drink. . . .[1]

[7] Boswell saw the completed picture for the first time in London in March 177
and both he and Sir Joshua Reynolds were disappointed by it.

[8] This letter and the one mentioned on 18 April are missing, but to judge fro
Lord Auchinleck's later letters he may have had some sharp things to say abo
Boswell's expenditures.

[9] Abbé Peter Grant was a member of the Scots College in Rome, a Catholi
seminary, and host to many distinguished British travellers of the period. Colo
nel Gordon is unidentified.

[1] Boswell is describing the ceremonies of Maundy Thursday. After mass cele
brated by a cardinal deacon in the Sistine Chapel, the Pope carried the sacra
ment in procession from the Sistine to the Pauline Chapel. He then pronounce
the benediction from the external loggia of St. Peter's, which was followed b
the *mandatum,* or washing of the feet. Finally the Pope served the representativ
priests with food and drink, blessed them, and left.

SATURDAY 6 APRIL. Yesterday far out for antiquities. Morison, ill-humoured Scot, disputed *matter.*[2] He near impertinent, but kept him right. Then owned [you were] Catholic once, as Rousseau [had been]. He quite stony. Dined late; called Gordon a little. Found self just as you could wish: reserved, and when you spoke, ingenious. — This day Gordon to dine. . . . Be well but *retenu,* and say you study hard and shun English. Be content to be known as Armstrong, and often silent but when business calls.[3] . . . Read all Virgil and Horace in Italy. Come, be active. Consult Deleyre how he could make you clever. . . .

SUNDAY 7 APRIL. Yesterday waited on Lumisden in his study. Found him quite a learned, pretty, honourable man. Got Queen Mary: quite royal. Went to Hamilton's; saw him paint. . . . Be devout *sans mélancholie.* Fine with Lumisden. Tell Morison no more ill manners.

MONDAY 8 APRIL. Yesterday morning went to St. Peter's. Immense crowd; fine day. Superb high mass.[4] Cardinal Alexander Albani; most grave and pious. Quite sure there must be some truth beyond skies. . . . Pope knelt and prayed. Whole crowd on knees. Universal silence; perfect devotion. Was quite in frame; thought it *one* way of adoring the Father of the universe, and was certain no hell for ever. Then up. Stood just by Pope's chair when he gave blessing. Grand. The whole place crowded with people. . . .

FRIDAY 12 APRIL. Yesterday walked to Genzano.[5] . . . Morison quite sulky; low to dispute with him. You have seen how vain, how impossible to make others as you. So from hence, never dispute. Be firm. — Night, new girl. Swear no women for week. Labour hard.

SATURDAY 13 APRIL. Yesterday . . . Dance dined with you; too rude. Why so free with him? Why own wildness at Naples? . . . Cold night and fire. Quite bad ideas; relaxed and hipped. — This day dress immediately, and do so always. Order twice as much milk a day. . . .

[2] That is, disputed the existence of matter.

[3] Like Dr. Armstrong; see p. 57 *n.* 9.

[4] The solemn papal mass, celebrated on Easter, Christmas, and St. Peter's day (June 29).

[5] Boswell had gone on a jaunt for a few days to Frascati with Hamilton and Morison. Genzano is nearby.

THURSDAY 18 APRIL. Yesterday morning saw Batoni draw Gord drapery.[6] . . . Reproved Morison and made him better. . . . Lumisden dined, tête-à-tête. LUMISDEN. "For some time, all uneasy things concealed from old man. Two weeks after Edward [Duke of] York at Florence, Cardinal [York] conducted by same people."[7] . . . Suppec light. Quite happy. Letter from Father; solid and kind. . . . Learn *du monde.* Write French every day, or you're gone.

SATURDAY 20 APRIL. . . . This day, up betimes, to work agains laziness which every man has if he neglects. Maintain Utrecht character. Never mind Jacob. . . .

SUNDAY 21 APRIL. Yesterday . . . dined tête-à-tête with Gordon [He said, "My life was] sad work till set on self; then gay, never sick or splenetic one moment. Well when waked; rise at any hou by self. Put out of way by nothing." Adultery. Said you, "Such people do it as child breaks a mirror: for want of reason." Night, letters, fine Up all night.

MONDAY 22 APRIL. Yesterday, after up all night, in brace nerves. Borghese Palace. . . . Then St. Peter's in grand frame. Prayer fervent to the unchangeable Father of all to drive away melancholy and keep clouds of Presbyterian Sundays from rendering mind gloomy. Hoped this, sure as God lives, and so to behave calm and decent, and at last die a worthy old laird, full of hopes. This is solemn period for life. Only be *retenu.* — Dined Lumisden. Talke much, but well and with grave force. . . .

TUESDAY 23 APRIL. Yesterday morning, Palais de Strozzi. . . Then Vatican library, superb. . . . Clarke fine fellow; kept in orde Colonel. Then Belvedere. "Meleager" well enough. "Laocoön" su

[6] It is not clear what Boswell saw Batoni drawing.

[7] Edward Augustus, Duke of York, was George III's brother; Henry Cardina York, the Old Pretender's second son. Lumisden's remark is clarified by a lette (22 September 1764) from Sir Horace Mann, British Envoy at Florence, t Horace Walpole. Cardinal York had complained of "the manner in which th Duke of York was received at Rome, but [the Cardinal] said his only concer had been to conceal it from his father who would have been much hurt, an that he had succeeded. I was forced to make a little complaint of the militar people here for showing certain honours to the Cardinal that could only con vene [to] the Duke of York, and they were reprimanded" (from the unpu lished manuscript, by kind permission of the owner, Wilmarth S. Lewis).

reme; equal to all ideas. Nerves contracted by it, so that beautiful Apollo" could not be felt.[8] . . . Had walked with Clarke in Medici. le fine country gentleman; quite restored by him. All old ideas reived. CLARKE. "The English royalists did not join, because [they vere] not [organized in] clans; so could not have a thousand men, ut go out themselves and lose all. Gave money; thus cleared up."[9] . . . 'his day, up active. . . . Speak little of Jacobitism for Father's sake.

[Boswell to William Johnson Temple][1]

Rome, 22 April 1765

MY DEAR TEMPLE, — When I concluded my letter at Naples, I romised to write you soon from this illustrious capital, and if I reiember right, gave some hints as if I intended to entertain you with arning and taste. By what means I proposed to myself to execute is design, I really cannot recollect. Perhaps it is better that I have rgotten, for I am now in a better frame of mind than when relaxed y the warm soft air of gentle Parthenope. As I have delayed it so ng, I shall not now fill up the large pages of my epistle with an acunt of my travels from Geneva to Rome. You will read it fully in y journal, which I continue with an assiduity and liberal humour eculiar to myself. I must only tell you that I have felt many a ange of sentiment since I crossed the Alps, and have not been so niformly strict in my conduct as when my blood was thickened in e fogs of Holland. Naples is now the retreat of Mr. Wilkes. He and lived much together. Many a social repast did we partake of and

The Belvedere court in the Vatican, according to J. J. de Lalande, "is perhaps e most remarkable place for art in all Italy, or perhaps in the whole unirse" (*Voyage d'un français en Italie fait dans les années 1765 & 1766*, 1769, . 184). The "Meleager" mentioned by Boswell is the statue which was ordirily called the "Belvedere Antinous," and is now thought to be of Mercury.

Godfrey Bagnal Clarke, a close friend of Edward Gibbon, and later M.P. for erbyshire. Clarke refers to the failure of the supporters of the Stuarts to rise expected when Prince Charles Edward invaded England in 1745.

William Johnson Temple, Boswell's old classmate at the University of Edinrgh and closest English friend. At this time he was studying for the ministry Cambridge, and was ordained in September 1766. Temple shared Boswell's thusiasm for politics and literature, but their intimacy was based on an unrstanding and acceptance of each other's temperament.

much classical gaiety we enjoyed, notwithstanding of our direct op
position of sentiment on every important subject. He is an exceptio
to all general rules, and his constant felicity shakes my solid specula
tions on human woe. He has an elasticity of mind that nothing ca
crush.

I am now wrapped up in the study of antiquities and fine arts.
have already surveyed most of the monuments of ancient grandeu
and have felt the true, venerable enthusiasm. What would I not giv
Temple, to have you here with me. How would we recall the day
when we used to climb Arthur Seat, when our minds were fresh t
all the charms of Roman poetry, and our bosoms glowed with a de
sire to visit the sacred shades. I have had many hours of rich enjoy
ment. But you must be sensible that a letter can give you but ver
imperfect accounts. My journal will be pretty well. But my conve
sation will be great. How I anticipate our mutual satisfaction.

I went lately and passed two days at Frascati, the Tusculum c
old. The weather was delicious. I felt the genius of the place, an
was supremely happy. In true philosophical frame I sat down an
wrote a Tusculan Question on happiness, in which I considered re
ligion. I was perfectly impartial, and calmly enquired how muc
more clear light has been imparted to the world during the eightee
hundred years that have rolled on since Cicero wrote his famous *Tu
culan Questions*. Of this genuine sketch I may perhaps make a ver
good essay. . . .[2]

Really, I am for laying aside the high-flown ideas of ambitio
which we have indulged. Had Nature intended us to execute an
such schemes, she would have inspired us with ardour sufficient
carry us rapidly on, without all this reasoning about the matter.
is better to please ourselves with imagining what we would hav
done than to regret our having failed upon trial. My present stud
is pictures. It is delightful. I am very fond of it, and I believe I sha
form a true taste. This study has a fine effect upon my mind. I a
good humoured and gay, and hardly ever gloomy.

[2] Boswell's essay, inspired by the spirit of Cicero, survives. In it, he accep
Christianity as one of the "three or four great systems said to be sent fro
heaven, all of which contain strong proofs and excellent doctrines but involv
with mystical ideas, many of which shock."

Morris (our old ostler) is not here unless he be actually in some stable. I should be glad to meet him and be better acquainted with him. I have very little connection with the British, except when I find some one from whom I can learn. Farewell, my dear Sir. I ever remain, most sincerely yours,

JAMES BOSWELL.[3]

[Boswell to Wilkes]

Rome, 22 April 1765

DEAR SIR, — The many pleasant hours which we passed together at Naples shall never be lost. The remembrance of them shall inspirit this gloomy mind while I live. Even your compliments were excellent, and had full effect. You told me I was "the most liberal man you had ever met with, a citizen of the world, free from the prejudices of any country, who would be liked in France as much as in Britain." You called me "My old Lord of Scotland," and you said I looked as if I had a thousand men at my back. Had it been your chiefest interest to make Boswell satisfied with himself, you could not have done it better. But I set a higher value on your parting words, which you pronounced with such a tone that I almost believed you: "I shall never forget your civilities to me. You are engraven upon my heart."[4] Was you really in earnest?

I wish much to hear how you live now you are got into the stately castle which we surveyed with so great attention. Yours is indeed a *nobile exilium*. I am afraid the punishment which you suffer for your evil deeds will hardly deter others from doing the like. You may think as you please, but I have no small pride in being able to write to you with this gay good-humour; for I do in my conscience believe you to be an enemy to the true old British Constitution, and to the order and happiness of society. That is to say, I believe you to be a very Whig and a very libertine. But philosophy can analyse human nature, and from every man of parts can extract a certain quantity of good. Dare I affirm that I have found cheerfulness, knowledge, wit,

[3] A long postscript concerning both Boswell's and Temple's matrimonial schemes is omitted.

[4] See 20 March 1765.

and generosity even in Mr. Wilkes? I suppose few crucibles are so happily constructed as mine; and I imagine that I have a particular talent for finding the gold in your Honour's composition. Certain it is the process must be performed very delicately. Some days ago, nothing would serve me but to write you an Heroic Epistle; and thus I began:

> To thee, gay Wilkes, though outlawed, still as gay
> As when Dan Armstrong wrote his German *Day*,
> Another Scot now sends his English rhymes,
> Spite of the Whiggish broils which mark our times,
> Spite of the rude *North Briton's* factious rage,
> And all the abuse of thy imputed page.
>
> *In magnis voluisse sat est.*[5]

In the Italian gazettes they have thought proper to give you the epithet of *Il Bruto Inglese. Bruto* in Italian may signify either "Brutus" or "ugly"; and you must know it is disputed between your friends and your enemies whether the epithet ought to be translated "the English Brutus" or "the ugly Englishman." "Much may be said on both sides."[6] Let Mlle. Corradini determine.

You are no doubt very busy preparing your expected works. At your hours of leisure I hope you think of your friends alive and dead. Of the first it is difficult to know which are which; of the last I know only two. Methinks I see Churchill bouncing into the regions below, making even Cerberus dread his brawny force, while poor Lloyd is lounging on the fatal shore, for want of a halfpenny to pay his freight. He would not want it long, could he who relieved him from the *Fleet* know where to find him.[7]

I have received from our friend Needham some philosophical remarks, which he desires may be communicated to you.[8] I enclose his

[5] "In great enterprises, it is enough to have made the attempt" (Propertius, *Elegies*, II. x. 6).

[6] Sir Roger de Coverley in *Spectator*, No. 122, "may" for "might."

[7] Robert Lloyd, the poet, died in the Fleet Prison where he had been jailed for debt in 1764. He was an important figure in the London literary world when Boswell met him in 1763, on the same occasion that he met Wilkes and Churchill. Wilkes had stood by him in prison.

[8] Needham had sent Boswell on 13 March a long defence of the Athanasian

letter, but beg you may return it me. I am, dear Sir, as much yours as a Scots royalist can be,

JAMES BOSWELL.

Pray write to me, *al Caffé Inglese.* I leave this soon.

[EDITORIAL NOTE: During the next few days Boswell gratefully cultivated Lumisden, while reminding himself to be prudent, since he might yet hold public office at home. On 29 April he was ill, and having called in Dr. James Murray, the Old Pretender's physician, discovered that he had a venereal disease. He tells himself to "resign to punishment, but be calm." On 30 April, he received a letter from Wilkes which "new stirred ideas" and "troubled the pool."]

[Wilkes to Boswell]

Naples, 27 April 1765

DEAR SIR, — I thank you very much for your most friendly letter of the 22nd from Rome, and still more for the many agreeable hours you favoured me with here. You have made me know halcyon days in my exile, and you ought not to be surprised at my cheerfulness and gaiety, for you inspired them.

You touch, however, in your letter a string which sounds most harsh and discordant to my ear, the death of poor Churchill. I endeavour by every way I can devise to divert my mind from the gloomy idea of so irreparable a loss, but your letter brought it back full upon me, and left me all yesterday after the arrival of the post quite melancholy. I will say no more on this head, but in the words of Tully, "Virum bonum et magnum hominem et in summa magnitudine animi multa humanitate temperatum perdidimus nosque

Creed to be handed on to Wilkes, whose religious scepticism had been publicized by his connection with certain obscene and blasphemous parodies, especially the "Essay on Woman" and the "Veni Creator," which was subtitled "The Maid's Prayer." Wilkes had defended himself in his "Letter to the Worthy Electors of the Borough of Aylesbury" (his constituency) by saying: "I am not the first good Protestant who has amused himself with the egregious nonsense and silly conceits of the strange, perplexed, and perplexing mortal . . . Athanasius" (*A Complete Collection of the Genuine Papers of John Wilkes*, 1769, p. 96).

malo solatio, sed nonnullo tamen, consolamur, quod ipsius vicem minime dolemus, immo hercule quia sic amabat patriam, ut mihi aliquo deorum beneficio videatur ex eius incendio esse ereptus."[9]

I thank you for the entertainment of Mr. Needham's letter. I hope to talk over those knotty points with that agreeable gentleman here at full leisure. To begin with the Athanasian Creed is taking the bull by the horns. I beg you to make my best compliments to him, and tell him of my impatience to see him here.

I took possession of this old crazy castle on the 3rd, and have since been only twice in Naples. I am in the bosom of philosophy and Corradini, calm and pensive, giving myself entirely to the two works I have in hand, the edition of my dear friend's Works and my History. The introduction will contain many things which I fear you will not approve respecting our Tarquins; the Stuarts I mean. I enclose you the first proof of the title.[1]

As to my punishment, &c., which you mention, the case is very different. I am outlawed, not for smuggling, nor for any crime, but that I may not have it in my power to continue my suits in the cause of liberty against a Secretary of State, who under a Brunswick has renewed all the arbitrary and illegal acts of a Stuart — and by my outlawry has done it with impunity.[2] Nothing but that could have stopped the proceedings. It was known that I was undaunted, and from the steadiness of my conduct must have succeeded where above

[9] "We have lost an excellent patriot and a great man, a man whose magnanimity was tempered by politeness. There is, however, one comfort left us, though a melancholy one, which should alleviate our grief at his death; I think that some favourable providence of the gods rescued a patriot like him from the conflagration of his country." (Slightly altered from Cicero's *Letters to Atticus*, iv. 6. The version given here is essentially that of William Guthrie, an eighteenth-century translator.) Wilkes quoted part of this passage in his fragmentary notes on Churchill's *Gotham*.

[1] The proof is missing.

[2] For Wilkes's successful fight for his release after being arrested under a general warrant, see Introduction, p. xiv. On an action for trespass against Robert Wood, Under-Secretary of State, arising from this illegal arrest, he was awarded £1000 damages on 6 December 1763. The sentence of outlawry, however, made it impossible for him to continue with a suit against Lord Halifax, Secretary of State, for damages for wrongful arrest. He finally collected £4000 in this suit in 1769.

two hundred others have failed. In such a cause have I any reason to be ashamed of my outlawry? I may triumph in it as a consequence of public virtue which has stood unshaken. The cause is the cause of all the Commons of England, and I hope they will take it up. You find by Clarendon how much they will bear, but at last they take a severe vengeance, witness Strafford, Laud, &c. So much for politics, to which the stream of your letter carried me.

I had rather you would tell me of your future schemes, of the Dutch *vrouw* you mentioned, who you may be assured is in love with you, of your tour from Rome, &c. If you choose it, you may have me for a regular correspondent, as regular as Italian posts will suffer us to be. I wish you would go on with your poem to me. It begins very spirited. You are an adversary worthy of the Whigs. I do not doubt but Rousseau and other champions of liberty will in time pluck out of your lairdish breast the black seeds of Stuartism, &c., with which you are now so strongly impregnated.

And do you intend to retire after all your peregrinations to the Ulubrae you spoke of with glee?[3] Let me know how you look into futurity, and I will give you my ideas on every part of it, if you wish to have them. You are a singular man. What you told Rousseau of yourself is exactly true, that you were *d'un mérite singulier*.[4] I hope too you will be *d'un bonheur singulier*. I am sure your merit demands it, but good Needham will tell us how unequal is the distribution of rewards and punishments here below.

*Il Bruto Inglese* of the Italian gazettes ought to be construed "the ugly Englishman," and not as you do, for what do these people know of Brutus? Our enemies are right. You are mistaken.

> E'en I, whom Nature cast in hideous mould,
> Whom, having made, she trembled to behold,

[3] A reference to the motto from Horace which Lord Auchinleck had placed on the front of his house at Auchinleck: "Quod petis, hic est, est Ulubris, animus si te non deficit aequus" (*Epistles*, I. xi. 29–30). Freely translated, it reads: "All you seek is here, here in the remoteness and quiet of Auchinleck, if you have fitted yourself with a good steady mind." Ulubrae, a small village near the Pontine marshes, is used by Horace as an example of an unpleasant residence.

[4] Boswell had introduced himself to Rousseau with this phrase (see *Boswell on the Grand Tour: Germany and Switzerland*, 3 December 1764).

Beneath a load of low abuse may groan,
And find that Nature's errors are my own.[5]

Cura ut valeas, et nos ames, et tibi persuadeas te a me fraterne amari.[6]

THURSDAY 2 MAY. Yesterday much better. Discovered beasts.[7] Shaved; ludicrous distress. . . . Swear conduct. Remember family. See Mountstuart often, as [he is a] good lad.

SATURDAY 4 MAY. Yesterday dined Lord Mountstuart's. He quite man of fashion, fine air; true Stuart. Immense crowd. Confused and tired and hipped. Honest Colonel mighty good. Then had drive with Mallet.[8] . . . Home and better — This day at nine, Willison's, and sit, a plain, bold, serious attitude.[9] . . . Drive off hypochondria, and pray God. . . . See often Lord Mountstuart and M. Mallet.

MONDAY 6 MAY. Yesterday morning called on Colonel Edmondstone. . . . Saw with him Colonna Palace and Falconieri. Was very bad but patient. . . . This day, Murray immediately. Then Willison, or first call Lumisden and talk over scheme, whether head or owl, &c.[1] Have Hamilton to dine, and talk to him of it. Talk to Lumisden of money affairs and get things settled, or speak to Edmondstone. One hundred pounds extraordinary will do all, and so stay less in France. . . .

TUESDAY 7 MAY. Yesterday began half-length at Willison's earnest desire. . . . Idle day. Durst not sit up for fear of heating blood. . . .

[5] Churchill, *Rosciad*, ll. 405–408. Line 407 actually reads: "Beneath the load of mimicry may groan."

[6] "Take care of yourself, continue to love me, and be assured that I love you as a brother." (Where no signature is appended to a letter, it is lacking in the original.)

[7] Crab-lice.

[8] For Mallet and "honest Colonel" (Colonel Edmondstone), see Introduction, p. xvi.

[9] Boswell had commissioned a portrait of himself from the young Scottish painter, George Willison. The portrait now hangs in the Scottish National Portrait Gallery. See C. B. Tinker and F. A. Pottle, *A New Portrait of James Boswell*, 1927.

[1] The question at issue was probably whether the portrait was to be a mere head or a half-length with a scenic background, including an owl. See the next entry.

[Boswell to Wilkes]

Rome, 7 May 1765

DEAR SIR, — My rogue of a *valet de place* has been the occasion of your not hearing from me three days sooner.[2] He told me on Friday that the Naples post did not go out till Saturday, and on Saturday I learnt that it goes out on Tuesdays and Fridays. Were it not that the fellow has a numerous family, I would turn him off.

I embrace you with joy as a regular correspondent, and although a certain weekly political tract has rendered you, as it were, *hackneyed* in punctuality, I doubt not to be as punctual as you. You have advised me to think of being a foreign minister. You shall judge how far I can be exact in my dispatches.

I am not displeased to find you can be melancholy. The loss of Churchill is no doubt the severest affliction that you could meet with. Pray let me be serious and advise you to seek consolation from the immortality of the soul, which your departed friend strongly defends in his *Duellist*. The arguments for that noble system which vindicates the divine justice are surely strong, and it depends on ourselves to cultivate elevating hope. It was the prospect of meeting the renowned and the worthy of former ages that made Cicero say, "Si in hoc erro, libenter erro."[3] I heartily wish that John Wilkes, who has his mind so well furnished with classical ideas, had this one in daily remembrance.

I am obliged to you for the title page of your History. The first motto is excellent for a furious Whig, and the second inimitably adapted to the years of our sovereign's reign.[4] I doubt not but you will

[2] The valet's name was Francesco, and Boswell described him as "small, stupid; a rascal."

[3] "If I am mistaken in this, I am willingly mistaken" (condensed from *De senectute*, xxiii. 85).

[4] The two mottoes, slightly altered from Livy's Latin, read: (1) "I shall seek in this work an additional reward, that of being able to avoid the contemplation of those evils which our age has evidenced for so many years, so long at least as I am absorbed by the memory of the brave old days. Thus I shall be free from every care which might cause the mind anxiety, even though they could not deflect it from the truth" (I, pref. 5). (2) "The Tarquins had grown too accustomed to rule.... Their very name was unpleasant and a danger to freedom" (II. ii. 3–4).

make more noise with the four first years of King George the Third than Dean Swift has done with the four last years of Queen Anne.

As to your evil deeds which I mentioned in my last, I beg you may not refuse the charge. Without entering into any long discussion, it is certain that you did all in your power to stir up jealousy and hatred between the southern and northern inhabitants of Britain, and that you treated with indecent irony our worthy monarch, for which I say you deserved to be *beaten with many stripes*.[5] You are now, it is true, connected with the great cause of general warrants. But for this you have reason to thank the blundering head of a statesman and cannot claim any real merit from it; for to be taken up without a name was surely no part of your plan.

Since you praise the lines which I sent you, and wish I would go on with the poem, I shall endeavour to do so; but I can tell you when my virtuous Tory soul grows warm, it will not be much to your credit.

In the course of our correspondence you shall have the various schemes which I form for getting tolerably through this strange existence. If you would think justly of me, you must ever remember that I have a melancholy mind. That is the great principle of my composition. Farewell,

JAMES BOSWELL.

THURSDAY 9 MAY. Yesterday . . . Abbé Winckelmann an hour.[6] Fine and classical taste. Lumisden and Willison at dinner; good. . . . Found *virtù* growing with all its bad passions.[7] Then Lumisden and saw prints. Resolved [to keep] busy to drive off gloom. Then Lord Mountstuart alone; pretty young man. . . . Try to be well with Lord Mountstuart.

FRIDAY 10 MAY. Yesterday . . . sat much to Willison all day, and at night wrote, but baddish. — This day finish letters and sit in all morning, and think, and see what you want, and prepare.[8] Have Mr.

[5] Luke 12. 47.

[6] Johann Joachim Winckelmann, the most influential art critic of his time.

[7] In his Accounts, the only item of *virtù* which Boswell mentions having bought in the previous week was a "boîte de lave de Vesuvius," which cost him three sequins, or about thirty shillings.

[8] According to his Register of Letters, Boswell sent off six letters on 11 May,

Lumisden to consult and fix all plans, and correspond with him sensibly for life. Think to stay at Durlach or in French province or Antwerp till spring; then London a little. Then home and at Auchinleck [for] health and law till June. Swear conduct more and more. But remember God gives us different powers. Marry not yet. Swear no risk with women, and drink little wine.

SATURDAY 11 MAY. Yesterday . . . at three with Abbé Winckelmann at Cardinal Alexander Albani's villa.[9] . . . Garden like spread periwig. Night, Lord Mountstuart's, easy. Wild stories. . . .

SUNDAY 12 MAY. Yesterday . . . after dinner went to Corso like one *enragé*, and amused for last time. You're never to go back. . . . Now swear no *libertinage*, except Florentine lady. Ask Lord Mountstuart for commission to Bob Temple.[1] . . . Little exercise for fear of fever. . . .

[Boswell to John Johnston][2]

Rome, 11 May 1765

MY DEAR SIR . . . While I tell you what I have been doing during my travels, I must not neglect to give you some account how I have been thinking. My natural sensibility and anxiety of mind has ever kept me exposed to the attacks of hypochondria; by the great exercise and entertainment which I have had, the foul fiend has been often chased away, but I have never been able to promise myself any long continuance of felicity. I have experienced during this last half year such changes of sentiment as would hardly be conceived to arise in a mind where judgment was not totally overthrown. I shall not enter into particulars, but leave you to imagine all the wild ideas which

---

including ones to Rousseau, Johnston, Needham, and the Margrave of Baden-Durlach. He had met the Margrave during his tour of Germany. See *Boswell on the Grand Tour: Germany and Switzerland.*

[9] Winckelmann was the Cardinal's librarian, and had helped to furnish the villa.

[1] Boswell had previously tried to get Temple's younger brother, an army officer, put back on full pay, but without success. He wished Mountstuart to intercede on his behalf with Lord Bute.

[2] This letter is not part of the long series which Boswell was writing to give to Johnston on his return, but was actually posted. A two-page review of Boswell's tour is omitted at the beginning.

your gloomy fancy can suggest on the wettest Sunday, while the bell is ringing for the Tolbooth Kirk,[3] and all the gay ideas which cheer your mind when the air is pure and the sun is bright, and you are lying luxuriously upon Arthur Seat or calmly musing in your wood at Grange.

My great comfort is that I am ever firm in my attachment to the old Family of Auchinleck, to my worthy parents, and to my bosom friends. Were it not for melancholy, I am one of the most fortunate young men alive, for I know none who has more real advantages than I have. I must, however, own that I am uneasy when I think of returning to Scotland. My father is very well satisfied with me at present, but I much fear he will not be so when he finds me at home with him. By his way of writing I can discover that he expects me to be a solid, steady man, who shall apply to business with persevering assiduity. But, my dear friend, you know that there is hardly any probability that I shall ever be such a man. Years, indeed, may render me steady, but I despair of having application. God bestows his gifts as he thinks fit, and long study of myself has convinced me that my constitution was never intended for great labour of mind. I can pore over books as long as any man. I did so at Utrecht. But the effect was not improvement but sickness and perturbation. I swear to you that I seriously think it my truest philosophy to be content with the powers which my Maker has assigned me, and not to torment myself by ineffectual struggles to change my nature. I find myself an amiable, pretty man of moderate abilities, but a soul truly noble, a soul which in reality sets me higher in the scale of being than if I had attained to the first honours which superior talents procure and been without such a soul.

I would, however, do what I can to promote the happiness of my fellow creatures. I shall put on the gown as an advocate, and endeavour to acquit myself faithfully towards those who entrust me with their causes. But I shall not lay myself out for very much em-

[3] At that time one section of St. Giles's Church in Edinburgh. The Tolbooth itself was the city prison, from which condemned criminals were taken to the Tolbooth Kirk for a special sermon on the Sunday before their execution. It was on such an occasion that the condemned Robertson escaped at the conclusion of the sermon, as told in Scott's *Heart of Midlothian*.

ployment. If I can get a seat in the House for a parliament, I shall like it much, but shall not absolutely set my heart upon it. I shall at all events hope to have a good Exchequer gown,[4] and so enjoy *otium cum dignitate*,[5] and have plenty of time to give to the cultivating our old estate and following out the studies which please me the most. The great point will be to begin properly when I return, and get my father to see me as I really am. Come, my good friend, encourage me. Who knows but I may yet rejoice my father's heart? I call God to witness that I wish most earnestly to do so. His civilities to you in my absence touch me sensibly. I hope to show him that I am grateful.

I am just now quite well and happy, and storing my memory with rich ideas which will give much pleasure to us both many years hence. To be in illustrious Rome itself and to walk the scenes of classical enthusiasm is indeed noble. When I give you my warm account of all this, you will enjoy it very near as much as if you had been here. I know how to make your soul feel joy. My journal will be a treasure to us. Were you but with me this evening, what store of entertainment would I pour forth! In a letter I can only give you a few ideas half-coloured.

You must know I have travelled through Italy under the protection of the Dominican friars. The King of Sardinia's antiquary recommended me to a Father of that order at Milan. I found him a learned, pretty man, and after having had some conversation with him, I discovered a very curious circumstance. This was the Father who converted to the Romish faith Sir Alexander Jardine. You may be sure I had a full account of that singular affair. This reverend monk recommended me to the convent at Bologna, and from thence I have had letters from convent to convent, and been treated with great distinction. The dress of this order is white with a black gown. This, Johnston, is being quite in my own romantic style. I have now been more than two months in Rome. I shall stay just a week longer. I have been presented to two cardinals, and on Monday I am to kiss the Pope's toe. I go from hence to Florence, then to Venice, and afterwards come round by Parma to Genoa, where I am to embark for France. How long I shall yet be abroad I cannot say. My father will

[4] A judgeship in the Scottish Court of Exchequer, an important position.

[5] "Dignified ease" (altered from Cicero, *Pro P. Sestio,* xlv. 98).

no doubt expect to see me before winter. But I am very desirous to pass some time in France, the country of gaiety, and afterwards intend to travel through Flanders, where are a great many places well worth seeing, and so return to Holland and see my good Dutch relations and friends. . . .

My dear friend, farewell,

JAMES BOSWELL.

[Boswell to Jean Jacques Rousseau. Original in French][6]

Rome, 11 May 1765

I HOPE, SIR, that you received a letter that I wrote to you from Geneva.[7] I have looked forward to the honour of a reply before this time, but I am far from imagining that I have the right to complain of him who on occasion takes his time in writing to M. Deleyre. I am for ever obliged to you for having introduced me to your worthy friend. I found in him the intelligence and knowledge which make him respected; but his heart, his soul have fascinated me in a way which you can well imagine in your gallant and singular Scot. I sent him your letter the same evening that I arrived in Parma, and although it was very late, he came immediately to see me. We poured out our hearts in mutual sympathy. We spoke of M. Rousseau with warmth. We are linked for ever. The next day I presented him with these verses:

Deleyre, I've seen thee only for an hour,
But of true worth so rapid is the power
That I, like Spaniard to determine slow,
Already own thee worthy of Rousseau.
Yes, friend of him whose glory Europe fills,
While he, retired amid Helvetia's hills,

[6] The original of this letter is in the Public Library of Neuchâtel. It is printed in French in the *Correspondance générale de J.-J. Rousseau,* xiii. 301–303, and in the *Letters of James Boswell,* i. 76–78, on which the translation is based. Boswell's draft among the Boswell papers at Yale exhibits only one major variation, which is noted below.

[7] This letter and the one from Rousseau to Deleyre mentioned below are printed in *Boswell on the Grand Tour: Germany and Switzerland,* 22 and 31 December 1764.

Can philosophic independence prize,
And show how far humanity may rise,
You share his heart, Deleyre — come boldly dare
To join his standard, and his glory share.

Here is a translation.[8] . . . I don't know what he has decided in regard to your proposal. He could not *restrain his own inclinations*.[9] He revealed his melancholy disposition, and thus endeared himself to me.

I have almost finished my tour of Italy. I have viewed with enthusiasm classical sites, and the remains of the grandeur of the ancient Romans. I have made a thorough study of architecture, statues, and paintings; and I believe I have acquired taste to a certain degree.

Dare I admit to you that my conduct has not been as virtuous as I expected when you gave me directions for my life?[1] At the moment the fever is past. I am as you would wish to see me. But this changeableness in character disturbs me a great deal. Patience is necessary.

I have promised M. Deleyre to return to Parma, and to spend several days there with him. I go from there to Genoa to embark for France; but I am determined first to go to Corsica, as I told you at Môtiers. I beg you then to send me at once, in care of Messrs. Vautier and Delarue at Genoa,[2] a letter of recommendation; and if you have any important orders, rely on me. I cannot restrain myself from paying a visit to those brave islanders who have done so much for their independence, and who have chosen M. Rousseau as their legislator.[3] If you do not write to me, I will show them the short letter which I received at Geneva from you, with your device, *vitam impendere*

[8] The verses are in English in the original. Boswell's French translation is omitted.

[9] Rousseau had asked Deleyre to write an introduction to a proposed edition of his works. Deleyre accepted this offer, but the project seems to have been abandoned. — The italicized phrase is from Rousseau's letter to Deleyre introducing Boswell. He had counselled Deleyre, in talking to Boswell, to resist his tendency to bring up melancholy subjects.

[1] Boswell's draft adds here a sentence missing from the letter as sent: "But this confused world is quite a different affair from your sacred retreat, and in truth I am a feeble man."

[2] Boswell's bankers.

[3] See p. 197 *n*. 1.

*vero,*[4] and I believe that will obtain a welcome for me. It will be singular if they hang me as a spy. If you care for me, Sir, then write me immediately. This is too romantic a project for me to forego. I am serious. My sincere respects to Mlle. Le Vasseur, and I am always yours as I was in your sacred retreat.

BOSWELL.

MONDAY 13 MAY. . . . This day, in silk, see Pope. Think old Presbytery. Be well with Lord Mountstuart, &c.

TUESDAY 14 MAY. Yesterday morning at ten went with Abbé, &c. to Monte Cavallo.[5] Waited. In antechamber, off sword, &c. Then in, and kneelings, and kiss of slipper rich with gold. "Signor Baron Boswell."[6] I, master of ceremonies. First Sir W., then I, then Clarke, then Rich.[7] POPE. "How long have you been away [from England]?" To all: "Very young." [We talked of] Naples, Genoa, *grande fête*, &c. CLARKE. "I have obtained letters, made preparations." Abbé, of me: "The Father is his friend." I: "Genoese Father." POPE. "Very pleasing manners," &c. I, like an idiot: "Made his acquaintance at Cav. Sal."[8] . . . Some more kneelings again. [Pope,] of me: "He begins to speak Italian." Had full thoughts of old Presbytery. Then Lord Mountstuart's; lazy. He and Mallet dined quite easy. . . . Mallet owned *noire*.[9] . . . Then drove in Corso. Supped Lord Mountstuart. . . . Bid my Lord be decent with Grant. Fine to be well with Wilkes and Lord Mountstuart.

THURSDAY 16 MAY. Yesterday . . . began Tasso. . . . Talked with

[4] "To stake one's life on the truth" (Juvenal, *Satires*, iv. 91).

[5] A papal palace on the Quirinal, later the residence of the kings of Italy.

[6] The title by which Boswell was presented to the Pope. While travelling in Germany, he had assumed the style of Baron as indicating his social status more justly in the Continental scale than the plain "Esquire" permitted him by British custom. The lands of Auchinleck were a barony, having been granted by James IV in 1504 to Boswell's ancestor, Thomas Boswell.

[7] Rich. (Richards or Richardson) is unidentified. Sir W. is probably Sir William Farrington, whom Boswell had visited previously.

[8] The conversation was conducted in Italian, with the exception of Clarke's remark, which is reported in French. The reconstruction given here is highly conjectural. Boswell apparently reproached himself for mentioning an enemy of the Pope.

[9] That he suffered from hypochondria.

Mallet. Told all story of Rousseau and Voltaire. Wrong to be so talkative; make him say he won't mention it. . . . Night, baddish. Supped my Lord's. Saw you fawned a little. 'Tis really better [to be] independent; by merit rise. His interest now and then.[1] Be prudent. . . . Send for Lumisden to dine, and Murray. . . .

[EDITORIAL NOTE: As the memoranda quoted above show, Boswell was becoming increasingly attached to Mountstuart. He accepted with pleasure an invitation to accompany Mountstuart to Tivoli, the seat of Horace's Sabine farm, where upon seeing the famous *Fons Bandusiae* he spouted Horace's ode on the spot. Mountstuart told him that he found a particular pleasure in his company, but the relationship was not all easy going. Mountstuart did not think his father would much like Boswell's association with Wilkes, and Boswell thought Mallet "a sad Genevois without subordination."]

WEDNESDAY 22 MAY. Yesterday morning still baddish. . . . Went to Casenove's and had third girl. Resolved no more. Swear it. Then Mr. Lumisden's. Saw drawings by Prince Charles. . . . Then Lord Mountstuart's. Lecture by Mallet on last wars. Then my Lord gave full account of his education, &c., and said: "There is not one Englishman to whom I could have talked in this way. I find a Scotsman better than, &c. Well, I have great hopes of myself. London for me; under my father's eyes; right people," &c. Was quite well with him. Up too late. This day . . . ask Colonel for lieutenancy to Bob Temple. Swear no more up late.

FRIDAY 24 MAY. Yesterday . . . met Mallet at Dance's; walked with him. MALLET. "Laziness is one argument against study; there are twenty in its favour. It is never too late — but you trifle." . . . My Lord and you up till 2½. Promised Bob Temple. . . .

[EDITORIAL NOTE: On 24 May, Boswell made another jaunt to Tivoli, this time with Lumisden.[2] On 27 May (Whitsunday) he drove

[1] That is, make use of his political influence occasionally.

[2] Boswell expressed his "classical enthusiasm" at seeing the countryside described by Horace in a letter to John Johnston (24 May 1765), and added: "I am sharing the classical satisfaction with an exiled countryman, Mr. Andrew Lumisden, secretary to the son and heir of King James the Seventh. Let cool poli-

with Abbé Grant to Frascati where he saw Cardinal York, the Old Pretender's second son, preside at mass, and thought him "majestic and elegant," with the face of an angel. On returning to Rome, he attended the burial of an acquaintance of Mountstuart, George Anthony Werpup, a Hanoverian baron who had been killed when his carriage overturned. He was buried in the Protestant cemetery at night, because the prejudice against Protestants was so strong that the authorities refused to allow daytime interments there. Mountstuart erected a monument (the first in the cemetery) to him, with a long Latin inscription.[3]]

TUESDAY 28 MAY. Yesterday better. At eleven, my Lord's, and with him &c. to Vatican. Apollo, baddish knees; Laocoön's sons too much formed: men in miniature. Dined my Lord. Then had history of Spain from him and Mallet. Was too agitated and made *outré* motions. . . . Night, my Lord said abjuration oath [like] signing "obedient servant," and would not be the first who took it. Would not have sworn to old King, but would to this.[4] Saw my Lord too feeble; loved him, but resolved to be manly character, worthy to do him good. This day . . . call my Lord between nine and ten. Get him up without joke, like ancient philosopher. . . . Swear sup no more; 'tis ruinous to health.[5] So beg my Lord manly, and say you'll show otherwise real regard. So be independent. . . . Pay debts. Settle affairs these days, or you're worthless.

---

ticians dispute as they may, I shall love and esteem the man who is generous, who acts from what he believes to be right, who exposed his life in the most dangerous civil war to support his prince, and who continues ever faithful to his old master. . . . Mr. Lumisden is learned, ingenious, and cheerful. He knows your character and wishes to see you." Lumisden found Boswell "a gentleman of great talents, and beloved by all his acquaintances" (James Dennistoun, *Memoirs of Sir Robert Strange and Andrew Lumisden*, 1855, ii. 33).

[3] The information about Mountstuart's connection with Werpup has been kindly supplied by Captain F. L. Pleadwell, M.D., who has in his possession several letters from Mountstuart to William Hamilton, including the one quoted below, p. 85 *n.* 9.

[4] All voters in Britain could be required to take an oath abjuring the Stuarts. Mountstuart maintains that it is a matter of form, like signing oneself "your obedient servant" at the end of a letter. The old King was George II.

[5] Supper was served about ten at night or later.

Andrew Lumisden (1720–1801), from the medallion by James Tassie; copyright by the National Galleries of Scotland, and reproduced by permission.

WEDNESDAY 29 MAY. Yesterday at ten my Lord abed. Two hours ere ready by sleeping and dressing. Mallet said, "A gardener who has tilled the soil for a long time knows better than a passer-by. But you do not go deep enough." BOSWELL. "I can conceal my complaints, but when I find other hypochondriacs, I speak of them." MALLET. "The Colonel pays attention neither to time nor money. Has no plan," &c.[6] Then my Lord, lesson on Charles V, &c. . . . Lumisden bid [you] accept of Lord Mountstuart's offer. . . .[7]

THURSDAY 30 MAY. Yesterday my Lord's at ten, and read history of Spain to him. . . . Dined Clarke, pretty well. Then my Lord. He read and repeated German constitution. Then drove hour in coach. BOSWELL. "My Lord, I'll do well if you take care." He said same: "You'll be odd man, very clever, liked by few, *too* honest; judge too by starts." . . . My Lord and Mallet; history. I ignorant; changed ideas. After all, Johnson would think you above Mallet. Ask my Lord.

FRIDAY 31 MAY. Yesterday with my Lord. . . . Be firm and tell him he must take you in your own way, with prejudices, &c. Fix to be well with him; only as independent philosopher. Colonel, good-humoured man: reads book as you eat all on plate. This morning send to Alves.[8] At nine, my Lord's. If not up, away, to learn to keep appointment. . . .

SUNDAY 2 JUNE. Yesterday . . . my Lord told all to Abbé of his amour, &c.;[9] really imprudent and weak. Advise him, and have his real regard. Go not with him except *pressed*, as 'tis better to see little,

[6] This memorandum reveals clearly how Boswell recorded only the "heads" of conversations in many instances, trusting to his memory for later reproduction of the conversation. The conversation probably began with the question of study, shifted to another favourite topic, hypochondria, and finally to Colonel Edmondstone.

[7] To travel with him and his party.

[8] James Alves was a Scottish painter whom Boswell had engaged to make a miniature of himself from Willison's portrait.

[9] Perhaps of his love for the Duchess of Guadignola, whom he "adored in vain." It was not she, but another of whom he wrote to William Hamilton at Naples (7 May 1765): "I also live with my belle, but a belle no longer so to me; for the Colonel, he and I at last have met, made a mutual confession of our grievances before a third person, and have agreed to live comfortably together, Lord Mountstuart being Lord Mountstuart and master of himself" (*Collection of*

lest [he] tire. You are too fiery with Mallet. 'Tis just bad habit. Swear restraint like Temple. Swear, prepare now. . . . Swear one week no supper; home regular. Try only two nights to come home firm, and see. Be serious.

MONDAY 3 JUNE. Yesterday . . . went with Hamilton to Vatican and saw pictures; most rich. In noble spirits, and thoughts of immortality and seeing Raphael, &c. . . . My Lord's, late. He again proposed (as before supper) to travel with him. You asked him to be politician and manage Father. He will. This day swear to be calm. . . . Remember you're old gentleman[1] and pretty man.

TUESDAY 4 JUNE. Yesterday morning sat to Alves. Dined my Lord's. Was too slovenly; guard against that. . . . Home, my Lord. With pleasure took his promise never to be offended, though you push him to history, &c. Talked to Mallet of going with them: "If you were in my place, would you not be charmed?" He was very fond of it.[2] After supper in room with Colonel; spoke of the affair to him. He said he had opposed others [joining], so would not appear just to favour Scotsman. He'd write to Lady Bute of a gentleman who had studied well but neglected history, whom my Lord lectures. Said this friendship might be of great use if King or Lord Bute lives. All well. . . .

WEDNESDAY 5 JUNE. Yesterday morning sat [to] Alves. Dined, great company my Lord's. King's birthday. Very well. After they went, you and he talked long then on Holland. . . . This day write Father, and Mother also. . . .

THURSDAY 6 JUNE. Yesterday morning wrote close, which dulled a little. . . . My Lord came; read his letter. Short and elegant; fine compliments. Yours strong, bold; he admired much. . . .[3]

---

*Autograph Letters . . . Formed by Alfred Morrison, Second Series: Hamilton and Nelson Papers* (1893), i. 4). The text is corrected from a transcript of the original supplied by Captain Pleadwell.

[1] Gentleman of an old family.

[2] He was strongly inclined to it.

[3] Presumably Boswell's letter to his father, which has not been recovered.

[Lord Mountstuart to Baron Mure][4]

Rome, 5 June 1765

Dear Mure, — Though four years and a half may have obliterated many things in the mind of a young man, yet they have not made me forget that I have a true friend in you, and that you would do everything in your power to serve me. To be very open with you, though I promised to write sometimes, my indolence and aversion to it would have always hindered me, had not an occasion presented itself of asking the following favour of you. Having got acquainted with Mr. Boswell here at Rome, our acquaintance soon grew into a strong intimacy — so much so, that I have desired him to go on with me in my tour through Italy, as long as it would be agreeable to him. He liked the scheme much, as well as Colonel Edmondstone, but says he is so much pressed by his father to go home that he durst not take such a step without his leave; but that you, being a great friend of my Lord's, might easily obtain permission. Boswell is an excellent lad, full of spirit and noble sentiments; and (as the world goes) it ought to be reckoned a fortunate thing for him going with me, and indeed fortunate for myself, as he goes on in the same studies as I do, and, if possible, rouses me up whether I will or no. He too has the advantage of being in company with one of the cleverest men in Europe, Mr. Mallet, the professor who attends me. Now, my dear Mure, I hope you will tell all this to his father; also that his cousin, the Colonel, wishes it much. You may tell him, too, that I am not so wild a man as I am generally supposed to be.

Adieu, dear Mure. I hear I am soon to be with you, when I shall endeavour not entirely to disappoint the hopes all my friends entertain of me, particularly you, being, with more friendship than I can express, ever sincerely yours,

Mountstuart.

FRIDAY 7 JUNE. Yesterday . . . my Lord at night spoke only bawdy, and told story of Colonel at Siena: "My God, I shot my piece," and then cunningly saying, "when I was in the army," &c. "She will

[4] The recipient of this letter was William Mure, Baron of Exchequer. The text is taken from *Selections from the Family Papers Preserved at Caldwell,* ed. William Mure, 1854, Part II, vol. ii. pp. 38–39.

never pardon you."[5] My Lord said: "You shall have lady in every town." Advised him, moderate abroad, and in England, good wife. . . . Swear no more late to ruin nerves. Swear keep up own firm character to surprise Father, &c.

SATURDAY 8 JUNE. Yesterday morning awaked to determine if Jacob should take bark.[6] In all morning and wrote, and dined at home. Grew dullish. . . . Then my Lord's. Colonel rough, like Scotsman; wants to be easy, [and is] rudely familiar. . . . At Clarke's be decent, so as never to make people always expect from you odd humour. Write what you remember of Mallet's lectures, no matter though imperfect. Swear piety. Swear independence and never to allow Colonel Edmondstone to be rough. Write plan to my Lord,[7] and not to mind fits of spleen. . . . Go on. Have *retenue*. Any man much seen loses esteem.

[ITALIAN JOURNAL][8] All great men who have written histories have begun their works with an introduction giving a brief statement of their intentions. I therefore advise my readers that I plan to write a concise account of the tour I had the honour to make through Italy with his Excellency, my Lord Mountstuart.

We left Rome on the fourteenth day of June 1765. The party consisted of my Lord, who was twenty years old; Colonel Edmondstone, who was more than forty; M. Mallet, sometime professor, who was more than thirty; and Baron Boswell, who was twenty-four. Thus our ages are all given; our characters will be revealed on the road.

FRIDAY 14 JUNE. My Lord and I were in the same carriage; we slept much, but we read some of the *Persian Letters*,[9] and talked about the characters of many men. At dinner, M. Mallet said he felt weak, but he ate a great deal and recovered his vigour; he said we would soon see a Turkish war. The Colonel was a little taciturn. We stayed

[5] Apparently a comment by Mountstuart.

[6] Quinine. Jacob was ill with a fever.

[7] Either an outline of Boswell's character and plan for future conduct, or perhaps a reference to his "Inviolable Plan" (printed in *Boswell in Holland*, Appendix I).

[8] From 14 to 22 June Boswell kept a separate journal in Italian. Events are those of the date under which they are entered.

[9] By Montesquieu.

at night at Terni, and talked to our innkeeper's son, a young tailor. We laughed a great deal.

In the middle of the night my Lord was troubled in his sleep, and he had the most fantastic dreams. He shouted continually at me, "Boswell, what are you upsetting your chamber-pot for? Why are you playing an air on your little bassoon, and why are you holding out your sword?"[1]

SATURDAY 15 JUNE. We arrived by evening at Foligno. The Colonel and I walked a little through the town. He promised me a good bowl of punch at his country-house in Scotland. My Lord was very angry to see us a little late for supper. My Lord told me many bawdy stories and we also talked about superstitions. I was afraid that ghosts might be able to return to earth, and for a time wished to get into bed with my Lord. But I lay quiet.

[Boswell to Wilkes]

Terni, 15 June 1765

DEAR SIR, — You was polite enough to say that I might have you for a regular correspondent, and I very gladly accepted of your offer. I wrote to you several weeks ago, and have not yet had an answer. Am I to impute your silence to the dejection of a forlorn swain whom the cruel Corradini has left to weep in solitude?[2] Or have you taken amiss the strong terms in which I declared my disapprobation of your conduct? As to the first, I suppose it is now pretty much over, and as to the second, you know I always talked the same language. I glory in being an enthusiast for my king and for my religion, and I scorn the least appearance of dissimulation. As the gay John Wilkes you are most pleasing to me, and I shall be fond to hear from you often. Let serious matters be out of the question and you and I can perfectly harmonize.

I have formed a great intimacy with my Lord Mountstuart, who

[1] The memorandum adds: "Beds in same room; always so. Never more read memorandums." Evidently Boswell was afraid he would lose caste if he were made to share rooms with Mallet or the Colonel.

[2] Corradini, irritated because Wilkes refused to settle £2000 on her, took advantage of his temporary absence at the end of May to steal what she could carry, and departed with her family for Bologna.

has insisted with me to accompany him in the rest of his tour of Italy. He is an amiable young nobleman, and I can tell you wants not the spirit of his ancient family. You see me then in my element. My liberal disposition will ever remain, should I even live in the very heart of a court. Gay Wilkes, adieu.

JAMES BOSWELL.

My address is *Chez M. Jean Watson à Venise.*

SUNDAY 16 JUNE [ITALIAN JOURNAL, CONTINUED]. I had taken too much of a medicine, which made me very sick. I was a poor companion, but after dinner I was very well. My Lord was in a childish mood, calling me *Jamie* continually.[3] I told him that the Stuart family had many weaknesses, one of which was to enjoy childish jokes. James I, though a man of learning and of wit, as wit was then understood, caused himself to be despised by his liking for low jokes. My Lord disputed this opinion strongly, and we were really excited. At night every one was tired. We stayed at Macerata, where we found a very good inn.

MONDAY 17 JUNE. We arrived at Loretto before noon, and the English Father Gillibrand came to see us at the inn. After dinner we went to look at the sights. We were accompanied by a doctor from Ravenna and his wife, a rather well-shaped woman with very beautiful black hair. There was also a canon from Ravenna, a tall, vigorous man, and I don't believe it is contrary to Christian charity to say that this canon was the favourite of the doctor's wife. We saw the Holy House and the treasure there. My Lord was not much pleased but very tired. I made him laugh by showing him the signboard of a barber who had the impudence to put outside his shop a very crudely drawn, ugly figure standing beside a wig, with the inscription, "Al Milordo Inglese."

TUESDAY 18 JUNE. The Colonel and I were very curious to see the Republic of San Marino. My Lord was in a bad humour, and at first thought he would wait for the Colonel and me in Rimini, but afterwards he changed his mind and wanted to go on to Bologna. I was very angry with his Excellency and in fact the whole party was divided in the most unpleasant way. We all wore sullen faces, espe-

[3] Boswell hated to be called by this familiar name, and later did not permit even his wife to use it.

cially Professor Mallet, that so wise, so learned, and now so discontented man.[4]

WEDNESDAY 19 JUNE. We went to San Marino. We found the best people in the world. I have written a particular report of this expedition, and therefore I do not choose to say anything here.[5] I need only say that it was an exceedingly warm day, and we were very tired.

[Mountstuart to Boswell]

Rimini, 19 June 1765

SIR: — I had the honour of receiving your very obliging letter[6] this morning at Pesaro and instantly set about what you desired, as you will soon see by the following lines. *To the purpose:* John, commonly called Lord Mountstuart,[7] has, after long examination, thought, and mature deliberation — I say, the same Lord has discovered James Boswell to be wrong in words, wrong in acts, and wrong in deeds; wrong without taste, and wrong in obstinacy, an obstinacy mistaken for firmness, an ideal thing with the said Boswell till he has got rid of the former. The above-mentioned Lord makes no doubt but that the said Boswell will have had the same thoughts on his way to San Marino, and that in cursing the stones and craggy

[4] The memorandum dated 18 June adds: "Resolve San Marino, and if his Excellency will be obstinate, no help for it. He is as one sick." For 19 June, Boswell goes on to say: "My Lord agreed to San Marino. At Pesaro, doubted. Would not go on to Rimini, but stayed after horses were [put] to. Irresolute and impolite. You in most sad ill-humour; could not speak. . . . Thought of leaving him at once, passion so strong. Was silent. He thought of going on [to] Bologna. Colonel said: 'It would be the most impertinent thing you could do to me.' My Lord, struck, agreed to wait [at] Rimini. Mallet wrong to join with his Excellency."

[5] Though Boswell's "particular report" is missing, the memorandum for 20 June testifies to the striking impression of sturdy independence which San Marino made on him. At the inn, for example, he asked the people whether they would be willing to give their lives for their republic, and they answered: "Yes, we will give our lives, blood, everything."

[6] Not recovered.

[7] This is the way Mountstuart would be designated in official documents, since his title was only a courtesy one. Its use is in keeping with the mock pomposity of the letter.

rocks of a free mountain, his monarchical spirit will flow back and make him curse himself for going to see so Gothic a thing as a free nation, and not following the advice of two unhappy people who take care to have no taste on proper occasions.

These, Sir, are the few dictates of an honest heart. I am sorry to have given you so much trouble, but am sure you would forgive me if you knew with what an interior satisfaction I have the honour to call myself, your most obedient and most humble servant,

MOUNTSTUART.

Excepting sickness we set out without fail tomorrow, three o'clock in the morning, for Bologna.

THURSDAY 20 JUNE [ITALIAN JOURNAL, CONTINUED]. All our differences were settled. My Lord laughed as usual and talked freely.

FRIDAY 21 JUNE. It was a very hot day. We stayed all morning at home, and after dinner we left for Ferrara, where we arrived late. We had a violent dispute as to whether it was necessary to stay to look at the city. Every one was in a bad temper. Some days before, the Colonel had offended M. Mallet by calling him insolent, and our Professor was terribly angry at the brave officer. But this evening the two were united in saying that I was the cause of all our confusion. I laughed at this display of human weakness.

SATURDAY 22 JUNE. More human weakness. We were all in a good mood, though nothing had really been changed. The Colonel, the Professor, and I viewed Ferrara as the beautiful remains of a great but ruined city. We had a bad day; at night we reached Rovigo.[8]

[EDITORIAL NOTE: The memoranda are resumed here as the party continued on its quarrelling way through Padua to Venice. Colonel Edmondstone told the two young men that they were honoured by having a distinguished man like Mallet with them, and that they had treated him badly, but Boswell was unable to contain his dislike for him. Mallet kept returning to one of Boswell's sore points, his lack of extensive learning. "MALLET. 'You know no one branch of learn-

[8] A few further details are provided by the memorandum: "Immense journey; rainy and dreary and bad roads. Night, joked Mallet too much; wrong. 'Tis below you. 'Tis bad habit. No more of it. Told my Lord of being Catholic. Wrong, for he has not studied it, and cannot understand."

ing. You never read. I don't say this to offend you, but of young men who have studied I have never found one who had so few ideas as you. . . . You have an eager mind and imagination; you can learn. I shall mention among the oddities of my travels that I found a man who had studied little and seen little of the world, who thought he knew a great deal.' " Boswell admitted, partly at least, the justice of these remarks, but they did not lessen his resentment of Mallet's assumptions of equality.[9] In Venice, General Graeme, a Scotsman who commanded the Venetian land forces, put them up, and Mallet, according to Boswell, had the "impudence to think of competing" with him for one of the better bedrooms.

Among the people whom Boswell met in Venice were Lady Bridget Wentworth, whose second husband John Murray was British resident (minister) at Venice,[1] and John Udney, the British Consul. The Corradini had been Udney's mistress and had contributed to his going into bankruptcy, before she met Wilkes.]

SATURDAY 29 JUNE. Yesterday morning out in gondola with Udney to his house. He showed me some pictures of the Venetian school. Also the letter which Corradini wrote Wilkes, and his answer. Thought him *now* worthless in private life; agreeable, to be sure, or he could not be so vicious, but in moral balance really good for nothing. Then went to island San Giorgio. Excellent place; fine superb convent by Palladio; large gardens. Benedictines here live like princes. In their refectory, "Marriage of Cana"; noble.[2] Dined General's; superb. Evening, Lady Wentworth's a little. Then home.

[9] In ironic contrast to Boswell, Mallet actually *was* a Baron, having been ennobled by the King of Denmark.

[1] Lady Mary Wortley Montagu, who got along very badly with Murray, described him in a letter (30 May 1757) to her daughter, Mountstuart's mother, as "such a scandalous fellow in every sense of that word, he is not to be trusted to change a sequin — despised by this government for his smuggling, which was his original profession, and always surrounded with pimps and brokers who are his privy councillors" (*Letters*, ed. Lord Wharncliffe and W. Moy Thomas, [1861], ii. 307). According to Casanova, who relates a repulsive anecdote about him, he looked like a handsome Bacchus painted by Rubens.

[2] Boswell is describing the church of San Giorgio Maggiore, begun by Palladio in 1565, and the old Benedictine monastery (now an artillery barracks) on the island. Veronese's famous picture is now in the Louvre.

My Lord and you on couch till two. He said you was a most odd character. All the English disliked you. Quite changeable: "Shall I put out that candle? 'No!' In two minutes. 'Yes!' " Pushing. Mallet said Rousseau had laughed at you. Voltaire writes to any young man well-recommended and of fire; then forgets him, "that English bugger." . . . MOUNTSTUART. "You are very honest, very honourable. I would do anything to serve you, and in a case of importance, entrust you. Yet you may be disagreeable. [You will be an] imperious husband and father."

TUESDAY 2 JULY. Yesterday morning went with my Lord, &c. to St. Mark's church. Old mosaic. Luckily, a solemn service. Saw also Doge's palace and in halls some good pictures. In council room roared out, "Cursed be your senate!" &c.[3] Had sad headache. After dinner agreed with Mallet no raillery for a week. He owned he could never be happy; knew its physical causes, which people ridiculously made moral. Madness [is] being struck with objects out of proportion to their distance of time, place, or connection with us. . . . Found tennis court; played a little. Home; sad distress of headache. Lay down, slept hour; better. Went to Lady Wentworth's; played whist ill. Home and had soup. Comfortable; better.

WEDNESDAY 3 JULY. Yesterday morning Mallet said, "We are four odd men." . . . Mme. Micheli dined; gay, lively, *appétissante.* Marked her.[4] Afternoon, called on her. Long alone; immediate amour. Chevalier and lady came in. — This day, out immediately. See Dominican's friend and Johnson's translator,[5] and at twelve, Mme. Micheli. Be easy and bold, and try fairly, and say you'll stay while you can, at any rate. She'll excuse, &c. See this fairly. . . .

[3] From Thomas Otway's *Venice Preserved:*

> Cursed be your senate, cursed your constitution,
> The curse of growing factions and division
> Still vex your councils, shake your public safety,
> And make the robes of government you wear
> Hateful to you, as these base chains to me.
>
> (IV. ii. 184–188.)

[4] Chiara Michieli, *née* Bragadini. She was a friend of Lady Mary Wortley Montagu. Boswell's conversations with her are recorded mainly in French.

[5] Giuseppe Baretti, a noted literary critic, who had translated Johnson's *Rasselas* into French.

Be dressed in brown silk. *Retenu*, and try gondolas and all expedients with Madame.

THURSDAY 4 JULY. Yesterday morning strolled in gondola till twelve. Then Madame's alone. By her on couch. Talked of religion, philosophy. BOSWELL. "[I would wish] to enjoy everything possible without causing harm to others." She said: "Libertines do not even get so much enjoyment out of — well, anything you choose. They are like drunkards who want merely to get brutally drunk. And do you know, Sir, I believe that all the exquisite notions which Aretino has left to us in writing and in pictures were invented by people who restrained their desires." Kissed hand often. She, half coy, said debauchery to yield before long time. Going away, [I] said, "I hope that your long time becomes short." . . . Mallet said, "I will describe your character as the greatest oddity to my children: a man with no system, and with false ideas. You have no attachments, no friends of long standing. They were your toadies not your friends." Shocked with wonder that a wretch could think so of you. Told him: "I have a very bad opinion of you. I have never lived quietly with a man of whom I had so bad an opinion. Perhaps I am wrong." At night, Madame's. Old noble there. Supped, and to bed late.

[Received 4 July, Wilkes to Boswell]

Naples, 22 June 1765

MY DEAR SIR, — I had yesterday the favour of your obliging letter from Terni. I regret that you have not yet received my last, which was serious enough for so solemn a soul as you call yours, and you know I am seldom in that mood. I therefore seized the opportunity, and I trust that curious letter will soon come to your hands, for I think it is wrote *ad hominem*.[6]

As to my dejection as a forlorn swain for the absence of Corradini, I will only say with Virgil, *O passi graviora*.[7] She had, like all the Italians, some points to carry for a father, a brother, and an uncle. The mother was already with me. I am not too fond of whole families.

[6] Boswell apparently never received this letter.

[7] Virgil, *Aeneid*, i. 199. The line from which it is taken reads: "Having endured heavier misfortunes," [we shall survive these also].

If there is one handsome or good in each, it is as much as we can expect in these latter times. You will see my firmness. I shall not stir one inch after her, and I have no reason to be pleased with some things which happened. I am however a laughing philosopher, and though I have a tolerable share of cullibility, it is only a sinking fund, which you may draw upon till it is exhausted. Mlle. Corradini has found this. Families and settlements are no favourite points with me, and though the gay Wilkes, as you and Armstrong call him, would exert himself *in many ways* for so pleasing, so elegant a form as hers was, yet there are lengths I will never go. Even in my amours you shall admire my firmness and strength of mind. Udney with whom she lived three years, our Consul at Venice, a most amiable man as I am told, called Corradini a *true fury*. I never regarded her temper, which indeed was not gentle, but I liked the delicacy and elegance of her Madonna figure. This is a great deal on such a subject to such a man as you, though you too like the thing almost as well as I do, but you dislike the talk and laugh about it, of which I am perhaps too fond.

My History and the edition of Churchill advance still the faster from my suffering no interruption whatever, except a few voluntary engagements with my old friend, Sir William Stanhope, &c. I wish you were here. I would give you some specimens would set your virtuous Tory soul in a rage, and how I should enjoy the noble storm!

I was very glad to hear that you had formed a great intimacy with Lord Mountstuart. He is by all accounts a most amiable young nobleman. I regretted exceedingly that political connections prevented my paying my respects to his Lordship both at Rome and here, for fame reports everything favourable of him. I congratulate you on that connection, which I hope will be advantageous to you, and particularly in the scheme which will make you the most happy in my opinion, that of being a foreign minister.

I wish to know all your schemes, and how happy should I be could I be of service to you in any of them! You see how punctual a correspondent I am, and I shall not be discouraged by the delay or loss of a letter or two. *Hope* shall always be my motto, and I continue to look forwards, though not quite so far as so good a Christian as Mr. Boswell. Posterity shall do justice to him as an excellent author, and to his friend Mr. Wilkes as a steady patriot, who bore the utmost efforts of ministerial rage even without peevishness.

I am so far from being disgusted at your freedom with me that it quite charms me. I regretted your last letter was so short. I beg you to write often and fully. Nothing can oblige me more. You are an enthusiast in your way for your king, as you say, and your religion. The French always called me an enthusiast for liberty. We have both the *vivida vis*,[8] which marks us.

I do not find that the mind is at all enervated even in this luxurious country, though the body is so much relaxed. I will prove likewise that it is not *otiosa Neapolis*,[9] and so Corradini knew while she was here. When I am ready for the greater of my two works, the History, I mean to go to Lausanne or Geneva, for I can only print here title-pages and specimens. No licence could be obtained for the entire work.

Poor Churchill often gives me that pleasing melancholy which I know not whether to call pleasure or pain. I indulge it sometimes for hours together, and I am sure I have not wrote one note he would disapprove, except indeed for the poorness of the matter or the badness of the style. I dwell upon his idea, which is the favourite one of my soul. ⟨Why⟩ do you not send me more lines of the epistle in verse, which you had begun ⟨so well? I⟩ hope it is finished before this. *Vale et me ama.*

My address is only *Monsieur Wilkes, à Naples.*

SATURDAY 6 JULY. Yesterday morning with her.[1] Pulled up petticoat and showed whole knees, &c. Said wretched. Cook only ten days — no.[2] Afternoon Lady Wentworth's till late. Then Cavaliera's. All shut. Angry. Away to Cort. Colon. Old woman alone in. [She called] my Lord "coglione briccone."[3] Ludicrous. My Lord valet,

[8] "Lively force" (Lucretius, *De rerum natura*, i. 72).

[9] "Idle Naples" (Horace, *Epodes*, v. 43).

[1] Mme. Michieli.

[2] That is, she said she would be wretched if she yielded to him; it would be like having a good cook for only ten days. See p. 10.

[3] An archaic approximation is "cullion knave." Cort. Colon. is perhaps an abbreviation for Corte delle Colonne, a street near St. Mark's. "Cavaliera" is presumably Mme. Michieli.

put you to bed; likes you, old Scots ideas. Take rhubarb and nitre, and never up at nights.

SUNDAY 7 JULY. Yesterday disputed plan. He changed to Milan by Mallet's advice, who with selfish cunning and impertinence opposed you. You was quite in rage and thought to go away. Evening Mme. Micheli's. She had sat up, &c. At supper my Lord and you told all whoring. Weak; can keep nothing. Resolve *retenu*. . . . This morning, up early and to work like Wilkes. Then Mallet and apologies. No more disputes ever. Twelve. Cavaliera. Take her on it fair, and ask to do her with hand. Settle papers or you're gone. Swear new conduct and try, &c.

MONDAY 8 JULY. Yesterday morning came Baretti, Johnson's friend; curious Italian. Copy.[4] At breakfast, disputed with Mallet, [with] Father's grand eloquence. Mallet said: "My valet will write like that. No miracles since the second century." Low joke. BOSWELL. "When you see him,[5] you will get down on your knees. David Hume a child in comparison to him. His *Dictionary* [is] great philosophy: all the axiomatical knowledge of the language; clear ideas." Hot dispute. BOSWELL. "M. Mallet, if you annoy me, I shall have to crush you." . . . Night, Madame; all lengths. MME. MICHELI. "I admit that I'm old-fashioned, but I would be wretched.[6] Never in my life. Once I was in danger, but escaped." Touched with her goodness. All other liberties exquisite. Quite bold. — This day, letter to Father, &c. Determine composure. Go to Mallet, and tell him once for all no more attacks. You're to let him alone, but remember you will not suffer one joke from him. Say it is impossible you could live easy with a man so totally different, and so little disposed to show you these *égards* which perhaps you are too fond of having, but 'tis your disposition. In history, you'll be glad to learn from him; that's all. Be firm and keep to this and be calm, and you'll see how he'll be ill with my Lord. Just till Florence, see. Ask my Lord to let you enclose a letter to Lord Bute; if [he does] not [agree] at once, say no more. See more things here.

[4] Baretti had promised Boswell a copy of a letter he was writing to Johnson, which may be the "copy" referred to here. Boswell received it on 18 July.

[5] Johnson.

[6] Presumably the conversation continued, "If I yielded to your desires." BOSWELL. "Have you never had a lover?"

Swear generous attention to Madame. Fond still, and if she'll give you hand, proof [all is] well.

TUESDAY 9 JULY. Yesterday . . . Baretti's, who showed you some letters of Johnson's; rich. Gave books. Was quite miserable, and said Devil had created us: "Why not die like dog?" &c., &c.[7] Pitied him. Home with Mallet a little, who said Fontenelle was insensible: "He used to dine twice a week with a friend. One took asparagus with butter, the other with oil and vinegar. One day the friend died. [Fontenelle said] 'Put all the asparagus in oil,' " &c. . . .

FRIDAY 12 JULY. Yesterday morning up betimes. Quite hipped. . . . Grand dinner; my Lord [had come] of age. Begged him new conduct, &c. — This day . . . swear care some weeks. See Mme. Micheli and give book. . . .

SATURDAY 13 JULY. Yesterday . . . resolved [to] alter conduct. Home and made speech: "We have lived as enemies, wrangling like children. From this time, I swear no more so." Quite happy with good resolve. Up late, but quite gone.

SUNDAY 14 JULY. Yesterday morning sick with being late up, but kept out. Told Mallet too resolution: no more jangling. MALLET. "We shall see how long that lasts." Set out at two. At Mestria, on coach alone, &c. To Smith's. . . . Pretty house and garden; elegant villa. Quite well. Curious old man, past eighty, resisted all attempts to dispute.[8] Colonel, worthy man, still at it. Arrived General's country-house.[9] . . . This day up; clear head. . . . Swear no more jangling. *Retenu*, and show firmness and so like Marischal, calm. Let alone my Lord; he'll come right, &c. Return to grand devotion. So proud, noble, and calm. Let us see how well you can execute plan and so be minister in London.

[7] See p. 281, where Baretti's remark is expanded.

[8] Joseph Smith, retired British Consul at Venice, was eighty-two when he married Murray's sister, a virgin of forty. Murray was supposed to have virtually sold his sister to Smith for an interest in the latter's fine collection of books and art objects. George III purchased this collection in 1763 for twenty thousand pounds. Smith, "a most lively and entertaining companion" according to Dr. McKinlay, was ninety-one when Boswell visited him.

[9] General Graeme's.

[Boswell to Wilkes]

Venice, 13 July 1765

Dear Sir, — I am very glad to find you have not been in the wrong to me, which I must own I could not help suspecting till your last agreeable letter arrived.

Your solemn epistle has not yet reached me, but I hope it is not lost. I suppose it has been delivered to my servant whom I left at Rome to recover of a fever. He is to meet me at Florence, and there I promise myself a singular pleasure in the perusal of a production whose rarity alone might entitle it to a place in the British Museum. You are seldom in a solemn humour. But you must be so sometimes; for without being in all humours it is impossible to know human nature. Would I had one half of your good humour, which is fresh at all hours, and cannot be hurt either by outlawry or by the loss of a mistress. I do admire your strength of mind, and look upon you as one of the vigorous few who keep up the true manly character in this effeminate age. With what a philosophical patience do you bear the flight of your beautiful Bolognese! Yet I can suppose you sometimes plaintive, and sometimes a little angry. If one may joke upon an old theme, I would ask if you have never exclaimed with the Mantuan swain, "Nec sum *adeo* informis, nuper me in litore vidi."[1] Since you must have a concubine, I am sorry that Corradini and you have differed, and I shall not be displeased to hear that you have made it up again. There was an idle report that she had robbed you. I cannot believe it; and if you think as I do, you will surely be generous enough to contradict it. After all, marriage is the real state of happiness. *Felices ter et amplius*, &c.,[2] can apply to nothing else. What we lawyers call the *consortium omnis vitae*[3] is the most comfortable of all ideas, and I hope I shall one day tell you so from experience. I mean not to triumph over you. Marriage is an excellent fruit when ripe. You have been unlucky enough to eat it green.

Your works must advance very fast. You will like Lausanne much, as the society there is very easy and agreeable. At Geneva you

[1] The complaint of the shepherd Corydon to the scornful Alexis: "Nor am I *so very* ugly; lately I saw myself down by the shore" (Virgil, *Eclogues*, ii. 25).

[2] "Thrice happy and more are those who are bound indissolubly together" (Horace, *Odes*, I. xiii. 17–18).

[3] Partnership for a lifetime.

will be very well received. The malcontents will flock around you, and borrow some of that fire which has blazed with such violence. As far as I can judge, the Geneva opposition is better founded than that in a certain great kingdom. I own to you, I love to see those republican dogs at variance among themselves. This, I fear, you will call a plume of the wing of Johnson. It may be so. My veneration and love for that illustrious philosopher is so great that I cannot promise to be always free from some imitation of him. Could my feeble mind preserve but a faint impression of Johnson, it would be a glory to myself and a benefit to mankind. O John Wilkes, thou gay, learned, and ingenious private gentleman, thou passionate politician, thou thoughtless infidel, good without principle and wicked without malevolence, let Johnson teach thee the road to rational virtue and noble felicity!

I have not made two verses these last two months. I have the most inconstant mind in the world. At times I can hardly help believing myself a man of considerable parts, but at other times I insensibly fall into a state little better than that of a blockhead. You have praised the beginning of my epistle to you, and I think with justice. I am afraid to go on with it for fear of the *fumum ex fulgore*.[4] However, if you insist upon it, I shall run all risks to entertain you with the completion of my small design.

I continue to like Lord Mountstuart. My intimacy with him has brought me acquainted with the character of Lord Bute, whom I shall ever admire. His letters to his son prove him to be a man of the most generous soul and most tender heart. I am sure he is one of the best friends and best fathers that ever lived. As a statesman, I am sure his intentions were grand and honourable. What his administration has been, upon my honour, I have not yet knowledge nor abilities enough to judge. He writes with an eloquence which would charm you.

Since you are willing enough to bear my honest freedom, our correspondence shall be as frequent as you please. Let us correspond, not as politicians but as men of wit and humour; and let us mingle about as much politics in our letters as politicians do wit and humour in theirs. Adieu, dear Sir,

JAMES BOSWELL.[5]

[4] "Fire first and then smoke" (Horace, *Ars poetica*, l. 143).

[5] The postscript that follows was written on a small scrap of paper which has

I have two favours to beg of you: one that your letters may be signed John Wilkes; another, that they may be sealed in such a manner that I may not tear a word in opening them.

My address is now *Locanda di Carlo, Firenze.*

Write soon.

MONDAY 15 JULY. Yesterday morning just Sunday in country without one Calvinist idea. Wrote well. . . . Afternoon, bowls. Plagued with jokes. Evening even General said, "By G——, the Baron thinks of nobody but himself." Mallet said, "Mentally, you are extraordinarily lazy. Write about Venice." Did so. MALLET. "But you have many more ideas than that, if you knew how to uncover them. Do you know them better than before you started to express them?" BOSWELL. "Yes." MALLET. "That's how one should study." — This day . . . get my Lord to write for Bob. Joke no more. Just let him live, and be not obstinate in impoliteness. With *ménagement*, profit by Mallet. Swear cure gleet.

TUESDAY 16 JULY. Yesterday morning my Lord went to Venice. You stayed fine and sung ballad and wrote. True Italy. Murray came and dined. Letters arrived. My Lord recalled; thunderstruck.[6] . . . Was really cast down, but so agitated as to feel it little. Night, whist. — This day, up. Swear manners. Get letters from my Lord to Sir Horace Mann, and to Siena. Prepare all. Take physic, and be as well as possible. Form in France, and after at home, be uniform. You remember your absurd prejudices against the French, and how you exposed yourself at Brunswick.[7] For these three days be quiet, and make

now become separated from the letter in which it was inserted. It seems to fit here better than anywhere else.

[6] On 22 May 1765 the Grenville Ministry forced George III to promise that he would no longer consult Bute on public affairs. This event, combined with the prospect of Grenville's imminent fall from power (which came on 16 July), apparently caused Bute to recall Mountstuart to the scene while he could still do something for him. Mountstuart was brought into the Commons in 1766 for Bossiney, a family pocket borough, but his father was not able to advance his career materially.

[7] Boswell presumably means Berlin, where he narrowly escaped a duel with a French captain over some insulting remarks he had made about the French (see *Boswell on the Grand Tour: Germany and Switzerland,* 15 September 1764).

true friendship with amiable Lord, and get him to give you full accounts from London. Try to get companion from Parma. Consult all with Deleyre, &c. Restrain weak openness, &c. . . .

THURSDAY 18 JULY. Yesterday after twelve hours abed, up. Fine morning. Had taken rhubarb. Drank bouillon. This air and reflection quite enough. . . . My Lord bad. Evening [he] said: "Sir, you behave ill to me. One day proud, one day flattering. Not to be depended on [to?] give little finger. Not told many things. From this day, no more to do with you." This day, [be] self. Let him come right. Prepare to go. Swear ⟨all⟩ day no jokes.

[Boswell to John Johnston][8]

Monigo, 19 July 1765

MY DEAR JOHNSTON . . . I intended to have left Rome before the middle of May, but I formed a great intimacy with Lord Mountstuart, who kept me on from week to week and at last insisted with me to accompany him in the rest of his tour of Italy. He removed the objections which I made on my father's account by assuring me that he would take care to have my conduct represented to him in such a manner that instead of being offended he should be highly satisfied with me. You may be sure this made me very happy, and on the fourteenth of June I set out with pride and pleasure as the distinguished friend of an amiable young nobleman, son to the favourite of our Sovereign. I promised myself a sure interest for life, and I felt my heart warm with affection to a branch of the royal house of Stuart. My Lord Mountstuart has with him Colonel Edmondstone, a worthy Scotsman who has attended him from the time that he left England, and M. Mallet of Geneva, who was preceptor to the Prince Royal of Denmark, and has a handsome pension from my Lord Bute for instructing his son in history. My dear friend, can you conceive anything more agreeable? We had a good journey to Venice, where we passed a fortnight. We lived at the house of General Graeme, brother to Bucklyvie. He is Commander-in-Chief of the troops of this Republic, and being an old friend of Lord Bute's and a very sensible polite

[8] This letter was not part of the series Boswell was to give Johnston on his return, but was actually posted.

man, we have been entertained by him with the greatest cordiality and ease.

We are now at his seat in the country, where fine air, regular living, and moderate amusement keep us in a state like what you have proved in your simple summer days at Shaw.[9] This is a new strong proof to me that a man ought never to despair; for after all my tossings in the variety of life, after all my dismal days of horrid gloom, I am now clear as when my mind was rural, young, and undisturbed except one day in seven. And yet, Johnston, I have reason to be unhappy, for my conduct of late has not been that of a sage. At Rome I ran about among the prostitutes till I was interrupted by that distemper which scourges vice in this world. When I got to Venice I had still some small remains of disease, but strange, gay ideas which I had formed of the Venetian courtesans turned my head, and away I went to an opera dancer and took Lord Mountstuart with me. We both had her; and we both found ourselves taken in for the punishment which I had met with at Rome. Pretty doings! Our evil has been recompensed but moderately but we are as much to blame as if we had suffered most sadly. I have blamed myself so much, and repented so sincerely, that I am now no more distressed. Besides I do assure you the climate of Italy affects me much. It inflamed my hot desires, and now it keeps my blood so warm that I have all day long such spirits as a man has after having taken a cheerful glass. . . .

I leave this in a day or two, and after going with my Lord as far as Verona, I shall separate from him and go to Parma, where I have an amiable French acquaintance, a man of knowledge and taste and sensibility to whom I was recommended by M. Rousseau. I may perhaps [spend] a little time at the Court of Parma and then go straight to Florence, and after seeing the curiosities there, jaunt through the rest of Tuscany, embark at Leghorn and sail to Genoa, where I shall embark for France. You must know I ⟨have⟩ been longer in Italy than my father intended and have spent £440 since the month of January. I hope my worthy father will not be uneasy; for I am determined ⟨to⟩ do what he inclines as far as may lie in my power.

I think, Johnston, you have here a pretty full account of me. Let

[9] Shaw in Hutton parish, Dumfriesshire, the home of the Grahams of Shaw, who were family friends of Johnston.

me add that my regard and affection for you is just as when we walked upon Arthur Seat, and that I will convince you of when we meet. Pray see Davie from time to time. My heart is bound up in him. He is the *flower of the flock.* I am uneasy to think that I am not yet master of myself, but I always hope to be better. Remember me kindly to all friends, and pray write soon. Adieu, my dear friend. I am ever yours,

JAMES BOSWELL.

My address is now *Chez Messrs. Vautier et Delarue à Gênes.*

[Boswell to Deleyre. Original in French]

Monigo, 19 July 1765

DEAR SIR . . . Your letter, my dear Sir, affected me deeply.[1] The elevation and delicacy of your sentiments moved me greatly. Believe me, I have never forgotten you, and in my most pleasant moments I have felt with enthusiasm all the worth of M. Deleyre. But the sincere compliments that you pay me are like reproaches when I examine myself impartially. Yes, Sir, I do not deserve your good opinion of me, since I have plunged into gross libertinism. Do not expect me to talk in sanctimonious fashion about repentance, but is it not humiliating to find myself a slave to sensual pleasures, and convinced that my[2] love of virtue is no more than a visionary admiration which one ardent desire or flash of ridicule can destroy?

Ah, Sir, what would you have me think? My misanthropy is only too well founded. Men are such feeble and changeable beings that all the merit which they can possess is insignificant in the eyes of a

[1] Deleyre's letter (dated 16 April 1765) was a long rhapsodic flight about the decadence of civilization, and the importance of "pure and modest virtue, which exhales her fragrance in obscurity like the violet hidden in the grass." Some shrewd comments about Boswell's character similar to those expressed in his letter of 18 February to Rousseau are interspersed among the platitudes, as well as the observant remark that "we suffer on all sides in trying to satisfy both duty and inclination, and become at the same time victims of remorse and self-sacrifice."

[2] Boswell wrote "son" for "mon," a fault resulting from hasty revision of his original sentence: "N'est-ce pas humiliant de me trouver un vil esclave de plaisirs sensuels, *un homme* convaincu que son amour. . . . "

metaphysician. Virtues that dwell in bodies like ours can scarcely be respected. Perhaps I am wrong; perhaps my troubled imagination ascribes to others what I experience in myself. I hope that is the case. I hope God has created great souls that are firm, constant, and superior to the physical. He was a noble Roman who rejoiced when three hundred of his fellow citizens were found more worthy than he. I would rejoice if thousands of men were found to be more worthy than I. I am coming to visit you in hopes of being consoled and strengthened. It is very probable that you will find me the same as him who pleased you so much last winter. I change for the better at least as often as I change for the worse. But, my dear Sir, I wish never to content myself with being intermittently good, or only so when I am with good men. The virtuous man must be always so.

Your ideas on the corruption of Italy have recurred to me many times. The worst is that in travelling there one becomes used to seeing people who think no more about the virtues of sensitive souls than an American savage thinks of the pleasures of civilized nations. The Italians as well as the savages appear to pass their time very agreeably. Why then reproach the former for not possessing elegant and sublime virtues, when we do not blame the savages for having neither brilliant ballets nor serious operas? Virtue may be regarded as a luxury which all the world need not possess. Leave others to live in peace according to their fancies and let us live according to ours, happy if we can find ways to pass without boredom or sadness this earthly existence of which we understand nothing. You see, my amiable philosopher, what sophisms present themselves when the heart is not warmed with sacred fire. You will answer all my difficulties and you will show me the road to the temple of constancy. . . . Adieu,

BOSWELL.

TUESDAY 23 JULY. Yesterday morning in fine, warm spirits. Took good breakfast and leave of worthy General, and again in chaise. My Lord sung much. My Lord was fine and said: "I shall miss you much on the road, Baron." Came to Vicenza; fine town. . . .

WEDNESDAY 24 JULY. Yesterday relaxed. Pissed fine in chaise. Talked only of a few English characters. Found conversation empty. Came to Verona. . . . Fine town here.

THURSDAY 25 JULY. Yesterday good journey. One post from Verona. Saw what the Republic prepares for Prince and Princess, &c. Just stop "to drink lemonade," [but had] four hundred cold dishes besides hot turkeys, &c.[3] . . . Rooms of wood new made; all elegant. Joked my Lord; curious to see confections more than antiquities. BOSWELL. "We'll make you a sugar Colosseum, ice Caracalla's Baths," &c. . . . Arrived Brescia. Saw fine walk. Ramparts. Dome. Full streets. MOUNTSTUART. "Lord Bute always [has] people below him with him, to keep up his dignity. Never familiar with any man. This great, but one loses much pleasure." My Lord said this well, and resolved to be great self. Talked of sheep and cows. What farm? Strange time this; over soon. — This day Milan; all well.

FRIDAY 26 JULY. Yesterday my Lord waked you boldly and showed *erect and tall.* Quite ludicrous this, but diverting. Drove briskly. Dined at Bergamo. . . . Disputes with my Lord. He said, "I shall always esteem you, but you're most disagreeable to live with. Sad temper," &c. Smiled to hear this. Was in strong spirits and afraid of nothing. Before dinner Mallet said, "The defect of hypochondriacs is that they seize upon an object so strongly from one aspect that they see none of the others. One must accustom one's self to correct that by reason — I mean, to keep one's self from always being convinced by each side of an argument in turn. Your logic is poor. It is more difficult to govern a hypochondriac than a kingdom, because one must be always starting again. You should have employment at Court, write verses, and not marry." . . . At night, Milan; curious sensations. Again dispute with Mallet. . . . This morning up immediately. Rinse well. Then wash feet and hands with warm water and soap, and all private parts with milk and water. Then have illustrious barber. . . . Have long conference with my Lord and own being in wrong, not for obstinacy but loose conduct. Say sorry, and you'll be on guard. Bid him be prudent not to say follies of you, as you've been free with him. Get Mallet to make you out character as he promised, neither keeping back bad nor good. . . .[4]

[3] The Infanta Maria Louisa of Spain and her escort were on their way to Innsbruck, where she was to be married to the Archduke Leopold of Austria, later Grand Duke of Tuscany. The party was welcomed by the Venetians at Castelnuovo on 29 July.

[4] A character sketch.

SATURDAY 27 JULY. Yesterday morning waked my Lord, quite happy. Strange. Loitered morning. Then great church, &c.; ideas changed. Then home. BOSWELL. "You have behaved ill to me. I'm sorry I did not put a stop to it at first. I'm glad we now quarrel. I wished it." Pretty this: afraid too sorry. Dinner; Colonel rough. COLONEL. "I intend it." Honest, homely man.[5] Resumed[6] your ill behaviour. You owned it partly. Leave.[7] MY LORD. "If you don't like me, you'll never anybody. Baron, are you sorry?" BOSWELL. "More than you thought." COLONEL. "You're geck[8] man. If you wanted to make friendship, [you should] not [have been] so familiar." BOSWELL. "True, for so you may destroy any man." . . . BOSWELL. "Draw my character." MALLET. "Yes, I promise you, if it's possible." BOSWELL. "To show you bear no malice?" MALLET. "No, I assure you. I shall never speak ill of you, and if I am asked about you, I shall say, 'But what do you expect from a lively mind?' "[9] After [they had] gone, dull an hour; weak. . . .

### [Boswell to Wilkes][1]

Mantua, 31 July 1765

DEAR SIR, — I must indulge myself in writing you a letter extraordinary from this consecrated seat of the Muses which I have come forty miles out of my road[2] to see. I know perfectly well how much most people laugh at the sort of enthusiasm which I now feel; but I also know that I am proud enough not to be affected by sentiments which I consider as the offspring of frivolous or of cold minds. Mr. Wilkes will probably smile at my having so much of the Pierian rage, but I am sure he will relish a few lines written on the spot where Virgil lived. I am at the village where he was born, and my vivacious fancy sees him sporting in the gay innocence of youth with the bees

[5] John Ramsay reported that on his return to Scotland Edmondstone commended Boswell to Lord Auchinleck for having undertaken his expedition to Corsica, but thought him in general "a mischief-making lad, vain, and penurious" (*Scotland and Scotsmen*, 1888, i. 172 *n.* 2).

[6] Summarized. [7] The moment of leave-taking. [8] Scots for "foolish."

[9] The distribution of these speeches is uncertain.

[1] This letter is printed from Boswell's draft. The original is not among the Wilkes papers in the British Museum.

[2] From Milan to Florence.

Oil painting in the collection of Sir Gilbert Eliott of Stobs, Bt., assumed to be a portrait of John Stuart, Lord Mountstuart, later 1st Marquess of Bute (1744–1814), by William Hoare of Bath.

flying around him in pleasing melody.[3] I date my letter from Mantua because he has been always called from it the Mantuan Bard, though his little native village is two Italian miles from the chief town of the territory. I don't know how this village, from being called Andes, has now got the name of Pietole.

I am happy enough to have as fine a day as Italy can give me. I set out when *primus equis Oriens adflavit anhelis*[4] and sailed softly down the *Mincius* who still *viridis tenera praetexit harundine ripas.*[5] I really see nothing improbable in supposing that beings of finer substance than we inhabit such delicious scenes as I now behold. Till you prove me the contrary, I shall believe this agreeable mythology. I do assure you that when I am at Auchinleck in a sweet summer season, my imagination is fully persuaded that the rocks and woods of my ancestors abound in rural genii. There is hardly a classical spot which I have not upon our own estate, and even after having travelled the enchanted land itself, I shall not be deprived of my romantic dreams. My having seen the realities shall not undeceive me. I have sought about here for the shade of the *patulae fagi*,[6] but could not find it. I am however sitting *sub umbra*, and *fronde super viridi.*[7] I look around me with delight, and I think I can trace the lands of Maro

qua se subducere colles
Incipiunt mollique iugum demittere clivo,
Usque ad aquam et veteris, iam fracta cacumina, fagi.[8]

[3] The Fourth of Virgil's *Georgics* deals with bee-keeping. According to Donatus, Virgil's father was a bee-keeper; and according to the versified biography of Virgil by Phocas, bees settled on Virgil's lips as a portent of the sweetness of his style.

[4] "First Aurora, with panting horses, breathes on us" (Virgil, *Georgics*, i. 250).

[5] Virgil, *Eclogues*, vii. 12–13:

Here wanton Mincius winds along the meads,
And shades his happy banks with bending reeds.
Dryden.

[6] "Spreading beech."

[7] "In the shade" . . . "on the green foliage." These phrases as well as the one in the preceding note are reminiscences of Virgil's First *Eclogue*.

[8] Virgil, *Eclogues*, ix. 7–9: "Where the hills begin to rise from the plain, and then descend in gentle slope to the waterside and the old beech with its battered top."

If you can suppose an old mulberry tree to be the beech here mentioned, you have a perfect picture.

Gay Wilkes, congratulate with me; an hour of felicity is invaluable to a man whom melancholy clouds so much. Here as I sit I am perfectly well. Time rolls back his volume. I am really existing in the age of Virgil, when man had organs framed for manly enjoyment and a mind unbroken by dreary speculation — when he lived happy and died in hope. Will you tell me, is humanity really the same now that it was then? And is it only our own faults that we are not as happy as the old Romans? Is it possible for us to regain those clear and keen sensations, that bright and elegant fancy, that firm and exalted soul which they certainly had? Bountiful Nature seems as kind as ever. Man alone is degenerated. Dear Wilkes, it is difficult to get you to think philosophically. Your active mind is so busy with what is, that you can hardly retire to think of what might be. But pray forget yourself; forget those elastic nerves, that free circulation, that resolved and daring spirit, and look upon the feeble, dull, and timid race of men whom you may see filling up the same age with yourself; and if you are a patriot, try to rouse them. I know it is too late for me to hope for great happiness. I may perhaps attain to a comfortable tranquillity. But did I think it possible to educate Romans, I would devote my life to a woman of beauty and worth, and give to other beings such an existence as I cannot have for myself. But I forget your being so wild a man. In serious truth I wish from my soul that you were a man of morality and religion. You have strength of mind to support both with dignity. I wonder what you will turn out at last when the heat of your youth is over.

Thus do I meditate on the Mantuan plains, and while I find no restraint upon my fancy, I rove with poetical licence in the bounds of conjecture. My prose is beginning to *run mad*,[9] and yet I feel no inclination to write verses. I will therefore get into my boat, and if any lines worthy of this scene present themselves, you shall have them as a postscript. Gay Wilkes, adieu.

JAMES BOSWELL.

P.S. I have tried in vain to rhyme. No Muse would come, although I begged very earnestly. Perhaps the divine sisters think that

[9] Pope, *Epistle to Dr. Arbuthnot*, l. 188.

they have already done enough for Mantua. Perhaps they refuse to inspire a bard who during his stay in the profligate Venice did not preserve a perfect purity. Perhaps winter is now the season of their visits; for then only the swans are found at Mantua. Lord Mountstuart is suddenly called home, I cannot say why. It seems the ministerial band is somewhat in confusion. I am now pursuing my journey as solitary as ever. I go to Parma on purpose to pass some days with M. Deleyre who, though one of *our worst enemies the French*, is my very accomplished and amiable friend.

THURSDAY 1 AUGUST.[1] I set out early and had a flow of spirits, repeating Johnson's noble lines, "What gave great Villiers to th' assassin's knife?" &c.,[2] and again being persuaded that there are some productions of humanity truly valuable. I got to Parma about one. It was curious to recollect my having left it just six months before. Don Philip's death threw a gloom on my mind, but a very slight one, for the sun shone warm and bright.[3] I dressed quite free and gay and saw Antonio as a genteel Tuscan, and casting back an eye to my boyish days, felt how I ought to be pleased at having an Italian servant.[4] After having dined lightly, I sent to the house of M. Deleyre to get notice if he was in town that I might go and wait upon him; but he heard I was arrived, and immediately came to my inn, where we embraced each other with affection. He was still the same amiable man; still melancholy, still delicate.

I disputed against Rousseau's notion that the savage life is the least unhappy, for the savages have none of the elegant pleasures of polished society to counterbalance their pains, and the quantity of enjoyment in an Indian tribe is hardly worthy existing for. Besides, the savages are torn with the fiercer passions, and are even tormented with ennui, for we are told by travellers that when the savage has killed his prey, roasted it, and eat it, and having no appetites to rouse him sees half a sun which he knows not how to employ, he sits down

[1] Two somewhat varying drafts of a fully written journal entry for 1 August survive, and are combined here. [2] *The Vanity of Human Wishes*, l. 129.

[3] The Duke of Parma had died of smallpox on 18 July.

[4] Antonio had been Mountstuart's servant. He accompanied Boswell from Milan to Florence.

pensive and sad by the seashore, and with a gloomy attention eyes the rolling of the waves.

M. Deleyre argued very justly against the system of Wilkes, insisting that morals were always necessary to preserve society in vigour, and that it could be proved geometrically that a virtuous nation must be happy.[5] We then went and waited on Mme. Deleyre, who was just the same good-tempered, well-bred woman as when I saw her last. It hurt me somewhat to be conscious of a total change of ideas. We called on an Irish Augustinian friar. His awkward, coarse manner hurt me so much that I sat quite uneasy, as if I had heard one sawing marble or scraping with a knife on a china trencher. My sensibility is so delicate that I must fairly own it to be weak and unmanly. It prevents me from having a decent and even conduct in the course of ordinary life. I would hope to be more firm as I grow older, though the ingenious Mr. Adam Smith is at the age of forty as tender as ever.[6]

Leaving the honest monk, who was really a very good sort of man, we went and walked in the Prince's garden. I soon started the interesting subject of God and immortality. M. Deleyre said that to think the world has been composed by a fortuitous concourse of material substances in continual motion from all eternity did not seem more improbable than to suppose a Being who created matter. All the arguments which I could recollect could not make M. Deleyre believe the existence of a Creator. I paused and thought with wonder, here is an atheist, the most virtuous and amiable of men. An atheist, whom I have always regarded with the horror which the multitude impute to that character. And have I an atheist for my friend? How much does the mind enlarge itself with years and experience! I was taught to think an atheist the most wicked of beings, a daring rebel against the Lord of the universe. But what is M. Deleyre? A candid philosopher whose mind is not convinced of the one eternal cause. I felt a strange sensation of doubt by no means unpleasing, as it filled me with a suite of ideas totally new to me. I however soon returned from this unbounded wandering. I thought that a bad education had given

[5] Alternately: "M. Deleyre convinced me that Wilkes was a bad politician in being a profligate man."

[6] Author of *The Wealth of Nations.* Boswell had attended his classes in moral philosophy and rhetoric at the University of Glasgow.

M. Deleyre so hideous a view of God that it was his interest to think there was none; and I am convinced that the inclination of philosophers for or against any truth makes the same arguments seem as different to them as the same colours seem to different eyes. I returned again to a calm persuasion of the existence of the glorious fountain of all mind, and I exulted in the hope of meeting M. Deleyre in a better world.

[EDITORIAL NOTE: In the "consolatory refuge" of Parma Boswell opened his soul to Deleyre, as the following extracts show. "Owned sad faults. He said, 'You were made to be unhappy. I would like to have your principles with my behaviour, and you my behaviour with your principles.' . . . BOSWELL. 'I wish people desired to overwhelm me with honours.' DELEYRE. 'You must have a rational pride. If you were constantly like this, it would be necessary to have you confined.' Showed journal. DELEYRE. 'When you are calm, you will get great pleasure and profit from reading this. Montaigne did likewise. He studied himself.' Told all history with Father. DELEYRE. 'You must tell him all your faults boldly, and begin as you are able to continue. . . . Take on yourself as much as you can without tormenting yourself.' " They parted "tender and sad" on 5 August, and Boswell then journeyed through Modena and Bologna to Florence, where he received the following letters from George Dempster and Rousseau.]

[Received 10 August, George Dempster to Boswell][7]

London, 1 July 1765

MY DEAR FRIEND . . . Now, Sir, as to the reprehensions with which your epistle opens, and which I called the overture of the opera, upon account of its blustering and noise with which very pretty songs, andantes, minuets, and jigs were introduced. Why not sign my name? Why sign it? It is as if after an hour's or a day's or a week's joyous chat, or as if in the midst of a period I should start all at once to my feet, make a low bow, and inform you that the gentleman with whom you had laughed, rampaged, and periodized was called George Dempster from Scotland; and then as if you should enquire how all

[7] George Dempster, M.P. for the Perth burghs, was a close friend of Boswell. Some time early in 1765 he had sent Boswell an undated, unsigned letter which concluded, "Adieu, you bitch."

my friends did, observe it was a fine day, and ask if you could be of any service to me. It is as if I was ashamed of my name, and as if you wished my letters to end as the Irish song begins, "My name's Paddy Grady, I care not who knows it."[8] Then you proceed to censure with more wit than justice the conclusion of my letter, or as we orators call it, the peroration: "Farewell, you bitch," which I thought both pathetic and laconic. Your ideas of intimacy and familiarity I perceive are quite absorbed in German ceremony and Italian finesse. Mr. James Boswell, Sir, when you have again crossed the narrow seas and my humble threshold, when I have contemplated you from head to foot, when I have been dazzled with your lace and embroidery, and have made the proper observations on the elevation of your chin, the stiffness of your neck, and the dignity of your character, perhaps I may vary the conclusion of my letter. But if I vary the end, tremble for the beginning and middle. No client ever approached his patron, Wauchope never address[ed] Lord Bute, in terms more full of respect than I shall do Mr. Boswell. When I visit you, I shall come in my chair and wait in your antechamber; when you repay the visit, I shall receive you with hat and sword. You shall be treated with all the respect and thought of with all the contempt due to pompous characters. In the mean time I'll continue bitching you and roguing you all over Europe. Whatever alteration your ideas may have undergone, mine are still the same. I still fancy myself admitted by Terry's maid, clambering up two pair of stairs, sitting on a rush chair drinking tea out of a tin kettle; I figure you in your greasy nightcap taking physic, or perhaps strutting in plain pompadour like an officer of the Horse Guards, or perhaps just returned with a week's provisions from the chandler's shop, or lampooning Michael Ramsay, or begging franks for Johnston or James Bruce, or waltering in my floor with *Fingal*, or — or — or, blanks to be filled with circumstances ten times more ludicrous if ever I hear a word more in your head upon the subject of dignity or decorum.[9] . . . Adieu, I will not sign my name, so farewell, you bitch.

[8] Above "Paddy Grady" Dempster has written "Bare Bosom," presumably the name of the melody. Neither words nor melody have been traced.

[9] Thomas Terry was Boswell's landlord in Downing Street, Westminster. See *Boswell's London Journal, 1762–1763.* — "Waltering" is an obsolete form of "weltering."

[Received 11 August, Rousseau to Boswell. Original in French][1]

Môtiers, 30 May 1765

THE STORMY CRISIS in which I have found myself since your departure from this[2] has not allowed me any leisure to answer your first letter, and hardly allows me leisure to reply in a few words to your second.[3] To confine myself to what is immediately pressing, the recommendation which you ask for Corsica; since you have a desire to visit those brave islanders, you may inquire at Bastia for M. Buttafoco, Captain of the Royal Italian Regiment; his house is at Vescovato, where he resides pretty often. He is a very worthy man, and has both knowledge and genius; it will be sufficient to show him this letter and I am sure he will receive you well, and will contribute to let you see the island and its inhabitants with satisfaction. If you do not find M. Buttafoco, and will go directly to M. Pascal Paoli, General of the nation, you may in the same manner show him this letter, and as I know the nobleness of his character I am sure you will be very well pleased at your reception. You may even tell him that you are liked by my Lord Marischal of Scotland, and that my Lord Marischal is one of the most zealous partisans of the Corsican nation. You need no other recommendations to these gentlemen but your own merit, the Corsicans being naturally so courteous and hospitable that all strangers who come among them are made welcome and caressed.

I have Mlle. Le Vasseur's thanks to give to you, and my own reproaches;[4] but I will await your return from Italy, when I hope you will come to receive both.

Do me the kindness, Sir, to deliver this letter for the Comte de Zinzendorf to the French Envoy (I cannot remember his name); I

[1] Boswell printed the greater part of this letter both in French and in English translation, at the beginning of his *Journal of a Tour to Corsica.* His translation is given here. Certain portions which he omitted are supplied from the original letter, which is among the Boswell papers at Yale.

[2] For Rousseau's troubles, see p. 259.

[3] See p. 80, and *Boswell on the Grand Tour: Germany and Switzerland,* 31 December 1764.

[4] Boswell had sent Mlle. Le Vasseur a garnet necklace. Rousseau may be reproaching Boswell for having given her such an expensive gift, or perhaps for his loose conduct in Italy.

am sure he will be willing to see that the Count gets it. I wish you agreeable and fortunate travels, health, gaiety, and a speedy return. I embrace you, Sir, with all my heart.

J. J. ROUSSEAU.

P.S. Since it may happen that you will not be at Genoa when you receive this letter, I have decided to send the one for M. de Zinzendorf by another hand.

[EDITORIAL NOTE: At Florence, Boswell fell in with a group of Englishmen, including Col. Isaac Barré, the famous politician (and the second half of Wilkes-Barre, Pennsylvania), Lords Beauchamp and Tylney, and the Scottish chaplain to Lord Hertford, James Trail, who was made Bishop of Down and Connor in this year. With Trail, Boswell discussed those metaphysical and psychological problems which fascinated him.[5] He also met John Dick, the British Consul at Leghorn, who was to become a lifelong friend and an active partner in his later schemes for assisting Paoli and the Corsican rebels.

Despite his immersion in society, Boswell was often unhappy in Florence. The goal he set for himself was a high, heroic one; he wrote, "I'm determined to try all experiments with a soul and body." But Boswell was too human to make a hero; his life at Florence was a mingling of comedy and pathos. His venereal disease recurred, and he reminded himself to "ask condoms for Siena." Among the English he found himself "just weak and young" or "awkward merely from vapours in head." He resumed his study of the flute, which alleviated his depression, but despite being pressed to stay he set out for Siena without great reluctance on the evening of 24 August.

The memoranda for 26 August to 8 September are missing — an unfortunate gap since they must have recorded the inception of two striking romantic adventures. To some extent, however, their story can be reconstructed from the materials printed below. Boswell arrived in Siena on 25 or 26 August (the thirty-six mile trip took nine and a half hours by post coach). He had asked Mountstuart for letters of recommendation, and had obtained one directed to Mountstuart's former mistress, Porzia Sansedoni. Though details are lacking, Bos-

[5] Boswell's notes of his conversations with Trail have been expanded by Robert Warnock in *Notes & Queries,* clxxiv (1938). 44–45.

well's approach to Porzia and to his other and more enduring object of affection, Girolama Piccolomini (or Moma), seems to have been as direct as it was to the ladies of Turin. As his letters to Porzia show, he got right to the point. Boswell's account of his Sienese adventures in his letter to Rousseau (p. 16) might well be used as a guide to this stage of his travels, since it summarizes and supplements the material printed below. His relations with Porzia and Moma are also discussed in the Introduction, p. xi.]

[Boswell to Porzia Sansedoni. Original in French][6]

[Siena, ? August 1765]

PERMIT ME, MY DEAR MADAME, to write to you. In a matter I have much at heart, you will judge better by quietly reading my letter than you can when we talk of it.

You are aware that I feel for you the strongest of passions, and one which is securely founded, since I foresaw it even before I came here when my Lord Mountstuart drew me a picture of your character. I found in you the very person my romantic soul had imagined; and that soul has begun to indulge in hopes that the time is come, at last, to enjoy the felicity of which it believed itself worthy.

But I see I am not born to be happy. I have declared my feelings towards you, and have learned that you are unable to reciprocate them. It is true, I have the honour to be not distasteful to you. You have displayed for me an esteem — I would even say a sort of tenderness — by which I am deeply flattered. But you insist that the delicacy of your attachment to my Lord precludes you from giving thought to any other man. I have told you, in all sincerity, how much I admired this romantic sentiment. But I have ventured to recall to you that it was a little too extravagant. My Lord is so formed that he is incapable of fidelity himself, and does not expect it from you; and believe me, Madame, did I imagine that my Lord would be vexed by

[6] All the letters to Porzia Sansedoni were published in the original French and in Geoffrey Scott's translations in the fifth volume of Colonel Isham's privately printed *Private Papers of James Boswell.* Scott's translations, slightly modified, are used here. The sequence of the first four letters to Porzia is optional, as Scott noted, but his arrangement has been followed.

your according me your friendship, there is nothing I would not endure sooner than to obtain it at the cost of a delicate point of honour. But I believe, on the contrary, my Lord would be generous enough to desire that his friend should possess the happiness he sighs for. It appears to me natural that you should be able to accord me a share of that love you have for my Lord, since, like yourself, I am a part of him. Ah, if that could happen, how much closer would be the bonds which knit me to my amiable friend, penetrated, as we should both be, with the same sentiments for yourself; beloved, as we should both be, by *la cara Porzia!* How beautiful would be the mixture of tender feeling between the three of us! Ah, Madame! When, in this brief existence, I see the possibility of such deep happiness, I pity myself greatly that it is scarce probable.

I entreat your advice, as my sincere friend; and, since your heart is untouched by passion, your judgment can be impartial. There is a lady here who has allowed me to see that she would gladly welcome me. Would you have me force myself into a gradual attachment to this lady, who, perhaps, would be able to distract me and help me to banish the memory of a passion by which, otherwise, I shall be tormented — for my temperament is sensitive, impatient, and prone to melancholy, and the consequences of uncertainty in an affair like this might be disastrous.

Or would you, rather, give me your assurance that you are not indifferent to me, that your affection for me is more lively than you imagined, and that you would be sorry to forego the opportunity of giving happiness to a gallant man — my Lord's friend — and one as romantic as yourself?

I know well that love is not in our control; if you tell me that I have nothing to hope from your heart, I shall not esteem you the less, and we shall be on the footing of friends, without passion. Only, I entreat you to tell me your feelings before it is too late; for I am philosopher enough to know that a passion which is still brief-rooted in the heart can be conquered. Whatever the event, I shall be, my very dear Madame, your eternal friend,

J. Boswell.

[Boswell to Porzia Sansedoni. Original in French]

[Siena, ? August 1765]

MY DEAR MADAME, — Allow me two or three words. In spite of all the anxieties I have suffered, I have some intelligence left to me. Your conduct persuades me that you are much interested in me. Madame, it is worth your while to stop and consider whether there is not something more in that interest than a cold friendship. I beg you to examine your heart, and I claim the right to know all in confidence. Believe me, I shall admire you more for generosity and a noble frankness than for any nicely calculated reserve. The romantic man really worthy of you is at Siena. Do not lose him. Time passes. A moment of despair may remove me for ever. Think seriously. I adore you. Be quite frank. Ah, Madame — I dare say no more.

[*c.* 2 SEPTEMBER. SIENESE REFLECTIONS][7] It seems to me that men have been much mistaken in their search for happiness, and I believe I see clearly the reason why. They have wished to establish the same general system of living for every one, without realizing that men differ as much in inclination as in appearance. It is not surprising that men who have devoted themselves to thought and who are honoured with the great name of philosopher — it is not surprising, I say, that their pride and ambition should make them wish that they could lay down the law to all their fellows and thus be almost kings of mankind. And it is not even surprising that the majority of men have submitted to this intellectual domination, since a great part of mankind are timid and lazy when it comes to thinking for themselves. As for me, who have found myself in every possible frame of mind and have experienced life in great variety, I think that the general rules are very badly conceived and hold men in a tiresome dependence, with no other advantage than to aggrandize certain famous names which have almost become oracles.

It is true that a society cannot exist without general rules. I agree.

[7] These reflections written in Italian are a counterpart of the French themes Boswell composed in Utrecht (see *Boswell in Holland*). They were written rapidly as linguistic exercises on any subject which came into his mind. Since they carry no dates, they have to be ordered on internal evidence and on the type of paper and ink used.

Let us therefore have laws, and let those laws be the general rules. But I want no others. The laws which are really necessary for public happiness are beyond all question very few. Men have many unwritten laws, and this is exactly the evil against which I am trying to argue. These are the laws of fashion, of custom, and of so many other particular sorts, that those who live "in the world," as the phrase goes, are little better than slaves. I wish every one to live naturally, as he himself pleases, and then possibly we might not hear so many people complaining of this evil world. To me these lamentations seem like the cries of animals in chains or in cages.

So I think when I live retired from the world and my spirit has complete liberty. So I think here at Siena, where I find myself in a pleasant Tuscan city in the midst of a simple and gay society; and if the moralist would judge some persons living here to be dissolute, then it must be said that the libertinism of Siena is like St. Paul's charity: it thinketh no evil. Marriage here is tacitly considered a different compact from that of civil law, for the *consortium omnis vitae* between married couples is never presumed. And really gentlemen and ladies here do nothing against their consciences, for their consciences are of quite another sort than those of people who live in a country where rigid morality is observed. So I can say philosophically that I have lived among very good people.

So I wish every man to live precisely according to his own inclination, without minding those of other people. I am living in this fashion now. I have been a week in Siena and have not as yet seen any *maraviglia*,[8] as the Italians say. I should not be able to say why to any one who demanded a proper reason, but I can explain it very well to myself: it is because I have been so busy with women that I have felt no curiosity about inanimate objects. I have resumed the study of Italian; I have read Ariosto with a fire worthy of that sublime author, and as I am making clear perhaps at this moment I have been trying to write a little in *la bella lingua*. I feel peaceful and happy, and though there may be more estimable people, I am sure there are none happier than I am. My philosophy aims no higher.

[8] "Sights," literally "marvel."

[Boswell to ?Porzia Sansedoni. Original in French][9]

[Siena] Wednesday [?4 September 1765]

I FEEL ALREADY that I am wholly yours. I am distressed by your absence this afternoon; for yesterday evening you said to me, "You must not be so melancholy," and from these words I drew some consolation. I am anxious to know if my hopes are merely vain. I shall wait on you this evening, for I cannot live a single day without the sight of you. If you return too late to talk with me, I shall at least have one moment of pleasure. Tomorrow morning I shall call upon you at the hour you appoint. I have still some difficulty in reading your handwriting. I hope to know it better. Adieu, my dear Madame,

J. BOSWELL.

[Boswell to Porzia Sansedoni. Original in French]

[Siena, ?5 September 1765]

GOOD MORNING, DEAR MME. SANSEDONI, I am very well and gay. And although I have some suspicions that you like me better when I am a melancholy cavalier, I refuse to dissimulate, even with a view to recommending myself to you. I refuse to feign a sadness I do not feel. If your heart declares itself for me, I shall be the happiest of mortals; and I shall think of you all my life with transport. If that cannot be, I have enough sense to be able to acquiesce in having failed to achieve the *impossible*. I shall, none the less, be your friend. I shall think of you all my life with tender esteem.

Judge, then, dear Madame. Be sincere. My resolution is fixed. I am myself. I am the proud Boswell. I am no wretched suppliant for your pity. No, Madame. I am a man who adores you and lays claim to your attachment. If you cannot love me, do nothing. I go.

The little favours which you granted me last evening ravished me. Ah, Madame, you have never seemed so beautiful to me as when you took off your glove and extended me your hand to kiss with romantic ardour. You said that I had accustomed you to think — you

[9] The absence of any superscription makes it possible that this letter was not addressed to Porzia, but the watermark and quality of paper are identical with Boswell's letter of 9 September to her.

would not tell me what thoughts. Think on, dear Madame; think those thoughts, and perhaps you will come to think more strongly. I will be with you between eleven o'clock and noon *to talk of my Lord*. Thank Heaven I am so well. Adieu.

[EDITORIAL NOTE: Boswell preserved in Italian the following account of a characteristic *conversazione* without indicating its place or date. Mention of Francis I's funeral, however, which occurred in Vienna on 28 August would seem to date it within ten days thereafter. The speakers are Giroloma (Moma) Piccolomini, Abbé Lorenzo Placidi, Placido Placidi, Giacomo Boswell, Tiburzio Spannocchi, Antonio Testa, Silvio Gori-Pannilini (Porzia's brother), and Bernardino (Bino) Ghini-Bandinelli.]

### SIENESE SCENE

MOMA. Good day, gentlemen. Good day, Tiburzio. You didn't go to the country? Sor[1] Silvio, another fan. That will do nicely. Bino, please wind this watch.

LORENZO. I saw a letter from Florence today that says flatly that there will be a detailed order for mourning, and that until it is published, no one should get any new clothes made. And that sounds reasonable, because it would surely be stupid to get a suit made today and be obliged to have it changed tomorrow. Then, too, it seems to me that there is no need of being in a hurry to get started on mourning that is going to be worn so long a time. Better, certainly, to take time to get it right.

PLACIDO. Certainly.

MOMA. Does your head ache, Placido?

PLACIDO. A little. I have not been sleeping well. But it's better today. — It's rather cold.

TIBURZIO. You are always working at something, Signora Girolama. You never seem to get tired.

MOMA. As a matter of fact, I enjoy knitting a few pairs of stockings; so I work and talk. It isn't hard, it doesn't tire me, it doesn't hurt my eyes.

GIACOMO. I wish I had a wife like you.

[1] *Sor*, an untranslatable familiar form like "marse" in Negro speech.

TIBURZIO. Bravo, Signor Giacomo. You are right. A most excellent lady.

MOMA. Good day, Tonino.[2] Have you been walking?

ANTONIO. No. I went to the café to pick up the news from Rome. The Pope is better. My brother is very busy, but it is not his understanding that there are many people there. Visitors from abroad prefer to stay in Florence.

SILVIO. The Mayor[3] told me that you are dining today at the Town Hall. If you feel sleepy afterwards, there's a good bed there.

MOMA. For shame, Silvio! You think of nothing but beds and sleeping. I want to go home at once.

GIACOMO. I shall go tomorrow to pay my respects to the Mayor.

MOMA. For shame! Come see me instead.

GIACOMO. Oh, no, Madame. I visit you a great deal. I must sometimes go call on Signor Orazio. You are jealous of your husband. I really enjoy being with him. We have argued with the most spirited keenness, and made the Town Hall ring. "Poh!" said he, "you are young." He was right.

MOMA. Well, tell us what you argued about.

GIACOMO. Ah, that's a secret.

BINO. I got today from Modena a gazette that contains a detailed account of all the ceremonial at the Emperor's funeral.

MOMA. It was magnificent?

BINO. Magnificent in the extreme.

LORENZO. There's no doubt of it. Who can expect magnificence if not a prince of such fame as the Emperor of Germany, our sovereign?

[*c.* 6 SEPTEMBER. SIENESE REFLECTIONS] It is true that Siena does not have great variety and may appear a little tedious to an active mind. The nobility is very ignorant, or if they have knowledge, they make very little use of it in conversation. I have often wondered how it is possible for human beings to live from day to day without cultivating the mind, without progressing in knowledge, without any increase in intellectual enjoyment. The philosophical systems which assert man to be an animal who is continuously improving are contradicted by this city.

[2] A Tuscan nickname for Antonio.

[3] Moma's husband.

The Emperor's death has been a great source of conversation for our ladies and gentlemen. The mourning which will have to be worn has been conceived of in a thousand different fashions, and the lively, fantastical imagination of the Italians has shown itself all in its splendour. . . .

I am naturally of a timid disposition, and my education has increased this timidity. Philosophy has cured this weakness somewhat, but occasionally it recurs and makes me feel ridiculous and miserable as before. The circulation of the blood is certainly what makes a man lively or sluggish, and yesterday my blood was circulating very badly. I sat then by Signora Girolama and looked at some ladies whom I saw for the first time, and I had an absurd but real anxiety. I could not escape this feeling, and I suffered like a man who has never been in company. . . .[4]

I am now in a beautiful town in Tuscany. I am well thought of by all the nobility. I enjoy the honest friendship of some pleasant ladies. I am studying the beautiful Italian language and making good progress. I am also studying music with an excellent teacher; I play my flute and sing with real enjoyment. I am enjoying good health. The weather is clear and agreeable. I can do everything I wish. I am in a situation which I imagined in my most delicious moments. And yet I cannot say I am happy. I am surprised at this. I don't know what to think. I don't know what to look for. Undoubtedly, in this world no man can be completely happy. Oh, no — sad thought! Abbé Crocchi, my esteemed instructor, advises me to consider this lack of happiness as a strong proof of the immortality of the soul, and of a better life in another world.

[Boswell to Porzia Sansedoni. Original in French]

[Siena] Friday 6 September 1765

Dear, dear Mme. Sansedoni, — After a night of apprehension, of sorrow, of tears — during which I have not closed my eyes except to think of you, and to be troubled by ideas more keenly melancholy than those which occupy my mind on the day succeeding such a night

[4] What follows may well have been written on a later day.

— dear, dear object of my celestial love, you will permit me to unlock to you, a little more, my afflicted heart.

My situation is indeed *dolorosa*, as you well said. I suffer bitter torments by a cruel fatality. For you are not cruel. No. You are sorry to see me so unhappy. Other women would look on me with triumph. You, with regret. Oh, my dear friend, give a thought on my behalf. I see myself sacrificed to a visionary idea; and yet I admire you the more for that idea. I feel all the force of your thoughts on fidelity, even to a faithless lover. It is such sentiments as these that ravish me, that cause me to adore *La Porzia* as a divinity. Ah sad, sad fate, that this admiration should cost me so many tears! I console myself with the certainty of your affection for me; but that disastrous passion, which can never be explained, leaves me no peace. Think *for* me, I entreat, as best you can. I still see a possibility. Perhaps, you said, in some moment of pity — Ah! Madame, do not forget that sentiment; it is from your pity alone that I have hopes.

You have told me, in that case, I should not be satisfied. Madame, I will tell that it is impossible for me to be wholly satisfied as long as I see that the woman who is the sole object of my desires is not wholly mine. So much I confess to you. But grant me the great proof I seek of your affection for me, and I shall retain all my life a grateful recollection, a sweet felicity mingled with a regret which, however, will be powerless to sadden me. It is not my wish to argue against your resolution of romantic fidelity; but I could desire that some angel should inspire you with another sentiment as romantic as that resolution. I should like to hear you say, "I have kept for my Lord an inviolate fidelity: I have only bestowed my pity on his worthy friend, who was in the saddest situation and will bless me the rest of his days. In so acting I have done my Lord no offence. Rather, I have proved the real strength of my serious attachment to him in thus contradicting my own fancy to save his friend."

My dear, dear friend, I am incapable of explaining my sentiments, but you can understand my way of thinking. Never have there been found circumstances more singular than ours. I ought to be content with your friendship, but I cannot be. I am in torment until I have that proof of your goodness towards me — and I swear to you that I desire it only as a proof.

I wish it were over. What a romantic idea! Yes, I could wish it were in the past; for it is not the ecstasy of a moment but the delicious memory of a whole lifetime that I so ardently desire. O dear, dear Madame, excuse, I entreat you, these extravagant ideas. I have entire confidence in you. I yield myself completely to you. Dispose of me as you will. I am nothing, independently of you; thus you are completely mistress of an honest Scot whose heart and soul breathe nothing but adoration for you.

Permit me to add one word more. To show you the delicacy of my ideas as to the proof which I desire from you, I should like to be with you late at night, and, in a modest darkness, to receive a tender pledge of your favour for an eternal friend. And, Madame, on the word of a man of honour, I shall never ask another. There you have the true romantic. I swear by everything that is sacred that after that single proof, no friend will be more respectful than I, or more chaste. I shall regard you with the liveliest gratitude. I shall adore you as my beneficent goddess and you will have in me the noblest of friends.

I entreat you, dear, dear Madame, think seriously of this, for never again will you find yourself in such circumstances as these. Consider well the nature of my passion. Consider well the generosity of my ideas. Your act, which it fills me with transport to picture, will but interrupt for a moment your romantic fidelity to my Lord, to grant a sublime and eternal happiness to his worthy friend.

Adieu, most adorable of women. I am wholly yours,

J. Boswell.

P.S. If you do not forbid it, I shall wait upon you a moment at five. You ought to see me like that, for a moment, every day.

P.P.S. Read this letter with care. It contains very, very romantic sentiments.

[Boswell to Porzia Sansedoni. Original in French]

[Siena] Friday midnight [6 September 1765]

I cannot go to bed without first writing a word to you. I have been happier this evening than ever. I thought you more tender. You have understood my romantic idea. That is a great deal. You are the only woman in the world who has sufficient delicacy and imaginaion to understand it. Yes, I shall be content. I swear to you, by all hat is holy, I shall never ask for more: only for that extraordinary proof of your pity, of your real eagerness to make me happy, and to win my gratitude for life.

When I was saying to you, "How if there be no other way of saving me from a state of bitter torment?" you replied, "Well, you must wait." And when I called out with transport, "Is it then possible?" your reply was, "You want to know too much." O my dear Madame, those are precious words. They have lit my heart with a joy which I hope you will not be cruel enough to extinguish. As I was telling you yesterday evening, I see that you are ready to judge for me. You are willing to take charge of a sick heart. I surrender myself to your gentle authority. My friend, protectress, goddess, remember that the eternal happiness of a worthy man is at stake. Consider that your slave, your subject, your romantic lover is truly so different from other men that his delicacy would not suffer him even to desire more than that one sacred night, and that his honour holds a far higher place than his desires. Heaven bless you! I repeat, dear Madame, *I wish that it were over*.

You feel a real esteem, a real friendship, for me: I am convinced of it. Take thought, O take thought, on your friend's behalf, and do not check the relenting impulse of your heart. Do not repress any gesture of tenderness.

[Boswell to Porzia Sansedoni. Original in French]

[Siena] Sunday 8 September [1765]

EVERY MORNING A LETTER! It is thus I say my orisons to my soul's goddess. Last evening's conversation was the most tender I have ever had with you. I flatter myself you begin to feel the worth of my romantic attachment. So you are *embarrassed!* Dear, dear Madame, I thank you a thousand times for the word. Yes, I am determined to put my interpretation on it: I am determined to hope. I am worthy of you. I can say no more. I have had a much better night than I have passed for some time. Gleams of joy flashed upon me, and filled me with transport; but perhaps they were deceitful. I dare not yet put my trust in them.

I seek relief in reading Ariosto. I am created to read that divine poet. I respond to all the force of his enthusiasm. At this moment my eyes fall on,

> Gli sdegni, le repulse, e finalmente
> Tutti i martir' d'Amor, tutte le pene,
> Fan per lor rimembranza, che si sente
> Con miglior gusto un piacer quando viene.[5]

*Gli sdegni e le repulse* have no application to us, for, dear Madame, you do not disdain me. *I martir'* are the result of circumstances which will not, I hope, be long lasting. I ask your pardon for having burdened you with the reading of so many of my distracted thoughts. I shall be at your *feet* between noon and one o'clock. I shall show the utmost possible discretion. I am eternally yours,

J. Boswell.

P.S. Adorable Porzia, do not fear the violence of my passion. Do not fear that it will grow cold if you show yourself tender to me. No, the heart of your brave Scot of ancient line has as much firmness as it has fire. You are the lady destined for his eternal constancy. His grateful soul will always be yours. It will be uplifted by a link with yours. Everywhere, and at all times, Boswell will be proud, and will have a dignity of character as the friend of Madame Sansedoni. Once more, good-bye.

MONDAY 9 SEPTEMBER. Yesterday dissipated morning. At 12½, Porzia. Music. She was pretty. Then toilet. Spoke French. She was indifferent.... After dinner, *billet* from Moma: Bandinelli threatens; "protect me from him."[6] Short answer: "We shall talk about what is worrying you." Was embarrassed.... Then strolled and tired. Then Lizza.[7] Porzia in coach; came to her. BOSWELL. "I am worse. I don't know what to do. I see you as one who torments me. I am generous." PORZIA. "No, for you want things your own way, and

[5] *Orlando Furioso,* xxxi. 4: "The recollection of the scornings and the repulses — in short of all the tortures of love, all its pains — causes pleasure, when it comes, to be felt with keener delight."

[6] Presumably Bernardino (Bino) Ghini-Bandinelli. Perhaps he was a *cavaliere servente* of Moma's, and threatened to reveal her love for Boswell to her husband.

[7] A promenade.

if you can't have them, you are angry." You was quite in gloomy passion. She said: "Come, don't fall into your melancholy fit. Be gay." BOSWELL. "You detest my gaiety." She was quite indifferent, and said, "I think now as I thought at first." Then home, quite sunk. Then thought: "This is a fine passion. Let us take all methods to preserve it, either by indulgence or restraint." Thought to go and have promise that if you was constant two years, [you should] return and enjoy. *Conversazione*, Casa Tai. Moma said, "Truly in love." Shunned talking; appointed tomorrow. Mme. Tai[8] at window with you, very gay. MME. TAI. "When a man has good manners, he needs no other recommendation." I. "I see that animals and mankind in general have material love. I want something superior." MME. TAI. "Do it little, and do it only in a frenzy, not thinking." Delicious this idea, to do it quite in ecstasy. Told her, "I shall think about this." Was gladdened by this mark of liking, and had heard from Moma how my Lord had said that Porzia after so many children would be *gouffre* and *bourreux*,[9] and that she had many intrigues and much art, and was growing old. You got great force and away to her. . . . Bowed. She turned away Abbé, but you approached not. A *marchese* whispered her. Then little dance. You felt spirited. Resolved to be free, and tell her so tomorrow. She came near you. You just talked indifferent subjects, and went away with rest. Bravo. You are now growing a man.

[Boswell to Porzia Sansedoni. Original in French]

[Siena] Monday 9 September [1765]

MADAME, — I have reflected as a philosopher. I have regained that strength of mind which is my pride. I rejoice to know myself once more. Your pity will give place to admiration, for you shall see

8 Boswell's form for the Italian *Taja,* the name of a prominent Sienese family. Mme. Agnese del Taja was about four years older than Boswell.

9 Greedy and fat; literally, as bottomless as a whirlpool and stuffed like a sofa. *Bourreux,* which does not appear in modern French dictionaries, is equivalent to *rembourré. Gouffre* as an adjective is most unusual, and Boswell certainly should have used the feminine form *bourreuse.* His "so many" probably means "a certain number," not "a great many." Porzia had had only three children by the time he visited Siena, the last having been born in August 1764.

how much I am master of myself. I shall have the honour to wait or
you a moment before dinner, or at six o'clock this evening. You wil
do me the favour of returning me those extravagant *billets* which
have taken the freedom to write you, and never shall you hear m
speak another word of that passion which has caused me so many tor
ments and kindled in me the hope of so much joy. I shall indulge my
self no more in vain interpretations. I shall no longer flatter mysel
to win, from your generosity of feeling, a noble and romantic happi
ness. I shall be, always, your sincere and respectful friend,

J. BOSWELL.

TUESDAY 10 SEPTEMBER. Yesterday morning sent bold, spir
ited, noble letter to Porzia. At 10½, Girolama. Alone; kind, con
certed. You went away. . . . Then Porzia at harpsichord. Was free
Got *billets*. Went out bold. Then Girolama. Quite agitated. Put or
condom; entered. Heart beat; fell. Quite sorry, but said, "A sign o
true passion." Dined full to have courage; was feverish after it anc
did little all day. Before five, Moma; father with her. Had near callec
him *fou*. Then fond with her. . . . She said: "I want to give myself up
to you, and I would lose[1] all the others for your sake." You swore pas
sion, but she laughed when you said, "But he has no inclination."
Was unquiet. At *conversazione*, Porzia came on purpose to talk witl
you. Said she had been surprised and "angry"; my "mistrust," &c
You assured her [you] had not thought a word of that; only resolu
tion. She feared evil tongues. BOSWELL. "No, Madame." Seemed in
different. She went to other room; you followed and assured no mor
passion. She said, "I am sorry," and made many advances. Saw he
clever woman of world, and (amazing!) had great coolness. You
talked with excellent address of eternal esteem, but regret not "grati
tude for a romantic happiness," and seemed moved.[2]

[Boswell to Porzia Sansedoni. Original in French]

[Siena, Sunday ?15 September 1765]

ADIEU, MY DEAR MADAME. Sunday is a lucky day for me. Tha
firmness of soul which I enjoyed a week ago is mine again today.

[1] *Perderai*, but possibly Boswell wrote *penderai*, hang.

[2] The memoranda for 11–28 September are missing.

hall speak clearly. I am almost sure, Madame, that you deceive
ourself in imagining that your cruelty towards me is occasioned by
our love for my Lord. No, Madame, it is caused by that same proud
ardness with which you tortured my Lord in the days when at the
ottom of your heart you loved him.

But, my dear Madame, all men have not the same character. The
ruelty which piques the fancy of a light lover pierces the heart of one
vho is in earnest. Although you do not know my merit, I dare assure
ou that I have a great deal. I confess, Madame, that at present you
ave the triumph of completely destroying it. You have the triumph
f troubling a noble and romantic soul, and of embittering the life of
worthy stranger.

Obdurate friend, give me the letter for Lucca![3] Give it, I implore
ou, without delay. Repeat to me one last time your cruel resolutions,
nd I will force myself, by the most solemn oath, to leave you for ever.
am vain enough to believe that, could I remain here a few months
onger, your arrogance would be sated, and you would make a formal
nd complete surrender.

But your brave Scot is not a professional gallant. He is all natural,
ll tender. His passions are genuine and strong. I adore you, Mad-
me. Resolve once for all. By my immortal soul I swear to you that
t last I am determined.

[Received 15 September, Mallet to Boswell. Original in French]

Geneva, 14 August 1765

YOU MADE ME PROMISE WHEN LEAVING, MY DEAR BARON, that I
vould write to you, and further that I would send your character
ketch. Although I have perhaps promised you this and although I
ave sufficient respect for my promise, I shall not be able to fulfill
nore than half of it this time. You will have a letter and no portrait,
nd moreover what a letter! I arrived here completely harassed,
ompletely heated; since I have been here I have been so distracted
nd wearied by paying and receiving calls and other petty miseries
hat I can truly say this time that I am *beaten down* and *prostrated*. It

This letter is probably the one for Anna Pallerini mentioned in the memo-
andum for 30 September.

is not in such a moment that I shall take up my pencils to make eve
the most feeble sketch. It is a great deal that I can hold a pen an
write flat prose on the most common subjects.

We left each other, my Lord Mountstuart, the Colonel, and I, sev
eral days ago with a promise to see one another soon in England. Be
fore this separation and especially during the rest of our journey, w
agreed, and I above all, that we had sometimes treated you too se
verely. I admit that a nervous man like myself should enter mor
fully than I often do into the various states of mind of his companions
but unfortunately the same frailty that puts one in need of indulgenc
is often the cause why one is little disposed to grant it to others. Ex
treme sensitivity to our own state of mind prevents us from consider
ing that of others, and people get along better if they do not resembl
each other.

M. de Voltaire is more the same man than ever. He works un
ceasingly to further the reign of reason. He wants to see its beginnin
before his death. Lately a young lady of quality from Savoy who pas
sionately wanted to see him was brought to his place. He sent out t
ask her if she were religious. The young lady having admitted he
guilt, he sent her word that recently he had shut his door to more tha
twenty deists, and that he would certainly not open it to a Chris
tian. . . .

Return by way of Geneva if it is possible. I dare promise you tha
we shall be able to amuse you for a few days at least, and you may b
assured that I shall not spare myself in any matter that depends o
me. You will see that despite my former complaints I find in yo
something to justify and inspire a great deal of esteem and friend
ship. . . .[4]

I cannot beg you too strongly to rely on me on all occasions as o
some one truly devoted to you. You are too philosophical not to prefe
this sincere and heartfelt assurance to the insipid compliments whic
are usual at the end of letters.

MALLET, PROFESSOR.

[4] A long paragraph is omitted here in which Mallet implores Boswell to try t
track down a chest of important papers which he has lost.

[Boswell to Mallet. Original in French][5]

[Siena, 15 September 1765]

LITTE BY LITTLE we shall get upon an excellent footing, in spite of all that has happened. In our letters there will be no room either for my tyrannical pride or for your gloomy moods and touchy sensibility. If you write much to me, you will be showing me an attention by which I shall be more flattered than you can imagine. Besides, you can do me good; for you have experienced all the varieties of hypochondria, and nevertheless preserved your judgment and reasonable tastes. Help me, I entreat you; for I cannot tell how I shall find myself able patiently to support the endless wretchedness to which I shall be exposed by my extreme sensibility. Those *petty miseries* of which you speak are like poisonous insects that gnaw a delicate soul. I have seen you unhappier at one of our dinners than if you had been in the galleys. My future life holds out a prospect of dinners, evenings, sermons, and tedious conversations without number. What is to be done? *Est mihi namque pater domi.*[6] It is both my duty and inclination to make him happy. But it is utterly impossible for me to succeed. He is a healthy, sound, hard-working man, who has never experienced one moment of hypochondria, and who regards the complaints of men like us as so much affectation. Conceive, then, what hours are in store for me. My plan will be to avoid being too much in his society, for trivial things are the great source of our suffering. His Highness[7] must procure me some employment in London where I shall pass the winter; my estate in Scotland will provide a romantic retreat for the summer months. I must enter Parliament. Whatever may be your present opinion, I shall make my mark there.

This morning I received an unexpected letter from our worthy General Graeme. He displays great esteem for me and affection also (in spite of all my faults), and desires to have my correspondence.

[5] This draft, probably an extract, was superscribed at a later date by Boswell, "To M. Mallet, from Siena, 1765." The original and Geoffrey Scott's translation, which is followed here, were published in the fifth volume of Colonel Isham's *Private Papers of James Boswell.*

[6] "I have a father at home" (Virgil, *Eclogues*, iii. 33, *domi pater*).

[7] Mountstuart.

Long live the Baron! Oh! all you — my fellow creatures of every degree — you cannot do other than love me!

[Girolama Piccolomini to Boswell. Original in Italian][8]

[Siena, ?18 September 1765]

ALLOW ME to indemnify myself to some extent for your absence by explaining the feelings I have about you. They ought to make you very happy if what you told me last night is true. My eyes cannot follow you in your little jaunt, but my longings can, and they are deputies more zealous than their principals. I saw you yesterday: morning, afternoon, and evening, and in spite of all that I long more than ever to see you again. O God, what shall I do when you are no longer here, if so short an absence is unendurable? But courage is always needed to conquer oneself; and instead of thinking of your good qualities I shall remind myself that you are a deceiver and a faithless lover, and then I shall laugh at you. But in the mean time I see you as lovable and, I would almost dare say, tender towards me. Were you playing a part even last night? If you are capable of carrying treachery to such a point, I must still love you because you are so good at the business.

You ordered me to think of you tonight, and I have obeyed you perfectly; you would have been quite satisfied with my docility if you had been here. If you return in time today I shall wait for you at home; otherwise we shall meet at the *conversazione*, where I beg you to talk to me with great discretion and on very general subjects, because every one is staying clear of me on your account and I should be the theme of all the gossip — besides being deserted, which in this city is of some consequence. Put this letter in your pocket, so that you can give it back to me when we meet.

[SIENESE REFLECTIONS] I must say that I am very happy today, for my soul is serene, my heart filled with gentle sweetness, my spirit bold, my imagination vivid. All that I lack is my native soil for

[8] Under 17 September in his Accounts Boswell records paying five sequins for "travelling expenses to Monte Oliveto," a Benedictine monastery about twenty-five miles south of Siena. The trip must have taken two days, and probably is the "little jaunt" mentioned in this letter, which is without address or signature.

which, as Virgil says, one always entertains loving thoughts. If I were now in the romantic woods of Auchinleck my happiness would be complete. I would see myself in the very place where Providence has established my residence, where I can honour the memory of my worthy ancestors, live happily cultivating my lands, doing good to my tenants, and showing a cordial hospitality to my neighbours. This is how I wish to live when my travels are over. In winter I shall go to London or Edinburgh, and in the summer I shall stay at my country-house and think many, many times of beautiful Italy. . . .

I am here in a room ornamented with a great number of paintings of all sorts: there are landscapes, fruit pieces, seascapes, pictures of buildings, of battles, of love. The portrait of a lady, hanging over my bedroom door, looks like my lady-in-waiting, for she stands with a majestic air and gestures with her hand as if to say, "There the gentleman sleeps." There are also some Biblical pictures cheaply engraved and horribly coloured. There is a large mirror and six small ones. And in my bedroom there are five mirrors, arranged with admirable skill over my bed. It is not an improbable supposition that these mirrors were placed here for his Excellency, my Lord Mountstuart, who loved to look at himself, like another Narcissus. . . .

Last night I paid a visit to the General Auditor,[9] with whom I stayed almost two hours. He showed me the French translation of Robertson's *History*.[1] I read some passages with pleasure, and wondered how I could have lived a great part of my life without enjoying liberal studies. But there is time for everything, and our inclinations must be followed as long as they are fresh, because the years of our youth pass so quickly. I see that I am falling back on the hackneyed sentiments of a hundred thousand men who have passed their lives before me. I dislike being a servile imitator, and I should like to flatter my pride of being original, but to be original is given to very few. Many pretend to enjoy this distinction, which is certainly something that infinitely increases one's self-regard. It seems as though a man possessing originality of mind is a better work of God, almost as though God bestowed particular pains on his creation. . . .

Love seems to me the most singular thing in this world, in this

[9] The principal minister of state in Siena. His name was Stefano Bertolini.

[1] Robertson's *History of Scotland*.

round of cause and effect. I am not talking about that pleasant instinct which the two sexes have to unite, but of that love which is called passion, which carries within itself a transport of spirit, anxiety, a delicate refinement, jealousy, in short all those feelings which have truly tormented poor mortals. I do not know whether animals make any discrimination among their females, nor do I know whether beauty exists among cows, hens, and bitches. I think rather that brutes aim directly at the grand finale without thinking much about the object of their desires. It is true I have seen brute males fighting for a female, but it was as if they were fighting for their food.

[Boswell to ?Porzia Sansedoni. Original in French][2]

[Siena, ?20 September 1765]

I HAVE THE HONOUR, MADAME, to give you back the *billets* which I had from you while we were treating of matters of which we think no longer. You have already returned some of my letters. I beg you will give back those which remain. Henceforth we shall write in a better style than when (in your words) my imagination was overheated. You shall find in me always a reasonable friend who admires you much.

I shall keep my own letters, and I shall read them with pleasure. They will recall to me an affair in which I gained some honour; for, although I was not victorious, I can boast at least of having made a brave attack.

Farewell, my dear Madame.

J. BOSWELL.

[2] Doubtfully assigned, both as to person and as to date. The mention of a considerable number of letters, however, points to Porzia. The date is based on the possibility that Porzia's letter which follows, if it is Porzia's, is a reply to this one.

[?Porzia Sansedoni to Boswell. Original in Italian][3]

[Siena] Saturday 21 [September 1765]

YOUR VERY KIND NOTE gave me great pleasure, and I am grateful for this attention of yours. I esteem your friendship very much, but it would give me still greater pleasure if I could assume that it was joined with a confidence that I have reason to fear [is lacking]. This is the reason why I shall be cautious, until I know how you feel about me at the moment. In some form or other, I hope to remain always your true servant and friend.

[Girolama Piccolomini to Boswell. Original in Italian][4]

[Siena, September 1765]

UP TO NOW I have flattered myself that the justice of my cause would have won your verdict for my manner of thinking, but I see that you are capricious and do not listen to the compelling arguments of justice. With you, the last advocate to speak always departs believing that he has won his case. Then, I am not pleased with a person who makes declarations to every woman he meets; and I would rather not have you at all than see you parcelled out; in a word, I prefer infidelity to the silly vanity that shows a person to be fickle and proud of his own parts. I beg you not to work up a feeling of repentance over your bad behaviour, for your relapses are so frequent that error must be becoming a habit with you, leaving no place for remorse. And meanwhile I shall try to alleviate my pain by thinking that I have erred in my choice of a lover, but not in that of a friend.

[Boswell to Girolama Piccolomini. Original in French]

[Siena] Friday [27 September 1765]

I AM STILL IN SIENA. I am leaving neither today nor tomorrow. Let us enjoy in peace the time remaining to us. Never in my life have

[3] Addressed to Boswell, but without signature. The handwriting is not Moma's, and the coy tone suggests Porzia.

[4] There is no way of dating this letter, but since it is addressed "A Monsieur, Monsieur Boswell" without any city specified, Boswell presumably received it while he was still in Siena.

I spent a more delicious day than yesterday. Yes, we are married. My heart and my soul cry out against unjust laws, and a sweet and generous emotion unites us for ever. I do not expect a reply. I simply wish to greet you.

SUNDAY 29 SEPTEMBER. Yesterday morning rose by eight. Was firm and philosophical and calm; put all in order. At ten, Momina. She was quite tendered down for she had not slept. You told her you was resolved. She said: "You go to greater and greater happiness, but you leave me here to go continually from bad to worse; for after a few years my youth will be gone, &c., and I am among people for whom I care nothing." His Excellency came.[5] You said, "I must be a Capitano di Popolo in my country." You was well with Orazio. They went. You took her to bed, and with mild courage did it fine. Both happy. She begged return from Leghorn, but you was reserved. She shed tears without affectation and promised fidelity. Her *allegria*[6] returned by fits. You was like Spanish cavalier and promised eternal friendship. You had been in Cathedral first. Leave quite in confusion. At twelve, found chaise at Porta. Half well, half ill all day. Night, bad inn.

MONDAY 30 SEPTEMBER. Yesterday had travelled all night. At seven, it rained heavy. You was all relaxed and slumbered sadly, and saw bad visions of Moma. Before twelve, arrived Lucca. Was quite sunk. Was just fit for falling into a melancholy as at Utrecht, had you been alone and had the same circumstances. Went to function and heard mass; then home and dined. Found the real advantage of an increase of ideas. Wrote Moma sickly and uncertain. At eight, opera: Bastardina,[7] delicious. . . . Went to Anna Pallerini; gave letter and saw her. Home, quite tired. . . .

[EDITORIAL NOTE: Despite his sadness at abandoning Moma, Boswell enjoyed his brief stay in Lucca. The memoranda demonstrate his talent for getting to know people quickly; his openness encouraged others to reveal their ideas frankly. Here Romano Garzoni, "a

[5] Orazio, Moma's husband.

[6] Gaiety.

[7] Lucrezia Agujari, otherwise known as La Bastardina. She was highly praised by Dr. Burney in his *History of Music.*

very sensible, civil man," became his friend, and soon they were discussing hypochondria and other topics of intense concern to Boswell. For 3 October he notes, "Romano came; you went to coffee-house with him. Always hipped in coffee-house. . . . Romano came home with you, and over burgundy said he had not the prejudice of jealousy, but if it was not known would give wife full liberty." Two days later, they were on the subject of ambition: "He said he had nothing of that prejudice which obliges every man to have an employment. Said it was unphilosophical, and that he would be like to kill himself if he thought he was bound to any constant employment, which was worse than galley-slave, who had only hands forced but mind free."

After viewing the Leaning Tower of Pisa, where he "with great modesty proposed doubt if the wind had not bowed it," Boswell arrived in Leghorn on 6 October. Here he made arrangements to sail to Corsica on a "merchant bark," and visited H.M.S. *Centurion*, on which Anson twenty years before had sailed on his famous expedition around the world. The commander of the British squadron in the Mediterranean, Commodore Harrison, who was also British Minister to Genoa, furnished him with what Boswell called a "passport," an elaborate document of identification in case his vessel was captured by Barbary corsairs. Count Antonio Rivarola, Sardinian Consul at Leghorn, but a Corsican by birth and son of a famous Corsican general, gave him four letters of recommendation. On 11 October Boswell started off.]

FRIDAY 11 OCTOBER.[8] After a few hours of sleep, was called at six by Signor Giuliano and another Corsican, who beat at my door. Was confused a little, but recollecting grand expedition, blood recovered bold circulation. Wrote Rousseau and Dempster; left also letters for Mme. de Spaen[9] and my dear Italian lady at Siena. At eight the little boat carried me to the bark, and we set sail. The good people had waited all night for me when the wind was so good that we should have been in Corsica ere morning. This day there was little wind. I was sick a very short while and threw up a little, but felt firm

[8] Only this one leaf, in the style of the fully written journal, survives from Boswell's trip to Corsica. It seems likely that most of his Corsican notes were written as extended memoranda and not in journal form.

[9] The Baroness von Spaen was one of Boswell's Dutch friends.

nerves in comparison of myself on the passage to Holland. A Corsican played a sort of guitar or lute, and I played my flute, and so did Jacob. The bark belonged to a Corsican of Pino. He carried wine to Leghorn. He spoke English. To save himself, he had the Tuscan flag (the Emperor's), and a Leghorn shipmaster, Ignazio Gentili. I lay down in the cabin bed, but was eat up by mosquitoes and other vermin. I eat cold tongue and bread and some of the crew's rice. There were ten aboard: two poor Corsican merchants, six Corsican sailors, the master, and a boy from Leghorn. I tried to read a little the disputes of Corsica, but could give no attention. Thought hardly any, and was content to be so. Jacob was firm and felt no sickness but wished to have a long voyage, and at night was delighted to see nothing but the sky and the sea. They laid a mattress on the provision chest, and hung a sail on the side of the bark and on four chairs, and under this tent you slept. At the Ave Maria they all kneeled, and with great fervency said their evening orisons to the Queen of Heaven. It affected you a good deal.

[Boswell to Rousseau. Original in French]

Leghorn, 11 October 1765

I HAVE RECEIVED YOUR LETTER, ILLUSTRIOUS PHILOSOPHER. I see that you do not forget me. Some time ago I started to write a very long letter to you entirely about myself.[1] At present, I account myself, my petty pleasures and petty anxieties, as nothing. In half an hour I embark for Corsica. I am going directly to the territories of Paoli. The worthy Count Rivarola has given me recommendations in plenty. I am all vigour, all nobility. If I perish on this expedition, think of your Spanish Scot with affection, and we shall meet in the paradise of imaginative souls. If I return safely, you will have a valuable account. I cannot write. I shall be able to speak. Death is nothing to me.

[1] Boswell refers to the letter printed above, p. 3.

# THE JOURNAL OF A TOUR TO CORSICA
# AND MEMOIRS OF PASCAL PAOLI

*Olim meminisse juvabit.* — VIRGIL

["One day you will rejoice to
remember" (*Aeneid*, i. 203)]

# The Journal of a Tour to Corsica and Memoirs of Pascal Paoli

Boswell and Corsica. One of the constant dreams of civilized man is to alter the state in which he lives, either by re-establishing a natural, harmonious society whose existence he discerns at one point or another in the past, or by working towards an ideal commonwealth of the future. Our own age looks forward more often than back, but the eighteenth century, which was also possessed by this dream, was still concerned with extending the Renaissance explorations of the spatial present and the temporal past. It tended to view its future in terms of the classical republicanism of the ancients — more than one Jacobin lived in the pleasing delusion that he was Cicero revived — or in the innocence of the savage state as reported by travellers. And in 1765, the imagination of Europe was aroused by an apparent fusion of these two concepts which was emergent in Corsica.[2]

At this time Corsica was under the rule of the Republic of Genoa, as it had been since the fourteenth century. Genoese domination, exacting and unpopular, was continually threatened by native revolts, and in 1738 the Genoese were obliged to import a French expeditionary force to subdue the island. On its withdrawal the Corsicans rose again and drove the Genoese back to the fortified towns on the coast, which proved difficult to capture without artillery and naval support. Yet even these towns might have fallen if the French in 1764 had not agreed to garrison them for four years in payment of a debt to Genoa. The French and Corsicans maintained reserved but friendly relations

[2] Chauncey B. Tinker's *Nature's Simple Plan*, 1922, offers a fine introduction to eighteenth-century interest in primitivism and in Corsica.

during this period, while the Genoese, now powerless, were despised and hated by their enemy.

European curiosity about this anomalous situation was increased by vague reports of the society and government of the Corsican rebels — or, in practical terms, the Corsican nation. In theory, Corsica was a republic governed by a nine-man Council and a General, life President of the Council, whose position was comparable to the Stadtholder's in Holland; in fact, as Boswell said, it was governed by "a species of despotism founded . . . on the affection of love,"[3] a manifestation of the ability and prestige of its General, Pasquale de Paoli.

Paoli, whose father and brother had been leaders of the nation before him, assumed the position of General in 1755 at the age of thirty. He was a tall, heavy, imposing man with reddish-blond hair and piercing blue eyes, whose personal ambition was swallowed up in an intense conviction that he was an instrument of God in Corsica's struggle for liberty. Energetic, pious, incorruptible, impatient with talkers and triflers, he never confused a firm regard for the dignity of his position with a sense of personal self-importance. His real achievement lay not in his victories over the Genoese, but in the establishment of order among the Corsicans themselves (a task which involved the suppression of the feudal lords and the vendetta), and in the encouragement of agriculture and commerce. In short he was the father of his country — the comparison to Washington is an easy and justifiable one — and, in Pitt's words, a hero out of Plutarch. So Boswell was to describe him, with just enough distinguishing traits to make an individual rather than a statue of him.

As a society, the Corsicans were as attractive as their leader. They were reputed to be hardy, brave, quick-tempered, and "uncorrupted" by civilization. What Europe saw was probably an uncomplicated feudal society; what it admired was a nation which seemed to embody in many ways Rousseau's ideal of political and social liberty, a nation to which Rousseau himself had referred approvingly in his *Social Contract*.[4]

[3] *Account of Corsica*, p. 190 (all page references to the *Account* are to the third edition). Boswell's striking phrase was lifted from Andrew Burnaby's Corsican journal. See p. 195 *n.* 4.

[4] Rousseau's statement is quoted on p. 195, and his connection with Corsica is discussed below, p. 197 *n.* 1.

Rousseau's reference had unexpected consequences, for it elicited an invitation from Matteo Buttafoco, a Corsican officer in the French service, to help prepare a constitution for the new republic, an invitation he was considering when Boswell arrived at Môtiers in December 1764. On hearing of it, Boswell jokingly proposed himself as Rousseau's Ambassador Extraordinary to Corsica, but the joke had serious overtones. The Corsican state was almost unknown, and although the British had traded with the island for many years, apparently no British gentleman had ever penetrated the interior. Such a trip would be a unique embellishment of his grand tour. But his project of visiting Corsica also arose from his serious interest in the political and social patterns of the new state. His journal (see, for example, the entry of 1 August) attests repeatedly to the uneasy attraction that Rousseau's theories of primitive man and the state of nature, in Boswell's simplified version, exerted upon him; Corsica might serve as a proving ground for these theories. In the excitement of the Italian tour his project disappears from view for some time after his visit to Rousseau, but his notation for 5 August 1765, "You must see Corsica," indicates that his determination to make the journey crystallized about then. He solved the problem of his father's assured displeasure at a further extension of his travels by simply failing to inform him of it.

Boswell's tour of Corsica is clearly outlined in the published *Journal* and needs only brief comment. By expanding and amalgamating his original condensed but extensive notes (only five pages of which appear to have survived), he made the week he spent with Paoli the focus of his six weeks' jaunt; other people and events are largely discussed in relation to Paoli and the political situation. The generous attentions paid him in Sollacarò demonstrated not only Paoli's genuine regard, but also a partly successful attempt to give substance to the rumour that he was an agent of the British government, an impression which Boswell confirmed in Genoa by smiling denials. As a tourist's record, the *Journal* is striking today because of its concentration on people rather than on the beauties and discomforts of the Corsican landscape. One would hardly be aware in reading this account that Corsica is impressively mountainous and that large sections of it are covered by the *maquis*, a dense undergrowth.

This shift in emphasis reflects in part the usual eighteenth-century indifference to romantic scenery, a point of view which Boswell fully shared. Human and not physical nature was his object; his assumption that the extensive observation of the traveller should primarily survey mankind and not his surroundings lay so deep that he would hardly have been able to conceive that it could be challenged. But in part the subject matter of the *Journal* was dictated by Boswell's purpose at the time of its publication in 1768.

A full history of the writing of *Corsica*, or to give its complete title, *An Account of Corsica; The Journal of a Tour to That Island, and Memoirs of Pascal Paoli*, would extend beyond the scope of this volume, but a few remarks on its nature and inception may help to put it in perspective. The first part, the *Account*, is a largely unoriginal survey of the history, geography, climate, and natural resources of Corsica, informative for contemporary readers but uninteresting in comparison to the second part, reprinted here. Johnson put the difference exactly: "Your *History* [*Account*] is like other histories, but your *Journal* is in a very high degree curious and delightful. There is between the *History* and the *Journal* that difference which will always be found between notions borrowed from without and notions generated within. Your *History* was copied from books; your *Journal* rose out of your own experience and observation. You express images which operated strongly upon yourself, and you have impressed them with great force upon your readers. I know not whether I could name any narrative by which curiosity is better excited, or better gratified."[5]

Boswell's notions were indeed generated within, but they were subjected to that process of moulding and revision, already evident in his private journal, which was to make his first important published work a finished piece of propaganda. Immediately upon leaving Corsica, he had started a newspaper campaign in which he hoped to arouse sympathy for the Corsicans, and to influence the British government to repeal its proclamation of 1763 in which the Corsicans were called rebels whom British subjects were forbidden to aid.[6] This declaration virtually prohibited trade between England and the

[5] *Life of Johnson*, 9 September 1769.

[6] See pp. 176 and 244.

Corsicans. In 1767, when *Corsica* was being written as the climax to this campaign, the situation had grown worse: the French had begun to make demands on Paoli and Genoa which hinted at their intention of taking over the island, and it seemed probable that Corsica would need official assistance if it was to survive as a nation. Boswell wanted to portray the Corsicans and their chief as democratic patriots struggling against Genoese oppression backed by the threat of French intervention; as a gallant, honest, simple people unjustly deprived of their independence. The model for his sketch was Sparta, Sparta under the actual rule of Lycurgus. The Genoese are treated with contempt, but the French with some delicacy since there was still a chance that they would come to terms with Paoli; Boswell also felt personally grateful for the care their commander, the Comte de Marbeuf, had taken of him during an illness. But the Corsicans were his subject; here was a people who hardly knew where England was, yet instinctively responded to Scottish airs and "Hearts of Oak" with cries of "Bravo Inglese!" He softened or suppressed details which would have blurred this image, and emphasized the quasi-idyllic primitivism of an unspoiled race.

Boswell's projection of himself against this background inspired the dislike of some of his contemporaries who saw in him a mixture of vanity, simple-mindedness, and self-importance, but they missed the point. Vanity there is, and a natural, rather innocent desire to exploit his considerable achievement in penetrating to the heart of Corsica and the Court of Paoli. But Thomas Gray's famous disparagement of *Corsica* as "a dialogue between a green-goose and a hero"[7] actually compliments Boswell's dexterity. He knew what he was about; he portrays himself as the young, ingenuous British traveller in the camp of a distinguished leader, and his awed respect mixed with a modest naïveté not only threw the stern and active virtues of

[7] In a letter to Horace Walpole, 25 February 1768, Gray also says: "Mr. Boswell's book . . . has pleased and moved me strangely, all (I mean) that relates to Paoli. He is a man born two thousand years after his time! The pamphlet proves what I have always maintained, that any fool may write a most valuable book by chance, if he will only tell us what he heard and saw with veracity. Of Mr. Boswell's truth I have not the least suspicion, because I am sure he could invent nothing of this kind" (*Horace Walpole's Correspondence*, ed. W. S. Lewis and others, 1937–     , xiv. 174).

Paoli into relief, but it established a character which permitted Boswell to wonder simply and passionately at the policy of his own government. With the strong incentives of idealism and commercial and military advantage, how can the British not come to the rescue of so promising a young state? More timid and, in retrospect, perhaps less practical heads prevailed, however; as Lord Holland said, "We cannot be so foolish as to go to war because Mr. Boswell has been in Corsica."[8] The French overwhelmed an isolated Paoli, and in June 1769 he boarded an English ship to begin his long exile.

---

## THE JOURNAL OF A TOUR TO CORSICA

Having resolved to pass some years abroad for my instruction and entertainment, I conceived a design of visiting the island of Corsica. I wished for something more than just the common course of what is called the tour of Europe; and Corsica occurred to me as a place which nobody else had seen, and where I should find what was to be seen nowhere else, a people actually fighting for liberty and forming themselves from a poor, inconsiderable, oppressed nation into a flourishing and independent state.

When I got into Switzerland, I went to see M. Rousseau. He was then living in romantic retirement, from whence, perhaps, it had been better for him never to have descended. While he was at a distance, his singular eloquence filled our minds with high ideas of the wild philosopher. When he came into the walks of men, we know alas! how much these ideas suffered.[9]

He entertained me very courteously, for I was recommended to him by my honoured friend the Earl Marischal, with whom I had the happiness of travelling through a part of Germany. I had heard that M. Rousseau had some correspondence with the Corsicans, and had been desired to assist them in forming their laws. I told him my scheme of going to visit them after I had completed my tour of Italy,

[8] Quoted in J. H. Jesse, *George Selwyn and His Contemporaries*, 1882, ii. 333.

[9] For Boswell's attitude towards Rousseau at the time *Corsica* was being written, see p. 297.

and I insisted that he should give me a letter of introduction. He immediately agreed to do so whenever I should acquaint him of my time of going thither, for he saw that my enthusiasm for the brave islanders was as warm as his own.

I accordingly wrote to him from Rome, in April 1765, that I had fixed the month of September for my Corsican expedition,[1] and therefore begged of him to send me the letter of introduction, which if he refused I should certainly go without it and probably be hanged as a spy. So let him answer for the consequences.

The wild philosopher was a man of his word, and on my arrival at Florence in August I received the following letter. . . .[2]

Furnished with these credentials, I was impatient to be with the illustrious chief. The charms of sweet Siena detained me longer than they should have done. I required the hardy air of Corsica to brace me after the delights of Tuscany.

I recollect with astonishment how little the real state of Corsica was known, even by those who had good access to know it. An officer of rank in the British navy,[3] who had been in several ports of the island, told me that I run the risk of my life in going among these barbarians; for that his surgeon's mate went ashore to take the diversion of shooting and every moment was alarmed by some of the natives who started from the bushes with loaded guns and, if he had not been protected by Corsican guides, would have certainly blown out his brains.

Nay at Leghorn, which is within a day's sailing of Corsica and has a constant intercourse with it, I found people who dissuaded me from going thither because it might be dangerous.

I was, however, under no apprehension in going to Corsica. Count Rivarola, the Sardinian Consul, who is himself a Corsican, assuring me that the island was then in a very civilized state; and besides that in the rudest times no Corsican would ever attack a stranger. The Count was so good as to give me most obliging letters to many people

[1] Boswell makes two errors here. His letter to Rousseau (printed on p. 80) was written in May 1765, and in it he says nothing about fixing September as the month for his expedition.

[2] Printed on p. 115.

[3] Keith Stewart, sixth son of the sixth Earl of Galloway, and Captain in the British navy. He had given Boswell this advice in Florence.

in the island.[4] I had now been in several foreign countries. I had found that I was able to accommodate myself to my fellow creatures of different languages and sentiments. I did not fear that it would be a difficult task for me to make myself easy with the plain and generous Corsicans.

The only danger I saw was that I might be taken by some of the Barbary corsairs, and have a trial of slavery among the Turks at Algiers. I spoke of it to Commodore Harrison, who commanded the British squadron in the Mediterranean and was then lying with his ship, the *Centurion*, in the bay of Leghorn. He assured me that if the Turks did take me they should not keep me long, but in order to prevent it he was so good as to grant me a very ample and particular passport; and as it could be of no use if I did not meet the corsairs, he said very pleasantly when he gave it me, "I hope, Sir, it shall be of no use to you."

Before I left Leghorn, I could observe that my tour was looked upon by the Italian politicians in a very serious light, as if truly I had a commission from my Court to negotiate a treaty with the Corsicans. The more I disclaimed any such thing the more they persevered in affirming it, and I was considered as a very close young man. I therefore just allowed them to make a minister of me till time should undeceive them.[5]

I sailed from Leghorn in a Tuscan vessel which was going over to Capo Corso for wine. I preferred this to a vessel going to Bastia, because as I did not know how the French General was affected towards the Corsicans I was afraid that he might not permit me to go forward to Paoli. I therefore resolved to land on the territories of the nation, and after I had been with the illustrious chief to pay my respects to the French if I should find it safe.

Though from Leghorn to Corsica is usually but one day's sailing, there was so dead a calm that it took us two days. The first day was the most tedious. However, there were two or three Corsicans aboard, and

[4] Professor Warnock has discovered from the correspondence of Rivarola, now in the State Archives in Turin, that he faithfully reported every move of Boswell to his masters.

[5] Boswell probably cultivated this impression himself, and he certainly took advantage of it. See p. 245.

one of them played on the *cetra*,[6] which amused me a good deal. At sunset all the people in the ship sung the Ave Maria with great devotion and some melody. It was pleasing to enter into the spirit of their religion, and hear them offering up their evening orisons.[7]

The second day we became better acquainted, and more lively and cheerful. The worthy Corsicans thought it was proper to give a moral lesson to a young traveller just come from Italy. They told me that in their country I should be treated with the greatest hospitality, but if I attempted to debauch any of their women I might expect instant death.

I employed myself several hours in rowing, which gave me great spirits. I relished fully my approach to the island, which had acquired an unusual grandeur in my imagination. As long as I can remember anything I have heard of "the malcontents of Corsica, with Paoli at their head." It was a curious thought that I was just going to see them.

About seven o'clock at night we landed safely in the harbour of Centuri. I learnt that Signor Giacomini of this place, to whom I was recommended by Count Rivarola, was just dead. He had made a handsome fortune in the East Indies; and having had a remarkable warmth in the cause of liberty during his whole life he showed it in the strongest manner in his last will. He bequeathed a considerable sum of money and some pieces of ordnance to the nation. He also left it in charge to his heir to live in Corsica, and be firm in the patriotic interest; and if ever the island should again be reduced under the power of the Genoese, he ordered him to retire with all his effects to Leghorn. Upon these conditions only could his heir enjoy his estate.

I was directed to the house of Signor Giacomini's cousin, Signor Antonio Antonetti at Morsiglia, about a mile up the country. The prospect of the mountains covered with vines and olives was extremely agreeable, and the odour of the myrtle and other aromatic

[6] An instrument comparable to the zither.

[7] This paragraph when compared to the journal entry for 11 October provides a minor but interesting illustration of Boswell's tendency in this book to generalize and tone down his first impressions when he came to publish them. Professor Warnock also suggests that what Boswell actually heard was the Corsican battle hymn of the Virgin Mary, the nation having been placed under her protection.

shrubs and flowers that grew all around me was very refreshing. As I walked along, I often saw Corsican peasants come suddenly out from the covert; and as they were all armed, I saw how the frightened imagination of the surgeon's mate had raised up so many assassins. Even the man who carried my baggage was armed and, had I been timorous, might have alarmed me. But he and I were very good company to each other. As it grew dusky, I repeated to myself these lines from a fine passage in Ariosto:

> E pur per selve oscure e calli obliqui
> Insieme van senza sospetto aversi.[8]

I delivered Signor Antonetti the letter for his deceased cousin. He read it, and received me with unaffected cordiality, making an apology for my frugal entertainment but assuring me of a hearty welcome. His true kindly hospitality was also shown in taking care of my servant, an honest Swiss who loved to eat and drink well.

I had formed a strange notion that I should see everything in Corsica totally different from what I had seen in any other country. I was therefore much surprised to find Signor Antonetti's house quite an Italian one, with very good furniture, prints, and copies of some of the famous pictures. In particular, I was struck to find here a small copy from Raphael of St. Michael and the Dragon. There was no necessity for its being well done. To see the thing at all was what surprised me.

Signor Antonetti gave me an excellent light repast and a very good bed. He spoke with great strength of the patriotic cause, and with great veneration of the General. I was quite easy, and liked much the opening of my Corsican tour.

The next day, being Sunday, it rained very hard; and I must ob-

[8] *Orlando Furioso*, i. 22:

> Together through dark woods and winding ways
> They walk, nor on their hearts suspicion preys.
> Boswell.

Boswell's general practice in *Corsica* was to print both originals and translations of foreign passages in the text itself; in this edition one or the other has been eliminated or removed to a footnote. Where Boswell's own footnotes involve more than the identification of sources, they are marked with his name.

serve that the Corsicans with all their resolution are afraid of bad weather to a degree of effeminacy. I got indeed a droll but a just enough account of this from one of them: "Sir," said he, "if you were as poor as a Corsican and had but one coat, so as that after being wet you could not put on dry clothes, you would be afraid too." Signor Antonetti would not allow me to set out while it rained, for, said he, "If a man finds himself abroad, there is no help for it. But to go deliberately out is too much."

When the day grew a little better, I accompanied Signor Antonetti and his family to hear mass in the parish church, a very pretty little building about half a quarter of a mile off.

Signor Antonetti's parish priest was to preach to us, at which I was much pleased, being very curious to hear a Corsican sermon. Our priest did very well. His text was in the Psalms: "Descendunt ad infernum viventes."[9] After endeavouring to move our passions with a description of the horrors of hell, he told us, "Saint Catherine of Siena wished to be laid on the mouth of this dreadful pit that she might stop it up, so as no more unhappy souls should fall into it. I confess, my brethren, I have not the zeal of holy Saint Catherine. But I do what I can; I warn you how to avoid it." He then gave us some good practical advice, and concluded.

The weather being now cleared up, I took leave of the worthy gentleman to whom I had been a guest. He gave me a letter to Signor Damiano Tomasi, Padre del Commune at Pino, the next village. I got a man with an ass to carry my baggage. But such a road I never saw. It was absolutely scrambling along the face of a rock overhanging the sea, upon a path sometimes not above a foot broad. I thought the ass rather retarded me, so I prevailed with the man to take my portmanteau and other things on his back.

Had I formed my opinion of Corsica from what I saw this morning, I might have been in as bad humour with it as Seneca was, whose reflections in prose are not inferior to his epigrams: "What can be found so bare, what so rugged all around as this rock? what more barren of provisions? what more rude as to its inhabitants? what in the very situation of the place more horrible? what in climate more intemperate? Yet there are more foreigners than natives here. So far

[9] "They go down alive into the pit." See Psalms 55. 15.

then is a change of place from being disagreeable, that even this place hath brought some people away from their country."[1]

At Pino I was surprised to find myself met by some brisk young fellows dressed like English sailors and speaking English tolerably well. They had been often with cargoes of wine at Leghorn, where they had picked up what they knew of our language, and taken clothes in part of payment for some of their merchandise.

I was cordially entertained at Signor Tomasi's. Throughout all Corsica, except in garrison towns, there is hardly an inn. I met with a single one about eight miles from Corte. Before I was accustomed to the Corsican hospitality, I sometimes forgot myself, and imagining I was in a public house called for what I wanted with the tone which one uses in calling to the waiters at a tavern. I did so at Pino, asking for a variety of things at once; when Signora Tomasi perceiving my mistake looked in my face and smiled, saying with much calmness and good nature, "One thing after another, Sir."

In writing this Journal, I shall not tire my readers with relating the occurrences of each particular day. It will be much more agreeable to them to have a free and continued account of what I saw or heard most worthy of observation.[2]

For some time I had very curious travelling, mostly on foot, and attended by a couple of stout women who carried my baggage upon their heads. Every time that I prepared to set out from a village, I could not help laughing to see the good people eager to have my equipage in order and roaring out, "The women, the women."

I had full leisure and the best opportunities to observe everything in my progress through the island. I was lodged sometimes in private houses, sometimes in convents, being always well recommended from place to place. The first convent in which I lay was at Canari. It appeared a little odd at first. But I soon learnt to repair to my dormitory as naturally as if I had been a friar for seven years.

The convents were small, decent buildings, suited to the sober ideas of their pious inhabitants. The religious who devoutly endeavour to "walk with God" are often treated with raillery by those whom pleasure or business prevents from thinking of future and

[1] Seneca, *Ad Helviam de Consolatione*, vi. 5–6.

[2] Also by this method Boswell is able to give readers the impression that he had spent a long time with Paoli. Actually he spent only about a week with him.

more exalted objects. A little experience of the serenity and peace of mind to be found in convents would be of use to temper the fire of men of the world.

At Patrimonio I found the seat of a provincial magistracy. The chief judge was there, and entertained me very well. Upon my arrival, the captain of the guard came out and demanded who I was. I replied "English." He looked at me seriously, and then said in a tone between regret and upbraiding, "The English — they were once our friends, but they are so no more." I felt for my country, and was abashed before this honest soldier.

At Oletta I visited Count Nicholas Rivarola, brother to my friend at Leghorn. He received me with great kindness, and did everything in his power to make me easy. I found here a Corsican who thought better of the British than the captain of the guard at Patrimonio. He talked of our bombarding San Fiorenzo in favour of the patriots,[3] and willingly gave me his horse for the afternoon, which he said he would not have done to a man of any other nation.

When I came to Murato,[4] I had the pleasure of being made acquainted with Signor Barbaggi, who is married to the niece of Paoli. I found him to be a sensible, intelligent, well-bred man. The mint of Corsica was in his house. I got specimens of their different kinds of money in silver and copper, and was told that they hoped in a year or two to strike some gold coins.[5] Signor Barbaggi's house was repairing, so I was lodged in the convent. But in the morning returned to breakfast and had chocolate, and at dinner we had no less than twelve well-dressed dishes, served on Dresden china, with a dessert, different sorts of wine, and a liqueur, all the produce of Corsica. Signor Barbaggi was frequently repeating to me that the Corsicans inhabited a rude,

[3] Acting as allies of the King of Sardinia, the English bombarded Bastia and San Fiorenzo in 1745, thus enabling the Corsicans to seize these towns from the Genoese. Count Domenico Rivarola, at that time a Colonel in the Sardinian service, accompanied the English on this expedition, and was shortly thereafter proclaimed Generalissimo of Corsica by the rebels. It is hardly surprising that his son should have been partial to the English.

[4] Seven miles south of Oletta. Boswell apparently arrived at Murato on 15 October.

[5] Boswell wrote while at Gotha: "I am somewhat of a virtuoso. Wherever I am, I make a collection of the silver specie struck the year in which I have been in the country" (*Boswell on the Grand Tour: Germany and Switzerland*, 20 October 1764).

uncultivated country and that they lived like Spartans. I begged leave to ask him in what country he could show me greater luxury than I had seen in his house; and I said I should certainly tell wherever I went what tables the Corsicans kept, notwithstanding their pretensions to poverty and temperance. A good deal of pleasantry passed upon this. His lady was a genteel woman, and appeared to be agreeable though very reserved.

From Murato to Corte, I travelled through a wild, mountainous, rocky country, diversified with some large valleys. I got little beasts for me and my servant, sometimes horses but oftener mules or asses. We had no bridles but cords fixed round their necks, with which we managed them as well as we could.

At Corte I waited upon the Supreme Council, to one of whom, Signor Boccheciampe, I had a letter from Signor Barbaggi. I was very politely received, and was conducted to the Franciscan convent where I got the apartment of Paoli, who was then some days' journey beyond the mountains, holding a court of sindacato[6] at a village called Sollacarò.

As the General resided for some time in this convent, the fathers made a better appearance than any I saw in the island. I was principally attended by the Prior, a resolute divine who had formerly been in the army, and by Padre Giulio, a man of much address who still favours me with his correspondence.

These fathers have a good vineyard and an excellent garden. They have between thirty and forty beehives in long wooden cases or trunks of trees, with a covering of the bark of the cork tree. When they want honey they burn a little juniper-wood, the smoke of which makes the bees retire. They then take an iron instrument with a sharp-edged crook at one end of it and bring out the greatest part of the honeycomb, leaving only a little for the bees, who work the case full again. By taking the honey in this way they never kill a bee. They seemed much at their ease, living in peace and plenty. I often joked with them on the text which is applied to their order: "Nihil habentes et omnia possidentes."[7]

I went to the choir with them. The service was conducted with

[6] The sindacatori were circuit judges.

[7] "Having nothing, and yet possessing all things" (II Corinthians 6. 10).

propriety, and Padre Giulio played on the organ. On the great altar of their church is a tabernacle carved in wood by a religious. It is a piece of exquisite workmanship. A Genoese gentleman offered to give them one in silver for it, but they would not make the exchange.

These fathers have no library worth mentioning, but their convent is large and well built. I looked about with great attention to see if I could find any inscriptions, but the only one I found was upon a certain useful edifice:

> Sine necessitate huc non intrate,
> Quia necessaria sumus.[8]

A studied, rhyming Latin conceit marked upon such a place was truly ludicrous.

I chose to stop a while at Corte to repose myself after my fatigues, and to see everything about the capital of Corsica. The morning after my arrival here, three French deserters desired to speak with me. The foolish fellows had taken it into their heads that I was come to raise recruits for Scotland, and so they begged to have the honour of going along with me; I suppose with intention to have the honour of running off from me as they had done from their own regiments.

I received many civilities at Corte from Signor Boccheciampe and from Signor Massesi, the Great Chancellor, whose son Signor Luigi, a young gentleman of much vivacity and natural politeness, was so good as to attend me constantly as my conductor. I used to call him my governor. I liked him much, for as he had never been out of the island his ideas were entirely Corsican.

Such of the members of the Supreme Council as were in residence during my stay at Corte I found to be solid and sagacious, men of penetration and ability well calculated to assist the General in forming his political plans and in turning to the best advantage the violence and enterprise of the people.

The University was not then sitting, so I could only see the rooms, which were shown me by the Abbé Valentini, Procurator of the University.[9] The professors were all absent except one Capuchin father

[8] "Do not enter here except in case of necessity, for we are the necessary [house]."

[9] In 1766 the University consisted of about twelve professors and one hundred fifty students.

whom I visited at his convent. It is a tolerable building with a pretty large collection of books. There is in the church here a tabernacle carved in wood, in the manner of that at the Franciscans', but much inferior to it.

I went up to the Castle of Corte. The Commandant very civilly showed me every part of it. As I wished to see all things in Corsica, I desired to see even the unhappy criminals. There were then three in the Castle: a man for the murder of his wife, a married lady who had hired one of her servants to strangle a woman of whom she was jealous, and the servant who had actually perpetrated this barbarous action. They were brought out from their cells that I might talk with them. The murderer of his wife had a stupid, hardened appearance, and told me he did it at the instigation of the devil. The servant was a poor despicable wretch. He had at first accused his mistress but was afterwards prevailed with to deny his accusation, upon which he was put to the torture by having lighted matches held between his fingers. This made him return to what he had formerly said, so as to be a strong evidence against his mistress. His hands were so miserably scorched that he was a piteous object. I asked him why he had committed such a crime; he said, "Because I was without understanding." The lady seemed of a bold and resolute spirit. She spoke to me with great firmness and denied her guilt, saying with a contemptuous smile as she pointed to her servant, "They can force that creature to say what they please."

The hangman of Corsica was a great curiosity. Being held in the utmost detestation, he durst not live like another inhabitant of the island. He was obliged to take refuge in the Castle, and there he was kept in a little corner turret, where he had just room for a miserable bed and a little bit of fire to dress such victuals for himself as were sufficient to keep him alive; for nobody would have any intercourse with him, but all turned their backs upon him. I went up and looked at him. And a more dirty, rueful spectacle I never beheld. He seemed sensible of his situation and held down his head like an abhorred outcast.

It was a long time before they could get a hangman in Corsica, so that the punishment of the gallows was hardly known, all their criminals being shot. At last this creature whom I saw, who is a Sicilian, came with a message to Paoli. The General, who has a wonderful talent for physiognomy, on seeing the man said immediately to some of the people about him, "Behold our hangman." He gave orders to ask the man if he would accept of the office, and his answer was, "My grandfather was a hangman, my father was a hangman. I have been a hangman myself and am willing to continue so." He was therefore immediately put into office, and the ignominious death dispensed by his hands hath had more effect than twenty executions by firearms.

It is remarkable that no Corsican would upon any account consent to be a hangman. Not the greatest criminals, who might have had their lives upon that condition. Even the wretch who for a paltry hire had strangled a woman would rather submit to death than do the same action as the executioner of the law.

When I had seen everything about Corte, I prepared for my journey over the mountains, that I might be with Paoli. The night before I set out I recollected that I had forgotten to get a passport, which in the present situation of Corsica is still a necessary precaution. After supper, therefore, the Prior walked with me to Corte to the house of the Great Chancellor, who ordered the passport to be made out immediately, and, while his secretary was writing it, entertained me by reading to me some of the minutes of the General Consulta. When the passport was finished and ready to have the seal put to it, I was much pleased with a beautiful, simple incident. The Chancellor desired a little boy who was playing in the room by us to run to his mother and bring the great seal of the kingdom. I thought myself sitting in the house of a Cincinnatus.

Next morning[1] I set out in very good order, having excellent mules and active, clever Corsican guides. My worthy fathers of the convent, who treated me in the kindest manner while I was their guest, would also give me some provisions for my journey, so they put up a gourd of their best wine and some delicious pomegranates. My Corsican guides appeared so hearty that I often got down and walked along with them, doing just what I saw them do. When we grew hungry, we threw stones among the thick branches of the chestnut trees which overshadowed us, and in that manner we brought

[1] Saturday, 19 October, since the passport, reproduced facing p. 160, is dated 18 October. Boswell had probably arrived in Corte on the evening of 17 October.

down a shower of chestnuts with which we filled our pockets, and went on eating them with great relish; and when this made us thirsty, we lay down by the side of the first brook, put our mouths to the stream and drank sufficiently. It was just being for a little while one of the "prisca gens mortalium,"[2] who ran about in the woods eating acorns and drinking water.

While I stopped to refresh my mules at a little village, the inhabitants came crowding about me as an ambassador going to their General. When they were informed of my country, a strong, black fellow among them said, "English! they are barbarians; they don't believe in the great God." I told him, "Excuse me, Sir. We do believe in God, and in Jesus Christ too." "Um," said he, "and in the Pope?" "No." "And why?" This was a puzzling question in these circumstances, for there was a great audience to the controversy. I thought I would try a method of my own, and very gravely replied, "Because we are too far off." A very new argument against the universal infallibility of the Pope. It took, however, for my opponent mused a while, and then said, "Too far off! Why, Sicily is as far off as England. Yet in Sicily they believe in the Pope." "Oh," said I, "we are ten times farther off than Sicily." "Aha!" said he, and seemed quite satisfied. In this manner I got off very well. I question whether any of the learned reasonings of our Protestant divines would have had so good an effect.

My journey over the mountains was very entertaining. I passed some immense ridges and vast woods. I was in great health and spirits, and fully able to enter into the ideas of the brave, rude men whom I found in all quarters.

At Bastelica, where there is a stately spirited race of people, I had a large company to attend me in the convent. I liked to see their natural frankness and ease, for why should men be afraid of their own species? They just came in, making an easy bow, placed themselves round the room where I was sitting, rested themselves on their muskets, and immediately entered into conversation with me. They talked very feelingly of the miseries that their country had endured, and complained that they were still but in a state of poverty. I happened at that time to have an unusual flow of spirits, and as one who

[2] "The primitive race of men" (Horace, *Epodes*, ii. 2).

GENERALE, E SUPREMO CONSIGLIO DI STATO

DEL REGNO DI CORSICA.

Desiderando il Sig. Giacomo Boswel di Nazione Inglese di passare nel Dila da monti per suo divertimento, Ordiniamo perciò a tutti quelli che dipendono dai nostri ordini di dover trattare detto Sig.re colla più possibile attenzione, e riguardi, e di prestarle tutta l'assistenza, e di farlo provvedere d'alloggiamento ove egli perverrà, siccome di cavalcature, e guide che richiederà per proseguire il suo viaggio, che tale è la nostra intenzione, e che tanto.

Dat. in Corti 18 Ottobre 1765.

[illegible]

Boswell's Corsican passport, issued 18 October 1765, from the original in the Yale University Library.

finds himself amongst utter strangers in a distant country has no timidity, I harangued the men of Bastelica with great fluency. I expatiated on the bravery of the Corsicans by which they had purchased liberty, the most valuable of all possessions, and rendered themselves glorious over all Europe. Their poverty, I told them, might be remedied by a proper cultivation of their island and by engaging a little in commerce. But I bid them remember that they were much happier in their present state than in a state of refinement and vice, and that therefore they should beware of luxury.

What I said had the good fortune to touch them, and several of them repeated the same sentiments much better than I could do. They all expressed their strong attachment to Paoli, and called out in one voice that they were all at his command. I could with pleasure have passed a long time here.

At Ornano I saw the ruins of the seat where the great Sampiero[3] had his residence. They were a pretty droll society of monks in the convent at Ornano. When I told them that I was an Englishman, "Ay, ay," said one of them, "as was well observed by a reverend bishop, when talking of your pretended reformation, 'Angli olim angeli nunc diaboli.' "[4] I looked upon this as an honest effusion of spiritual zeal. The fathers took good care of me in temporals.

When I at last came within sight of Sollacarò, where Paoli was, I could not help being under considerable anxiety. My ideas of him had been greatly heightened by the conversations I had held with all sorts of people in the island, they having represented him to me as something above humanity. I had the strongest desire to see so exalted a character, but I feared that I should be unable to give a proper account why I had presumed to trouble him with a visit, and that I should sink to nothing before him. I almost wished yet to go back without seeing him. These workings of sensibility employed my mind till I rode through the village and came up to the house where he was lodged.

Leaving my servant with my guides, I passed through the guards and was met by some of the General's people, who conducted me into

[3] Sampiero di Ornano, a sixteenth-century Corsican hero who fought against the Genoese.

[4] "The English, formerly angels now devils."

an antechamber where were several gentlemen in waiting. Signor Boccheciampe had notified my arrival, and I was shown into Paoli's room. I found him alone, and was struck with his appearance. He is tall, strong, and well made; of a fair complexion, a sensible, free, and open countenance, and a manly and noble carriage. He was then in his fortieth year. He was dressed in green and gold. He used to wear the common Corsican habit, but on the arrival of the French he thought a little external elegance might be of use to make the government appear in a more respectable light.

He asked me what were my commands for him. I presented him a letter from Count Rivarola, and when he had read it I showed him my letter from Rousseau. He was polite but very reserved. I had stood in the presence of many a prince, but I never had such a trial as in the presence of Paoli. I have already said that he is a great physiognomist. In consequence of his being in continual danger from treachery and assassination, he has formed a habit of studiously observing every new face. For ten minutes we walked backwards and forwards through the room hardly saying a word, while he looked at me with a steadfast, keen, and penetrating eye, as if he searched my very soul.[5]

This interview was for a while very severe upon me. I was much relieved when his reserve wore off and he began to speak more. I then ventured to address him with this compliment to the Corsicans: "Sir, I am upon my travels, and have lately visited Rome. I am come from seeing the ruins of one brave and free people; I now see the rise of another."

He received my compliment very graciously, but observed that the Corsicans had no chance of being like the Romans, a great conquering nation who should extend its empire over half the globe. Their situation, and the modern political systems, rendered this impossible. "But," said he, "Corsica may be a very happy country."

[5] Fanny Burney, several years later, recorded Paoli's version of this first meeting: "He came to my country, and he fetched me some letters of recommending him, but I was of the belief he might be an impostor, and I supposed in my minte he was an espy; for I look away from him, and in a moment I look to him again and I behold his tablets. Oh! he was to the work of writing down all I say! Indeed I was angry. But soon I discover he was no impostor and no espy, and I only find I was myself the monster he had come to discern" (*Diary and Letters of Mme. D'Arblay*, ed. Austin Dobson, 1904–1905, ii. 100).

He expressed a high admiration of M. Rousseau, whom Signor Buttafoco had invited to Corsica to aid the nation in forming its laws. It seems M. de Voltaire had reported, in his rallying manner, that the invitation was merely a trick which he had put upon Rousseau. Paoli told me that when he understood this, he himself wrote to Rousseau enforcing the invitation. Of this affair I shall give a full account in an after part of my Journal.

Some of the nobles who attended him came into the room, and in a little we were told that dinner was served up. The General did me the honour to place me next him. He had a table of fifteen or sixteen covers, having always a good many of the principal men of the island with him. He had an Italian cook who had been long in France, but he chose to have a few plain substantial dishes, avoiding every kind of luxury and drinking no foreign wine.

I felt myself under some constraint in such a circle of heroes. The General talked a great deal on history and on literature. I soon perceived that he was a fine classical scholar, that his mind was enriched with a variety of knowledge, and that his conversation at meals was instructive and entertaining. Before dinner he had spoken French. He now spoke Italian, in which he is very eloquent.

We retired to another room to drink coffee. My timidity wore off. I no longer anxiously thought of myself; my whole attention was employed in listening to the illustrious commander of a nation.

He recommended me to the care of the Abbé Rostini,[6] who had lived many years in France. Signor Colonna,[7] the lord of the manor here, being from home, his house was assigned for me to live in. I was left by myself till near supper time when I returned to the General, whose conversation improved upon me as did the society of those about him, with whom I gradually formed an acquaintance.

Every day I felt myself happier. Particular marks of attention were shown me as a subject of Great Britain, the report of which went over to Italy and confirmed the conjectures that I was really an envoy.

[6] The Abbé Carlo Rostini later furnished Boswell with some information for the historical part of the *Account of Corsica* from his considerable collection of historical materials.

[7] Pier Andrea Colonna d'Istria is described by Boswell in the *Account of Corsica* as "a worthy, sensible man, and very zealous in the great cause" (p. 99).

In the morning I had my chocolate served up upon a silver salver adorned with the arms of Corsica. I dined and supped constantly with the General. I was visited by all the nobility, and whenever I chose to make a little tour I was attended by a party of guards. I begged of the General not to treat me with so much ceremony, but he insisted upon it.

One day when I rode out, I was mounted on Paoli's own horse with rich furniture of crimson velvet, with broad gold lace, and had my guards marching along with me. I allowed myself to indulge a momentary pride in this parade, as I was curious to experience what could really be the pleasure of state and distinction with which mankind are so strangely intoxicated. When I returned to the Continent after all this greatness, I used to joke with my acquaintance and tell them that I could not bear to live with them, for they did not treat me with a proper respect.

My time passed here in the most agreeable manner. I enjoyed a sort of luxury of noble sentiment. Paoli became more affable with me. I made myself known to him. I forgot the great distance between us, and had every day some hours of private conversation with him.

From my first setting out on this tour, I wrote down every night what I had observed during the day, throwing together a great deal that I might afterwards make a selection at leisure.

Of these particulars, the most valuable to my readers, as well as to myself, must surely be the memoirs and remarkable sayings of Paoli, which I am proud to record.

Talking of the Corsican war, "Sir," said he, "if the event prove happy, we shall be called great defenders of liberty. If the event shall prove unhappy, we shall be called unfortunate rebels."

The French objected to him that the Corsican nation had no regular troops. "We would not have them," said Paoli. "We should then have the bravery of this and the other regiment. At present every single man is as a regiment himself. Should the Corsicans be formed into regular troops, we should lose that personal bravery which has produced such actions among us as in another country would have rendered famous even a marshal."

I asked him how he could possibly have a soul so superior to interest. "It is not superior," said he; "my interest is to gain a name.

I know well that he who does good to his country will gain that, and I expect it. Yet could I render this people happy, I would be content to be forgotten. I have an unspeakable pride. The approbation of my own heart is enough."

He said he would have great pleasure in seeing the world and enjoying the society of the learned and the accomplished in every country. I asked him how with these dispositions he could bear to be confined to an island yet in a rude uncivilized state, and instead of participating Attic evenings, "noctes coenaeque Deum,"[8] be in a continual course of care and of danger. He replied in one line of Virgil: "Vincet amor patriae laudumque immensa cupido."[9] This, uttered with the fine open Italian pronunciation, and the graceful dignity of his manner, was very noble. I wished to have a statue of him taken at that moment.

I asked him if he understood English. He immediately began and spoke it, which he did tolerably well. When at Naples, he had known several Irish gentlemen who were officers in that service. Having a great facility in acquiring languages, he learnt English from them. But as he had been now ten years without ever speaking it, he spoke very slow. One could see that he was possessed of the words, but for want of what I may call mechanical practice he had a difficulty in expressing himself.

I was diverted with his English library. It consisted of some broken volumes of the *Spectator* and *Tatler*, Pope's *Essay on Man*, *Gulliver's Travels*, a *History of France* in old English, and Barclay's *Apology for the Quakers*. I promised to send him some English books.[1]

[8] "The nights and banquets of the gods" (Horace, *Satires*, II. vi. 65).

[9] "The love of country will prevail, and the overwhelming desire for praise" (*Aeneid*, vi. 823).

[1] I have sent him the works of Harrington, of Sidney, of Addison, of Trenchard, of Gordon, and of other writers in favour of liberty. I have also sent him some of our best books of morality and entertainment, in particular the works of Mr. Samuel Johnson, with a complete set of the *Spectator*, *Tatler*, and *Guardian;* and to the University of Corte, I have sent a few of the Greek and Roman classics, of the beautiful editions of the Messrs. Foulis at Glasgow. — BOSWELL. Boswell must have altered his opinion of Algernon Sidney, since he had previously condemned his works (*Boswell on the Grand Tour: Germany and Switzerland*, 30 November 1764).

He convinced me how well he understood our language, for I took the liberty to show him a memorial which I had drawn up on the advantages to Great Britain from an alliance with Corsica, and he translated this memorial into Italian with the greatest facility.[2] He has since given me more proofs of his knowledge of our tongue by his answers to the letters which I have had the honour to write to him in English, and in particular by a very judicious and ingenious criticism on some of Swift's works.[3]

He was well acquainted with the history of Britain. He had read many of the Parliamentary debates, and had even seen a number of *The North Briton.* He showed a considerable knowledge of this country, and often introduced anecdotes and drew comparisons and allusions from Britain.

He said his great object was to form the Corsicans in such a manner that they might have a firm constitution, and might be able to subsist without him. "Our state," said he, "is young, and still requires the leading strings. I am desirous that the Corsicans should be taught to walk of themselves. Therefore when they come to me to ask whom they should choose for their Padre del Commune or other magistrate, I tell them, 'You know better than I do the able and honest men among your neighbours. Consider the consequence of your choice, not only to yourselves in particular but to the island in general.' In this manner I accustom them to feel their own importance as members of the state."

After representing the severe and melancholy state of oppression under which Corsica had so long groaned, he said, "We are now to our country like the prophet Elisha stretched over the dead child of the Shunammite, eye to eye, nose to nose, mouth to mouth. It begins to recover warmth and to revive. I hope it shall yet regain full health and vigour."

I said that things would make a rapid progress, and that we should soon see all the arts and sciences flourish in Corsica. "Patience, Sir," said he. "If you saw a man who had fought a hard battle, who was much wounded, who was beaten to the ground, and who with diffi-

[2] Neither memorial nor translation has been recovered.

[3] No letters from Paoli to Boswell during the period 1765–1768 have been recovered, but Boswell printed the text of one (p. 203).

culty could lift himself up, it would not be reasonable to ask him to get his hair well dressed and to put on embroidered clothes. Corsica has fought a hard battle, has been much wounded, has been beaten to the ground, and with difficulty can lift herself up. The arts and sciences are like dress and ornament. You cannot expect them from us for some time. But come back twenty or thirty years hence, and we'll show you arts and sciences, and concerts and assemblies, and fine ladies, and we'll make you fall in love among us, Sir."

He smiled a good deal when I told him that I was much surprised to find him so amiable, accomplished, and polite; for although I knew I was to see a great man, I expected to find a rude character, an Attila King of the Goths, or a Luitprand King of the Lombards.

I observed that although he had often a placid smile upon his countenance, he hardly ever laughed. Whether loud laughter in general society be a sign of weakness or rusticity I cannot say; but I have remarked that real great men, and men of finished behaviour, seldom fall into it.

The variety, and I may say versatility, of the mind of this great man is amazing. One day when I came to pay my respects to him before dinner, I found him in much agitation, with a circle of his nobles around him and a Corsican standing before him like a criminal before his judge. Paoli immediately turned to me, "I am glad you are come, Sir. You Protestants talk much against our doctrine of transubstantiation. Behold here the miracle of transubstantiation, a Corsican transubstantiated into a Genoese. That unworthy man who now stands before me is a Corsican, who has been long a lieutenant under the Genoese in Capo Corso. Andrew Doria and all their greatest heroes could not be more violent for the Republic than he has been, and all against his country." Then turning to the man, "Sir," said he, "Corsica makes it a rule to pardon the most unworthy of her children when they surrender themselves, even when they are forced to do so as is your case. You have now escaped. But take care. I shall have a strict eye upon you, and if ever you make the least attempt to return to your traitorous practices, you know I can be avenged of you." He spoke this with the fierceness of a lion, and from the awful darkness of his brow one could see that his thoughts of vengeance were terrible. Yet when it was over he all at once resumed his usual appearance, called out "Come along," went to dinner, and was as cheerful and gay as if nothing had happened.

His notions of morality are high and refined, such as become the father of a nation. Were he a libertine his influence would soon vanish, for men will never trust the important concerns of society to one they know will do what is hurtful to society for his own pleasures. He told me that his father had brought him up with great strictness, and that he had very seldom deviated from the paths of virtue. That this was not from a defect of feeling and passion, but that his mind being filled with important objects, his passions were employed in more noble pursuits than those of licentious pleasure. I saw from Paoli's example the great art of preserving young men of spirit from the contagion of vice, in which there is often a species of sentiment, ingenuity, and enterprise nearly allied to virtuous qualities. Show a young man that there is more real spirit in virtue than in vice, and you have a surer hold of him during his years of impetuosity and passion than by convincing his judgment of all the rectitude of ethics.

One day at dinner he gave us the principal arguments for the being and attributes of God. To hear these arguments repeated with graceful energy by the illustrious Paoli in the midst of his heroic nobles was admirable. I never felt my mind more elevated.

I took occasion to mention the King of Prussia's infidel writings, and in particular his *Epistle to Marshal Keith*. Paoli, who often talks with admiration of the greatness of that monarch, instead of uttering any direct censure of what he saw to be wrong in so distinguished a hero, paused a little, and then said with a grave and most expressive look, "It is fine consolation for an old general when dying, 'In a little while you shall be no more.' "[4]

He observed that the Epicurean philosophy had produced but one exalted character, whereas Stoicism had been the seminary of great men. What he now said put me in mind of these noble lines of Lucan:

> . . . Hi mores, haec duri inmota Catonis
> Secta fuit, servare modum finemque tenere,

[4] Frederick the Great's *Épître au Maréchal Keith* is subtitled in French, "an imitation of the third book of Lucretius." Paoli summarized it accurately.

Naturamque sequi patriaeque inpendere vitam,
Nec sibi sed toti genitum se credere mundo.[5]

When he was asked if he would quit the island of which he had undertaken the protection, supposing a foreign power should create him a marshal and make him governor of a province, he replied, "I hope they will believe I am more honest, or more ambitious; for," said he, "to accept of the highest offices under a foreign power would be to serve."

"To have been a colonel, a general, or a marshal," said he, "would have been sufficient for my table, for my taste in dress, for the beauty whom my rank would have entitled me to attend. But it would not have been sufficient for this spirit, for this imagination" — putting his hand upon his bosom.

He reasoned one day in the midst of his nobles whether the commander of a nation should be married or not. "If he is married," said he, "there is a risk that he may be distracted by private affairs and swayed too much by a concern for his family. If he is unmarried, there is a risk that not having the tender attachments of a wife and children, he may sacrifice all to his own ambition." When I said he ought to marry and have a son to succeed him; "Sir," said he, "what security can I have that my son will think and act as I do? What sort of a son had Cicero, and what had Marcus Aurelius?"

He said to me one day when we were alone, "I never will marry, I have not the conjugal virtues. Nothing would tempt me to marry but a woman who should bring me an immense dowry, with which I might assist my country."

But he spoke much in praise of marriage, as an institution which

[5] Lucan, *Pharsalia,* ii. 380–383:

These were the stricter manners of the man,
And this the stubborn course in which they ran;
The golden mean unchanging to pursue,
Constant to keep the purposed end in view;
Religiously to follow Nature's laws,
And die with pleasure in his country's cause.
To think he was not for himself designed,
But born to be of use to all mankind.
Nicholas Rowe.

the experience of ages had found to be the best calculated for the happiness of individuals and for the good of society. Had he been a private gentleman, he probably would have married, and I am sure would have made as good a husband and father as he does a supreme magistrate and a general. But his arduous and critical situation would not allow him to enjoy domestic felicity. He is wedded to his country, and the Corsicans are his children.

He often talked to me of marriage, told me licentious pleasures were delusive and transient, that I should never be truly happy till I was married, and that he hoped to have a letter from me soon after my return home, acquainting him that I had followed his advice and was convinced from experience that he was in the right. With such an engaging condescension did this great man behave to me. If I could but paint his manner, all my readers would be charmed with him.

He has a mind fitted for philosophical speculations as well as for affairs of state. One evening at supper he entertained us for some time with some curious reveries and conjectures as to the nature of the intelligence of beasts, with regard to which he observed human knowledge was as yet very imperfect. He in particular seemed fond of inquiring into the language of the brute creation. He observed that beasts fully communicate their ideas to each other, and that some of them, such as dogs, can form several articulate sounds. In different ages there have been people who pretended to understand the language of birds and beasts. "Perhaps," said Paoli, "in a thousand years we may know this as well as we know things which appeared much more difficult to be known." I have often since this conversation indulged myself in such reveries. If it were not liable to ridicule, I would say that an acquaintance with the language of beasts would be a most agreeable acquisition to man, as it would enlarge the circle of his social intercourse.

On my return to Britain, I was disappointed to find nothing upon this subject in Dr. Gregory's *Comparative View of the State and Faculties of Man with Those of the Animal World*, which was then just published. My disappointment, however, was in a good measure made up by a picture of society, drawn by that ingenious and worthy author, which may be well applied to the Corsicans: "There is a certain period in the progress of society in which mankind appear to the greatest advantage. In this period, they have the bodily powers and all the animal functions remaining in full vigour. They are bold, active, steady, ardent in the love of liberty and their native country. Their manners are simple, their social affections warm, and though they are greatly influenced by the ties of blood, yet they are generous and hospitable to strangers. Religion is universally regarded among them, disguised by a variety of superstitions."

Paoli was very desirous that I should study the character of the Corsicans. "Go among them," said he, "the more you talk with them, you will do me the greater pleasure. Forget the meanness of their apparel. Hear their sentiments. You will find honour and sense and abilities among these poor men."

His heart grew big when he spoke of his countrymen. His own great qualities appeared to unusual advantage while he described the virtues of those for whose happiness his whole life was employed. "If," said he, "I should lead into the field an army of Corsicans against an army double their number, let me speak a few words to the Corsicans to remind them of the honour of their country and of their brave forefathers — I do not say that they would conquer, but I am sure that not a man of them would give way. The Corsicans," said he, "have a steady resolution that would amaze you. I wish you could see one of them die. It is a proverb among the Genoese, 'The Corsicans deserve the gallows, and they fear not to meet it.' There is a real compliment to us in this saying."

He told me that in Corsica criminals are put to death four and twenty hours after sentence is pronounced against them. "This," said he, "may not be over-catholic, but it is humane."

He went on and gave me several instances of the Corsican spirit:

"A sergeant," said he, "who fell in one of our desperate actions, when just a-dying, wrote to me thus: 'I salute you. Take care of my aged father. In two hours I shall be with the rest who have bravely died for their country.'

"A Corsican gentleman who had been taken prisoner by the Genoese was thrown into a dark dungeon, where he was chained to the ground. While he was in this dismal situation, the Genoese sent a message to him that if he would accept of a commission in their service, he might have it. 'No,' said he. 'Were I to accept of your offer, it would be with a determined purpose to take the first opportunity of returning to the service of my country. But I will not accept of it. For I would not have my countrymen even suspect that I could be one moment unfaithful.' And he remained in his dungeon." Paoli went on: "I defy Rome, Sparta, or Thebes to show me thirty years of such patriotism as Corsica can boast. Though the affection between relations is exceedingly strong in the Corsicans, they will give up their nearest relations for the good of their country, and sacrifice such as have deserted to the Genoese."

He gave me a noble instance of a Corsican's feeling and greatness of mind. "A criminal," said he, "was condemned to die. His nephew came to me with a lady of distinction, that she might solicit his pardon. The nephew's anxiety made him think that the lady did not speak with sufficient force and earnestness. He therefore advanced, and addressed himself to me: 'Sir, is it proper for me to speak?' as if he felt that it was unlawful to make such an application. I bid him go on. 'Sir,' said he, with the deepest concern, 'may I beg the life of my uncle? If it is granted, his relations will make a gift to the state of a thousand zechins. We will furnish fifty soldiers in pay during the siege of Furiani. We will agree that my uncle shall be banished, and will engage that he shall never return to the island.' I knew the nephew to be a man of worth, and I answered him, 'You are acquainted with the circumstances of this case. Such is my confidence in you, that if you will say that giving your uncle a pardon would be just, useful, or honourable for Corsica, I promise you it shall be granted.' He turned about, burst into tears, and left me, saying, 'I would not have the honour of our country sold for a thousand zechins.' And his uncle suffered."

Although the General was one of the constituent members of the court of sindacato, he seldom took his chair. He remained in his own apartment, and if any of those whose suits were determined by the sindacato were not pleased with the sentence they had an audience of Paoli, who never failed to convince them that justice had been done them. This appeared to me a necessary indulgence in the infancy of government. The Corsicans, having been so long in a state of anarchy, could not all at once submit their minds to the regular authority of justice. They would submit implicitly to Paoli, because they love and venerate him. But such a submission is in reality being governed by their passions. They submit to one for whom they have a personal regard. They cannot be said to be perfectly civilized till they submit to the determinations of their magistrates as officers of the state entrusted with the administration of justice. By convincing them that the magistrates judge with abilities and uprightness, Paoli accustoms the Corsicans to have that salutary confidence in their rulers which is necessary for securing respect and stability to the government.

After having said much in praise of the Corsicans, "Come," said he, "you shall have a proof of what I tell you. There is a crowd in the next room waiting for admittance to me. I will call in the first I see, and you shall hear him." He who chanced to present himself was a venerable old man. The General shook him by the hand and bid him good day, with an easy kindness that gave the aged peasant full encouragement to talk to his Excellency with freedom. Paoli bid him not mind me, but say on. The old man then told him that there had been an unlucky tumult in the village where he lived, and that two of his sons were killed. That looking upon this as a heavy misfortune, but without malice on the part of those who deprived him of his sons, he was willing to have allowed it to pass without enquiry. But his wife, anxious for revenge, had made an application to have them apprehended and punished. That he gave his Excellency this trouble to entreat that the greatest care might be taken, lest in the heat of enmity among his neighbours anybody should be punished as guilty of the blood of his sons who was really innocent of it. There was something so generous in this sentiment, while at the same time the old man seemed full of grief for the loss of his children, that it touched my heart in the most sensible manner. Paoli looked at me with complacency and a kind of amiable triumph on the behaviour of the old man, who had a flow of words and a vivacity of gesture which fully justified what Petrus Cyrnaeus hath said of the Corsican eloquence: "Diceres omnes esse bonos causidicos."[6]

I found Paoli had reason to wish that I should talk much with his countrymen, as it gave me a higher opinion both of him and of them. Thuanus has justly said, "Sunt mobilia Corsorum ingenia."[7]

[6] "You would say they are all good pleaders." — BOSWELL. Petrus, a priest, wrote a history of Corsica in the early sixteenth century.

[7] "The dispositions of the Corsicans are changeable." — BOSWELL. Thuanus (Jacques Auguste de Thou) published a history of his own times in the early seventeenth century.

Yet after ten years, their attachment to Paoli is as strong as at the first. Nay, they have an enthusiastic admiration of him. "This great man whom God hath sent to free our country," was the manner in which they expressed themselves to me concerning him.

Those who attended on Paoli were all men of sense and abilities in their different departments. Some of them had been in foreign service. One of them, Signor Suzzoni, had been long in Germany. He spoke German to me, and recalled to my mind the happy days which I have passed among that plain, honest, brave people, who of all nations in the world receive strangers with the greatest cordiality. Signor Gian Quilico Casabianca, of the most ancient Corsican nobility, was much my friend. He instructed me fully with regard to the Corsican government. He had even the patience to sit by me while I wrote down an account of it, which from conversations with Paoli I afterwards enlarged and improved. I received many civilities from the Abbé Rostini, a man of literature, and distinguished no less for the excellency of his heart. His saying of Paoli deserves to be remembered: "We are not afraid that our General will deceive us, nor that he will let himself be deceived."

I also received civilities from Father Guelfucci of the order of Servites, a man whose talents and virtues, united with a singular decency and sweetness of manners, have raised him to the honourable station of secretary to the General. Indeed all the gentlemen here behaved to me in the most obliging manner. We walked, rode, and went a-shooting together.

The peasants and soldiers were all frank, open, lively, and bold, with a certain roughness of manner which agrees well with their character and is far from being displeasing. The General gave me an admirable instance of their plain and natural solid good sense. A young French marquis, very rich and very vain, came over to Corsica. He had a sovereign contempt for the barbarous inhabitants, and strutted about with prodigious airs of consequence. The Corsicans beheld him with a smile of ridicule and said, "Let him alone, he is young."

The Corsican peasants and soldiers are very fond of baiting cattle with the large mountain dogs. This keeps up a ferocity among them which totally extinguishes fear. I have seen a Corsican in the very heat of a baiting, run in, drive off the dogs, seize the half-frantic animal by the horns, and lead it away. The common people did not seem much given to diversions. I observed some of them in the great hall of the house of Colonna where I was lodged amusing themselves with playing at a sort of draughts in a very curious manner. They drew upon the floor with chalk a sufficient number of squares, chalking one all over and leaving one open alternately; and instead of black men and white, they had bits of stone and bits of wood. It was an admirable burlesque on gaming.

The chief satisfaction of these islanders, when not engaged in war or in hunting, seemed to be that of lying at their ease in the open air, recounting tales of the bravery of their countrymen, and singing songs in honour of the Corsicans and against the Genoese. Even in the night they will continue this pastime in the open air, unless rain forces them to retire into their houses.

The *ambasciatore inglese*, as the good peasants and soldiers used to call me, became a great favourite among them. I got a Corsican dress made, in which I walked about with an air of true satisfaction. The General did me the honour to present me with his own pistols, made in the island, all of Corsican wood and iron and of excellent workmanship. I had every other accoutrement. I even got one of the shells which had often sounded the alarm to liberty. I preserve them all with great care.

The Corsican peasants and soldiers were quite free and easy with me. Numbers of them used to come and see me of a morning, and just go out and in as they pleased. I did everything in my power to make them fond of the British, and bid them hope for an alliance with us. They asked me a thousand questions about my country, all which I cheerfully answered as well as I could.

One day they would needs hear me play upon my German flute. To have told my honest natural visitants, "Really, gentlemen, I play very ill," and put on such airs as we do in our genteel companies, would have been highly ridiculous. I therefore immediately complied with their request. I gave them one or two Italian airs, and then some of our beautiful old Scots tunes: *Gilderoy*, *The Lass of Patie's Mill*, "Corn rigs are bonny." The pathetic simplicity and pastoral gaiety of the Scots music will always please those who have the genuine feelings of nature. The Corsicans were charmed with the specimens I gave them, though I may now say that they were very indifferently performed.

My good friends insisted also to have an English song from me. I endeavoured to please them in this too, and was very lucky in that which occurred to me. I sung them "Hearts of oak are our ships, Hearts of oak are our men."[8] I translated it into Italian for them, and never did I see men so delighted with a song as the Corsicans were with the *Hearts of Oak*. "Cuore di quercia," cried they, "bravo Inglese!" It was quite a joyous riot. I fancied myself to be a recruiting sea officer. I fancied all my chorus of Corsicans aboard the British fleet.

Paoli talked very highly on preserving the independency of Corsica. "We may," said he, "have foreign powers for our friends, but they must be friends at arm's length. We may make an alliance, but we will not submit ourselves to the dominion of the greatest nation in Europe. This people who have done so much for liberty would be hewn in pieces man by man rather than allow Corsica to be sunk into the territories of another country. Some years ago, when a false rumour was spread that I had a design to yield up Corsica to the Emperor, a Corsican came to me and addressed me in great agitation: 'What! shall the blood of so many heroes, who have sacrificed their lives for the freedom of Corsica, serve only to tinge the purple of a foreign prince!' "

I mentioned to him the scheme of an alliance between Great Britain and Corsica. Paoli with politeness and dignity waived the subject by saying, "The less assistance we have from allies, the greater our glory." He seemed hurt by our treatment of his country. He mentioned the severe proclamation at the last peace, in which the brave islanders were called the rebels of Corsica. He said with a conscious pride and proper feeling, "Rebels! I did not expect that from Great Britain."

He however showed his great respect for the British nation, and I could see he wished much to be in friendship with us. When I asked him what I could possibly do in return for all his goodness to me, he replied, "Only undeceive your Court. Tell them what you have seen here. They will be curious to ask you. A man come from Corsica will be like a man come from the Antipodes."

[8] The words of this song are by David Garrick, the music by William Boyce.

I expressed such hopes as a man of sensibility would in my situation naturally form. He saw at least one Briton devoted to his cause. I threw out many flattering ideas of future political events, imaged the British and the Corsicans strictly united both in commerce and in war, and described the blunt kindness and admiration with which the hearty, generous common people of England would treat the brave Corsicans.

I insensibly got the better of his reserve upon this head. My flow of gay ideas relaxed his severity and brightened up his humour. "Do you remember," said he, "the little people in Asia who were in danger of being oppressed by the great king of Assyria, till they addressed themselves to the Romans; and the Romans, with the noble spirit of a great and free nation, stood forth and would not suffer the great king to destroy the little people, but made an alliance with them?" He made no observations upon this beautiful piece of history. It was easy to see his allusion to his own nation and ours.

When the General related this piece of history to me, I was negligent enough not to ask him what little people he meant. As the story made a strong impression upon me, upon my return to Britain I searched a variety of books to try if I could find it, but in vain. I therefore took the liberty in one of my letters to Paoli to beg he would let me know it. He told me the little people was the Jews, that the story was related by several ancient authors, but that I would find it told with most precision and energy in the eighth chapter of the first book of the Maccabees.

The first book of the Maccabees, though not received into the Protestant canon, is allowed by all the learned to be an authentic history. I have read Paoli's favourite story with much satisfaction, and as in several circumstances it very well applies to Great Britain and Corsica, is told with great eloquence, and furnishes a fine model for an alliance, I shall make no apology for transcribing the most interesting verses. . . .[9]

I will venture to ask whether the Romans appear in any one instance of their history more truly great than they do here.

Paoli said, "If a man would preserve the generous glow of patriotism, he must not reason too much. Marshal Saxe reasoned, and carried

[9] Boswell's extended quotation, comprising most of the eighth chapter of I Maccabees, is omitted.

the arms of France into the heart of Germany, his own country.[1] I act from sentiment, not from reasonings.

"Virtuous sentiments and habits," said he, "are beyond philosophical reasonings, which are not so strong, and are continually varying. If all the professors in Europe were formed into one society, it would no doubt be a society very respectable and we should there be entertained with the best moral lessons. Yet I believe I should find more real virtue in a society of good peasants in some little village in the heart of your island. It might be said of these two societies, as was said of Demosthenes and Themistocles, 'Illius dicta, huius facta magis valebant.' "[2]

This kind of conversation led me to tell him how much I had suffered from anxious speculations. With a mind naturally inclined to melancholy, and a keen desire of enquiry, I had intensely applied myself to metaphysical researches, and reasoned beyond my depth on such subjects as it is not given to man to know. I told him I had rendered my mind a *camera obscura*, that in the very heat of youth I felt the *non est tanti*, the *omnia vanitas*[3] of one who has exhausted all the sweets of his being and is weary with dull repetition. I told him that I had almost become for ever incapable of taking a part in active life.

"All this," said Paoli, "is melancholy. I have also studied metaphysics. I know the arguments for fate and free will, for the materiality and immateriality of the soul, and even the subtle arguments for and against the existence of matter. But let us leave these disputes to the idle. I hold always firm one great object. I never feel a moment of despondency."

The contemplation of such a character really existing was of more service to me than all I had been able to draw from books, from conversation, or from the exertions of my own mind. I had often enough formed the idea of a man continually such as I could conceive in my best moments. But this idea appeared like the ideas we are taught

[1] Hermann Maurice, Comte de Saxe, was a natural son of Augustus II of Saxony. Having served in his youth under Marlborough and Prince Eugene, he later became a marshal of France and was the victorious general at Fontenoy in 1745.

[2] "The one was powerful in words, but the other in deeds." — BOSWELL.

[3] "It is not worth while. . . . All is vanity." The first phrase is proverbial; the second is from Ecclesiastes 1. 2.

in the schools to form of things which may exist, but do not: of seas of milk and ships of amber. But I saw my highest idea realized in Paoli. It was impossible for me, speculate as I pleased, to have a little opinion of human nature in him.

One morning I remember I came in upon him without ceremony while he was dressing. I was glad to have an opportunity of seeing him in those teasing moments when according to the Duc de La Rochefoucauld no man is a hero to his *valet de chambre*.[4] That lively nobleman, who has a malicious pleasure in endeavouring to divest human nature of its dignity by exhibiting partial views and exaggerating faults, would have owned that Paoli was every moment of his life a hero.

Paoli told me that from his earliest years he had in view the important station which he now holds, so that his sentiments must ever have been great. I asked him how one of such elevated thoughts could submit with any degree of patience to the unmeaning ceremonies and poor discourse of genteel society, which he certainly was obliged to do while an officer at Naples. "Oh," said he, "I managed it very easily. I was known to be a singular man. I talked and joked and was merry, but I never sat down to play; I went and came as I pleased. The mirth I like is what is easy and unaffected. I cannot endure long the sayers of good things."

How much superior is this great man's idea of agreeable conversation to that of professed wits, who are continually straining for smart remarks and lively repartees. They put themselves to much pain in order to please, and yet please less than if they would just appear as they naturally feel themselves. A company of professed wits has always appeared to me like a company of artificers employed in some very nice and difficult work which they are under a necessity of performing.

Though calm and fully master of himself, Paoli is animated with an extraordinary degree of vivacity. Except when indisposed or greatly fatigued, he never sits down but at meals. He is perpetually in motion, walking briskly backwards and forwards. Mr. Samuel Johnson, whose comprehensive and vigorous understanding has by

[4] The *Maxims* of La Rochefoucauld do not contain this saying. It is sometimes attributed to Mme. Cornuel, sometimes to Mme. de Sévigné.

long observation attained to a perfect knowledge of human nature, when treating of biography has this reflection: "There are many invisible circumstances which, whether we read as enquirers after natural or moral knowledge, whether we intend to enlarge our science or increase our virtue, are more important than public occurrences. Thus Sallust, the great master of nature, has not forgotten in his account of Catiline to remark that 'his walk was now quick, and again slow,' as an indication of a mind revolving something with violent commotion."[5] Ever mindful of the wisdom of the Rambler, I have accustomed myself to mark the small peculiarities of character. Paoli's being perpetually in motion, nay his being so agitated that as the same Sallust also says of Catiline, "Neque vigiliis, neque quietibus sedari poterat,"[6] are indications of his being as active and indefatigable as Catiline, but from a very different cause: the conspirator from schemes of ruin and destruction to Rome, the patriot from schemes of liberty and felicity to Corsica.

Paoli told me that the vivacity of his mind was such that he could not study above ten minutes at a time. "My head is like to break," said he. "I can never write my lively ideas with my own hand. In writing, they escape from my mind. I call the Abbé Guelfucci, 'Come quickly, take my thoughts,' and he writes them."

Paoli has a memory like that of Themistocles, for I was assured that he knows the names of almost all the people in the island, their characters, and their connections. His memory as a man of learning is no less uncommon. He has the best part of the classics by heart, and he has a happy talent in applying them with propriety, which is rarely to be found. This talent is not always to be reckoned pedantry. The instances in which Paoli is shown to display it are a proof to the contrary.

I have heard Paoli recount the revolutions of one of the ancient states with an energy and a rapidity which showed him to be master of the subject, to be perfectly acquainted with every spring and movement of the various events. I have heard him give what the French

[5] *Rambler*, No. 60. Boswell enlarged on this quotation, which he took as a basis for his own biographical method, in his opening remarks to *The Life of Johnson*. The quotation from Sallust is from the *Bellum Catilinae*, xv.

[6] "He could not be quieted either by watching or by repose." — BOSWELL. See *Bellum Catilinae*, xxvii.

call *un catalogue raisonné* of the most distinguished men in antiquity. His characters of them were concise, nervous, and just. I regret that the fire with which he spoke upon such occasions so dazzled me that I could not recollect his sayings so as to write them down when I retired from his presence. He just lives in the times of antiquity. He said to me, "A young man who would form his mind to glory must not read modern memoirs, but Plutarch and Titus Livius."

I have seen him fall into a sort of reverie, and break out into sallies of the grandest and noblest enthusiasm. I recollect two instances of this. "What a thought: that thousands owe their happiness to you!" And throwing himself into an attitude as if he saw the lofty mountain of fame before him: "*There* is my object! (pointing to the summit). If I fall, I fall at least *there* (pointing a good way up); *magnis tamen excidit ausis*."[7]

I ventured to reason like a libertine, that I might be confirmed in virtuous principles by so illustrious a preceptor. I made light of moral feelings. I argued that conscience was vague and uncertain, that there was hardly any vice but what men might be found who have been guilty of it without remorse. "But," said he, "there is no man who has not a horror at some vice. Different vices and different virtues have the strongest impression on different men, but virtue in the abstract is the food of our hearts."

Talking of Providence, he said to me with that earnestness with which a man speaks who is anxious to be believed: "I tell you on the word of an honest man, it is impossible for me not to be persuaded that God interposes to give freedom to Corsica. A people oppressed like the Corsicans are certainly worthy of divine assistance. When we were in the most desperate circumstances I never lost courage, trusting as I did in Providence." I ventured to object; "But why has not Providence interposed sooner?" He replied with a noble, serious, and devout air, "Because His ways are unsearchable. I adore Him for what He hath done. I revere Him in what He hath not done."

I gave Paoli the character of my revered friend Mr. Samuel Johnson. I have often regretted that illustrious men, such as humanity produces a few times in the revolution of many ages, should not see

[7] "It was, however, in a great venture that he failed" (Ovid, *Metamorphoses*, ii. 328).

each other; and when such arise in the same age, though at the distance of half the globe, I have been astonished how they could forbear to meet.

"As steel sharpeneth steel, so doth a man the countenance of his friend,"[8] says the wise monarch. What an idea may we not form of an interview between such a scholar and philosopher as Mr. Johnson and such a legislator and general as Paoli![9]

I repeated to Paoli several of Mr. Johnson's sayings, so remarkable for strong sense and original humour. I now recollect these two. When I told Mr. Johnson that a certain author[1] affected in conversation to maintain that there was no distinction between virtue and vice, he said, "Why, Sir, if the fellow does not think as he speaks, he is lying; and I see not what honour he can propose to himself from having the character of a liar. But if he does really think that there is no distinction between virtue and vice, why, Sir, when he leaves our houses let us count our spoons." Of modern infidels and innovators, he said, "Sir, these are all vain men, and will gratify themselves at any expense. Truth will not afford sufficient food to their vanity, so they have betaken themselves to error. Truth, Sir, is a cow which will yield such people no more milk, and so they are gone to milk the bull."[2] I felt an elation of mind to see Paoli delighted with the sayings of Mr. Johnson, and to hear him translate them with Italian energy to the Corsican heroes.

I repeated Mr. Johnson's sayings as nearly as I could in his own peculiar forcible language, for which prejudiced or little critics have taken upon them to find fault with him. He is above making any answer to them, but I have found a sufficient answer in a general remark in one of his excellent papers: "Difference of thoughts will produce difference of language. He that thinks with more extent than another will want words of larger meaning."[3]

[8] See Proverbs 27. 17.

[9] Paoli and Johnson took to each other when Boswell introduced them in 1769. In *The Life of Johnson*, Johnson is reported as saying that Paoli had "the loftiest port of any man he had ever seen" (10 October 1769).

[1] James Macpherson, the "translator" of Ossian.

[2] Johnson made this remark apropos of David Hume and "all other sceptical innovators" (*Boswell's London Journal, 1762–1763*, 22 July 1763).

[3] *Idler*, No. 70.

I hope to be pardoned for this digression, wherein I pay a just tribute of veneration and gratitude to one from whose writings and conversation I have received instructions of which I experience the value in every scene of my life.

During Paoli's administration there have been few laws made in Corsica. He mentioned one which he has found very efficacious in curbing that vindictive spirit of the Corsicans of which I have said a good deal in a former part of this work.[4] There was among the Corsicans a most dreadful species of revenge, called *vendetta trasversa*,[5] which Petrus Cyrnaeus candidly acknowledges. It was this: if a man had received an injury and could not find a proper opportunity to be revenged on his enemy personally, he revenged himself on one of his enemy's relations. So barbarous a practice was the source of innumerable assassinations. Paoli, knowing that the point of honour was everything to the Corsicans, opposed it to the progress of the blackest of crimes fortified by long habits. He made a law by which it was provided that this collateral revenge should not only be punished with death, as ordinary murder, but the memory of the offender should be disgraced for ever by a pillar of infamy. He also had it enacted that the same statute should extend to the violators of an oath of reconciliation once made.

By thus combating a vice so destructive he has by a kind of shock of opposite passions reduced the fiery Corsicans to a state of mildness, and he assured me that they were now fully sensible of the equity of that law.

While I was at Sollacarò, information was received that the poor wretch who strangled the woman at the instigation of his mistress had consented to accept of his life upon condition of becoming hangman. This made a great noise among the Corsicans, who were enraged at the creature and said their nation was now disgraced. Paoli did not think so. He said to me, "I am glad of this. It will be of service. It will contribute to form us to a just subordination. We have as yet too great an equality among us. As we must have Corsican tailors and Corsican shoemakers, we must also have a Corsican hangman."

I could not help being of a different opinion. The occupations of a

[4] In the *Account of Corsica*.

[5] Collateral revenge. — BOSWELL.

tailor and a shoemaker, though mean, are not odious. When I afterwards met M. Rousseau in England and made him a report of my Corsican expedition, he agreed with me in thinking that it would be something noble for the brave islanders to be able to say that there was not a Corsican but who would rather suffer death than become a hangman; and he also agreed with me that it might have a good effect to have always a Genoese for the hangman of Corsica.

I must, however, do the Genoese the justice to observe that Paoli told me that even one of them had suffered death in Corsica rather than consent to become hangman. When I, from a keenness natural enough in a Briton born with an abhorrence at tyranny, talked with violence against the Genoese, Paoli said with a moderation and candour which ought to do him honour even with the Republic, "It is true the Genoese are our enemies, but let us not forget that they are the descendants of those worthies who carried their arms beyond the Hellespont."

There is one circumstance in Paoli's character which I present to my readers with caution, knowing how much it may be ridiculed in an age when mankind are so fond of incredulity that they seem to pique themselves in contracting their circle of belief as much as possible. But I consider this infidel rage as but a temporary mode of the human understanding, and am well persuaded that ere long we shall return to a more calm philosophy.

I own I cannot help thinking that though we may boast some improvements in science and, in short, superior degrees of knowledge in things where our faculties can fully reach, yet we should not assume to ourselves sounder judgments than those of our fathers. I will therefore venture to relate that Paoli has at times extraordinary impressions of distant and future events.

The way in which I discovered it was this. Being very desirous of studying so exalted a character, I so far presumed upon his goodness to me as to take the liberty of asking him a thousand questions with regard to the most minute and private circumstances of his life. Having asked him one day when some of his nobles were present whether a mind so active as his was not employed even in sleep, and if he used to dream much, Signor Casabianca said with an air and tone which implied something of importance, "Yes, he dreams." And upon my asking him to explain his meaning, he told me that the

General had often seen in his dreams what afterwards came to pass. Paoli confirmed this by several instances. Said he, "I can give you no clear explanation of it. I only tell you facts. Sometimes I have been mistaken, but in general these visions have proved true. I cannot say what may be the agency of invisible spirits. They certainly must know more than we do, and there is nothing absurd in supposing that God should permit them to communicate their knowledge to us."

He went into a most curious and pleasing disquisition, on a subject which the late ingenious Mr. Baxter had treated in a very philosophical manner in his *Inquiry into the Nature of the Human Soul*, a book which may be read with as much delight and surely with more advantage than the works of those who endeavour to destroy our belief. Belief is favourable to the human mind, were it for nothing else but to furnish it entertainment. An infidel I should think must frequently suffer from ennui.

It was perhaps affectation in Socrates to say that all he had learned to know was that he knew nothing. But surely it is a mark of wisdom to be sensible of the limited extent of human knowledge, to examine with reverence the ways of God, nor presumptuously reject any opinion which has been held by the judicious and the learned because it has been made a cloak for artifice or had a variety of fictions raised upon it by credulity.

Old Felltham says, "Every dream is not to be counted of; nor yet are all to be cast away with contempt. I would neither be a stoic, superstitious in all; nor yet an epicure, considerate of none." And after observing how much the ancients attended to the interpretation of dreams, he adds, "Were it not for the power of the Gospel in crying down the vains[6] of men, it would appear a wonder how a science so pleasing to humanity should fall so quite to ruin."[7]

The mysterious circumstance in Paoli's character which I have ventured to relate is universally believed in Corsica. The inhabitants of that island, like the Italians, express themselves much by signs. When I asked one of them if there had been many instances of the General's foreseeing future events, he grasped a large bunch of his hair and replied, "So many, Sir."

It may be said that the General has industriously propagated this

[6] He means vanity. — BOSWELL.

[7] Owen Felltham, *Resolves*, cento i, resolution 52.

opinion in order that he might have more authority in civilizing a rude and ferocious people, as Lycurgus pretended to have the sanction of the oracle at Delphos, as Numa gave it out that he had frequent interviews with the nymph Egeria, or as Marius persuaded the Romans that he received divine communications from a hind. But I cannot allow myself to suppose that Paoli ever required the aid of pious frauds.

Paoli, though never familiar, has the most perfect ease of behaviour. This is a mark of a real great character. The distance and reserve which some of our modern nobility affect is because nobility is now little else than a name in comparison of what it was in ancient times. In ancient times noblemen lived at their country seats, like princes, in hospitable grandeur. They were men of power, and every one of them could bring hundreds of followers into the field. They were then open and affable. Some of our modern nobility are so anxious to preserve an appearance of dignity which they are sensible cannot bear an examination that they are afraid to let you come near them.[8] Paoli is not so. Those about him come into his apartment at all hours, wake him, help him on with his clothes, are perfectly free from restraint; yet they know their distance and, awed by his real greatness, never lose their respect for him.

Though thus easy of access, particular care is taken against such attempts upon the life of the illustrious chief as he has good reason to apprehend from the Genoese, who have so often employed assassination merely in a political view and who would gain so much by assassinating Paoli. A certain number of soldiers are continually on guard upon him, and as still closer guards he has some faithful Corsican dogs. Of these five or six sleep, some in his chamber, and some at the outside of the chamber door. He treats them with great kindness, and they are strongly attached to him. They are extremely sagacious, and know all his friends and attendants. Were any person to approach the General during the darkness of the night, they would instantly tear him in pieces. Having dogs for his attendants is another circumstance about Paoli similar to the heroes of antiquity. Homer repre-

[8] In an outline, or summary of materials, which Boswell made in preparing *The Journal of a Tour to Corsica* for the press, this observation on the decline of the nobility is credited to Adam Smith.

sents Telemachus so attended: *δύω κύνες ἀργοὶ ἕποντο.*[9] But the description given of the family of Patroclus applies better to Paoli: *ἐννέα τῷ γε ἄνακτι τραπεζῆες κύνες ἦσαν.*[1]

Mr. Pope in his notes on the second book of the *Odyssey* is much pleased with dogs being introduced, as it furnishes an agreeable instance of ancient simplicity. He observes that Virgil thought this circumstance worthy of his imitation, in describing old Evander. So we read of Syphax, General of the Numidians, "Syphax inter duos canes stans, Scipionem appellavit."[2]

Talking of courage, he made a very just distinction between constitutional courage and courage from reflection. "Sir Thomas More," said he, "would not probably have mounted a breach so well as a sergeant who had never thought of death. But a sergeant would not on a scaffold have shown the calm resolution of Sir Thomas More."

On this subject he told me a very remarkable anecdote, which happened during the last war in Italy. At the siege of Tortona, the commander of the army which lay before the town ordered Carew, an Irish officer in the service of Naples, to advance with a detachment to a particular post. Having given his orders, he whispered to Carew, "Sir, I know you to be a gallant man. I have therefore put you upon this duty. I tell you in confidence, it is certain death for you all. I place you there to make the enemy spring a mine below you." Carew made a bow to the general, and led on his men in silence to the dreadful post. He there stood with an undaunted countenance, and having called to one of the soldiers for a draught of wine, "Here," said he, "I drink to all those who bravely fall in battle." Fortunately at that instant Tortona capitulated, and Carew escaped. But he had thus a full opportunity of displaying a rare instance of determined intrepidity. It is with pleasure that I record an anecdote so much to the honour of a gentleman of that nation on which illiberal reflections are too often thrown by those of whom it little deserves them. What-

[9] *Odyssey*, ii. 11: "Two dogs, a faithful guard, attend behind" (Pope).

[1] *Iliad*, xxiii. 173: "Nine large dogs domestic at his board" (Pope).

[2] "Syphax standing between two dogs called to Scipio." I mention this on the authority of an excellent scholar and one of our best writers, Mr. Joseph Warton, in his notes on the *Aeneid* [viii. 461–462]; for I have not been able to find the passage in Livy which he quotes. — BOSWELL. The passage is not in Livy, and its source is still unknown. Warton later deleted the note.

ever may be the rough jokes of wealthy insolence or the envious sarcasms of needy jealousy, the Irish have ever been and will continue to be highly regarded upon the Continent.

Paoli's personal authority among the Corsicans struck me much. I have seen a crowd of them with eagerness and impetuosity endeavouring to approach him, as if they would have burst into his apartment by force. In vain did the guards attempt to restrain them, but when he called to them in a tone of firmness, "No audience now," they were hushed at once.

He one afternoon gave us an entertaining dissertation on the ancient art of war. He observed that the ancients allowed of little baggage, which they very properly called "impedimenta"; whereas the moderns burden themselves with it to such a degree that fifty thousand of our present soldiers are allowed as much baggage as was formerly thought sufficient for all the armies of the Roman empire. He said it was good for soldiers to be heavy-armed as it renders them proportionably robust, and he remarked that when the Romans lightened their arms, the troops became enfeebled. He made a very curious observation with regard to the towers full of armed men which we are told were borne on the backs of their elephants. He said it must be a mistake, for if the towers were broad, there would not be room for them on the backs of elephants; for he and a friend who was an able calculator had measured a very large elephant at Naples, and made a computation of the space necessary to hold the number of men said to be contained in those towers, and they found that the back of the broadest elephant would not be sufficient, after making the fullest allowance for what might be hung by balance on either side of the animal. If again the towers were high, they would fall; for he did not think it at all probable that the Romans had the art of tying on such monstrous machines at a time when they had not learned the use even of girths to their saddles. He said he did not give too much credit to the figures on Trajan's pillar, many of which were undoubtedly false. He said it was his opinion that those towers were only drawn by the elephants; an opinion founded in probability and free from the difficulties of that which has been commonly received.

Talking of various schemes of life fit for a man of spirit and education, I mentioned to him that of being a foreign minister. He said he thought it a very agreeable employment for a man of parts and address during some years of his life. "In that situation," said he, "a man will insensibly attain to a greater knowledge of men and manners and a more perfect acquaintance with the politics of Europe. He will be promoted according to the returns which he makes to his court. They must be accurate, distinct, without fire or ornament. He may subjoin his own opinion, but he must do it with great modesty. The ministry at home are proud."

He said the greatest happiness was not in glory but in goodness, and that Penn in his American colony where he had established a people in quiet and contentment, was happier than Alexander the Great after destroying multitudes at the conquest of Thebes. He observed that the history of Alexander is obscure and dubious, for his captains who divided his kingdom were too busy to record his life and actions, and would at any rate wish to render him odious to posterity.

Never was I so thoroughly sensible of my own defects as while I was in Corsica. I felt how small were my abilities and how little I knew. Ambitious to be the companion of Paoli and to understand a country and a people which roused me so much, I wished to be a Sir James Macdonald.[3]

The last day which I spent with Paoli appeared of inestimable value. I thought him more than usually great and amiable when I was upon the eve of parting from him. The night before my departure a little incident happened which showed him in a most agreeable light. When the servants were bringing in the dessert after supper, one of them chanced to let fall a plate of walnuts. Instead of flying into a passion at what the man could not help, Paoli said with a smile, "No matter"; and turning to me, "It is a good sign for you, Sir. *Tempus est spargere nuces.*[4] It is a matrimonial omen; you must go

[3] Sir James Macdonald, Baronet, of the Isle of Skye, who at the age of one and twenty had the learning and abilities of a professor and a statesman, with the accomplishments of a man of the world. Eton and Oxford will ever remember him as one of their greatest ornaments. He was well known to the most distinguished in Europe, but was carried off from all their expectations. He died at Frascati, near Rome, in 1765 [1766]. Had he lived a little longer, I believe I should have prevailed with him to visit Corsica. — BOSWELL.

[4] "It is time to scatter walnuts." — BOSWELL.

home to your own country and marry some fine woman whom yo
really like. I shall rejoice to hear of it."

This was a pretty allusion to the Roman ceremony at weddings
of scattering walnuts. So Virgil's Damon says,

> Mopse, novas incide faces: tibi ducitur uxor.
> Sparge, marite, nuces: tibi deserit Hesperus Oetam.[5]

When I again asked Paoli if it was possible for me in any way t
show him my great respect and attachment, he replied, "Remembe
that I am your friend, and write to me." I said I hoped that when h
honoured me with a letter, he would write not only as a commande
but as a philosopher and a man of letters. He took me by the han
and said, "As a friend." I dare not transcribe from my private note
the feelings which I had at this interview. I should perhaps appea
too enthusiastic. I took leave of Paoli with regret and agitation, no
without some hopes of seeing him again. From having known inti
mately so exalted a character, my sentiments of human nature wer
raised; while by a sort of contagion I felt an honest ardour to dis
tinguish myself, and be useful as far as my situation and abilitie
would allow; and I was, for the rest of my life, set free from a slavis
timidity in the presence of great men, for where shall I find a ma
greater than Paoli?

When I set out from Sollacarò, I felt myself a good deal indis
posed. The old house of Colonna, like the family of its master, wa
much decayed, so that both wind and rain found their way into m
bedchamber. From this I contracted a severe cold, which ended in
tertian ague.[6] There was no help for it. I might well submit to som
inconveniences where I had enjoyed so much happiness.

I was accompanied a part of the road by a great swarthy pries
who had never been out of Corsica. He was a very Hercules fo
strength and resolution. He and two other Corsicans took a castle gar

[5] *Eclogues*, viii. 29–30:

> Thy bride comes forth! begin the festal rites.
> The walnuts strew! prepare the nuptial lights!
> O envied husband, now thy bliss is nigh,
> Behold for thee bright Hesper mounts the sky!
> Joseph Warton.

[6] Malaria.

Pasquale de Paoli (1725–1807), engraved by John Raphael Smith from the original painting commissioned by Boswell from Henry Benbridge; from a print presented to the Yale Art Gallery by Chauncey Brewster Tinker.

isoned by no less than fifteen Genoese. Indeed, the Corsicans have
uch a contempt for their enemies that I have heard them say, "Our
omen would be enough against the Genoese." This priest was a
luff, hearty, roaring fellow, troubled neither with knowledge nor
are. He was ever and anon showing me how stoutly his nag could
aper. He always rode some paces before me, and sat in an attitude
alf turned round with his hand clapped upon the crupper. Then he
ould burst out with comical songs about the devil, and the Genoese,
nd I don't know what all. In short, notwithstanding my feverish-
ess, he kept me laughing whether I would or no.

I was returning to Corte, but I varied my road a little from the
ay I had come, going more upon the low country and nearer the
estern shore. At Cauro I had a fine view of Ajaccio and its environs.
Iy ague was some time of forming, so I had frequent intervals of
ase, which I employed in observing whatever occurred. I was lodged
t Cauro in the house of Signor Peraldi of Ajaccio, who received me
ith great politeness. I found here another provincial magistracy.
efore supper, Signor Peraldi and a young abbé of Ajaccio enter-
ined me with some airs on the violin. After they had shown me their
iste in fine improved music, they gave me some original Corsican
irs, and at my desire they brought up four of the guards of the
iagistracy and made them show me a Corsican dance. It was truly
ivage. They thumped with their heels, sprung upon their toes, bran-
ished their arms, wheeled and leaped with the most violent gesticu-
itions. It gave me the idea of an admirable war dance.

During this journey I had very bad weather. I cannot forget the
orthy Rector of Cuttoli, whose house afforded me a hospitable re-
eat when wet to the skin and quite overcome by the severity of the
orm, which my sickness made me little able to resist. He was di-
ectly such a venerable hermit as we read of in the old romances. His
gure and manner interested me at first sight. I found he was a man
ell respected in the island, and that the General did him the honour
correspond with him. He gave me a simple collation of eggs, chest-
uts, and wine, and was very liberal of his ham and other more sub-
antial victuals to my servant. The honest Swiss was by this time
ery well pleased to have his face turned towards the Continent. He
as heartily tired of seeing foreign parts, and meeting with scanty

meals and hard beds in an island which he could not comprehend th pleasure of visiting. He said to me, "If I were once more at home i my own country, among those mountains of Switzerland on whic you have had so many jokes, I will see who shall prevail with me t quit them."

The General, out of his great politeness, would not allow me t travel without a couple of chosen guards to attend me in case of an accidents. I made them my companions to relieve the tediousness o my journey. One of them called Ambrosio was a strange iron coloured, fearless creature. He had been much in war; careless o wounds, he was coolly intent on destroying the enemy. He told me as a good anecdote, that having been so lucky as to get a view of tw Genoese exactly in a line, he took his aim and shot them both throug the head at once. He talked of this just as one would talk of shooting couple of crows. I was sure I needed be under no apprehension; but don't know how, I desired Ambrosio to march before me that I migh see him.

I was upon my guard how I treated him. But as sickness frets one' temper, I sometimes forgot myself and called him "blockhead"; an once when he was at a loss which way to go, at a wild woody part o the country, I fell into a passion and called to him, "I am amazed tha so brave a man can be so stupid." However, by afterwards calling hin friend and speaking softly to him I soon made him forget my il humour, and we proceeded as before.

Paoli had also been so good as to make me a present of one of hi dogs, a strong and fierce animal. But he was too old to take an attach ment to me, and I lost him between Lyons and Paris. The General ha promised me a young one to be a guard at Auchinleck.[7]

At Bocognano I came upon the same road I had formerly trav elled from Corte, where I arrived safe after all my fatigues. My goo fathers of the Franciscan convent received me like an old acquaint ance, and showed a kind concern at my illness. I sent my respect to the Great Chancellor, who returned me a note of which I insert translation as a specimen of the hearty civility to be found among th highest in Corsica.

"Many congratulations to Mr. Boswell on his return from beyon

[7] The younger dog had no sooner arrived in London in March 1768 than it ra away. Apparently it was recovered.

ıe mountains from his servant Massesi, who is at the same time very •rry for his indisposition, which he is persuaded has been occasioned y his severe journey. He however flatters himself that when Mr. oswell has reposed himself a little, he will recover his usual health. ı the mean time he has taken the liberty to send him [by the mes-:nger] a couple of fowls, which he hopes he will honour with his ac-:ptance, as he will need some refreshment this evening. He wishes im a good night, as does his little servant Luigi, who will attend im tomorrow to discharge his duty."[8]

My ague distressed me so much that I was confined to the convent r several days. I did not, however, find myself weary. I was visited y the Great Chancellor and several others of the civil magistrates, ıd by Padre Mariani, Rector of the University, a man of learning ıd abilities, as a proof of which he had been three years at Madrid . the character of secretary to the General of the Franciscans. I re-.ember a very eloquent expression of his, on the state of his country. Corsica," said he, "has for many years past been bleeding at all her :ins. They are now closed. But after being so severely exhausted, it ill take some time before she can recover perfect strength." I was so visited by Padre Leonardo, of whose animating discourse I have .ade mention in a former part of this book.[9]

Indeed I should not have been at a loss though my very reverend thers had been all my society. I was not in the least looked upon as heretic. Difference of faith was forgotten in hospitality. I went about ıe convent as if I had been in my own house, and the fathers without ıy impropriety of mirth were yet as cheerful as I could desire.

I had two surgeons to attend me at Corte, a Corsican and a Pied-ontese; and I got a little Jesuit's bark from the *spezeria* or apothe-.ry's shop of the Capuchin convent. I did not, however, expect to be fectually cured till I should get to Bastia. I found it was perfectly fe for me to go thither. There was a kind of truce between the Corsi-

The original of this letter has survived, and is dated 31 October, so Boswell obably left Sollacarò, ninety miles away, on the morning of 29 October. He ıs scheduled to depart on 27 October, according to a letter from Paoli to Mas-si which Professor Warnock has discovered in the Corsican archives in Ajaccio. ıe words in brackets translate a phrase in Massesi's letter which Boswell ıitted.

Padre Leonardo Grimaldi da Campoloro was professor of philosophy and math-ıatics at the University of Corte. See *Account*, p. 205.

cans and the French. Paoli had held two different amicable confe
ences with M. de Marbeuf, their Commander-in-Chief, and was s
well with him that he gave me a letter of recommendation to him.

On one of the days that my ague disturbed me least, I walke
from the convent to Corte purposely to write a letter to Mr. Samu
Johnson. I told my revered friend that from a kind of superstitio
agreeable in a certain degree to him as well as to myself, I had durin
my travels written to him from *loca sollennia*, places in some measu
sacred. That as I had written to him from the tomb of Melanchthon
sacred to learning and piety, I now wrote to him from the palace
Pascal Paoli, sacred to wisdom and liberty, knowing that howev
his political principles may have been represented, he had always
generous zeal for the common rights of humanity. I gave him a sketc
of the great things I had seen in Corsica, and promised him a mo
ample relation.[2]

Mr. Johnson was pleased with what I wrote here, for I received
Paris an answer from him which I keep as a valuable charter. "Whe
you return, you will return to an unaltered, and I hope unalterabl
friend. All that you have to fear from me is the vexation of disappoin
ing me. No man loves to frustrate expectations which have bee
formed in his favour; and the pleasure which I promise myself fro
your journals and remarks is so great that perhaps no degree of a
tention or discernment will be sufficient to afford it. Come hom
however, and take your chance. I long to see you and to hear yo
and hope that we shall not be so long separated again. Come hom
and expect such a welcome as is due to him whom a wise and nob
curiosity has led where perhaps no native of this country ever w
before."[3]

[1] Boswell decided that this letter was "at once too superstitious and too enthu
astic" and did not send it to Johnson until 1777 (see *Boswell on the Grand To*
*Germany and Switzerland*, 30 September 1764).

[2] The original has not been recovered, but Boswell describes it in *The Life*
*Johnson* (14 January 1766) as "full of generous enthusiasm." He continu
"After giving a sketch of what I had seen and heard in that island, it proceed
thus: 'I dare call this a spirited tour. I dare to challenge your approbation.' "

[3] Johnson's entire letter is published in *The Life of Johnson* (14 January 176
Boswell published this paragraph here without Johnson's permission, but Joh
son, though displeased, soon forgave him.

I at length set out for Bastia. I went the first night to Rostino, oping to have found there Signor Clemente de Paoli. But unluckily e had gone upon a visit to his daughter, so that I had not an oppor- unity of seeing this extraordinary personage of whom I have given ) full an account, for a great part of which I am indebted to Mr. urnaby.[4]

Next day I reached Vescovato, where I was received by Signor uttafoco, Colonel of the Royal Corsicans in the service of France, ith whom I passed some days.[5]

As various discourses have been held in Europe concerning an ıvitation given to M. Rousseau to come to Corsica, and as that affair as conducted by Signor Buttafoco, who showed me the whole cor- spondence between him and M. Rousseau, I am enabled to give a istinct account of it.

M. Rousseau, in his political treatise entitled *Du Contrat social*, as the following observation: "There is yet one country in Europe ıpable of legislation, and that is the island of Corsica. The valour ıd the constancy with which that brave people hath recovered and efended its liberty would well deserve that some wise man should ach them how to preserve it. I have some presentiment that one day ıat little island will astonish Europe."[6]

Signor Buttafoco, upon this, wrote to M. Rousseau, returning him

Clemente de Paoli, Pasquale's elder brother, was noted both for his extraordi- ıry religious zeal and his bravery in battle. Boswell's description of him in the *ccount of Corsica* (pp. 247–250) is taken from the unpublished journal of a ur to Corsica made in 1766 by the Rev. Andrew Burnaby, who lent a copy of s manuscript to Boswell for his use. This journal, supplemented by letters om Pasquale de Paoli to Burnaby, was published in 1804.

The first two editions of the *Journal* contain at this point some sentences in hich Buttafoco is highly praised. These were deleted in the third edition, and e following footnote added to that portion of Rousseau's letter (p. 115) hich mentions Buttafoco: "This man's plausibility imposed upon M. Rousseau ıd me. But he has shown himself to be mean and treacherous, having betrayed ısinca to the French, for which his memory will ever be infamous. They who e possessed of the former editions of this book are entreated to erase what I ıve said of him." In Buttafoco's defence, it must be pointed out that he had rved most of his life in the French army and believed in French control of ›rsica, so he can hardly be called a traitor.

Book 2, chapter 10.

thanks for the honour he had done to the Corsican nation, an
strongly inviting him to come over and be that wise man who shoul
illuminate their minds.

I was allowed to take a copy of the wild philosopher's answer t
this invitation; it is written with his usual eloquence. "It is supe
fluous, Sir, to endeavour to excite my zeal for the undertaking whic
you propose to me. The very idea of it elevates my soul and transpor
me. I should esteem the rest of my days very nobly, very virtuousl
and very happily employed. I should even think that I well redeeme
the inutility of many of my days that are past if I could render the
sad remains of any advantage to your brave countrymen; if by an
useful advice I could concur in the views of your worthy chief, an
in yours. So far then you may be sure of me. My life and my hea
are devoted to you."[7]

Such were the first effusions of Rousseau. Yet before he conclude
even this first letter, he made a great many complaints of his advers
ties and persecutions, and started a variety of difficulties as to th
proposed enterprise. The correspondence was kept up for some tim
but the enthusiasm of the paradoxical philosopher gradually sub
siding, the scheme came to nothing.

As I have formerly observed, M. de Voltaire thought proper t
exercise his pleasantry upon occasion of this proposal, in order to ve
the grave Rousseau, whom he never could bear.[8] I remember he use
to talk of him with a satirical smile, and call him "ce garçon"; I fin
this among my notes of M. de Voltaire's conversations when I wa
with him at his Château de Ferney, where he entertains with th
elegance rather of a real prince than of a poetical one.[9] To have Vo
taire's assertion contradicted by a letter under Paoli's own hand wa
no doubt a sufficient satisfaction to Rousseau.

From the account which I have attempted to give of the prese
constitution of Corsica and of its illustrious legislator and General,
may well be conceived that the scheme of bringing M. Rousseau in
that island was magnified to an extravagant degree by the reports

[7] This letter is printed in its entirety in the *Correspondance générale de J.-*
*Rousseau,* xi. 297–299, where most — perhaps all — of the letters that pass
between Rousseau and Buttafoco may be found.

[8] See p. 163.

[9] His notes of Voltaire's conversations, now at Yale, do not contain any refe
ences to Rousseau, but it is known that some pages are missing.

the Continent. It was said that Rousseau was to be made no less than a Solon by the Corsicans, who were implicitly to receive from him a code of laws.

This was by no means the scheme. Paoli was too able a man to submit the legislation of his country to one who was an entire stranger to the people, the manners, and in short to everything in the island. Nay, I know well that Paoli pays more regard to what has been tried by the experience of ages than to the most beautiful ideal systems. Besides, the Corsicans were not all at once to be moulded at will. They were to be gradually prepared, and by one law laying the foundation for another, a complete fabric of jurisprudence was to be formed.

Paoli's intention was to grant a generous asylum to Rousseau; to avail himself of the shining talents which appeared in his writings by consulting with him and catching the lights of his rich imagination, from many of which he might derive improvements to those plans which his own wisdom had laid down.

But what he had principally in view was to employ the pen of Rousseau in recording the heroic actions of the brave islanders. It is to be regretted that this project did not take place. The father of the present Colonel Buttafoco made large collections for many years back. These are carefully preserved, and when joined to those made by the Abbé Rostini would furnish ample materials for a history of Corsica. This, adorned with the genius of Rousseau, would have been one of the noblest monuments of modern times.[1]

[1] The whole question of Rousseau's relations with Buttafoco and Paoli is extraordinarily complicated. It is discussed in detail in Ernestine Dedeck-Héry, *Jean-Jacques Rousseau et le projet de constitution pour la Corse*, 1932, and in Joseph Foladare's unpublished dissertation, "James Boswell and Corsica" (Yale, 1936). Buttafoco, apparently without consulting Paoli, suggested to Rousseau that he become the legislator of Corsica. Rousseau was hesitant from the start, but eventually asked for shelter in Corsica, and in return offered to attempt a history of Corsica. Shortly thereafter, Rousseau changed his mind about going to Corsica — according to David Hume, at the insistence of Thérèse. Rousseau, in his *Confessions*, gives a number of reasons emphasizing the difficulties involved in making the trip. Paoli does not seem to have had any part in this proposal until after the original offer was made. Since with one possible exception no letter from him to Rousseau has survived, we cannot be sure what Paoli had in mind, but from Boswell's account (which he got mostly from Burnaby) it may perhaps be assumed that Paoli restricted himself to politely seconding Buttafoco's offer of hospitality.

Signor Buttafoco accompanied me to Bastia. It was comfortable to enter a good warm town after my fatigues. We went to the house of Signor Morelli, a counsellor-at-law here, with whom we supped. I was lodged for that night by a friend of Signor Buttafoco in another part of the town.

Next morning I waited on M. de Marbeuf. Signor Buttafoco introduced me to him, and I presented him the letter of recommendation from Paoli. He gave me a most polite reception. The brilliancy of his levee pleased me; it was a scene so different from those which I had been for some time accustomed to see. It was like passing at once from a rude and early age to a polished modern age, from the mountains of Corsica to the banks of the Seine.

My ague was now become so violent that it got the better of me altogether. I was obliged to ask the French General's permission to have a chair set for me in the circle. When M. de Marbeuf was informed of my being ill, he had the goodness to ask me to stay in his house till I should recover. "I insist upon it," said he; "I have a warm room for you. My servants will get you bouillons and everything proper for a sick man, and we have an excellent physician." I mention all these circumstances to show the goodness of M. de Marbeuf, to whom I shall ever consider myself as under great obligations. His invitation was given in so kind and cordial a manner that I willingly accepted of it.

I found M. de Marbeuf a worthy, open-hearted Frenchman. It is a common and a very just remark that one of the most agreeable characters in the world is a Frenchman who has served long in the army and has arrived at that age when the fire of youth is properly tempered. Such a character is gay without levity and judicious without severity. Such a character was the Count de Marbeuf, of an ancient family in Brittany, where there is more plainness of character than among the other French. He had been *gentilhomme de la chambre* to the worthy King Stanislas.[2]

He took a charge of me as if he had been my near relation. He

[2] Stanislas I was King of Poland (1704–1709, 1733–1735). His son-in-law, Louis XV, helped to restore him to the throne in 1733, but he was driven out by Augustus III of Saxony. Louis XV arranged that he be given the duchies of Lorraine and Bar in 1737, while Francis, Duke of Lorraine, received the Grand Duchy of Tuscany in exchange.

furnished me with books and everything he could think of to amuse me. While the physician ordered me to be kept very quiet, M. de Marbeuf would allow nobody to go near me, but paid me a friendly visit alone. As I grew better he gradually increased my society, bringing with him more and more of his officers; so that I had at last the honour of very large companies in my apartment. The officers were polite, agreeable men; some of them had been prisoners in England during the last war. One of them was a Chevalier de St. Louis of the name of Douglas, a descendant of the illustrious house of Douglas in Scotland by a branch settled near to Lyons. This gentleman often came and sat with me. The idea of our being in some sort countrymen was pleasing to us both.

I found here an Englishwoman of Penrith in Cumberland. When the Highlanders marched through that country in the year of 1745, she had married a soldier of the French picquets in the very midst of all the confusion and danger, and when she could hardly understand one word he said. Such freaks will love sometimes take.

> Sic visum Veneri, cui placet inpares
> Formas atque animos sub iuga aenea
> Saevo mittere cum ioco.[3]

M. de La Chapelle was the physician who attended me. He had been several years physician to the army at Minorca, and had now the same office in Corsica. I called him the physician of the isles. He was indeed an excellent one. That *gaieté de cœur* which the French enjoy runs through all their professions. I remember the phrase of an English common soldier who told me that at the Battle of Fontenoy his captain received a shot in the breast "and fell," said the soldier, "with his spontoon in his hand, as prettily killed as ever I see'd a gentleman." The soldier's phrase might be used in talking of almost everything which the French do. I may say I was prettily cured by M. de La Chapelle.

[3] Horace, *Odes,* I. xxxiii. 10–12:

> So Venus wills, whose power controls
> The fond affection of our souls;
> With sportive cruelty she binds
> Unequal forms, unequal minds.
> Philip Francis.

But I think myself bound to relate a circumstance which shows him and his nation in the genteelest light. Though he attended me with the greatest assiduity, yet, when I was going away, he would not accept of a single louis d'or. "No, Sir," said he, "I am nobly paid by my King. I am physician to his army here. If I can at the same time be of service to the people of the country or to any gentleman who may come among us, I am happy. But I must be excused from taking money." M. Brion, the surgeon-major, behaved in the same manner.

As soon as I had gathered a little strength, I walked about as well as I could, and saw what was to be seen at Bastia. Signor Morelli was remarkably obliging. He made me presents of books and antiques, and of every other curiosity relating to Corsica. I never saw a more generous man. Signor Caraffa, a Corsican officer in the service of France, with the order of St. Louis, was also very obliging. Having made a longer stay in Corsica than I intended, my finances were exhausted, and he let me have as much money as I pleased. M. Barlet, secretary to M. de Marbeuf, was also very obliging. In short, I know not how to express my thankfulness to all the good people whom I saw at Bastia.

The French seemed to agree very well with the Corsicans. Of old those islanders were much indebted to the interposition of France in their favour. But since the days of Sampiero, there have been many variances between them. A singular one happened in the reign of Louis XIV. The Pope's Corsican guards in some fit of passion insulted the French Ambassador at Rome. The superb monarch resolved to revenge this outrage. But Pope Alexander VII, foreseeing the consequences, agreed to the conditions required by France, which were that the Corsican guards should be obliged to depart the Ecclesiastical State, that the nation should be declared incapable ever to serve the Holy See, and that opposite to their ancient guardhouse should be erected a pyramid inscribed with their disgrace.

Le Brun, whose royal genius could magnify and enrich every circumstance in honour of his sovereign, has given this story as a *médaillon* on one of the compartments of the great gallery at Versailles. France appears with a stately air, showing to Rome the design of the pyramid; and Rome, though bearing a shield marked S.P.Q.R., receives the design with most submissive humility.

I wish that France had never done the Corsicans greater harm than depriving them of the honour of being the Pope's guards. Boissieux and Maillebois cannot easily be forgotten;[4] nor can the brave islanders be blamed for complaining that a powerful nation should interpose to retard their obtaining entire possession of their country and of undisturbed freedom.

M. de Marbeuf appeared to conduct himself with the greatest prudence and moderation. He told me that he wished to preserve peace in Corsica. He had entered into a convention with Paoli mutually to give up such criminals as should fly into each other's territories. Formerly not one criminal in a hundred was punished. There was no communication between the Corsicans and the Genoese, and if a criminal could but escape from the one jurisdiction to the other he was safe. This was very easily done, so that crimes from impunity were very frequent. By this equitable convention justice has been fully administered.

Perhaps indeed the residence of the French in Corsica has, upon the whole, been an advantage to the patriots. There have been markets twice a week at the frontiers of each garrison town, where the Corsican peasants have sold all sorts of provisions and brought in a good many French crowns which have been melted down into Corsican money. A cessation of arms for a few years has been a breathing time to the nation to prepare itself for one great effort, which will probably end in the total expulsion of the Genoese. A little leisure has been given for attending to civil improvements, towards which the example of the French has in no small degree contributed. Many of the soldiers were excellent handicraftsmen, and could instruct the natives in various arts.

M. de Marbeuf entertained himself by laying out several elegant pieces of pleasure-ground; and such were the humane and amicable dispositions of this respectable officer that he was at pains to observe what things were most wanted in Corsica, and then imported them from France in order to show an example to the inhabitants. He introduced in particular the culture of potatoes, of which there were none in the island upon his arrival. This root will be of considerable

[4] The Comte de Boissieux and the Marquis de Maillebois were the two French generals responsible for subduing Corsica for the Genoese in 1738–1740.

service to the Corsicans; it will make a wholesome variety in their food, and as there will thereby of consequence be less home consumption of chestnuts, they will be able to export a greater quantity of them.

M. de Marbeuf made merry upon the reports which had been circulated that I was no less than a minister from the British Court. The Avignon *Gazette* brought us one day information that the English were going to establish *un bureau de commerce* in Corsica. "O Sir," said he, "the secret is out. I see now the motive of your destination to these parts. It is you who are to establish this *bureau de commerce*."

Idle as these rumours were, it is a fact that when I was at Genoa, Signor Gherardi, one of their secretaries of state, very seriously told me, "Sir, you have made me tremble, although I never saw you before." And when I smiled and assured him that I was just a simple traveller, he shook his head, but said he had very authentic information concerning me. He then told me with great gravity, "That while I travelled in Corsica, I was dressed in scarlet and gold, but when I paid my respects to the Supreme Council at Corte, I appeared in a full suit of black." These important truths I fairly owned to him, and he seemed to exult over me.

I was more and more obliged to M. de Marbeuf. When I was allowed by my physician to go to his Excellency's table, where we had always a large company and everything in great magnificence, he was so careful of me that he would not suffer me to eat anything or taste a glass of wine more than was prescribed for me. He used to say, "I am here both physician and Commander-in-Chief, so you must submit." He very politely pressed me to make some stay with him, saying, "We have taken care of you when sick; I think we have a claim to you for a while when in health." His kindness followed me after I left him. It procured me an agreeable reception from M. Michel, the French *chargé d'affaires* at Genoa, and was the occasion of my being honoured with great civilities at Paris by M. l'Abbé de Marbeuf, *conseiller d'état*, brother of the Count, and possessing similar virtues in private life.

I quitted Corsica with reluctance when I thought of the illustrious Paoli. I wrote to him from Bastia informing him of my illness, which I said was owing to his having made a man of so much consequence that instead of putting me into a snug little room, he had lodged me in the magnificent old palace where the wind and rain entered.

His answer to my first letter is written with so much spirit that I begged his permission to publish it, which he granted in the genteelest manner, saying, "I do not remember the contents of the letter, but I have such a confidence in Mr. Boswell that I am sure he would not publish it if there was anything in it improper for public view; so he has my permission." I am thus enabled to present my readers with an original letter from Paoli.[5]

Patrimonio, 23 December 1765

MUCH ESTEEMED MR. BOSWELL, — I received the letter which you wrote to me from Bastia, and am much comforted by hearing that you are restored to perfect health. It is lucky for you that you fell into the hands of an able physician. When you shall again be seized with a disgust at improved and agreeable countries, and shall return to this ill-fated land, I will take care to have you lodged in warmer and better-finished apartments than those of the house of Colonna at Sollacarò. But you again should be satisfied not to travel when the weather and the season require one to keep within doors, and wait for a fair day. I expect with impatience the letter which you promised to write to me from Genoa, where I much suspect that the delicacy of the ladies will have obliged you to perform some days of quarantine for purifying you from every the least infection which you may have carried with you from the air of this country; and still more so, if you have taken the whim to show that suit of Corsican velvet[6] and that bonnet of which the Corsicans will have the origin to be from the ancient helmets, whereas the Genoese say it was invented by those who rob on the highway in order to disguise themselves — as if during the Genoese government public robbers needed to fear punishment. I am sure, however, that you will have taken the proper method with these amiable and delicate persons, insinuating to them that the hearts of beauties are formed for compassion and not for disdain and tyranny, and so you will have been easily restored to their good graces.

Immediately on my return to Corte, I received information of the

[5] Original in Italian. The translation is by Boswell.

[6] By Corsican velvet he means that coarse stuff made in the island, which is all that the Corsicans have instead of the fine velvet of Genoa. — BOSWELL.

secret landing of Abbatucci,[7] on the coast of Solenzara. All appearances make us believe that he is come with designs contrary to the public quiet. He has, however, surrendered himself a prisoner at the Castle, and protests his repentance. As I passed by Bocognano, I learned that a disbanded Genoese officer was seeking associates to assassinate me. He could not succeed, and finding that he was discovered, he betook himself to the woods where he has been slain by the party detached by the magistrates of the provinces on the other side of the mountains in order to intercept him. These ambuscades do not seem to be good preliminaries towards our accommodation with the Republic of Genoa. I am now holding the sindacato in this province of Nebbio. About the 10th of next month I shall go for the same object into the province of Capo Corso, and during the month of February I shall probably fix my residence in Balagna. I shall return to Corte in the spring to prepare myself for the opening of the General Consulta. Wherever I am, your friendship will be present to my mind, and I shall be desirous to continue a correspondence with you. Meanwhile, believe me to be your most affectionate friend,

PASCAL PAOLI.

Can anything be more condescending and at the same time show more the firmness of an heroic mind than this letter? With what a gallant pleasantry does the Corsican chief talk of his enemies! One would think that the queens of Genoa should become Rival Queens for Paoli. If they saw him, I am sure they would.

I take the liberty to repeat an observation made to me by that illustrious minister whom Paoli calls the Pericles of Great Britain:[8] "It may be said of Paoli, as the Cardinal de Retz said of the great Montrose, 'He is one of those men who are no longer to be found but in the *Lives* of Plutarch.' "

[7] Abbatucci, a Corsican of a very suspicious character. — BOSWELL. Giacomo Pietro Abbatucci opposed Paoli, but later fought with him against France, and resisted even after Paoli's departure. After the French victory he joined the French army, and eventually was general of a division in Italy under Napoleon, who said he was not fit to command fifty men.

[8] William Pitt, Earl of Chatham.

# THE VOYAGE HOME

*1765–1766*

# *The Voyage Home, 1765–1766*

THE VOYAGE HOME. Many years after the completion of his grand tour, Boswell remarked to Paoli that it was wonderful what Corsica had done for him: "I had got upon a rock in Corsica, and jumped into the middle of life."[1] This remark epitomizes what every student of Boswell knows, that his experiences in Corsica affected him in a profound and vital manner, and that they were a turning-point in his life. Paoli's acceptance of him gave him confidence and a cause, and the success of *Corsica* identified him as "Corsica Boswell" throughout his life.

Yet changes of character take time to manifest themselves, and the Boswell who sailed and walked and rode back to England was not much different superficially from the Boswell who, like Hannibal anticipating conquest, had crossed into Italy a year before. On the road to Paris domestic Boswell was to the fore: he was variously tortured by ingrown toe-nails; by Jachone, the mastiff given him by Paoli; and by Jacob, his Swiss servant. The last of these trials he saw depart at Lyons with some relief; to his own annoyance, Boswell had never really absorbed the convention that masters have places as well as servants, and Jacob in his republican obstinacy returned with persistence to this point. Gentlemen who are gentlemen, he informed Boswell, are not stingy, behave in a dignified manner, and do not converse in a familiar fashion with their servants. From Jachone, whom he seems to have disliked from the start, Boswell apparently expected the responses of a human. When the dog failed to exhibit supernatural intelligence, he treated him with a cruelty that was probably not uncommon in his age, but which he later found so excessive that he inked out its details, one of the relatively few expurgations which he himself ever made in his journal. It is hardly surprising that

[1] *Boswelliana*, ed. Charles Rogers, 1874, p. 328.

Jachone ran away near Auxerre. The ingrown toe-nails, which were probably acquired by walking along the mountainous trails of Corsica in riding-boots, slowed his progress and recurred to trouble him in later years.

Once in Paris, his interest in Zélide, the belle of his Dutch student days, revived with great intensity, and he forwarded a very tentative proposal to her through her father with the intention of following the matter up by returning home through Flanders and Holland.[2] But one day on a visit to Wilkes, of whom he saw a great deal in Paris, he read in a London newspaper that his mother had died, and he prepared instead to set out directly for England and home. His companion on the trip was Thérèse Le Vasseur, who was following Rousseau to London; the story of their relationship is a fitting flourish to the end of his tour.

Boswell's revaluation of people in London demonstrates his development during the two and a half years he had spent on the Continent. The apprehensive boy to whom Johnson had waved good-bye at Harwich returned a man of poise and some consequence. He had acquired a knowledge of the world and men that reduced his heroes to more normal proportions: Rousseau had diminished in his eyes, and even Johnson momentarily appeared "not so immense as before." After having known Paoli, as Boswell wrote in *Corsica*, "I was, for the rest of my life, set free from a slavish timidity in the presence of great men, for where shall I find a man greater?" These brave words contained a substantial if not complete truth. Yet if Corsica was the central factor in his new attitude towards himself and others, his journey as a whole had contributed to this change. It had been not only a tour of Europe but an exploration of his own capacities, and he was gratified at their extent. The great conversations with Johnson and especially with Pitt at the end of this volume show that, with due allowance for differences in ability and rank, Boswell now felt himself any man's equal.

---

[2] Boswell's letter and M. de Zuylen's reply are printed in *Boswell in Holland*, Correspondence, Nos. 19, 20.

[EDITORIAL NOTE: Boswell set sail for Genoa and home on 20 November, but his ship was immediately forced by violent contrary winds to take harbour at the small, rocky island of Capraja, about eighteen miles east of the northern tip of Corsica. During the six days that he was detained there, he lodged in a friary of Franciscans, who obligingly took him in after he had declined the "one inconvenient bed" that the inn in the village afforded. The fathers he found "hospitable without cunning," a "new race of men," but very simple, so much so that the Father Superior professed himself unable to understand the Rousseauistic "universal creed" that Boswell expounded to him. Apart from their simplicity and kindness, he was chiefly impressed by the extreme frugality of their living, which stood out even on this almost soilless rock where everybody was poor. To keep off the ennui, he wrote a minute account of the island, picking up his information with as much care, he said, as he would have if he had been treating of an empire. Even so, he was not able to preserve serenity. He argued hotly with the fathers in favour of the Corsicans (Capraja was entirely controlled by the Genoese), and wrangled with Jacob, who had scolded him for being so stingy. He finally worked himself up to a magnificent outburst. Two Genoese officers, marooned like himself in Capraja, had promised him a place in their felucca. The master, one Ruggero Semedei, after various postponements, announced that they must all come aboard on the night of the 27th, and that he would sail when the moon rose. "Evening took leave of good convent, and thought how soon one is accustomed to a place. Ruggero sent he did not go till four. Down you went in fury — called him to land — trembled with passion. BOSWELL. 'You stupid bugger, I won't be ballocksed around any more. I want absolutely to leave this evening. I'll write to M. de Marbeuf. Damn! If it wasn't a sin to tie a man in a sack and drown him, I'd do it to you this instant!' "[3] He then went aboard — and in five minutes was so sick he had to beat a retreat to the guardroom on shore. The wind changed at four, as Ruggero had predicted, and Boswell, retching and terrified ("Vastly sick; afraid too when sails lashed sea"), finally escaped from Capraja.]

[3] The unusual coarseness of Boswell's invective is due to the fact that he is speaking Italian: "Bestia bugerone! Non voglio esser più coglionato; voglio partire assolutamente questa sera. Io scriverò a M. de Marbeuf. Cospetto! Si non fosse un peccato di mazzare un uomo, vi mazzarei in questo momento!"

SATURDAY 30 NOVEMBER. At two in morning, with clear moon, saw noble gulf fit for —— ships of war. Pretty good wind; coasted away. Still sick. Four last hours on deck. Saw views from river:[4] villages extending, then Genoa, most delicious show. Land, overjoyed. To inn. Sent to consul and bankers. Letters: Father, ill, seriously recalling [you]. Hipped with old ideas. [From] Dick, kind; Signora, all love. What variety! Dined with immense pleasure.

[Lord Auchinleck to Boswell][5]

Edinburgh, 10 August 1765

MY DEAR SON, — I received a letter from you dated from Rome the 4th of June, and your mother received another from the same place dated the 12th of that month; and these are the last letters we have had from you. This is really an inexcusable neglect. For after I had condescended to allow you to travel a little longer in Italy to attend Lord Mountstuart, you must be sensible it was highly proper to inform me of your progress and intended route, not only to give me a reasonable satisfaction, but also to let me know what — and where — credit I should order for you. And what adds to the fault is that I got communicated to me this day a letter from Herries & Cochrane at London, to Coutts & Company here, acquainting that they had got a letter from you dated from Venice, the 17 of July, in which you wrote to them that, besides the £100 from Rome, you had drawn for £60 from Venice, and desired them to send you a credit upon Lyons and upon Paris. And as these gentlemen, you might be sure, would furnish no credit without my ordering it, and have wrote to Coutts & Company here to know what my directions are, by this strange conduct of yours I am not in condition to say anything with judgment for want of information. This much I can say, that you have spent a

[4] Along the east coast or littoral, translating Italian *la riviera di Genoa.*

[5] Three letters from Lord Auchinleck, recalling his son to Scotland, form, with their hard Northern irony, a perfect contrast to Boswell's essays in Italian warmth. They require no introduction and tell their own story; being at once classic examples in the paternal style — any father to any son — and replete with individual comedy. No documents in the collection shed a clearer light on that contrariety between the pair which is an essential element in Boswell's biography. — GEOFFREY SCOTT.

vast deal of money, for since you left Geneva in January last you have got no less than £460 sterling, which is much beyond what my income can afford, and much beyond what the sons of gentlemen near double my estate have spent on such a tour; and that makes it quite necessary now to put an end to peregrination. You have had full opportunity to be satisfied that pageantry, civil and ecclesiastic, gives no entertainment to thinking men, and that there is no end nor use of strolling through the world to see sights before unseen, whether of men, beasts, birds, or things, and I hope are, with the poet, saying "Utinam remeare liceret ad veteres casas,"[6] and will return with a proper taste and relish for your own country. For if that were not to be your disposition, I should most heartily repent that ever I agreed to your going abroad, and shall consider the money spent in the tour you have made as much worse than thrown away. But I choose to banish all such gloomy suspicions, and hope to my infinite satisfaction to see you on your return a man of knowledge, of gravity and modesty, intent upon being useful in life. If this be so, your travelling will be a little embellishment to the more essential talents, and enable you to make a better figure in your own country, which is the scene of action Providence has pointed out for you.

And now to return to what route you are now to follow. I said I was quite at a loss how to write. I don't know whether you are still with Lord Mountstuart or not; I have been informed that Lord was to come straight home from Italy. If so, I think you should return with him. If, again, his Lordship is to make a tour through France, you must make your excuse to him and come off by yourself. There is nothing to be learned by travelling in France. I can say this from my own experience. So what I propose and insist on is that you come directly from Lyons to Paris, which as the metropolis of France is worth while to say you have seen, and which you may see fully in three or four days; and you should see Versailles, Marly, and Trianon — the King's three palaces — all very near Paris, which won't take up above three or four days more. In short, stay at Paris and the environs of it ten days or a fortnight at farthest, and then set out for Calais and so come over to London, from which, after staying eight or

[6] "I wish I could go back to the old dwelling" (Claudian, *De bello Gildonico*, ll. 108–109, *casas* for *fines*).

ten days, set out for Scotland. This is the plan which I propose and expect is to be exactly followed with all expedition; and in order to it, as you have yet £40 remaining of your last credit on Italy, that should do well, with that you'll have of your £60, to execute it; but lest you should run short, I have ordered a credit for you on Lyons for £50. And when you come to London, you shall have a credit there for answering your expenses home, where I long to see you, and where, as I hope, you are to set up on a decent, sensible footing. I dare say you shall be very happy, and may expect all encouragement that I can give you.

On Monday comes on the trial of Mrs. Ogilvy and Lieutenant Ogilvy for incest and poisoning her husband, his brother, of which I wrote you in my last. I suppose it will last thirty or forty hours.

Your mother and David are both well and remember you with affection. We propose to set out for Auchinleck on Wednesday first; there's a good deal of new work carried on there since you left us. I have some little buildings to make for some kind of offices near the house, and have got home a good many stones for them, but you shall assist in fixing the plan and situation of them, so will have an opportunity of showing your Italian taste; for, though the buildings are small, *ex ungue leonem*.[7] If you still are with Lord Mountstuart, present my most respectful compliments to his Lordship and Colonel Edmondstone.

Edinburgh, 14 August 1765

What is above was wrote on Saturday, but delayed to be sent off in expectation yet of a letter from you, but there is none. The trial I mentioned came on Monday at seven in the morning and did not end till this morning at one o'clock. The jury by a great plurality of voices found the panels guilty both of the incest and of the murder by poison, which they returned as their verdict to us this afternoon.

Edinburgh, 15 August

This day we resumed the consideration of this melancholy affair and repelled sundry pleas for arrest of judgment, and thereafter adjudged the Lieutenant to be hanged the 25 of September and his body to be delivered to the surgeons to be anatomized. This we preferred to

[7] "From the claw of a lion one can imagine what the whole beast would look like."

the hanging in chains, as we wished to have no memorial of such shocking crimes. Mrs. Ogilvy pleaded she is with child, so a jury of midwives is to examine and report tomorrow, and if it is true, we shall delay sentence till November.[8] I have only to add that I hope we shall have the pleasure of meeting soon. I am your affectionate father,

ALEXR. BOSWEL.[9]

[Lord Auchinleck to Boswell]

Glasgow, 16 September 1765

MY DEAR SON, — I have received yours from Parma, which surprised me greatly, for I expected you had got to Paris, and would be home directly; and never imagined that you would have been returning to places where you had formerly been. It is no great wonder therefore that you have received none of my letters these several months; for though I wrote severals[1] and sent them off, I could not divine where to find you, so left it to Herries, Cochrane & Company, bankers, and it seems they have been equally uncertain with me. I

[8] This was one of the most notorious Scots trials of the century. Katharine Nairn, nineteen-year-old daughter of Sir Thomas Nairn of Dunsinane, married on 30 January 1765 Thomas Ogilvy, the laird of Eastmiln, a bachelor of forty. According to the verdict of the jury (which appears to have been quite just) she began almost immediately a guilty intrigue with the laird's younger brother, Patrick, an officer on half-pay, and in the following June, with Patrick's connivance, poisoned her husband with arsenic. Patrick was hanged in a bungling but effective manner on 13 November. Mrs. Ogilvy having proved pregnancy, her sentence was deferred to the following March, but on 15 March (about two weeks after the birth of a daughter, who died within the month) she escaped from the Tolbooth and got to France. It was generally believed that her escape was arranged by her uncle, William Nairn, advocate, later Sir William and a judge in the very court whose sentence he helped to cheat. For a full and authoritative account of the Ogilvy case see *The Trial of Katharine Nairn*, ed. William Roughead, 1926. — During the examination of the principal witness for the prosecution in this trial, Lord Auchinleck sat nine hours without rising from his seat. This was believed to have brought on the serious ailment which he reports in his next letter, and from which he suffered all the rest of his life.

[9] "Boswel" was Lord Auchinleck's spelling of his own name. James followed the general practice of his family in using two l's.

[1] Obsolete for "a number."

have some hopes, however, that the last I wrote you would come to your hand, as it was sent to them in consequence of a letter they wrote transmitting one from you to them desiring a further credit, and inquiring if or not I would agree to give the further credit. In that letter I let you know I had ordered a small credit for bringing you to London by the way of Paris, and that you were to make dispatch and spend but about a fortnight at Paris and its environs, which is sufficient for all the purpose.

Since that letter, I came to Auchinleck, where I was taken dangerously ill and was a' death's door; indeed, for a day or two I expected every hour would have been my last. My distemper was a total suppression or obstruction of urine. At length by the assistance of Mr. Parlane, a surgeon of this place, I got the water drawn off. He stayed with me there about eight days but could not stay longer, and therefore as the operation required to be repeated twice a day, I came in with him here eight days ago. I bless God that I enjoy now a great deal of ease except during the operation; but as the distemper remains, God only knows what may be the event. This my state, I should think, will make you incline to accelerate your return; because I hope you have impressions of filial duty, besides knowing of what consequence it is to you in after life that I, before I die, come to be satisfied, from what I see of your conduct, that you are become a man such as I and your other friends could wish you to be.[2]

Your mother, who is here with me, is troubled with rheumatisms. She remembers you with affection. David is well. I had a letter from him since I came here. He is careful and I hope will do well. As for John,[3] he is still in England, full of pride and ill nature, and disposed to follow no sort of business that he is capable for, so to be an idle load upon the earth and discontented with the station, place, and people that he happens to be in and with; which is the necessary consequence of having no business nor settled way of employing time. I am your affectionate father,

ALEXR. BOSWEL.

[2] Lord Auchinleck talked of disinheriting Boswell, but he actually did not have the power to do so, since his marriage contract had settled the estate on his eldest son (see *Boswell's London Journal*, Introduction).

[3] Lord Auchinleck's second son. He had been injured by a fall on a flight of stairs in 1762, and suffered periodically from insanity for the rest of his life.

[Lord Auchinleck to Boswell]

Edinburgh, 1 October 1765

Dear Son, — Your conduct astonishes and amazes me. You solicited liberty to go for four months to Italy. I opposed it as altogether useless; but upon your pressing importunity, contrary to my own opinion, I agreed to it, and thereafter allowed you one month more. You went there January last. Upon your writing that Lord Mountstuart was anxious you should stay some time with him in Italy, and upon his Lordship's desiring that I might agree to it, by a letter to Baron Mure, as you noticed the advantages might attend a friendship with that Lord and the benefit of having Colonel Edmondstone and M. Mallet's counsel, I agreed readily to the thing. But when I heard of Lord Mountstuart's coming over, how surprised was I that you had not come along with him, but stayed in a country where you had nothing to do, and where all you could learn could be of no use in after life. I flattered myself, however, you would haste away, take a passing view of France, and be home about this time or before it. I have wrote letters on the back of letters to you, telling you to come home. Whether any of them have reached you I cannot say. It is possible not, for one thing is most extraordinary in your conduct; you give me no notice where you will be when any letter I can write may reach you, but leave me to guess. I have this day got a letter of yours which had the London postmark on it, so that I hoped you had got there. But when I came to open it, I found it was from Siena; and you tell me you were to stay there three weeks or a month, and this in order, as you write, to learn the Italian language. As you don't say where you are to go after this, or what your scheme is, I must suppose you intend fixing in Italy, where that language can only be of use to you; for in this country it is no better than Arabic. If you have any view of returning home, I desire, as I did in my former letters, you may do so speedily; that you don't stop in France, except about ten days or a fortnight about Paris and its environs, that you may say you have been there, which is all the benefit travellers have over others. I wrote in my last I have been, and still am, under great distress with a stoppage of urine, that has forced us to come in to Edinburgh for the aid of physicians. Your mother, who is equally astonished at your conduct with me, remembers you. So does your brother David; which is all from your affectionate father,

A.B.[4]

[Girolama Piccolomini to Boswell. Original in Italian]

Siena, 3 October 1765

I WAITED AND WAITED for the hour and the moment of the arrival of the mail from Lucca, expecting your dear letter.[5] I had it at last, and in transports of joy I printed a thousand k——s on it without knowing its contents. Then I sat down to read it; and as I read the first pages I thought you felt a little of the love I feel for you. But the page written on Monday shows no more than that you feel friendship for me, since you tell me you have enjoyed peace of mind and have slept well at night. Happy you who can make such changes so readily; I prove the contrary only too well. I have not had a moment of peace since you left Siena. I try to assume an air of ease, and I feel all the burden of having to compel myself; I give way to melancholy, and I realize the necessity of arousing myself from this state. I read your letter over and over, and I find in it sentiments which a man in love would not utter; I think of how you wanted to deceive me, and it horrifies me. I remember that you left me in the depths of despair

[4] Lord Auchinleck's attitude towards Continental jaunts seems much the same as that expressed in Burns's "The Twa Dogs," where the laird goes off

> To mak a tour an' tak a whirl,
> To learn *bon ton*, an' see the worl'.
>
> There, at Vienna or Versailles,
> He rives his father's auld entails;
> Or by Madrid he taks the rout,
> To thrum guitars an' fecht wi' nowt; [fight with cattle]
> Or down Italian vista startles,
> Whore-hunting amang groves o' myrtles.
> Then bowses drumlie German-water [drinks muddy]
> To mak himsel look fair an' fatter,
> An' clear the consequential sorrows,
> Love-gifts of Carnival signoras.

[5] This letter is missing, as are all the subsequent letters except one from Boswell to Moma. He may have been moved by prudence to make no copies. In his Register of Letters, she is listed simply as "Signora ——."

without being willing to promise that you would return; I flattered myself that I had won your heart at the moment when I was losing it.

All these considerations leave me not a moment of calm, and your mind is at rest? Does my condition give you no uneasiness? You slept well Monday night? Perhaps at this very moment some other woman is making an impression on your heart? And you call that philosophy?

I shall answer in particular certain points in your letter. You tell me that your constitutional melancholy is subject to fluctuations, to which I reply that a melancholy nature when it has truly been impressed, is not as likely to be impressed again so easily as is a cheerful temperament which wastes itself in every trifle. I say rather that you are inconstant, and are carried away by novel objects; but do not attribute this weakness to a melancholy temperament which is by its very nature steady and firm in all its resolutions.

Let us turn to another of your statements: that the frankness with which you tell me everything ought to convince me that you are telling the truth. But do you not remember having told me many times that in order to deceive well one must show a certain ingenuousness? And how did you behave with me for two weeks?

At another point of your letter, you exclaim, "Happy night." What did you mean? For my part, since your departure I have been happy neither by night nor day, and what is worse, I despair of ever being able to recover my peace of mind, for your memory will always be before me, and the knowledge of how lovable you are will make me look with disdain on others, seeing them much inferior to you — in good qualities as in bad.

As to what Signor Muzio told you about Bino and Placido, I am not at all surprised, since they are two young men who are attentive to me, and the whole town must believe that there is gallantry between us. I am only surprised that *you* can doubt my truthfulness; ask for whatever evidence you please on this point and I will do all I can to convince you of the truth, but do not do me the injustice of believing that I am a hypocrite, and of judging my conduct by your own.

You advise me to rest during the day on the sofa, in the dark, but this is the one thing in which I cannot obey you. I try to avoid those places where I have been with you in order to escape gloomy ideas, for there is no greater sorrow than to remember happiness in a time of misery.[6] So forgive me if I do not do as you ask.

My health holds up, and is sufficient to combat the turmoil in my soul. At night I follow the usual round. I play *tressetti*,[7] and the remaining time seems very long to me. Days I pass alone, and I am spending today in writing to you. Mornings all the abbés are here; they generally play *tressetti*, with Pietro, Tiburzio, and Tono. Auditor Arrighi comes very often. — I would not tell you about these little trifles if you had not asked me to tell you everything. Your asking it makes me believe that you are enough my friend to be interested in everything concerning me; and writing to you is like talking to my most faithful bosom friend. At the moment, I can give you no more news about myself. You are my sweetest and entire occupation, the sole good that I desire; I am indifferent to everything else, and if I reach out for anything, it is only for a distraction necessary to remain alive.

I dare not say what passion I feel for you, and how dear you are to me, and how much I fear you do not love me in return. O God, that doubt harrows me! And a word from you that my doubts are justified would reduce me to utter despair.

Tell me frankly whether you clearly understand this letter, and the one I wrote to you while you were at Lucca.[8] I understand your letter wonderfully; and if it is practice for you to write in Italian, do it by all means, though for other reasons it might be better to write in French. Letters can be lost, and if they were in French it would not be so easy to read them. But the important thing is to write to me often and tell me exactly what you do and everything you do. I shall never fail to keep you informed of what is happening to me, not merely for your sake, but also to console myself with the pleasure of writing. Dearest, continue to be my friend. I deserve it.

[6] "Non vi è maggior dolore che ricordarsi delle felicità in tempo di miserie." Moma has reworded Francesca's touching remark in the *Divine Comedy* (I. v. 121–123).

[7] A Tuscan card game, still current.

[8] This earlier letter to Boswell has not survived, and perhaps never reached him.

If I have no letter from you by Monday, I shall not write again, because I do not know how long you plan to stay at Leghorn. Therefore always tell me where I am to direct my letters so that they may not fall into the wrong hands. Remember that I am yours with all my heart.

There are two Germans here at Siena. Charlottina has a high fever, which is believed to be smallpox. Good-bye. I long for you.

[Girolama Piccolomini to Boswell. Original in Italian]

Siena, 7 October 1765

IN MY LETTER TO YOU of last Friday,[9] which I addressed to Leghorn, I told you that I was not going to write to you this morning unless I had first received a letter from you telling me how long you were to stay in Leghorn, and where I should direct my letters. But I flattered myself that this morning I would certainly have found word from you at the post-office — a single line might have been enough to calm my anxiety. After such neglect, I ought to persuade myself that twenty years from now I shall still be receiving letters from you? And you had the effrontery to assure me of that? And you said that I should grow satisfied with you, because your continued friendship would have indemnified me for all my sufferings? I must say that I am experiencing the effects of all that friendship you told me about. If you were good-hearted, you would not leave me in this uncertainty. But what a thought — that you might have a heart! As though I could not recall all the jealousy you caused me to suffer when you were here — and if I complained about it then, face to face, I could obtain no satisfaction. And now you are far away should I think of you as faithful, and eager to calm the violence of my passion? Should I weigh my feelings against your cruelty, and give you credit for any part of them you are not responsible for, since the name of Boswell and inconstancy are one and the same thing? Continue on this system, and I shall be convinced at last that a constant though disagreeable man is worth more than one who is inconstant and lovable.

[9] 3 October was a Thursday, but Moma's long letter may well have been written partly on the next day.

I do not know whether this letter will reach you, so I dare not tell you the details of my misery. Even if you find it at the Leghorn post-office, where I am directing it, I do not know how it will be received by a man who knows nothing of real passion, who at this very moment is laughing at me with some coquette or other, with women who are scheming to increase their triumphs at my expense. Ah, if they knew you better they would not be proud of their conquest, but would see their ruin as I see mine. Let me know, for my peace of mind, if you have received one letter at Lucca and two at Leghorn, including this one.

Bianconi arrived Saturday, to place two little girls at the convent, and he will stay here for the whole month, I believe. I sometimes see him but he is not much pleased with me, as he found me very melancholy, and because I receive him very seldom.

Have a good time, and do not be afflicted by remorse for having brought unhappiness to a woman who did not deserve it.

Charlottina has a very mild case of smallpox, and her mother is well.

Write me a line only, but tell me whether you sympathize with my wretchedness, and then go visit the barbarians, which is just the right place for you. In spite of your treatment of me, it distressed me that you are undertaking this voyage.[1]

I forgot to tell you that you can spare yourself the trouble of writing ostensible letters, for I have announced freely that I have received a letter from you. So write rather with complete intimacy, since it is unnecessary to show any letter.

Tell me whether women's silk stockings can be had in Leghorn, and at what shop.

Remember me, for I am truly unhappy, and remind yourself in the midst of your diversions that you have left one who loves you in a deplorable state. If I find no consolation in what you write, my condition is irremediable. I cannot live in this manner.

[1] The following paragraphs, which are on a separate piece of paper, may belong to this letter.

[Girolama Piccolomini to Boswell. Original in Italian]

Siena, 21 October 1765

AFTER HAVING CONDEMNED YOU A THOUSAND TIMES because I had received only one letter, and because I knew you had written one to Porzia in which you offered to come back to Siena if she would have pity on you — in that turmoil of spirit I finally received your dear, dear letter[2] telling me that you have not received mine. I cannot understand how such a thing can have happened, for I wrote three letters, one of which you should have received at Lucca at the same time that I received yours, and the other two at Leghorn, at the address you gave me.

After these, I dared not write anywhere else because I did not know whether you welcomed them, or whether you might not have left for Corsica. Do inquire about these letters through some of your friends, because, aside from my wish to show you my good faith, I should not like them to fall into the wrong hands, for they revealed my feelings to you without sufficient disguise. I was afraid that my servant, in order to avoid paying the postage, had not taken them to the post-office, but I made inquiry and was assured that the post-office had forwarded them to their destination. So please hunt for them diligently — if an evil fate does not keep you from getting this one, too.

Dear Boswell, if you knew with what anxiety I waited for the mail from Lucca or Leghorn (since I did not know where you were), saw it come without bringing me the news of you I wished for, did not know what to think, dared not blame you for fear of being unjust! To torment myself, to become enraged was all I could do. I was afraid that some accident had occurred, that you were ill, or that you no longer loved me. However terrible that thought might be, I unhesitatingly preferred it to the former.

To give you news of myself as to my health, today I have a little fever but it will come to nothing; as to my heart, I love you more than ever, if that were possible. My sole consolation since your departure from Siena has been to read over and over the letter that you sent me from Lucca; and the thought that you once told me you loved me makes my sorrows dearer to me. Of all the faculties of the mind I find

[2] According to his Register of Letters, Boswell wrote to Moma on 10 October.

at present that imagination is the most useful and the most necessary. O God, what an immense difference there is between imagination and reality! Yet imagination at present furnishes the only pasture where my pleasures can feed, and is the only consolation left to me. I enchant myself with your doubtful promise to return to me again within a few weeks; in the name of charity I beg you to come back if you have any human feelings.

The thought of your departure for Corsica still distresses me and makes me envisage all the dangers that such a fantastic voyage involves. I believe I suffer more, fixed here on my sofa, than you at sea in the midst of a raging storm.

I shall say no more, since I do not know what will happen to this letter. The bad luck that dogs me says that it will meet the same fate as the other three. I am directing it to the Consul of His Britannic Majesty, as you told me to. Good-bye. I am expected by a number of people whom in any other circumstances I should like to see, but whom I now feel like sending to the devil.

Answer this letter, and believe that neither time nor space will change my feelings for you, not till death itself. Can you promise as much?

[Boswell to Wilkes]

Genoa, 1 December 1765

Dear Sir, — You are a very sad man indeed. I wrote you a long letter from Venice, and a most classical one from Mantua. I directed them both *à M. Wilkes à Naples*, according to your desire, and am sure that I did not neglect to give you my address at this place. After making a very singular tour to the island of Corsica, I arrived at Genoa in full hopes of finding a packet of your wit and gaiety, but to my great disappointment there is not a line from you. If you have received the letters I mention,[3] I must be very angry with you; for although I have heard that you have been running over the world, and trying the keenness of your wit with that of Voltaire, I cannot excuse your forgetting an ancient laird.

I have had a flow of spirits, and have written above a hundred and fifty lines of my Epistle to you.[4] I am in hopes it will be a piece that may do us both some honour.

[3] Wilkes had sailed from Naples for Marseilles on 27 June.

[4] About 220 lines of Boswell's "Epistle to Wilkes" survive among the Boswell

I set out for Paris in a week hence. My father is ill and anxious to see me. If I do not hear that he is better, my stay in France at this time must be very short. Pray write to me immediately at Lyons, by the address which you will find on the opposite page.[5] It will please me to be thus met by you on my road to Paris. Adieu, dear Sir,

JAMES BOSWELL.

[EDITORIAL NOTE: Boswell landed in Genoa in the sustaining glow of a unique experience. Other men made Continental tours, other men scribbled and published, other men boasted of familiar intercourse with Samuel Johnson and Jean Jacques Rousseau. But nobody else had been over the mountains to Paoli; nobody else could talk with authority of the little isle that was to astonish Europe. On the morning after his arrival, he called on the British consul, James Hollford, and set him right ("Talked of Corsican affairs plainly"); then waited on the French *chargé d'affaires* and was invited to dinner. It was here that he met the Genoese secretary of state whom he had caused to shake in his shoes, and learned, with considerable increase in his self-esteem, that Genoese spies had had him under surveillance all the time he was in Corsica. "Do you know," he wrote delightedly to John Johnston on 9 December, "I have had my own fears at Genoa, for, being just arrived from Corsica, where I was very intimate with their terrible enemy, Paoli, I am pretty certain that the noble merchants of this despicable republic would have been well pleased to have had a stiletto slipped into my back, or to have got me into prison and very quietly given me a little poison. But the British flag makes them tremble, and good Captain Robinson of the *Vulture* rides at anchor in their port." The dagger, the chain, and the poisoned bowl are a bit romantic, but there is no doubt that he had caused a great flurry in the foreign offices. Michel, the French *chargé d'affaires*,

---

papers. It is not known whether Boswell ever showed Wilkes this poem except for the first six lines, which were enclosed in his letter of 22 April (p. 70). Curiously enough the two stanzas of a poem by Boswell which are among the Wilkes papers in the British Museum, and which were printed as Appendix II in Chauncey B. Tinker's *Letters of James Boswell*, are not from this poem but from the earlier "Parliament: A Poem" which Boswell wrote for George Dempster (see *Boswell on the Grand Tour: Germany and Switzerland*, 6 August 1764).

[5] "A Monsieur, Monsieur Boswell, Gentilhomme Écossais, Chez Messrs. Condère, Père et Fils, et Passavant, à Lyons."

was probably forwarding to Paris reports which had been sent over from Corsica by *his* spies; Count Antonio Rivarola in Leghorn was certainly having Boswell shadowed and was reporting all his movements to Turin — for the King of Sardinia had designs on Corsica too. These newly recovered reports of Rivarola — voluminous and very accurate so far as they can be tested — say in fact that the Doge of Genoa had Boswell in for questioning. It seems odd that Boswell should have recorded so important an event only obliquely, but his notes say nothing about the interview, and merely record his uneasiness later when he was told that he had kept the Doge waiting.

His remarks on pictures and buildings seem to show a new self-confidence, as for example this comment on a picture in the Palazzo Durazzo: "Rubens's Juno putting Argus's eyes into peacock's tail[6] — Juno all dignity, but action bad. Girl picking out eyes with a thing like skiver,[7] as a cookmaid, and Juno holding them like mussels to clap into [peacock's] tail. Mean. Should have been done by a wand — a sudden transmigration."

He seems while in Genoa to have been best pleased with the society of a group of now obscure British "captains" — Captain Robinson of the *Vulture*, a young artillery officer named Duncan Drummond, and others unnamed — but he had his usual luck in meeting men whose names can easily be turned up in modern biographical dictionaries. The French astronomer Joseph Jérôme Lalande, to whom he had secured a letter of introduction, had the misfortune to observe the planet Neptune and to record it as a star;[8] John Symonds was Thomas Gray's successor in the chair of Modern History at Cambridge; Count Hessenstein was an illegitimate son of King Frederick I of Sweden; Henry Ellis, explorer of Hudson Bay, was successively Governor of Georgia and of Nova Scotia; the ambiguous Frederick Augustus Hervey, son of Pope's "Sporus," later became both Bishop

[6] Rubens's "Juno and Argus," now in the Wallraf-Richartz Museum in Cologne.

[7] A variant of *skewer*, now dialectal.

[8] He made two observations of the planet on the 8th and 10th of May, 1795. When he found that the observations did not agree, he rejected one as probably in error. If only he had taken one more look with the telescope to see *which* observation was wrong, he would have found that his "star" really was moving, and thus would have been put in the way of discovering the planet more than fifty years before it was actually recognized.

of Derry and Earl of Bristol. Hervey and Symonds were so roused by Boswell's accounts of Corsica that they made visits there themselves.

Boswell had resolved in Capraja to discharge Jacob as soon as they got to Genoa, but instead he only went on wrangling with him. Serious thoughts of Belle de Zuylen recurred ("Thought to offer marriage to Zélide — mad"). He read *The Rambler*, and "after long intermission felt all the force and fancy of illustrious Johnson." He had his sore toe attended to ("Yesterday morning *valet de place* brought surgeon who cut down nail above, and by cutting and pulling got him out. Was much relieved"). The Genoese notes end with an account of his going to see a young lady take the veil.]

TUESDAY 10 DECEMBER. Yesterday morning Prince[9] politely insisted to take you with him to ceremony. You was quite at ease with him. You went and saw beautiful lady of first family (nineteen) richly dressed. Old Dominican preached, [called her] a "valiant maiden." Then at gate with crown and nuns a-singing. Then church and before altar deshabilled and hair cut, &c. *Camerieres*[1] — neat one and young. Ladies all looked at you; [heard one say] "I've seen him." Strutted by Grimaldi proud, and looked full[2] . . . Took Jacob. . . . Found self poor. Viewed conduct — bad. Rouse.

TUESDAY 10 DECEMBER.[3] After a tolerable night's sleep, I was called at seven by the sailors and went with them to the port, but the courier was not yet come; so I strolled about a little in the city, and went into a church and paid my devotions to Him who rules the sea. At eight we sailed. The felucca was a very good, well-built vessel. It had a *railing* of wood to cover it in, over which might be thrown canvas to defend the passengers from the sun or from rain, and from the night air when they choose to sleep aboard. It had twelve sailors: the master and boy and ten rowers. The *courier de France*, with whom I embarked, was a young, round, lively little fellow. He had the com-

[9] Count Hessenstein. Boswell says he was a "sweet, lively young man."

[1] Properly *cameriere:* the lady's maids who helped "deshabille" the "valiant maiden."

[2] Grimaldi was one of the Genoese officers who had helped him escape from Capraja.

[3] With this entry Boswell began again to keep a fully written journal and continued it with some exceptions through 6 January 1766. Events belong to the date under which they are entered.

mon cant: "There is no country like France." He told me that Prince Charles was expected at Rome every day, and that apartments were prepared for him in his father's palace. He told me, "The Queen is very beautiful." I asked him if she was still alive.[4] "Oh, yes, Sir," said he, and told me her picture was in St. Peter's. By this he meant the bust of the Queen which is upon her monument, and from which I suppose he has concluded her to be very beautiful. We had a fine calm sea, and for an hour and a half we had a brisk gale directly for us; the motion of the felucca was sound and smooth and I was not sick, but had a very good appetite and eat a bit with great pleasure. Between three and four the wind changed against us, so we were obliged to put ashore at Vado, ten leagues from Genoa. My dog began to grow sick, so I threw him into the sea, thinking that when he had swum ashore he would follow the boat; but instead of that he ran off like a criminal back to Savona. The courier went off by land, and I was left to manage as I could with the master of the felucca.

I found a very tolerable inn at Vado and got some fresh fish. A poor young fellow, a stocking weaver of Nîmes, who told me there were not many curiosities in his town, was with us in the felucca. He said at the inn he had no inclination to eat, and though I pressed him to taste my fish, he would not. Upon being asked a livre for his bed, he threatened going back to the felucca. But the landlady lodged him for twelve sols.[5] I sent an express to Savona who brought me for answer that my dog had been seen at the butchers' stalls; but it was too late to find him. However, as the gates were shut, he could not be gone out of the town, and therefore I might have him by sending next morning before the gates could be opened. Jacob slept in the same room with me. He told me he had bought malaga at two livres, four sols a bottle. I was in a great passion with him and said, "It makes me angry to have a servant who spends money in such a fashion." Upon this he told me he had bought a capon which cost him two livres, and said, "All the other gentlemen buy provisions. They are

[4] Maria Clementina Sobieski, wife of the Old Pretender, died in 1735.

[5] The value of currencies varied from one Italian state to another. Usually a sol or sou was worth about an English halfpenny. Twenty sols made a livre, six livres an écu, and twenty-four livres a louis d'or, which was worth about a pound. A franc and a livre were the same.

right-thinking people. I shall always preserve my health, since I see that I am to be given nothing to pay the doctors." (This was a hint to me that I had not paid for the curing of his fever at Rome; however, as he has made enough by me, I took no notice of what he said.) I found myself so fortified by agitation that, although I was conscious that I had neither a genteel nor rational conduct in being thus levelled with my own servant, who really thought with more justness than I did, it gave me no concern, and I fell asleep in most easy indifference.

WEDNESDAY 11 DECEMBER. Early this morning I dispatched my servant with a guide to Savona. I had here (at Vado) as good a clean bed as I could wish; so I lay comfortably till near nine, when my envoys returned without the dog, who had not been heard of since last night. I composed myself, thinking that Mr. Hollford would get him for me and send him by sea to England. The sea was so rough that the felucca could not go. I inclined to go by land; but, as I heard the roads were so bad that I could not get to Antibes in less than four days, I thought it better to wait a day for the chance of going by sea in four and twenty hours. The master and I had some dispute about what I should pay. It was at last agreed that I should give six sequins[6] (one less than the courier), and, if bad weather stopped us, I should pay only as far as I went with him. At eleven came three men from Savona bringing my dog along with them. The principal person among them said he had bought my dog for *six francs* from a butcher. I, overjoyed to have him again, gave the money without considering that the fellow had no right to sell a dog which was not his own. Thus was I cheated by a crafty Ligurian. I considered, however, that if I had made him be sent after me, it would have cost more. I was in rage against the brute for running away and plaguing me, and I resolved to punish him sufficiently, so I took him to the inn, tied him to a bedstead, and beat him without mercy.[7]

I went out and walked in the village. The church took my eye. It had a light, airy steeple, and was painted with different colours in the Genoese taste, which I own I cannot help being pleased with. No matter why; I am pleased and want no more. I know it is against prin-

[6] About three pounds.

[7] Boswell later crossed out this sentence.

ciple; I know Lord Kames and other cool analysers of feeling could tell me, "Pray, Sir, what should a building be? Strong, to be sure, and therefore of stone. What colour has stone? Surely never green and blue, and certainly it is never diversified with figures of the Roman emperors, with St. George and the dragon, with the whimsical, fantastical zigzags which adorn the panels of a drawing-room, with terrible arms, or with elegant flowerpots; therefore this plastering and painting system is absurd, as it would make a thing appear what it never was nor never can be." "Very well argued, master metaphysician. But I cannot feel by reason, and therefore, when an object excites pleasure in me, I call it pleasing, be it a dance at Sadler's Wells, a ballad sung by porters against the ministry, a roasted apple from a stand at Temple Bar, a Methodist sermon, or a print of the world turned upside down." Thus I philosophize.

I called upon the curate, who very obligingly showed me the inside of the church. I spoke to him in Italian and he answered me, "Monsieur, je ne vous comprends pas." I then talked to him as a Frenchman. But he told me he was not of that country, but Italian. I asked him why he could not understand me. He said, "Je parle Génois, le patois d'ici." I entered a garden which pleased me much. The gardener, who was gathering olives, came up to me and asked me if I would have *milk* — "latte," added he. "Ho venduto molto di questo alle barche inglesi e hanno detto sempre *milk*."[8] I was delighted to have thus by chance my most agreeable regale. I went home with him and his wife, and had bread and three large vessels of fine, sweet milk and enjoyed life. The gardener showed me his little cow-house where the cows were constantly kept and fed, without ever being taken out except to the bull. He said they were so accustomed to this life that, take them to the meadow and they would not know how to eat.

Jacob was very rude in talking of my severity to Jachone: "If my brother did a thing like that, I would thrash him." Thus talked with rough manner my Swiss peasant. I made him hold his tongue, but was really fretted. I continued to beat Jachone from time to time, and gave him nothing to eat, so that I humbled him very well.

I thought a religious life is difficult only because it is a constant

[8] "I have sold much of this to English boats, and they have always said *milk*."

conformity to a regulated system, to fulfil which one is anxious. The life of a toast, or a perfect coquette, is as difficult, and so is that of a man who insists on being respected every moment of his existence. I considered how very pleasant my life now was when I followed purely the inclination of each moment without any manner of restraint. I thought, however, this could not last. Scotland stared me full in the face, but seemed comfortable. I wished to be home. I had Erskine's *Institutes* with me and read him clearly and soundly; I rejoiced to find that as I acquired strength of mind, I could take in even law as an object of philosophy. I dreaded my worthy father's death, and thought how hard it would be if I should become a man that could rejoice his heart, and he not live to see it, to be consoled after all that my miserable sallies of hypochondria have made him suffer.

Thinking of Jacob's republican obstinacy, I was of opinion that, lest stubborn nature should rebel, that a gentleman may by natural as well as civil right exercise despotism over his domestics. He ought never to engage a servant without having beat him at a fair boxing-match or at hard cudgels. I also thought that in my Scots Dictionary it might not be amiss to give little cuts of particular words, as *quaich*  , *luggie*  .[9] At night I had from my gardener fresh butter and charming buttermilk.

THURSDAY 12 DECEMBER. Early this morning the sailors called me. The master told me it was good wind, and I, eager to go, agreed to pay him six sequins passage, and, if we could not advance, four. The rogue took me in; for the wind fell as we advanced and then was contrary, and this he must have known.

We went up three leagues and put in at Noli. I still starved Jachone, and discharged[1] Jacob to give him any victuals. I stepped down on shore (after being drawn to land by the sailors, which I called [the] best manner of going in [a] boat), and when I returned

[9] Boswell had started to gather material for a dictionary of Scots English while in Holland. It was never completed. A quaich (or quaigh) is a kind of shallow drinking-cup, formerly common in Scotland, usually made of wooden staves hooped together, but sometimes of silver. A luggie is a small wooden vessel with a "lug" or handle.

[1] Scots for "forbade."

I found Jacob feeding my dog. I called to him, "How dare you give anything to that dog when I forbade it?" He replied, "Yes, I have given him something, *sacré dieu!*" as if he had been speaking to a brother peasant. I said, "Upon my word, you are a fine man!" "Well," said he, "I *am* a man. I am not a fool." You said, "You are the most impertinent rascal I have *ever* known." He said, "Sir, you knew that long ago. You should not have taken me with you." Such changling passed between a master and his servant. Shameful! I could do nothing as I owed the fellow thirty louis, but I resolved if possible to borrow money at Antibes and turn him off from thence.

I determined to go by land, so left Jacob and my baggage in the felucca, and desired the master to call in at Razzi[2] and Monaco and one or two of the other ports, if I should make him a sign from any of them. I took Jachone with me, pulling him along with a good cord, and, whenever he was rebellious, beating him sorely. I even hung him fairly up twice upon trees for half a minute, but he grasped them with his feet and saved his neck.[3] I walked five miles to Finale (the first post, which a punster would say should be the last).

Here I saw a sort of Genoese triumphal arch erected on I don't know what occasion. There was a Latin inscription upon it, as how thunder had set the sand on fire, which did not pass the arch, and this happened during the magistracy of Signor somebody. The same meaning was put into verse below, and the poet took the license of paying a compliment to the magistrate by hinting that it was owing to him that the kindled sand went no farther. I began to copy this inscription, but the Commandant, a suspicious fool, came up and told me that he could not allow me to do it without an order from the Governor, and very gravely did he write to his Excellency desiring to know if it should be permitted to a stranger to copy the inscription on the triumphal arch. When he had done, I told him that as I must wait half an hour for the answer it was not worth while, for indeed I would not wait ten minutes for it. I wished to have copied out my inscription by force, or have made a riot. I should have done so in any other state, where I was sure that the government would take to task

[2] Probably Alassio.

[3] Boswell later crossed out this sentence and the preceding one from "pulling him along."

a foolish commandant, but I considered that the Genoese would hardly do me the justice which I had a right to expect.

I eat a bit and then got a horse and a postilion to run afoot with me to Pietra. Here the post would oblige me to take two horses. I went to a little inn where the people seemed civil and got me a quiet fellow who agreed to go with me cheap, but insisted on taking two horses as there was much water on the road. I set out at ten. It was very dark. I began to ruminate on Italian robberies and assassinations and was vastly uneasy. I took my louis and put them loose in my pocket, leaving two in my purse for the rogues if they should come. I rode in most disagreeable anxiety, but was three or four times comforted by passing snug, smoky towns.

At last I arrived at Razzi at one in the morning, and knocked up the landlord and landlady of a little inn. I found I had let my purse with two louis drop by the way, so I dispatched the landlord's two sons with a lantern to seek it for me, their father having charged them to pray to the Virgin that it might be found. I did not much like this Genoese inn. My room had two doors, one of which opened on a room where I saw one or two stout fellows. That door I bolted very well; the other, which opened on my landlord's room, I attempted to shut. He called to me that I had locked it, while I heard the sound of a lock, but I knew I had not turned the key, and discovered that he had bolted it on his side and would make me believe that I had locked it. This looked ugly. The sequel, however, proved that he had no other intention but merely to humour my resolution to have my door locked, for I was obliged to content myself with matters as they were. It was three o'clock before I got to bed. I did not throw off my clothes, but laid Jachone on the foot of my bed and took my *couteau de chasse* and laid it at my side.

FRIDAY 13 DECEMBER. At six some of the stout fellows I had seen set out with mules on their intended plan for the day and made a terrible noise. I was waked suddenly, and in a fright I started up with my *couteau de chasse* in my hand and ran to the window, where I found I had no reason to be apprehensive, so went and slumbered disagreeably enough till nine, when I got up and walked out to the shore from whence I saw my felucca pass in full sail, so that she could not come to land to take me up. I walked to the next village, where I got a horse to the first post-town, and from thence took a post-horse to Porto Maurizio, passing in my way through several villages very well built and remarkably well paved, with generally half a dozen lines of larger stones cutting the street into pretty sections from end to end.

At Porto Maurizio the postmaster told me that my horse and guide were ready; so that I supped at my ease on fried eggs, without care. But when I was ready to set out, he came and told me that there was another postmaster besides himself who would not consent to give me one horse, as the night was dark and there were rivers in the way which in the day-time could be passed in boats, but in the night there was no getting over but ahorseback. He therefore insisted on my taking two horses, or waiting till it should be light. I took him to be lying and demanded my horse and guide afoot. He refused, and I in a great passion groped my way some gunshots to the town and got a man to show me to Signor Sicardi, the British Vice-consul. I told him my story and imagined he could force the postmaster to give me what I wanted, but he knew nothing of the matter, and his stupidity enraged me. He offered to lodge me in his house, but I could not bear to stay with him. The other postmaster had been sent for, and came and talked with us. I had seen him indeed before; but he also refused me one horse. He lighted me along the street, and showed me to two different inns, the outside of which I disliked. I was quite fretted and did not know what I would be at. At last I thought of the Vice-consul of France, as M. Michel had given me a circular letter to all of them. I was informed he was a Frenchman, and that was enough. I went to him, followed by the second postmaster. I found him just the obliging second-rate Frenchman. He told me that I really would do wrong to travel in the night, and that I could not force a single horse. Our postmaster talked reasonably. I said, "Si dice una mezza dama. Lei è un mezzo galantuomo ma giunto con un briccone."[4] The Vice-consul assured me that the other was a drunken rascal and had been complained of to him often and often. I talked of writing against him to Commodore Harrison and Mr. Hollford and M. Michel, but the Vice-consul said I had better have no more of it, and he was right.

I agreed to wait till six next morning and then set out with one

[4] "People use the expression, *mezza dama* (almost a lady). I should call you almost an honest man, though you are in league with a scoundrel."

horse. The Vice-consul said frankly, "You will do me the kindness to eat a little supper here and accept a bed which will be better than what you will find at the inn." I gladly accepted his offer. His name was M. de La Selle, a native of Orléans. He lived here in a large house with two Genoese and their sister, all oldish, fat people. He himself was plump and hearty and had a daughter well married at Paris, where his wife was gone for some time.

We had a neat little supper, and talked well. All the villages in this neighbourhood are supported by the commerce of oil. At Porto Maurizio they export in a good year one hundred thousand barrels of oil at two louis a barrel. There are here many good houses and a number of people who have tolerable good fortunes. Their figs are the best I ever eat. I drank here a wine little inferior to madeira, and my landlord assured me that, by corking close the fermenting juice, he made what could not be known from true champagne. I got an excellent bed here. I was ill-dressed but quite the man of fashion. M. de La Selle was quite occupied in showing me *des politesses*. There are people who from good habits delight in serving others. I have little of this, and therefore view with admiration the obliging attention, the alert civility, of others. I thought it would be no bad life to go about profiting by this happy disposition of mankind.

SATURDAY 14 DECEMBER. I mounted early and went briskly on and was convinced that a foot-guide could not have passed in the night. About a league before I came to San Remo, I saw a curious grotto, a cave just by the side of the road. It is now a chapel dedicated to the Madonna Annunziata. It is fifty foot in length from the great altar (there being three) to the door in front (having also a side door), and thirty-three foot broad. A poor hermit lives on the brow of the declivity which overhangs this chapel, which he shows to such as are curious, though my guide told me I was the first he had seen examine it with attention. The hermit lighted me with a torch up a little stair cut in the rock till we got above the great altar. We advanced along a passage in the rock four or five foot broad, but diminishing as we advanced both in breadth and heigth. We were above a hundred foot from the front door. The hermit told me the passage had no end, and indeed I saw a vast way beyond where we were, but advanced no farther, as we were obliged to creep upon all four and I began to want fresh air. There is from the roof of this chapel and the passage a continual dropping of water, which it seems is looked upon as a kind of miracle. I inquired of the hermit and of my guide how this curious grotto had been made, supposing that there would certainly be some singular tradition with regard to it; but all the information they could give me was that the Madonna had made it herself. I gave the hermit some money. He very seriously asked me if I intended it for the Madonna or for him, a piece of scrupulous honesty, this, which I am afraid is not to be found in the greatest number of the mendicant religious, nor in those ragged laymen who in white iron boxes collect from passengers their charity for the souls in purgatory. As I considered the hermit to have more need of money than the Virgin had of masses, I told him what I gave was for himself.

I found San Remo to be, as Mr. Addison remarks, a "pretty little town."[5] The noble family of Borea has a very large palace there, the size of which struck me much, but I saw nothing remarkable in the architecture. Nothing is more agreeable in travelling up the river of Genoa than to find oneself gradually transported from a cold air to an agreeable warmth. By the time I got to San Remo I had entirely changed climate. At Genoa we were shivering over large fires, and at San Remo I sat with the windows open in a room without fire and basked in the rays of a benign sun. This town is remarkable for the immense quantity of oranges and lemons which grow in its territories. I went with the postmaster to his garden and had the pleasure of pulling in December sweet oranges to eat and lemons to squeeze in my wine. I was just at Naples. I liked San Remo so much I regretted its being in the Genoese dominions. On the other side of it, on the brow of a pleasant hill, is a college of Jesuits, very genteel, and, as Thomson says, "embosomed soft in trees."[6]

Walking in the streets of San Remo, I observed a barber's sign, *Alla Perrucca Trionfante;* a hand held aloft a periwig, and three or four fleurs-de-lis marked the master French. It made me laugh so much that I sent for the master and made him shave me. I asked him how he durst enter a foreign state in that manner, with periwig

[5] *Remarks,* p. 15. The poor are lucky, Addison felt, to live in this climate.

[6] James Thomson, *Spring,* l. 953.

triumphant, and if he was not afraid of drawing upon himself the vengeance of the Republic. I plagued the fellow so much that he at last denied its being his sign, calling himself the barber *vis-à-vis*.[7]

At night I arrived at Ventimiglia, an old town situated on a steep hill. They frightened me here so much with robbers being on the frontiers, and assured me besides that the gates of Mentone were never opened in the night-time, that I lay at the post-house, where the landlord and landlady were Spaniards; and vastly courteous was mine host, a fine young fellow. I slept in my clothes with Jachone in my arms.

SUNDAY 15 DECEMBER. I set out before six. My guide bid me hold high the bridle, saying that the horse was "like a vessel" that when the sails were hoised up went well. The frontiers of the Genoese state are very rocky and seem most proper fastnesses for banditti. They have placed a tower with forty soldiers for security. I had some very bad road, particularly the steep Passo di Teodoro. I made my guide tell me when I stepped into the territories of Monaco. I felt most comfortable to have escaped safe from the rascally Genoese. Mentone made me think myself in France, my landlord talking French and treating with the address which the lively nation is remarkable for.

I went out of my road a few miles to see the little town of Monaco, or rather indeed the Prince's palace, where Mr. Addison had been. I mounted an immense steep mountain to get up to it, but I had an excellent road made in the reign of Antonius I,[8] as an inscription bore. The French have a garrison here, as it is of consequence for them to take care of the frontiers of Italy. The Commandant, to whom I was carried, gave me permission to walk about freely. The court of the palace pleased me. The outside of this building is not good, but I saw some very good apartments and the pictures that Mr. Addison talks of. They made me think of old Scots families. The present Prince of Monaco lives almost always at Paris, so that the palace looked desolate, like the house of a Scots laird who lives in England.

I passed a prodigious mountain and then went on to Nice, where I walked about a little but saw nothing but a procession. I called on Jullien, the French Consul, taking him to be one of my circular vice-

[7] The barber across the street.

[8] Antoine I, Prince of Monaco from 1701 to 1731.

consuls. He undeceived me and was stiffly civil, being a formal Frenchman, which is horrid. I heard Lord Breadalbane and Lord and Lady Glenorchy were here. With true Scots excellent ceremony I sent them a polite card excusing myself for not waiting on them, having no clothes and being in a great hurry. They sent me a polite answer, and Dr. Ramsay of Edinburgh, who was of their party, came and sat an hour with me. We talked away very well. He quite revived my Scots ideas.

MONDAY 16 DECEMBER. I took a phaeton and post-horses for Antibes. A little way out of Nice I saw a marble cross erected on the place where the Pope [Paul III] stopped.[9]

For these two days I let Jachone run loose, and he followed me very well. I got to Antibes at noon, and found that my servant and baggage had been there two days before me. I put up at St. Jacques sur la Place, where I was pretty well. After dinner I called on M. Vial, *procureur du roi à l'amirauté*, to whom M. Michel had recommended me. He engaged a chaise to carry me to Marseilles, being a very expert little man in those matters. I called on Capitaine Bellini, a Corsican who was recruiting, or rather receiving recruits, for the Royal Corsicans.[1] He was a good, talkative little man. I also called on M. Campion, *contrôleur des fermes*. He painted and engraved prettily and read English. Caraffa had recommended me to both these last-named gentlemen. I was surprised to find Antibes so small and so poor-looking a place. Jacob was very civil. I reminded him of his strange behaviour at Noli. He asked pardon, saying that he was always sorry after such sallies.

TUESDAY 17 DECEMBER. Julien La Fleur, my *voiturin*, made me set out betimes. I expected that French carriages could never go slow, but I found the vivacity of the airy nation did not appear in its *voiturins*, for he walked me along more slowly than my Italian vetturinos, and very discontented I was. Jachone went back to the inn where I dined, for which I beat him till his nose bled, and then letting

[9] Boswell left a blank for the name of the Pope. Paul III concluded a truce there in 1538 between the Emperor Charles V and Francis I of France. The cross seen by Boswell was torn down in 1796.

[1] The French Royal-Corse regiment, of which Buttafoco had just been made colonel.

him loose, he run off from me before the chaise. A sergeant of the Régiment de Languedoc, who had just come from Bastia for his health, walked along with us. He informed Jacob that the honest fellow, the *frotteur*[2] *chez M. de Marbeuf* who served me so carefully during my fever, had been turned off because he would not divide with the others the two gros écus which I left him. On my arrival at Fréjus, Jachone was found waiting at the gate of the town. I found a most excellent inn here, a good table d'hôte, and a bedroom as if in a private house in Britain.

WEDNESDAY 18 DECEMBER. Jogged most sluggishly along. Disputed with Jacob, who said he knew me perfectly and that it was impossible for servants to live well with me, as I was not, like other gentlemen, content with external acquiescence, but would always show them clearly that they were wrong. He is very right. I am always studying human nature and making experiments on the lowest characters, so that I am too much in the secret with regard to the weakness of man in reality, and my honest, impetuous disposition cannot take up with that eternal repetition of fictitious minutiae by which unthinking men of fashion preserve a great distinction between master and servant. By having Jacob so free with me, I have felt as servants do, and been convinced that the greatest part of them laugh in their sleeve very heartily at the parade of their lords, knowing well that eating, drinking, sleeping, and other offices of nature are common to all. Jacob said, "I believe, Sir, that you have been badly brought up. You have not the manners of a nobleman. Your heart is too open." I confessed to him that I was two and twenty before I had a servant. Said he, "The son of a gentleman ought to be accustomed early to command a servant, but reasonably, and never to joke with them; because each must live in his state according to his quality. You, Sir, would live just like a peasant. And you force a servant to speak in a way he shouldn't, because you torment him with questions. You want to get to the bottom of things. Sir, I do not think you should marry. At least, if you marry, you should not live in the same house with your wife; otherwise, *ma foi!* there will shortly be disputes, and a quarrel which cannot be made up. Sir, this is what you should do: marry a lady, give her a certain allowance, and let her

[2] Apparently a bootblack.

have her house where you can go when you find it agreeable and not be inconvenienced; and you must never see your children, or otherwise they will be as badly brought up as you. I hope, Sir, you will not take this in bad part." The fellow talked thus with so much good sense, so much truth, and with so natural an air, that upon my word I admired him; I however hoped that a few years more would temper all that impetuosity and remove all that weakness which now render me inconstant and capricious. At any rate, I have a singular kind of philosophy which will make me content to be whatever I shall turn out.

I came at night to a tolerable inn.[3] I sat up too late writing, and I suppose astonished the people of the house, who are used to see their guests tumble into bed immediately after supper. By the by, the French soft feather beds are destroying me by relaxing my nerves. The inns of this light-headed nation are very seldom good, for the rooms are cold and comfortless and dirty, the sheets damp, and snuffers difficult to be found. Old England live for ever, for thy inns are more excellent than are palaces anywhere else.

THURSDAY 19 DECEMBER. The noble highway which leads from the country near Antibes to Toulon is admirable, like what is in the Scots Highlands. This evening I arrived at Toulon. At the gate a soldier made me come out of my chaise and conducted me to the Marquis de Coincy, the Commandant, to be examined, as all strangers are. He very politely asked me a few questions. When I was found no fault with, I presented him a letter from M. de Marbeuf begging him to show me civilities, and if possible to get me a sight of the arsenal, but this he told me could not be done; but he would try.

I put up at the Croix de Malte and was tolerably well. Three posts before I arrived, Jachone was a-missing. I enquired of all passengers before us on the road, but he had not advanced. I was quite uneasy, quite feverish with anxiety about him. Jacob said, "Sir, you are getting yourself in a fever over a wretched cur." I sent an express for him three posts.

FRIDAY 20 DECEMBER. Before I got up, my express returned with Jachone. The voracious brute had returned to where I dined and had eat a whole hare which was hung up before a window. I insisted

[3] At Le Luc, from which Boswell wrote to Johnston.

with Jacob that Jachone had laid a plan for this, and that his inclination was to dine at the tables d'hôte at thirty-five sous *par repas*. The sergeant from Corsica said I should give Jachone so much a week, as I did to my servant. I saw that it was to no purpose to beat the brute as he did not understand what I meant, being very stupid. I therefore resolved to carry him along with me just like a trunk or a packet that could move of itself.

I found at the inn here Captain Keith Stewart, who had frightened me so much with regard to my Corsican expedition.[4] He joked me very heartily and really did not enter into the spirit of my singular tour. He conducted me to see the harbour. I made my *valet de place* follow. "Sir," said Stewart, "you are so much accustomed to guards in Corsica that you cannot walk out except you have several attendants." I saw here Captain Elliot who had brought Mr. Grenville, the Ambassador, from Constantinople.[5] How manly these captains looked, while I was conscious of having no firm hold of any plan. Upon my word it is owing to my philosophy, which sees too clearly the vanity of all the pursuits of mortals. Yet, had I that noble force which Johnson has, I might embrace life firmly although I am convinced of its vanity, for there is still reality. I set out at noon and went a few leagues to a poor inn.[6]

SATURDAY 21 DECEMBER. I arrived at Marseilles about eleven. A little way before you come to it, on the Toulon road, is the best *vin cuit* in France. This is a particular sort of wine, which, after having been boiled is excellent to drink a glass of with a crust of bread, by way of breakfast. At Marseilles I put up at the Nouvelle Rose, a very bad inn; the table d'hôte was dirty, and through the room where it was held were some of us obliged to pass to our rooms. The service was bad and the master impertinent. Some honest Irish gentlemen dined with me at the table d'hôte and then we went all and drank coffee. Before dinner I went and saw Mr. Pennant, who had taken an apart-

[4] See p. 149.

[5] Captain Elliot's ship, the *Thames,* on which the Hon. Henry Grenville was returning, was laid up for repairs in Toulon. Since they had been there for two months, the French were afraid that they wanted to find out too much about the arsenal, to which they were forbidden admittance. The English claimed that the reason for their stay was to perfect themselves in the French language.

[6] At Cuges.

ment here and had his cook and lived comfortably.[7] Antonio, Lord Mountstuart's *volante*, my travelling companion from Milan to Florence, whom I had recommended to Pennant, was now advanced to be *valet de chambre*, and a very genteel one he made. I had neither money nor credit, but trusted to Pennant, an ancient Welshman of very large fortune. I asked him to answer for me for fifty louis, which he most readily agreed to. Nothing is to be had in this world as one would have it. By making Pennant answer for my fifty louis, I deprived myself of one excellent subject of my satire, for he is indeed a most absurd mortal; and now it would be shocking in me to portray him as I well could. Oh, no matter; sure one need not regret being forbidden to laugh at one absurdity in a world where there are so many, unless one had the perversity of Adam who eat of the one forbidden tree.

At five Pennant introduced me to Mr. Osborn (Sir George's brother), and to a Major Langham; genteel men. Osborn had been an Oxonian of Sir J. Macdonald's time. We went to the theatre, which at Marseilles is a very handsome one and generally has very good comedians. Let me here ask myself how, in the name of all that is strange, was I, when nineteen and more, so enthusiastic an admirer of plays and players? I can explain it. My education had been the most narrow. I had a scanty share of ideas; I had no freedom of thought. The stage of Marseilles is always crowded with gentlemen, a sad abuse which destroys the very essence of a dramatic entertainment: the reality. I met here Colonel Ross (of Inverchasley) whom I had known a little in Scotland. He served me as a proof how much I must be improved since I came abroad, for I used to look sheepish before him like a poor scholar at a country school, and now I was rather superior to him, at least in assurance. I could not attend to the comedy. There was a little piece after it where was some singing, which without affectation tortured me. The French squeaking and grimaces were insufferable to a man just come from the operas of Italy. O Italy! Land of felicity! True seat of all elegant delight! My mind shall ever soothe itself with the image of thy charms. Thy divine music has harmonized my soul. That nature, that sweet sim-

[7] Not Thomas Pennant, the famous traveller, but Edward Pennant, whom Boswell had met in Florence.

plicity, that easy grace which has pleased me so often in thy theatres, shall never fade from my memory.

The gallant Duncan Drummond had told me at Genoa of a very good girl whom he kept a long time, and had with him eight months at Minorca. Since I arrived at five and twenty,[8] I have determined never again to risk my constitution with women. But Drummond having assured me that Mlle. Susette was honest, safe, and disinterested, and counselled me to put in at that port, I went to her after the comedy. My *valet de place* was a German who spoke French and English, a tall and decent pimp. He showed me her lodgings. I found her a fine little lively girl, with hardly any of the vile cant of prostitutes. After examining me very shrewdly if I was really a friend of Drummond's, she agreed to let me pass the night with her. I went home and supped, and returned to her. She had a handsome bedroom prettily furnished. She was so little that I had an idea as if she was a child, and had not much inclination for her. I recalled my charming Signora at Siena, and was disgusted at all women but her, and angry at myself for being in the arms of another. Susette chatted neatly and diverted me. I sacrificed to the graces. I think I did no harm.

SUNDAY 22 DECEMBER. I found I was now above being taken in by whores. I viewed with pity the irregularities of humanity. I went to hear mass, but was too late. I looked at the front of the Maison de Ville, on which is some carving by Puget. I went and sat half an hour with Colonel Ross. I had been in the morning to visit Mr. Grenville, who was stately but affable. He pleased me. I have attained such a happy frame of mind that envy never disturbs me, and I can calmly admire a man of merit just as I admire a fine picture. It is merit which engages me, be it in myself or in others.

I dined with Pennant, who entertained me well. He had a genteel young Frenchman who lived in the house, and, as Pennant said, charged himself with the detail of his *ménage.* I could see that the young rogue lived upon him and laughed in his sleeve. Ross came in, and he and I went to wait on Mrs. Grenville.[9] She was gay and easy

[8] On 29 October 1765, the day of his parting from Paoli.

[9] Peggy Banks, a celebrated beauty, mentioned frequently in the correspondence of Horace Walpole.

as a foreign woman, and said I had seen nothing, as I had not seen Turkey, the true paradise on earth. She was very fond to hear my anecdotes from Corsica.

At the *comédie* I maintained to Ross the influence of spirits on us, as we have a power to affect other animals who know not how we do it (just Baxter's doctrine). I ridiculed the reasonings of the modern minute philosophers: a lobster thrown by a cook into a kettle of boiling water concludes probably that Nature is in convulsions, views his dreadful fate as occasioned by some tremendous accident in the jumble of things; and, at a *petit souper* of French lobsters, Crébillon le fils and other vivacious disputants would laugh at all suppositions of a superior agent.[1] But our confined knowledge is no argument against any reasonable conjecture. Thinking of the Duke of Cumberland's death, I said to myself, "He was too sad a barbarian to have the privilege of dying, and, by that solemn change, to be protected from satire. He ought to have lived in everlasting infamy, detested by all humane men."[2] The *comédie* did not amuse me a bit.

Birkbeck, our Consul here, or a merchant at least, made difficulty to find me louis to set off with next morning. I made Ross give me what he had, saying, "Every man give me his purse. Collect for the poor." That happy facility which Mr. Adam Smith allows me to possess is of vast value.[3] I was anxious to get off in order to pass my Christmas at Avignon. I went to Pennant and desired him to supply me with what louis he could. He looked wild and seemed to suspect I was in some disagreeable circumstance which obliged me to fly. He joked and asked me if I had murdered anybody in Corsica. He however offered to go to Solicoffre, another merchant, and raise me the louis I desired if I insisted on going off instantly. I chose to wait.

MONDAY 23 DECEMBER. I returned Ross his money. He had been this morning at his banker's and had got more gold to give me. This will do him honour while I live. Birkbeck furnished me twenty louis, which made me easy. I breakfasted with Pennant. I heard that my

[1] A reference to the dinners of the "Caveau," of which Boswell had no doubt heard from Wilkes, who had attended as Crébillon's guest.

[2] George III's uncle, who died on 31 October 1765. As commander of the government forces in the Rebellion of 1745, he earned the nickname of the "Butcher" for his severity.

[3] Boswell treasured Smith's compliment that he was "happily possessed of a facility of manners."

cousin Willy Cochrane lived in the same stair. I went up to him and found him very bad of a consumption. I am grown hard. I regret the distress of a relation, but do not feel it much. I was sorry not to have heard of him sooner. I used rather to dislike his manner. Sickness had softened and bettered it. I liked him. All is changes, and odd ones too.[4]

Pennant made me dine with him. But first I went and saw the galleys. It was curious to see a row of little booths, with signs, all occupied by slaves, many of whom looked as plump and contented as any decent tradesman whatever. I went into one of the galleys where the slaves were mostly working in different ways in order to gain some little thing. I was told that many of them make rich, as they are allowed a great deal of time for themselves when lying in the harbours.[5] I talked with one who had been in the galleys twenty years. I insisted with him that after so long a time custom must have made even the galleys easy. They came about me, several of 'em, and disputed my proposition. I maintained that custom made all things easy, and that people who had been long in prison did not choose to come out. "Ah," said the slaves, "it is otherwise here. It is two prisons. If we could escape, we should certainly do it. A bird shut up in a cage desires freedom, and so much the more should a man desire it. At first we shed tears, we groaned, but all our tears and groans availed us nothing." I was touched with the misery of these wretches, but appeared firm, which made them not show much grief. Mallet, who used to joke me on being an eternal disputer, might now say, "Baron, you dispute even with galley-slaves." One of them gave me a very full account of their manner of life. When he would tell me of their being out at sea, he said "Quand nous sommes en campagne."[6] This it seems is a galley phrase. I could not but smile at it. They said, "Nous aimerons mieux les campagnes des bois."[7] I was much satisfied with having seen a galley. I gave the slaves something to drink.

I went to Pennant's in my fur coat. He introduced me as the Rus-

[4] Cochrane, who was a second cousin of Boswell's mother, died in Marseilles at the age of twenty-six about a month later, and was buried in the Cemetery for Foreigners of the Pretended Reformed Religion.

[5] Actually they now "lay in harbour" almost permanently. Since 1748 the galleys at Marseilles had been no more than prison-ships for convicts at hard labour, which is no doubt what Boswell means by "slaves."

[6] "When we are in the field," or "on cruise."

[7] "We shall like the real fields better."

sian Ambassador. Between four and five I set out for Aix. I now found it proper to part with Jacob. I desired him to go by *voiturin* to Lyons, where I should meet him. I was now prepared to go post ahorseback, but I got a chaise as cheap to carry me to Aix, where I arrived just in time to sup at the table d'hôte, where was a French sea officer who had been aboard of Thurot.[8]

[Editorial Note: An entry in Boswell's Register of Letters for this date marks the beginning of one of the most elaborate and extended campaigns of puffing and propaganda ever to engage the attention of a man of letters. The entry is "Mr. Wilkie," and it is repeated just a month later, when Boswell was in Paris. John Wilkie was the editor of an English newspaper of wide circulation, *The London Chronicle;* and what Boswell was sending him was a series of news paragraphs which were to be "released" separately in successive issues of the paper. They began to appear on 7 January 1766, more than a month before Boswell landed in England, and were — to use the terminology which Boswell himself later employed in indexing his contributions in his own file of the *Chronicle* — a medley of "fact" and "invention." The serious, persisting object of this campaign was to work up so much public sympathy for the Corsican cause in England that the Government would be forced to reverse its policy of non-intervention; the immediate object was to puff the book on Corsica which Boswell already planned to write, and to make England and Europe aware of the existence of James Boswell, Esq. We are here concerned only with that phase of the campaign which ended when Boswell arrived in London in February 1766.

Since the Peace of 1763, in which Great Britain had agreed to consider the Corsicans as malcontents and rebels, very little concerning Corsica had appeared in the English newspapers. Boswell's strategy, therefore, was to start with a letter, unsigned but purporting to have been sent in by a correspondent in England, briefly summarizing the political situation in Corsica, and pointing out the importance of the island in a military way. Then a narrative of intrigue and dramatic suspense was to be developed in a series of letters purportedly sent

[8] That is, had served under Captain François Thurot, the intrepid French privateer who harried the coasts of Scotland and Ireland, and was killed in 1760.

from various Italian cities, all actually originating in the fertile brain of James Boswell, Esq., and written from Marseilles and Paris. The "inventions" would become more and more romantic and interesting as Boswell drew near home, and then would be blown away as baseless rumours, leaving only the "facts," of which there had actually been a considerable quantity. So far as Boswell's part in the business is concerned, all this has a quite twentieth-century ring, but one is shocked to find that a responsible newspaper should have printed such paragraphs as news. The fact is that all eighteenth-century papers did print such paragraphs, and were glad to get them. "I do believe," wrote Boswell later in his *Account of Corsica* (p. 225), "an English newspaper is the most various and extraordinary composition that mankind ever produced. An English newspaper, while it informs the judicious of what is really doing in Europe, can keep pace with the wildest fancy in feigned adventures, and amuse the most desultory taste with essays on all subjects and in every style." In the vulgar idiom of our day, he would know.

The paragraphs are printed in Appendix D (p. 322); the following summarizes the more striking parts of the saga so far as Boswell himself is concerned:

Rome, 5 December (appearing in London on 9 January, Boswell on the road from Lyons to Paris). There have been rumours that Great Britain was planning to send an embassy to Corsica; well, a British subject has actually been there. He is Mr. Boswell, a Scots gentleman upon his travels over Europe. He met Paoli, he was treated with every mark of distinction. He *says* he went to Corsica merely out of curiosity, but the politicians of Italy think they can see more important reasons for his visit. The Genoese are not a little alarmed. People in this part of the world are curious to know what will really be the consequence of Mr. Boswell's tour to Corsica.

Florence, 16 December (appearing in London on 23 January, Boswell in Paris). *We* know all about the true motives of the late expedition into Corsica. It was a scheme to do something for the Young Chevalier, Charles Stuart. Mr. B., with some of his friends, had worked out a plan for getting that unfortunate prince made King of Corsica, and Mr. B. went over to sound out Paoli. The Chevalier, we are assured, knew nothing of this notable scheme.

Genoa, 2 January (appearing in London on 6 February, Boswell at Calais). Our officèrs, Colonel Matra and Captain Grimaldi, who took refuge in Capraja in company with the Sieur Boswell, say they could learn nothing from him as to his motives, but he *did* have a good many papers about which he seemed anxious.

Leghorn, 3 January (appearing in London on 11 February, Boswell on the road from Dover to London). Nothing could prove the weakness of the Genoese more than their present fears about Mr. Boswell's tour. Why must we suppose that Great Britain has any serious designs on Corsica? Isn't the curiosity of an observing traveller reason enough for such a tour?

Turin, 6 January (appearing in London on 13 February, Boswell in London). There is no truth whatsoever in the rumours that Mr. Boswell is a desperate adventurer whose real name is M'Donald. He is a gentleman of fortune upon his travels and a friend of the celebrated Rousseau. *We* don't think he had any instructions from his Court to treat with Paoli, but all the same we hope he will be able to undeceive his countrymen with regard to the Corsican nation.

London, 15 February. Yesterday [actually on 11 February] James Boswell, Esquire, arrived in town from his travels.

This summary has carried us some seven weeks ahead of the narrative of the journal, to which we now return.]

TUESDAY 24 DECEMBER. The French officer and I walked about a little and saw Aix. I stopped to get my shoes cleaned. He paid I suppose a denier for me, saying, "As they say in England, I'll pay the little expenses and you'll pay the big ones." So we went to a café, where I paid for breakfast. French easy impudence is amazing.

At ten I mounted with my great jack-boots to *courir à franc étrier — à bidet*,[9] as they say. Both the nails of my great toes were now in the flesh and made me suffer sadly. The ostlers and postilions were impertinent dogs, crying always, "Foutre! sacré dieu!" without rhyme or reason. At one stage they gave me small stirrups, which hurt me. I insisted with the postilion to give me his, which he refused, and galloped off, thinking I would chase him and so end the stage; instead of which I very coolly made my horse step along at a slow walk. Nothing tortures a Frenchman so much as retarding the cur-

[9] To ride at full speed — pony express.

rent of his animal spirits. So my postilion turned back and gave me his stirrups, and then — *allons!* I was enlivened and fortified by strong exercise, eating now and then bread and cheese and drinking wine.

At night I came to the ferry where you pass over to the territories of Avignon. The man who waited at the *bureau des droits* would not pass me, but would send his son for the *patron du vaisseau.* I asked him if he would pass me if the *patron* was there. He said yes. Upon which I ordered the postilion to mount, and away we went a mile to the next village, where was the *patron*, for so they call the master in Provençal, that detestable corruption of Italian and French. He who takes the bark by the year entertained me well with bread and figs and almonds baked with honey, as is the custom in the country in the Christmas holidays. I carried the master with me; but when I arrived, my friend of the bureau desired a particular order to pass me. I had been informed that he would play that trick, and was prepared for him. I talked with a voice like an Indian chief and beat my staff upon his floor and asked him, "Did you not say that you would pass me if the master were here? Postilion, take note of his words. I will see the end of this affair." Thus did I threaten the rogue, though I knew well I could do him no manner of harm. He was frightened and agreed to pass me, so over I went and paid genteelly. Poor Jachone runs along with me, but is sadly covered with mud and greatly fatigued. The night was very cold.

I arrived at Avignon about eleven. It was comfortable to enter a good warm town. I put up at St. Omer's, the table d'hôte excellent, but my room was cold and smoky and I was ill off. The want of a servant was hard upon me. I however served myself wonderfully well, and by doing duty as a *valet de chambre* learnt to command well as a master, just as young officers learn by doing the duty of common soldiers. I had some warm wine and bread to comfort me, and then went to the Cathedral and heard the midnight mass. This was a most perfect satisfaction to me. I recollected how Dr. Boswell[1] told my mother of the splendid solemnity in Roman Catholic countries on Christmas Eve. I saw this now in France, and in a town under the dominion of the Pope. I was truly devout.

WEDNESDAY 25 DECEMBER. I rose in good frame to keep the

[1] Dr. John Boswell, his uncle.

feast of the Nativity of Jesus, and went and heard mass in the Cathedral. Yet I examined myself and found that my faith had been for some time very feeble. No help for it. I keep my doubts to myself, and, as I am very regular in acts of piety, I keep up external decency and preserve internal peace.

I sent to the Earl of Dunbar a respectful card with a letter from Mr. Lumisden. He answered me, "I wait with impatience, Sir, for the pleasure to embrace you, and am very sincerely your most obedient humble servant, Dunbar." I had only my *couteau de chasse*, so was obliged to appear in half dress. I entered his door with great pleasure. His first appearance was that of a very elegant man of fashion. He took me in his arms and kissed me on both sides of the face in the old Scots way, and his sister, my Lady Inverness, saluted me also with a kiss. I was just in the castle of some respected Scots lord. Lord Dunbar was a genteel, middle-sized man, rather thin, with a good deal of Lord Mansfield's look. He was a sensible, pretty, worthy man, and did honour to him who made him a peer.[2] Lady Inverness had been very handsome. She was a lively, clever, agreeable woman. Although both the brother and sister were old, they showed no marks of age. His Lordship had something of Lord Marischal's manner, and something peculiar to Scotland which pleased me mightily. He asked me to stay and eat a soup *sans façon*, which I most willingly agreed to do. I gave him an account of my Corsican tour, with which he was much entertained, and observed of Paoli's authority over his countrymen, "That could not be obtained by chance." His Lordship showed great curiosity and I had the happiness to give him satisfaction. At dinner was with us Mr. Stafford, an Irish gentleman who was of Prince Charles's train, a good, blunt, worthy fellow. Lady Inverness, helping me to soup, said, "Are you a kail-supper?"[3] — just the true Scots kindliness.

His Lordship said, "Lord Marischal was the most inconstant man. He differed with King James because he would not follow his advice. 'Your reasons, my Lord?' 'That's what I think, Sir.' And he

[2] James Murray, a Jacobite who took part in the Rebellion of 1715, was created Earl of Dunbar by the Old Pretender in 1721. He was a brother of Lord Mansfield, Lord Chief Justice of the King's Bench. Lady Inverness was the widow of a Jacobite peer.

[3] "Are you fond of broth?"

would say no more." My lady said he was vastly negligent and had many things lost, and going to Paris put Spanish gold pieces into chocolate pot which went really to pot. Lord Winton was from his youth crazy. When on his travels, had whim not to write name, even to draw for money; worked two years at Lyons as blacksmith till Dr. Pitcairne sent over money and brought him home.[4] When Prince Charles was born, Lord Winton fell upon his knees and remained so for an hour by the cradle, swearing fidelity and attachment, &c., to the Prince of Wales, and would not stir till he should see the King; "for," said he, "he may suspect." Lady Inverness was obliged to go into his room and say, "Sir, pray come and deliver us from Lord Winton." He came, and Lord Winton kissed hand and said although he had the greatest attachment for the Prince, yet that did not any how prejudice the allegiance to H.M. The King made him a gracious speech, which he could well do, for he was the best-bred, amiable man; wrote as well as any man. Had now and then vapours. Said, "I'm not master [enough of myself] not to think myself dying, but [I am] master [enough of myself] to think 'tis equal whether I die here or in street, so I can order my coach and go out." Prince never could study, except the fine arts, and cannot write well nor spell. Has the noble soul of his family; told Lady Inverness, who asked if he would marry; "No. Would you have me bring children into the world to be as miserable as I am? There is but one thing can make me happy; all between that and brown bread is just the same." When in favour with King of France, the King said, "Sir, you ask a great deal for all your friends, but nothing for yourself." PRINCE CHARLES. "I should consider it wrong to ask your Majesty; it is for you to think of that." Now he says, "I will have nothing to do with them. I despise them." Lady Inverness asked him, "Well, how do you like your old principality of Lochaber?" — which it seems belonged to them before they came to the crown. He gave her a hasty look, and said, "It is not so bad a country as you imagine. And let me tell you, I have walked over more Scots ground than most Scotsmen." In such good old conversation did the time pass till late in the evening, when I

[4] George Seton, fifth Earl of Winton, was one of the three rebel lords sentenced to death for their share in the Rebellion of 1715. He escaped from the Tower to France and then to Rome where he died in 1749. Dr. Archibald Pitcairne was a famous Edinburgh physician, Jacobite, and wit.

went home to my inn, wrote a little, and then supped at the table d'hôte, where the company was so disagreeable that I resolved never to sup more with them. I forgot that Lord Dunbar said he hoped I was come to pass some time with them. I said I was obliged to go next day. But in the afternoon, when we had talked cordially, the good old man's heart warmed and he said to me, "You're not absolutely pressed?" BOSWELL. "No." DUNBAR. "Will you give us another day?" BOSWELL. "Indeed will I, my Lord, with all my heart."

THURSDAY 26 DECEMBER. I went and looked at one or two churches. I was much pleased with that of St. Laurent, which the nuns had finely adorned with hangings of elegant lace, like that of Brussels. Avignon is a very agreeable place to live at. The air is excellent and there are there many nobles.

I went early to my Lord Dunbar's. There were many servants there, quite the old grandeur. He said he had advised Prince Charles always to speak to everybody, and by that means he had none of that *mauvaise honte* which makes many people so awkward. This King of Spain could speak well upon all occasions but where it was necessary for him to speak. (This struck me as being just myself.) He had made Prince Charles, when at Naples, a present of two horses with handsome rich furniture. Prince Charles next day at Court paid him some polite compliments of thanks, to which he could not answer a word. But immediately after, talked with great ease of anything else.

Lord Dunbar said that a man of true ambition fixed betimes a great point in view. And this was the case with Lord Mansfield. Lady Inverness had him up from Oxford and asked why he would not marry the lady that Lord George Murray afterwards did, saying she was a fortune.[5] "Fortune!" said he, "I'll make a fortune that you have no idea of."

Lord Dunbar had been this morning to wait on me, but I was gone out. He told me one or two curious stories of Peter Stewart, who was always called "the Protestant line," because when the stupid Hanoverians who pressed back on the army were fired upon he called out, "Take up the Protestant line"; and to Mungo Smith, brother of

[5] Lord George Murray, sixth son of the first Duke of Atholl, was one of the ablest generals under Prince Charles Edward in the Jacobite uprising of 1745. He married Amelia, daughter and heir of Dr. James Murray of Glencarse and Strowan.

Letham, who had been a broken silk merchant and of the reversion of his sale had bought commission, "Mungo, ye wad gie an inch to the ell to be off"; and when a *valet de chambre* whom Lord Orkney had made officer and aide-de-camp was killed galloping before the lines, "My Lord, my Lord! That makes guid the auld proverb, 'Set a beggar on horseback and he'll ride to the deil.' "[6] We recalled the ancient days of Scottish glory. They showed me the Battle of Luncarty done by an Italian painter vastly well: Hay and his sons well expressed, and the King seeing them, stately.[7] My Lord asked me seriously, "Are the greatest part of the people in Scotland reconciled to the Union?" BOSWELL. "My Lord, I fear they are; that is to say, they have lost all principle and spirit of patriotism."

Stafford carried me to his lodgings and showed me some papers with regard to Scotland, and promised me a copy of them. We returned to Lord Dunbar's where I sat an hour more. A marquise came in. Lady Inverness talked of somebody *qui gardait son lit*. "Pouf," said the Marquise, "quand on a des lits, il faut bien les garder."[8] She took quantities of snuff and pulled up her gown and warmed her legs, and in short was offensive. The French women may be virtuous, but they look like strumpets. The Italian women may be licentious, but they look modest. I said to Lord Dunbar and my Lady that I'd make their compliments to Lord Mansfield. They made no answer; but Lady Inverness said, "You'll see my sister at Edinburgh, and tell her you saw us well."[9] They either don't correspond with Lord Mansfield, or don't wish it should be known. I took leave of them cordially.[1]

[6] Probably events of the battle of Malplaquet in Flanders fought on 11 September 1709. George Hamilton, Earl of Orkney, was Colonel of the First Foot (Royal Scots) in which Stewart and Smith were officers.

[7] According to legend, Hay, a Scottish farmer, with the aid of his two sons, routed the Danes at the Battle of Luncarty in the latter half of the tenth century. Lady Inverness's late husband, the titular Earl of Inverness, was a Hay. "The King" is Kenneth II.

[8] Lady Inverness should have said, "qui gardait *le* lit" (who was keeping to his bed). The Marquise managed to see an indelicate reference in Lady Inverness's words and replied, "When one has beds, it's necessary to watch them well."

[9] Probably Nicolas Helen Murray (the "Miss Nicky Murray" who ruled the dancing assemblies of Edinburgh), but Lady Inverness had several other sisters.

[1] Dunbar wrote to Andrew Lumisden on 28 December: "We have at present, Sir, very cold weather, which I suspect has retarded the courier, but I have re-

FRIDAY 27 DECEMBER. I intended to have set out early, but a strong wind hindered the boat to pass the Rhône. I breakfasted on coffee and bread and butter with good Stafford. I was shown at Avignon the house where the Duke of Ormonde lived. It looked Gothic and venerable. Stafford said he was by no means a man formed for the important post which he filled. He was much the man of fashion and had a great deal of what the French call *du monde*, but no more.[2] I set out before noon and galloped along pretty well. At night I reached Nîmes where I put up A l'Orange.

SATURDAY 28 DECEMBER. Early this morning a brisk little fellow who officiated as antiquary showed me the Baths, which are elegant, but I could not distinguish what is ancient from what is modern. The Temple of Diana, fine remains; the Maison Carrée, the most beautiful remain in the world; the amphitheatre, most magnificent but sadly filled up with smoky houses. It looked large when I viewed the space of so many houses. I enjoyed well Nîmes.[3] At night I arrived at Montpellier and put up at Cheval Blanc.[4]

SUNDAY 29 DECEMBER. I had sent a card to Mr. Ray, merchant here, to whom Mr. Lumisden had recommended me. He had passed some time at Rome, and was so much of the antiquarian that they gave him the name of Dr. Ray. He was a free, sensible, good-humoured man with a variety of agreeable knowledge. After breakfasting he carried me a-walking. At a corner of one of the streets he showed me a singular thing. Not to encroach on the street, the corner

---

ceived yours by Mr. Boswell. I am extremely obliged to you for procuring me so valuable an acquaintance, having passed two days in his company with great pleasure" (Stuart papers, Royal Archives, Windsor Castle).

[2] James Butler, second Duke of Ormonde, held high appointments under James II, William and Mary, and Anne. He was impeached on the accession of George I for supposed Jacobite sympathies, fled to France, and joined the Old Pretender.

[3] "Nîmes is another Rome in regard of antiquities. I have seen here some as magnificent remains of Roman grandeur as are in the world over which these noble conquerors ruled. The contemplation of those antiquities banishes from my mind every frivolous and mean idea, and gives me a manly and virtuous tone which makes me happy in myself, and estimable to others" (Boswell to John Johnston, 28 December 1765).

[4] Smollett, who had stopped at this inn two years before, called it "a most wretched hovel, the habitation of darkness, dirt, and imposition" (*Travels*, i. 168).

The Maison Carrée at Nîmes, engraved by Louis Pierre Baltard; from Charles Louis Clérisseau, *Antiquités de la France*, Paris, 1804.

house, instead of having its corner fully built, retires at the bottom into the shape of a *clam*[5] shell, and supports the weight as an arch. Mr. Lumisden could write a dissertation upon this. We also saw a statue of the present King of France on horseback, very well done, and an aqueduct of very elegant taste, something Roman.[6] Ray and I talked Italian. I dined with him comfortably. I observed how absurd it was because a man has written a good book to make a travelling governor of him.[7] As well because a man has made a good watch, may you give him the command of an expedition. "Certainly," says Ray, "if a man has written a good book, encourage him to write another, and take him not from what he excels in." At five he carried me to see Lady St. John. I was tired with the dull talk of English ordinary plain kind of women. Ray and I had visited a Mr. Vives in the morning, a very pretty young man. This evening we visited Abemaar and Boeterheim, two Dutch young men; stupid enough work, for the one was a sort of fine gentleman and talked *prettily* to be sure, and the other was consumptive and coughed most hollowly. Ray and I returned to his house and eat eggs and talked on religion vastly well. He was full of the great plan of universal felicity at last, and had no doubt of his rising in the scale of immortal being.

MONDAY 30 DECEMBER. You[8] breakfasted with Ray and, I know not from what caprice, would defend the system of chance producing all things. To oppose his argument of constant uniformity in the productions of nature, I by chance found an orange of a very odd shape, with little excrescences on it like claws. I saw this at a fruit stand, bought it and held it up to the Doctor. Such sallies can I sometimes have. But you had not the least doubt of Supreme Existence, nor even appeared to have it; I only would show that the arguments which convince most people are not of such force as is the strong sentiment

[5] Scots for "scallop."

[6] The statue was actually of Louis XIV, not Louis XV. The aqueduct, which resembled a Roman one, had been finished just three weeks before Boswell's arrival.

[7] Boswell was probably thinking of Mallet, whose fame was derived from his *History of Denmark*.

[8] Here Boswell slips into the style generally used in the notes and memoranda. In most of this entry he originally wrote "you," but later changed it, in all but two instances, to "I."

of conviction that *God is*, which the mind naturally has impressed upon it, and I remember M. Deleyre told me that even the devout Rousseau had owned that he believed in the Divinity more from sentiment than from proof. Yet surely Dr. Clarke's argument for one great first cause is most noble and convincing.

I in vain sought at Montpellier the sweet ideas of fine air and pleasing amusement which I had associated with it. The frost was so intense that I thought myself in Russia. I had great pleasure in being able to say that I had felt much severer cold in the south of France than I had ever felt in Scotland. Ray begged I would stay longer. "I want to get more out of you," said he. "I grudge that you carry away anything that I have a right to have from you." I told him he paid me a compliment which I did not deserve, for my knowledge was very confined. I promised to send him from Scotland now and then a good production of his ingenious countrymen. I left this worthy fellow cordially.

The Cheval Blanc was a very dear inn. My *valet de place*, Pierre, had served my Lord Cassillis. He said, "My Lord is gentle as a lamb." My nails tormented me. I sent for a good surgeon. There came to me a *garçon* who was as awkward and bouncing a dog as if he had been bred a blacksmith. I set him off when I found how he looked at my toes.

I took the *brouette de la poste*[9] for six livres to Nîmes where I arrived about midnight, after having been jumbled to death in a confounded cart in company with a by-post[1] and a little jackanapes who in all probability was a travelling packman. I was much tired, and rather than go on to ——,[2] where I could wait for the Marseilles *brouette* to carry me on to Lyons, I chose to repose me quietly at the Orange, where I had formerly been, and my by-post carried thither my portmanteau, for which *onerous cause*[3] I made him sup with me in the kitchen, and he and I drank our couple of bottles of wine.

TUESDAY 31 DECEMBER. I had a great dispute with the mistres of the inn because she charged me too much. I was, however, obliged

[9] The mail wagon.

[1] A man carrying a post subsidiary to the regular mail.

[2] Probably Pont St.-Esprit.

[3] A legal term meaning "valuable consideration."

to pay her more than I ought to have done; after which she had the impudence to tell me that she heard there was an order for all the English to leave the country, and that she would be sorry. "Yes," said I, "sorry at not being able to rob them as you have robbed me." The ostler was a true Gaul. He asked *pour boire*. I told him he would hardly rise the night before to let me in. He said, "I did not know that it was you. If I had known that, I should have hastened to serve you." What an impudent rascal, when I am sure he did not know me from any other. He asked me if I would send him back by the postilion *pour boire*. I joked and said, "Perhaps." He thought I refused him, and, from licking the ground beneath my feet, he cried, "I hope to God that your horse falls with you." Notorious villain.

At the first post from Nîmes was a little horse, which, when I passed before, pleased me so much that I thought of buying him, and so riding quietly to Paris; but my toes were so bad that the great post-boots hurt me terribly and I suffered severely. Besides, I saw it was an idle scheme to buy a French post-horse which had probably many faults. At ——,[4] I found the Marseilles courier arrived. I agreed to go with him to Lyons for three louis, he paying for me at the inns. I paid for our dinner here. One of my feet was now swelled prodigiously, by reason of an inflammation in the toe. The courier was a fine, open, hearty fellow, a *bourgon.*[5] I saw in him what good health can do. His *brouette* was not a bad machine, though it went pretty rough. We drew our curtains and had wrappings enough to keep us warm. The landlord where we dined fell upon an excellent contrivance for my swelled foot. He bought me a hare's skin into which I put it, and so kept it as easy and warm as could be. My courier and I talked away very well on war and on peace; on his German wife. "For," said he, "je trouvais à Strasbourg à peu près ce qui me fallait."[6] I gave him great praise for his *à peu près*, for all that *nous faut* can hardly be found in marriage. We supped plentifully on game and drank good wine. We drove on all night.

[4] Pont St.-Esprit.

[5] Boswell was perhaps confused between *bourgogne* (Burgundy wine) and *bourguignon* (Burgundian).

[6] "I found at Strasbourg practically all that was necessary to me."

# *1766*

WEDNESDAY 1 JANUARY. We rumbled along, never stopping but to devour wild fowl and drink wine. Poor Jachone had sad work of it. The icy road hurt his feet and he used to whine most grievously. I was hard-hearted enough to let him suffer. We drove along still all night. I slept now and then tolerably.

THURSDAY 2 JANUARY. This morning we came to a very steep hill. The horses tried to pull us up, but could not. The courier attempted to put a stone under one of the wheels, but the wheel went back with such rapidity that it cut the point of his forefinger so that he was obliged to have a joint cut off. He bore it with great good humour and we drove along merrily to Lyons. I went to his house, where I saw his German wife, who was very handsome, and was most complacent to her husband. I took a fiacre and put my baggage into it and drove immediately to the bureau of the Lyons diligence. Finding that the best places were taken for Saturday, I engaged the first place for Monday. I then went to the Auberge au Parc and asked if my servant was arrived, as he had agreed to wait there till I should come and find him. He was not come. I therefore went to the house of Le Blanc, *baigneur*,[7] where I paid three livres a day, for which I had my room and wax candles, and was shaved and dressed. I sent a note to M. Bertollon, merchant here, a jolly dog whom I had seen at Mainz and journeyed with from thence to Mannheim.[8] He came to me. A restaurant keeper just by Le Blanc's furnished me dinner and half a bottle of wine for three livres, and Étienne, my *valet de place*, was very active and had the name of "l'éveillé." My feet were so bad that I could not walk across my room, so I hopped about as well as

[7] Literally, "bath keeper."

[8] Boswell described this "merchant of fine stuffs" as a "great lubberly dog with a head like a British tar," who "sang most outrageously" and was given to crying, "Damn, but I'm bored!" (*Boswell on the Grand Tour: Germany and Switzerland*, 2–4 November 1764).

my lameness would allow. La Marie, an old maid of the inn, was my *gouvernante*, and I let myself be taken care of by her, and went early to sleep in a soft bed with the curtains drawn, and was as much a lazy old man as if I had been sixty and never had seen Paoli. Poor Jachone had his feet swelled and sore with fatigue. I caused make a bed of hay for him in the corner of my room, where he lay very snugly. Jacob arrived this very day and came to me in the evening. He was just as glad to see me as if he had been with me all his life: but he said he would not go to Paris even if I should insist on it, for he saw that he should spend what money he had gained. He also told me that he had really suffered from seeing my stinginess. I made him wait a day here but was well persuaded that it was better to part with him at Lyons.

FRIDAY 3 JANUARY. The surgeon of a *charité*[9] here came and dressed my feet. He was a fat and an alarming dog, for he very gravely advised me to pull out my nail altogether, "because," said he "in so doing, you will have no more risk of ever being troubled with it." As well might he have advised me to cut off my hand, had I hurt it. He gave me a softening plaster for my toe and bid me wait till I got to Paris to have it cured. I sent to a Mme. Boy de la Tour,[1] for whom her sister, Mlle. Roguin at Yverdon, had given me a recommendation a year ago. I knew she was a friend of M. Rousseau and begged she would inform me where he was. She let me know that he was at Paris. This gave me a bounce of joy, for I now saw him just before me, and pleased myself with talking to him fully of the noble affairs of Corsica. I immediately wrote him a most spirited letter. I also wrote to Dr. Pringle begging he would settle my being on an independent and genteel footing on my return to Scotland. I enclosed open for his perusal, a letter for my father in which I talked strongly of my views and promised to do my best. Jacob came and received all that I owed him, and took leave of me. I told him that I regarded him as a very worthy man, but that I was, however, glad that he left me for, after having rebelled and been so free, it was impossible he could be a good servant for one of my disposition. He seemed angry a little at this. He made awkward speeches as how he wished to have served

[9] A religious establishment for the care of the sick.

[1] She was the owner of the house in which Rousseau lived at Môtiers.

ne better, and was sorry for having ever offended me, and was much obliged to me for my goodness to him, &c. Thus was I at last separated rom my Swiss governor. I wished him sincerely all happiness.[2]

[EDITORIAL NOTE: With the following letter, Boswell tried to establish contact again with Rousseau, who had become involved in ery serious difficulties. His *Lettres écrites de la montagne*, an attack n the magistrates of Geneva, had been answered in December 1764 shortly after Boswell's visit to him) by *Sentiment des citoyens*, an nonymous pamphlet which maintained that his reputation for strict norality was a fraud, and specifically charged that he and Thérèse ad had five illegitimate children, who had been deposited in a founding hospital. This pamphlet, which Rousseau attributed to a Genevan minister named Vernes though it was actually by Voltaire, so pset him that he had it republished in Paris in January 1765 with efutatory notes of his own. His denials were not fully convincing nd even his haste to defend himself was suspicious; the accusation, he truth of which he was later to admit, severely damaged his posiion as a man of austere virtue.

A more important consequence was that it brought the author of *mile*, one of the great works on the education of children, face to ace with a terrible divergence between his theory and practice. He vas forced to question his own self-estimation, a process which both rove him close to madness and engendered that masterpiece of revlatory defence, the *Confessions*.

Rousseau's feelings of persecution were excessive, but they did ave very practical bases. Forbidden to return to France or Geneva, e was safe only for the time being in the Principality of Neuhâtel. The local clergy were incensed that the wicked could live eacefully in their midst, and one of their number, M. de Montmolin, by a sermon so aroused the population of Môtiers against him in eptember 1765 that his house was stoned. The official protection of rederick the Great, obtained through his friend Lord Marischal, no onger sufficed, and Rousseau fled to the little island of Saint-Pierre n the neighbouring canton of Berne. After six weeks here, the Berese authorities told him to leave, and he hurried off to Strasbourg un-

Boswell furnished Jacob with a letter of reference in which he is described s "extremely active, careful, and honest upon all occasions."

decided where to settle next and with death in his heart.[3] Finally h
determined to go to England at the cordial invitation of David Hume
the two did not know each other but Hume had long admired him
In Paris he joined Hume, who was serving as secretary to the Britis
Ambassador, and on 4 January 1766, the same day on which Boswel
wrote the letter printed below, they left together for England wher
they arrived nine days later.]

[Boswell to Rousseau. Original in French][4]

Lyons, 4 January 176

ILLUSTRIOUS PHILOSOPHER! At last the darkness has lifted. Fo
several months I have had no idea into what corner you had fled, an
I did not know how to address a letter to you. Have you received on
that I wrote to you from Leghorn, before I embarked for Corsica?
spent five weeks in the island. I saw a great deal of its people. I ac
quired information with an attention which you would not believ
me capable of. I became intimately acquainted with General Paol
that noble man. I have treasures to communicate to you. If you sti
have as warm feelings for the brave islanders as you had when yo
wrote to the gallant Buttafoco, you will embrace me with enth
siasm. You will forget all your sorrows for many an evening. I a
under the deepest obligations to you for having sent me to Corsic
That voyage has done me a wonderful amount of good. It has affecte
me in the same way that Plutarch's *Lives* would if they were fus
into my mind. Paoli has given a temper to my soul which it will nev
lose. I am no longer the tender, anxious being who complained to y
in your Val de Travers. I am a man. I think for myself. You will s
with your own eyes.

I arrived here yesterday, and this evening Mme. Boy de la To
told me that you are in Paris. I would give a great deal if you cou
have seen the joy with which I received this information. I take t
Monday diligence and shall be in Paris Saturday. I never swea

[3] See Rousseau's two letters to Thérèse printed in Appendix B.

[4] Printed from the original, owned by Frederick W. Hilles. Boswell's co
which has fewer corrections than the original, is in the Yale collection. Si
the letter was in the collection of Duchesne, Rousseau's Parisian bookseller a
friend, he may never have received it.

otherwise you would have a volley of those oaths by which the mad English express extraordinary satisfaction.

I am bound to the Corsicans heart and soul. If you, illustrious Rousseau, the philosopher whom they have chosen to aid them by his insight to conserve and to enjoy the liberty they have won so heroically — if you have grown cold towards these brave islanders, I am enough of a man to be able to regard you with pity. But generosity constitutes a part of your being, and I am not one of those who believe that the noble qualities of the soul can be destroyed.

I am told that you are going to England. What a wonderful prospect for me! I am sure there is no man on earth more keenly disposed to contribute to your happiness than I, and you will be sure of it too; and in time you will rely on the young friend of my Lord Marischal. I propose a perfect satisfaction for myself in introducing Mr. Johnson to you, about whom I told you so much at Môtiers, and of whom you said, "I should love that man, I should respect him" — and that after having heard that he would scarcely respect you.[5] But I know you both, and although the one employs his powers to uphold the wisdom of the centuries, and the other to feed the fires of his own sublime and original spirit, I am sure that your great souls will acknowledge each other with warmth. And you shall go to Scotland, and you shall visit our romantic country-seat; and Rousseau shall meditate in the venerable woods of my ancestors, and he shall share my belief that nymphs, genii, angels, and all kinds of benevolent and happy spirits hold their choirs there. Farewell, my dear Sir. How impatient I am to see you, and to tell you a thousand enchanting anecdotes of Corsica. The moment I arrive in Paris I shall send to Mme. Duchesne's, where I hope to find a line from you. I am ever yours, as I was at Môtiers,

BOSWELL.

SATURDAY 4 JANUARY. I regretted being confined to the house at Lyons, where are several Roman remains. I had always an idea that my father had passed some time here. I know not if it was true. But this idea made me look on Lyons with a degree of reverence. The son of Mme. Boy de la Tour came and saw me. He was a merchant here, young, pock-pitted, and repeating sentences as if he had got

[5] See *Boswell on the Grand Tour: Germany and Switzerland*, 15 December 1764.

them by heart. At four I went and visited his mother. She was dull enough, but her daughter was a fine, healthy, sentimental girl. I don't know how, she engaged me to be quite free and open with her. I supped there, but the French small talk and made airs irritated me.

SUNDAY 5 JANUARY. Bertollon dined with me. I called again at Mme. Boy de la Tour's. I know not why, I was quite rustic these two days, with my hair undressed. I went to bed early as the diligence set out next morning. I had been to see it. The coachman took me into the yard where it stood. The strength and size of it struck me much. I exclaimed, "Ma foi, c'est une voiture respectable!"

MONDAY 6 JANUARY. At four I was at the *bureau de la diligence*. The company were a Chevalier de St. Louis who had served in America, a Chevalier de Malte who had served in Germany, a Norman, a Parisian, the French Consul at Barcelona, with his wife, who was vapourish and in constant fear of death, and a little daughter of five or six years. I cannot mark precisely each day of our journey. I will therefore just lump these six days together. We were all very soon acquainted.[6]

[Received 12 January 1766, Lumisden to Boswell][7]

12 October 1765

As I AM PERSUADED you have left Leghorn, I address this, as I did my former letter, to Genoa. You will probably receive both at the same time. I need not tell you what an agreeable entertainment your letter from Lucca of the 30th past gave me. I am indeed at a loss which to admire most in it, the stern philosopher or the sprightly lover. The latter listened to the siren, but the former soon got the better of the spell. How much labour did it cost Ulysses to get rid of

[6] There are no entries for 7–11 January. From Auxerre, on 9 January, Boswell wrote to Johnston that he was enjoying the trip, and had "great vigour and a pure absence of thought." He stopped at Sens to see his relative John Nairne, a Jacobite.

[7] The manuscript of this letter in the Boswell papers at Yale is oddly enough a copy, though in Lumisden's hand. Lumisden, fearing that the original letter sent to Genoa would miscarry, probably enclosed a copy in another letter which he sent to Boswell at Paris. A text from Lumisden's letter-book, practically identical with the text given here, is printed in *Memoirs of Sir Robert Strange*, i. 206–207.

Circe! In these cases it is dangerous to trust so feeble a counsellor as reason. The safest measure is to fly the temptation. I blame you not, my dear friend, for what has happened. Youth, passion, even novelty apologizes for you. Let me, however, congratulate you on your happy escape; for I flatter myself that you have not risked a second separation. It is enough you have once tasted Italian gallantry. It will serve to embellish your history. Your warm, unsuspicious heart might easily feel a real passion. But I know too much of the ladies of this country to suppose that your fair one felt the same. Accustomed to change, they are strangers to this passion. Amidst variety it never can be properly felt. Artful in a science in which art should not enter, they can pretend ardours, sighs, and flames when their hearts are perfectly at ease. Trust them not. Preserve your vigour for some healthful, innocent Scots lass, a stranger to intrigue, who will make you a happy father of a family, and continue the race of those worthy ancestors, whose memories you so justly esteem. . . .

[Received 12 January 1766, Girolama Piccolomini to Boswell. Original in Italian]

Siena, 12 December 1765

After your return from Corsica I received your two very kind letters,[8] in which you give me an exact account of all that has happened to you. You cannot imagine how relieved I felt, especially since I had not heard from you for so long. Letters from you will always be dear to me, and I thank you a thousand times for having sent me these, as reading them is at present the sweetest relief I have from the continual vexations that surround me. I swear to you that your letters have been the most agreeable pleasure that I have tasted since your departure from Siena, and I promise you that they will remain my sole pleasure in the future. Although at times the feelings you express appear to me more ingenious than sincere, nevertheless I abandon myself to all the tender agitation which they arouse in me. I cannot think of the time I have spent with you without the strongest perturbation; in this very moment in which I write to you, I feel a violent resurgence of the strong impression that you made on me, and

[8] Boswell wrote to Moma on 31 [sic] November and 6 December 1765 (Register of Letters).

I experience the effects of that sweet memory. I am sorry that you cannot observe the excitement with which I write this letter, and the emotions I feel in this very process; but you can imagine them if you have ever been in love, as you know the strength of desire, and you know what desperate remedies must be taken when lovers are separated.

I am glad that you made the tour of Corsica safely and that Signor Paoli did justice to your merits, as anyone must do who knows you. Though I had strong doubts about your returning to Siena, the smallest of hopes sustained me in my distress; so that when I lost it (to quote your own unfeeling words) I could not help being overcome by a deep melancholy, without hope of ever rousing from it all the days of my life. Nevertheless, I would not advise you ever to come to Siena with the slightest presumption of my favour, for I wish rather to be your friend than your mistress. From that you will know that my love is not based on a mere whim, and that I place your happiness above my own quiet and repose.

Tell me all about your tour of France, of your arrival and of your stay there. I shall be delighted to hear of your diversions whatever they may be. Even if they are enjoyed at the expense of my feelings I shall willingly suffer them, provided they make you happy. In short, tell me everything that happens to you, especially about your health which concerns me very deeply. Take care of yourself — which you have not done in the past — and be moderate in your pleasures, so as to enjoy them longer. My concern for you cannot seem suspicious because of any personal interest which I may have in participating in your pleasures. Though my desires are always directed towards you, the great distance between us prevents me from summoning you thence, did nothing else stop me. But it gives me the greatest consolation to hear that you are in a state to enjoy some diversions.

By way of giving you an exact account of myself, let me tell you that after you left I was seized with bad convulsions accompanied by fever, which obliged me to keep to my bed for some weeks. I took purges, which did me a great deal of good and put my machine in its usual state, but my spirits are more disordered than ever. As to my amusements, they consist of knitting a stocking, in reading a book, and at night, in going the old round. Since your departure Bino has not left me, but he is always in a vile humour. Placido comes very seldom, and I do not bother myself with winning him back. Bianconi stayed here a long time, and I confessed to him my passion for you.

I gave your compliments to Porzia, telling her that you were corresponding with me, and that you had seen nothing of any reply to a letter you had written to her. She told me that she had thought many times of writing to you, since you had favoured her with a most obliging letter. As to the revenge that you put in my power to take against Porzia, I did not think it right to put it into effect, knowing that you had deceived me many times while dealing candidly with her. And although at present your kindness for me is greater, yet it is not right to laugh at one who trusts you. Therefore, on this point I cannot approve your conduct, for an honourable man ought not to say what he does not feel in his heart. Does what I say convince you? Or do you believe it to be the advice of an interested party who wants always to hear from you nothing but the truth? You are right in holding me slightly suspect, because of the interest I take in everything you say to me about myself, and for the doubt which stirs in me when I hear that you are capable of writing to flatter. But all of this aside, I do not like a man with that sort of character. If Porzia accepted your proposal, how would you clear yourself? And do you feel no remorse at such proceedings? Do you feel justified in instituting them because she was willing to use the same weapons against you? Judge for yourself.

I send a little note with a commission for me,[9] which you do not have to execute if it is a bother. In case you are willing to take the trouble, you must apply to a lady who is skilled and accurate. The bill should run to about thirty sequins. Advise me how to remit the money, whether through the courier himself, or through the Astini bank.

You correct me for an *ha* which I write in places I should not. In return I urge you to scan the sense of my letters, never the word order nor the spelling. But in the future, I shall banish all *h*'s from my letters, which shows the importance I attach to your advice.[1] I con-

[9] The "little note" is the enclosure printed below.

[1] Moma sometimes added an *h*, writing *ha* for *a* (to), and sometimes dropped one, writing *anno* for *hanno* (they have). In at least one case she wrote *Ho Dio* for *O Dio*. This indicates nothing about her pronunciation, for in Italian *h* is always silent.

gratulate you on writing our language very well. If you made no mistakes in the tenses, you would be perfect. But since you are so clever you need not make fun of a poor woman who lives merely because she eats.

Dear Boswell, give me your friendship as I give you all my love. Command me if you wish to oblige me, for neither time nor distance shall make me forget you. If you find another who loves you as much as I do, I shall be content if you return her love. Farewell, farewell.[2]

[Enclosure:] A pair of ear-rings with three drops of flat pearls. Thirty-two ells of cloth of the latest fashion with a watered ground; the colour of the ground should be throat-of-pigeon; or if that colour cannot be had, the nearest to it. Accessory materials for making up the said cloth, according to the fashion, with chemisette, flounces, knots on the sleeves, flowers, and *sclavage*[3] rather high in the neck.

A pair of sleeves of silk point-lace, all of one piece, and six ells of matching lace to make the pieces surrounding the neck.

SUNDAY 12 JANUARY.[4] Yesterday, after being up night with Nairne, set out again in old diligence, and rolled comfortable. Passed by Fontainebleau; immense numbers of hares and partridges. By bad weather, nothing to be seen. Approached Paris, Invalides appeared as St. Paul's does, coming to London. Was not affected much. Came to bureau, got baggage, and in fiacre to Mme. Duchesne's; Rousseau gone. Asked for next *baigneur's;* [directed to] Le Clerc, Rue de Pierre Sarrazin; little, cold, high room. Submitted to fate, hardy.

MONDAY 13 JANUARY. Awaked tolerable; no change of ideas from being in Paris. Had some milk; in fiacre went to Scots College.[5]

[2] The remaining correspondence between Moma and Boswell is printed in Appendix A.

[3] Presumably this word, whose meaning is uncertain, is related to the French *esclavage* or "choke collar."

[4] From this point to 23 February, Boswell kept only a condensed journal, or journal notes. — Boswell's news paragraphs in *The London Chronicle* (see p. 244) have now begun to appear, and form an amusing counterpoint to his private record.

[5] A Catholic seminary for Scots, which developed from a foundation for students established by Bishop David of Moray in 1325. Its purpose was to provide priests for the Scottish missions, but because of financial difficulties and its supposed Jansenist tendencies it was not flourishing at this time.

Felt the good old sentiments. Principal Gordon, a tall, stately man, sensible and obliging.[6] Saw many pictures of House of Stuart. Made me stay dinner. Had servant for me, Joseph, who had served Hon. George Stuart. Dined well; old Mr. Riddoch, Mr. Patullo, [who spoke] braid Scots. After dinner Mr. Macdonald, &c. [and had] just old ideas. Had heard mass at St. Stephen's.[7] Evening went to[8] Hôtel de Dauphin, Rue de Taranne. Was well satisfied.

TUESDAY 14 JANUARY. Yesterday little surgeon dresses my toes. In all day writing; send to De Tuyll.[9] He comes, and seems genteel. You talk of sister. He says, "I am not sure, but I think you will make a very good husband for my sister." He said Bellegarde's marriage was merely "convenable." He set you a-thinking of old scheme.

WEDNESDAY 15 JANUARY. Yesterday had black suit, and looked most lawyer-like. Paid visits; was hipped, however. Saw nobody but Tuyll. Resolved to write to father[1] and put confidence in him to propose marriage [for you] if she still preferred [you]. You was agitated.

THURSDAY 16 JANUARY. Yesterday in all day and wrote magnificent letter to De Zuylen. Was quite *étourdi;*[2] would set out immediately. Wrote Father of seeing end of this affair.[3]

[6] "I was carried up another pair of large, dirty stairs to the Principal, who was a tall, raw-boned man about sixty years of age, seemed to be much broken with the gout, who talked a medley of a language between Scotch and French; he received me in his chamber, which was hung all round with pictures of the unhappy and unfortunate family of Stuart" (William Cole's *Journal of My Journey to Paris in 1765,* ed. F. G. Stokes, 1931, p. 193).

[7] St.-Étienne-du-Mont.

[8] That is, moved to.

[9] Willem René van Tuyll, Zélide's eldest brother. Boswell had received a letter from Willem René's father on 12 January telling him that his son was at Paris, and also that Zélide might soon marry the Marquis de Bellegarde, a colonel in the Dutch service. The letter is printed in *Boswell in Holland,* Correspondence, No. 18.

[1] Zélide's father, Diederik Jacob van Tuyll, Lord of Zuylen. Boswell's letter and M. de Zuylen's friendly reply of 30 January saying that he could not take up Boswell's proposal until M. de Bellegarde's case was settled are printed in *Boswell in Holland,* Correspondence, Nos. 19, 20. Ultimately, of course, Zélide married neither of them.

[2] Giddy.

[3] Boswell's letter to Lord Auchinleck is missing, but he gives its substance in his letter to M. de Zuylen. He had received a letter (not recovered) from Lord

FRIDAY 17 JANUARY. Yesterday visited Hon. Alexander Murray; heard all his story. Quite Lord Elibank.[4] Was pleased to revive such ideas. Surgeon [said cure would be] slow; set in for long process. Agreed [fee should be ——] louis. Sent letter to De Zuylen; was like man of great business.

SATURDAY 18 JANUARY. Yesterday went to Luxembourg. Not day to see gallery. Admired much the fabric in the Tuscan style. Then to Palais Royal. Mind was revived at the sight of palace with pictures, but it was so dark could see nothing, and the cold was intense. Went to an hotel to dine. They asked three livres *sans vin;* you would not stay. Mean. Went to Café de Conti; [met] Clarke of London. Home and dined with him and his wife. Colonel Gordon came in after dinner in his usual spirits.[5] You had plenty of animal spirits, and easily showed him how superior you was. Went to Scots College and eat bread and cheese. Abernethy, an officer, was there; was at burial of Sir William Gordon of Park,[6] on ramparts at Douai, a six and twenty pounder at his head and sentry at his foot. John Bain pronounces oration: "Pretty man of Scotland. [Let] nae mon seek for justice; [he'll] gae awa' wi' sair heart. March!"

SUNDAY 19 JANUARY. Yesterday morning Wilkes, for whom you had left card, had the assurance to send his *valet de chambre* to ask you to dine. You sent answer he had not been here. "I must thresh him. Say there's a fencing-master with me." Soon after he came, and was just the usual courteous man. You felt yourself above him. He had the effrontery to tell you Paoli offered him a regiment. You was

---

Auchinleck on 12 January saying that his health was better and that Boswell had his permission to spend a month in Paris. Boswell in reply asked for permission to go back to England via Flanders and Holland. Lord Auchinleck replied on 30 January strongly opposing any match with a *bel esprit* and foreigner like Zélide, but Boswell did not receive this letter until the following July (*Boswell in Holland,* Correspondence, No. 21).

[4] Murray, brother of the fifth Lord Elibank, was an active but cautious Jacobite. He retired to France in 1751, and was created Earl of Westminster by the Old Pretender in 1759. He was recalled from exile in 1771.

[5] Whether this was the same Colonel Gordon whom Boswell had known in Rome is uncertain.

[6] A Jacobite who had gone over to France and died in 1751, after taking part in the '45.

struck, but laughed it off: "Come, come, come, don't tell me so. Don't play upon me. You have been diverting yourself by telling over Switzerland that you had choice of three places to be minister." He looked odd. BOSWELL. "You must know, Sir, that there are no regiments in Corsica." "Oh," said he, "an equivalent to a regiment, a command. Signor —— offered it me at Naples." BOSWELL. "Oh, he has been sounding you." WILKES. "Signor —— is not a man to sound people." Agreed to dine with him. A Burke there.[7] Wilkes talked of Corsica: "I wonder you could leave it. As I passed by it in tartane,[8] pulled off hat and drunk his[9] health." "French conversation, light,[1] not as in English book where you prove clearly Lord Bute the most abandoned minister."[2] When he took leave of Voltaire, the old poet told him, "Sir, you must either live in London, or Paris, or Heaven, or — Hell. You must be in one of these four places — no matter which." Wilkes chose the last, "Because," said he, "the wittiest poem I ever read, the *Pucelle d'Orléans*,[3] puts there the very best company: most of the popes, many cardinals, almost all kings." Wilkes said, "We are not only the most brave, but the most generous nation. We have given you all [our conquests?] back." VOLTAIRE. "But your generosity would be more esteemed were there not some among you that grumble at it."[4] Wilkes showed you some notes on Churchill. Did not think them so clever.

Had been morning with De Tuyll; made him come to you at

[7] Richard Burke, Edmund Burke's brother.

[8] A small one-masted vessel used in the Mediterranean.

[9] Paoli's.

[1] This word is uncertain.

[2] Probably a remark of Voltaire to Wilkes. The "English book" is apparently a reference to the collected edition of *The North Briton.* Wilkes wrote in *The North Briton,* No. 45, in regard to the King's speech at the opening of Parliament: "This week has given the public the most abandoned instance of ministerial effrontery ever attempted to be imposed on mankind."

[3] Voltaire's ribald poem on Joan of Arc.

[4] The Peace of Paris (1763) ending the Seven Years' War had been chiefly managed for the British by Lord Bute. Current English feeling that certain possessions had been unnecessarily restored to the French is reflected by Wilkes's statement in his notes to Churchill's *Gotham,* that the Peace of Paris "proved more ruinous to England than all the swords of all our enemies" (*Correspondence of John Wilkes,* iii. 16).

night. Talked of scheme on Zélide, was hipped a little, afraid to venture. Saw all fretful situations. Recalled force; [thought of] variety of life. You and Tuyll pleased with this. Thought you'd undertake to live well with her on honour. He joked, and bid you be *sage:* "I am concerned in this." His melancholy speculations of Supreme Being did not affect you. Curious consciousness. God may make you any kind of being. Said to Tuyll, "When one is too delicate, door opening offends, and you speculate, 'Why are doors made to give wind?' But in health you don't think so. Thus tender mind is hurt by [notions of] moral evil." Bid him farewell like father: "Heer Van Zuylen, onderdanighste dienaar."[5]

MONDAY 20 JANUARY. Mass, Scots College, Strange.[6]

TUESDAY 21 JANUARY. Stayed in all day writing. Received a letter from Mr. Johnson, treating you with esteem and kindness.[7] Was nobly elated by it, and resolved to maintain the dignity of yourself.

WEDNESDAY 22 JANUARY. Morning went to Wilkes. Sir Harry Echlin with him. Wilkes appeared a little sunk by distress, but had always Catullus[8] and *Pucelle d'Orléans* with him. Went and found Horace Walpole, whom you had treated with by cards,[9] lean, genteel man. Talked to him of Corsica. He said you should give something about them, as there are no authentic accounts. You said you intended to do so. He had seen Theodore,[1] but, whether from pride or stupidity,

[5] "Most obedient servant."

[6] Robert (later Sir Robert) Strange, the engraver, who was Lumisden's brother-in-law. Lumisden had sent Alves's miniature of Boswell to him to forward to Scotland.

[7] See p. 194.

[8] Wilkes published an edition of Catullus in 1788.

[9] Walpole's evasive card is printed in the seventh volume of Colonel Isham's private edition of the *Private Papers of James Boswell:*

"Mr. Walpole is extremely thankful to Mr. Boswell for his obliging note, and shall be very glad of the honour of his acquaintance, and will endeavour to find him at home or hopes to meet him. Is very sorry it has not happened, but as Mr. Walpole, from conforming to the French hours while he is here, and living much with the people, rises very late, and is seldom at home afterwards till very late too, he has been so unlucky as not to see Mr. Boswell, but flatters himself he shall soon have an opportunity of being acquainted with him."

[1] Theodore, Baron von Neuhoff, was a fantastic adventurer who arrived in Corsica in 1736 and persuaded the Corsican leaders to proclaim him King. He

he hardly spoke any. Horace has the original writing for getting him out of prison, and the great seal of the kingdom. He said the Pretender had best title [to the British throne,] but not right. He looked on Rousseau as mountebank with great parts.[2] Dined with Wilkes and Sir Harry. Then Lady Berkeley's.

THURSDAY 23 JANUARY. Yesterday Principal Gordon and Mr. Strange dined with you. All went well. You saw pass by a procession of ransomed captives. At five came in Caffarena and talked sensibly and sung. But you tired of him.

FRIDAY 24 JANUARY. You paid visits yesterday morning. Wilkes and Caffarena dined. You said Ramsay wickedly said Strange would not do pictures as Jacobite. WILKES. "No objection to my Lord Bute."[3] Wilkes was so bad [you was] obliged to go. Drove Caffarena about. Found self mean, but your mind was so fortified you stood all.

SATURDAY 25 JANUARY. Yesterday taken up all day to get trunk

---

brought magnificent promises of support with him, but little material aid. After a chequered career, he abandoned Corsica and went to England, where he ended in debtor's prison. Walpole exerted himself on Theodore's behalf, and after his death in 1756, erected a tablet to him in St. Anne's, Soho.

[2] Walpole wrote to Gray on 18 February 1768, "Pray read the new *Account of Corsica*. . . . The author, Boswell, is a strange being, and . . . has a rage of knowing anybody that ever was talked of. He forced himself upon me at Paris in spite of my teeth and my doors, and I see has given a foolish account of all he could pick up from me about King Theodore [*Account of Corsica*, pp. 137–138]. He then took an antipathy to me on Rousseau's account, abused me in the newspapers, and exhorted Rousseau to do so too: but as he came to see me no more, I forgave all the rest. I see he now is a little sick of Rousseau himself, but I hope it will not cure him of his anger to me. However, his book will I am sure entertain you" (*The Yale Edition of Horace Walpole's Correspondence*, xiv. 170–171). For Gray's answer, see p. 147. Boswell sent Walpole a presentation copy and letter dated 23 February 1768, in which he politely said that Walpole's advice to publish something to show the Corsicans in a proper light was his first incitement to undertake the *Account of Corsica.*

[3] In 1759 George III (then Prince of Wales) offered Strange one hundred pounds to engrave his portrait and Lord Bute's. Strange had made other plans, and felt as well that the remuneration was inadequate for a possible two years of work, so he declined, only to discover that Allan Ramsay, who was involved in the affair, was misrepresenting him and saying that Strange had declined because of his strong Jacobite principles. Wilkes is suggesting that Bute was a Jacobite at heart.

out of *douane*, except with Strange, who told James's death.[4] Was dull a little. Met there[5] a young fellow who gave you names of good bordellos. Went to fiacre [and said] "Do you know any of these?" [He knew] Mme. Hecquet; went. Mlle. Constance, tall, quite French lady. Feigned simplicity. [She said,] "I'll show you all the sights."

SUNDAY 26 JANUARY. Yesterday evening Montigny's; sad work.[6]

MONDAY 27 JANUARY. Heard mass at Théatins. Went to Ambassador's Chapel; old ideas of Church of England, in some measure. Sermon made you gloomy, or rather tired. At Wilkes's saw in *St. James's Chronicle*, Mother's death.[7] Quite stunned; tried to dissipate [grief.] Dined Dutch Ambassador's; much of Corsica. At six Mme. Hecquet's as in fever. Constance elegant.

TUESDAY 28 JANUARY. Yesterday morning sent to Foley; got letter from Father, written by David. Too true; Mother gone. Was quite stupefied. In all morning. Wept in bursts; prayed to her like most solemn Catholic to saint. Roused philosophy; sung Italian gently to soothe. But would not have hurt prejudices by doing so before others. Called on Principal Gordon, told him privately sad news. Had company with him who had said mass for requiem to old James. Lord Alford (Sir John Graham) genteel man. Curious feelings; was prudent, but with true philosophy sustained your distress; was decent. Had strong enthusiasm to comfort Father all his life.

[Lord Auchinleck to Boswell]

Edinburgh, 11 January 1766

MY DEAR SON, — In my last I acquainted you that your dear mother was indisposed, and was to get a vomit that evening on which

[4] The Old Pretender died on 1 January 1766. Strange had just received a letter from Lumisden describing the funeral.

[5] At the customs.

[6] The Hotel Montigny, a well-known brothel, was run by a Mlle. Dupuis. Charlotte Geneviève Hecquet, mentioned in the previous entry, ran a couple of establishments.

[7] The notice appeared in *The St. James's Chronicle* for 18 January 1766: "At Edinburgh, Lady Auchinleck, spouse to the Hon. Alexander Boswell of Auchinleck, Esq., one of the Senators of the College of Justice."

my letter was wrote; I did not then apprehend her to be in any danger, but from that time forward she daily turned worse of a slow and obstinate fever, which at length put a period to her valuable life this morning half an hour after seven. This melancholy event you'll easily believe affects me deeply; I have lost my friend, my adviser and assistant in everything, and that has made me agree to use your brother's hand, which he out of compassion made offer of to me. My dear Jamie, had you seen and heard what we have been witnesses to these last three weeks, you would have agreed with us that many useful lessons were to be learned. Your dear mother, who from the beginning of her illness had a fixed persuasion that she was to die of it, and in that view spoke to me seriously on different subjects and particularly in relation to you, for whom she had always a great affection, and who she hoped would return with proper dispositions — I say notwithstanding this her persuasion of approaching death, she was so far from showing any terror that she expressed a pleasure in the thoughts of it; and indeed nothing could be a greater proof of the reality and efficacy of true religion than what appeared in her conduct during the whole time of her indisposition; and notwithstanding the many medicines, blisterings, and other operations she underwent, she never once complained; on the contrary, said that she thought she was likely to have an easy passage. This her conduct was not owing to insensibility, or to a disbelief or the least doubt of her immortality or of a future state, but to her most serious, constant, and habituated attention to her duty both to God and to the world, and to a full persuasion in and through the merits of our blessed Redeemer of attaining endless bliss in the other world. Among her last words, a very little time before her death she audibly though with a faltering tongue said, "I have fought the good fight of faith, I have finished my course, henceforth is prepared for me a crown of glory,"[8] and when she had expressed a longing for death and was asked if she did not wish to recover to be a comfort to her family, she answered she wished to be with Christ, which is far better. She left us without any struggle or even a groan, and as it were fell asleep. She was one who all her life long was intent and diligent in doing her duty both to God and the world. You know her attachment to devotion and serious re-

[8] See II Timothy 4. 7–8.

ligion, and you know that she managed all my private affairs with the utmost accuracy, and was anxious to serve all her friends and acquaintances. I am now reduced to a destitute state; I have lost my friend, I have lost my adviser in all things which concerned both worlds. You have lost a most affectionate and kind mother, and will doubtless be affected deeply with this awful stroke as we and all your friends here are; and as upon the back of this, diversions of any kind cannot have any relish with one of your sensibility, it will occur to you how much I need your assistance, this irreparable breach made upon me besides the having my old bodily trouble still hanging about me; and therefore, it will be needless to tell you that I expect you home with all speed. Your brother remembers you with great affection. I am, my dear son, your affectionate father.

ALEX. BOSWEL.

P.S. The contents of this letter are not to be shown, being intended for yourself. Since writing this letter I have had the pleasure of yours from Marseilles and rejoice to hear of your arrival in France. Do not disquiet yourself about the money you have spent; if you turn out in the way I expect, I shall never grudge these expenses. You have got £100 credit on Paris. Farewell, my dear Jamie, may God bless and preserve you.[9]

WEDNESDAY 29 JANUARY. Yesterday felt more the sad news. Recalled her kind, affectionate concern. Was deeply touched, but

[9] Lord Auchinleck's attitude was elaborated in a letter to Boswell from his brother David. (The letter is dated 3 February 1766, but Boswell has endorsed it: "This letter arrived at Paris after I had left it, and lay at Foley's till July 1766, when I got it over to Scotland.") David warns him against writing their father any further in his "gay, volatile, romantic manner," and says that Boswell's letter to Lord Auchinleck of 15 January had "almost ruined your character with him for discretion and good sense." Furthermore, he reports that the Edinburgh papers were reprinting items from *The London Chronicle* about Boswell's Corsican expedition, and this had enraged Lord Auchinleck. The item which spoke of Boswell's "warm and ill-judged zeal" for Prince Charles Edward (see p. 325) David had persuaded the Edinburgh papers to omit, but Sir David Dalrymple had mentioned it to Lord Auchinleck, for whose strong Whig sympathies it had been close to the final straw. Finally David reminds Boswell that their mother, who had been his greatest advocate, is now dead, and begs him to return quickly.

thinking of her being in heaven, was easy. Was pious and had manly hope. Had heard Mlle. Le Vasseur was arrived, and had sent to her; went this morning to Hôtel de Luxembourg. She was with Mme. de la Roche, *première dame de la Maréchale.*[1] She was just as at Môtiers. Told her sad news. She told you her anxiety about journey, and [said], "Mon Dieu, Monsieur, if we could go together!" You said you came to propose it to her. She showed you Rousseau's letter from Paris, where he agrees to her coming, and gives directions to wash his new shirts, &c., [adding,] "Do nothing hastily," and another from London, [saying,] "Resign yourself to suffering a great deal." Made a long story of it. Quackery this.[2] Went to Scots College, and Principal showed you, in little cabinet with British arms, many volumes of King James's own hand:[3] royal letters, &c., &c., and then showed you cartulary of Glasgow, Queen Mary's letters and testament, her prayer-book, &c., &c. You was truly pleased, and thrown into reverend humour which kept off grief. Wilkinson, a priest, dined. Then paid visits to Lord Alford, &c. Wilkes said Christian religion gave you nothing new but the resurrection of the body. WILKES. "I care no more to be raised in the same body than in the same coat, waistcoat, and breeches. Incarnation absurd." STRANGE.[4] "Sir, if [you admit] one spirit in body, why not superior one?" Carlotti, Italian Marquis, [once said] to Wilkes, "But my soul — ." WILKES. "G–d damn your soul."

THURSDAY 30 JANUARY. Yesterday morning found Strange. Picture by Teniers with heads like Paul Veronese.[5] [Took] leave of

[1] First lady-in-waiting to the Maréchale Duchesse de Luxembourg. Her residence, the Hôtel de Luxembourg, was in the Rue St.-Marc.

[2] These two letters apparently have not survived, but two others from Rousseau to Thérèse are printed in Appendix B. The beginnings of Boswell's disillusionment with Rousseau are apparent even before this, as a discarded portion of the first draft of his long letter to Rousseau (3 October 1765) shows. This portion is printed in Appendix C.

[3] James II. These manuscript memoirs were destroyed during the French Revolution.

[4] From a cancelled passage in the manuscript, it seems likely that this speech should be attributed to Strange.

[5] Probably "A Man Caressing a Woman" by David Teniers the elder (Robert Strange's *Catalogue of Pictures,* 1769, p. 132).

him till London. Dined Abbé de Marbeuf. Little man there, lively and forward, disputed Corsican affairs. You held them up to glory, and forgot distress by heat of argument, but like man in despair. Discovered little man to be Genoese minister, [son] of father at Ajaccio. He maintained to be with Genoa best for Corsica. The island must be dependent; [the] smaller [the] state on which it depends the better, and [thus] less liable to be enslaved. New this, and clever, but you maintained that Corsica might be free and only protected by another. HE. "Where is the liberty of a protected state?" You then argued for alliance. He asked you whether you admired more those who had struggled for liberty (alluding to the noble efforts of Genoese), or those who were struggling at the moment. You replied, "Do you admire more a woman who was beautiful, or one who is at the moment?" He was put to it, [but said,] "But if she preserves her beauty?" Blockhead! Genoa preserves its independency, 'tis true, but not the bold spirit as when struggling for it. Comtesse de Marbeuf was there. You was vastly well. Told sad news and took leave. Abbé said, "When you return, do not forget the Rue St. Dominique." You went and paid visit to Principal Gordon. Marshall there. Felt superiority over one you had not seen for long time, as Brown said you should. Was just as you could wish. Went for third time to Mlle. Le Vasseur; tired of her complaints. Ordered matters prudently. Went to Wilkes; company with him. He asked you, "Have you letters [from home]? I dare not ask you." Took him aside; told him melancholy affliction. He was affected, or decently seemed to be so. Bid you write immediately from home, and he'd write you regularly.[6] Promised him "Lines on Wilkes." [He] said, "Consider how you have avoided the pain of seeing mother dying, and how you'll go back and comfort father, and amuse him by telling of all you've seen." He said, "You're made for active life." You said, "You'll think as I do one day." HE. "You'll probably think as I in state, and I as you in church."[7]

[6] Boswell wrote to Wilkes from Auchinleck on 6 May 1766 to thank him for his kindness in Paris, and added: "I have often thought of you with affection. Indeed, I never admired you more than when you tried to alleviate my affliction; for whether it be from self-interest or not, I set a higher value on the qualities of the heart than on those of the head" (*Letters of James Boswell*, i. 90).

[7] A partly undecipherable marginal passage is omitted here.

FRIDAY 31 JANUARY. Yesterday morning after having been up all night and written sixteen or seventeen letters,[8] and felt spirits bound in veins, kept post-horses waiting from six till nine, then was still in confusion. Cried, "Is it possible that my mother is dead?" Set out, and at Hôtel de Luxembourg took up Mademoiselle. Was serious and composed. Passed by castle at ——,[9] [asked,] "Whose is that château?" Duc de Fitzjames.[1] [You said,] "God be blessed! The blood of the Stuarts has always some distinction. It is the most illustrious blood in the world." Dined ——;[2] was mild but gloomy, and now and then thought Mother alive and gave starts.[3] Night was manly, but hurt by Mademoiselle's mean kindness to servants, &c. Talked much of Rousseau always.

[EDITORIAL NOTE: The entries for the first eleven days of February 1766, which are said to have filled some twelve pages of manuscript, are now missing from Boswell's journal, having been destroyed just prior to the transference of the papers to Colonel Isham. They narrated in detail the progress of an amorous episode with which Boswell and Thérèse Le Vasseur occupied the time of their leisurely crossing from Paris to London. A small slip of paper, bearing the words "Reprehensible Passage" in the hand of Sir William Forbes (one of Boswell's literary executors) and signed with his initials, was found within the wrapper which enclosed this portion of the journal, and must have referred to something in the missing pages. Colonel Isham was fortunate enough to have read the whole passage before it was destroyed, and from him are gleaned the following notes on one of the most extraordinary episodes of Boswell's career.

It does not appear that before leaving Paris Boswell had formed any scheme of seducing Thérèse, and the day of his departure found

[8] Including letters to Lord Auchinleck, Temple, Dr. Johnson, Rousseau, Moma, Deleyre, M. de Zuylen, and Lumisden (Register of Letters). They must have been mainly short letters with the news of his mother's death. Only the letter to Temple has been recovered.

[9] Blank in manuscript. The place was Clermont (Oise).

[1] Charles Fitzjames, Duc de Fitzjames, was the fifth son of the Duke of Berwick, an illegitimate son of James II.

[2] Blank in manuscript.

[3] That is, "gave starts" of grief when he recalled that she was dead.

him tense and harassed by difficulties in getting started, and deeply unhappy over his mother's death. But the intimacy of travel and the proximity in which the pair found themselves at inns at night precipitated an intrigue almost immediately. On the second night out they shared the same bed; Boswell's first attempt, as often with him, was a fiasco. He was deeply humiliated, the grief he was trying to repress came back upon him, and he wept. Thérèse, with a Frenchwoman's tenderness and sympathy, put her arm around him to console him and laid his hand on her shoulder. His grief and embarrassment waned; as he recorded on another occasion, his powers were excited and he felt himself vigorous. Next day he was very proud of himself, and in the coach he congratulated Thérèse (who was almost twenty years his senior) on her good fortune in having at last experienced the ardours of a Scotch lover. Thérèse stunned him by denying that she had great cause for gratitude: "I allow," she said, "that you are a hardy and vigorous lover, but you have no art." Then, with quick perception seeing him cast down, she went on, "I did not mean to hurt you. You are young, you can learn. I myself will give you your first lesson in the art of love."

Since Boswell's success as a lover depended on his maintaining a feeling of superiority, this announcement filled him with terror. The apartment in which they were lodged that night was in the shape of an L: a private dining-room with the bed in an alcove at one end. As bedtime approached, he grew more frightened. In the earlier period of his life, as the journal printed in the present volume shows, he drank little, but on this occasion he secured from the servant a full bottle of wine and concealed it in the dining-room. Thérèse retired; Boswell remained reading. Thérèse called him; he went in clutching the wine, but instead of joining her, he paced up and down asking questions about Rousseau. At last, when no further diversion would avail, he drained the bottle and reluctantly slipped into bed.

He gave some details of her instruction. He must be gentle though ardent; he must not hurry. She asked him, as a man who had travelled much, if he had not noticed how many things were achieved by men's hands. He made good technical progress, though he was not wholly persuaded of her right to set up for a teacher; he said she rode him "agitated, like a bad rider galloping downhill." After a while her lectures bored him, and he brought up the subject of Rousseau, hoping at least to gather a few *dicta philosophi* for his journal. Thérèse in her turn found that dull. It was a mistake, he finally reflected, to get involved with an old man's mistress.[4]

The first entry of the journal on the other side of the hiatus not only furnishes unequivocal evidence of the liaison, but also vindicates Boswell's claim to vigour.]

WEDNESDAY 12 FEBRUARY [Dover]. Yesterday morning had gone to bed very early, and had done it once: thirteen in all. Was really affectionate to her. At two set out in fly; breakfasted Rochester on beefsteaks.[5] Mrs. Morrice, a woman who had been married to a sergeant, and a bluff, true Englishman sat with you. Mademoiselle was much fatigued. Came to London about six, to Swan at Westminster Bridge. Was now so firm that London made no impression. You was good to her. Sent to Stewart, and then went to his house.[6] You was quite easy. Macpherson was there.[7] You was talked to much of Corsica, but said nothing but calm account of what you saw, and when they said, "Who could send over this intelligence?" you said, "You must ask Gazetteer."[8] Carried her to David Hume. Then went to

[4] In a letter to the Comtesse de Boufflers (12 February 1766), Hume anticipated Boswell's relations with Thérèse on their trip in startlingly accurate fashion, though he intended no more than a joke: "A letter has also come to me . . . by which I learn that Mademoiselle sets out post in company with a friend of mine; a young gentleman, very good-humoured, very agreeable, and very mad. He visited Rousseau in his mountains, who gave him a recommendation to Paoli, the King of Corsica; where this gentleman, whose name is Boswell, went last summer in search of adventures. He has such a rage for literature that I dread some event fatal to our friend's honour. You remember the story of Terentia, who was first married to Cicero, then to Sallust, and at last, in her old age, married a young nobleman, who imagined that she must possess some secret which would convey to him eloquence and genius" (*Letters of David Hume*, ed. J. Y. T. Grieg, 1932, ii. 11).

[5] Apparently Boswell and Thérèse landed at Dover very early in the morning of 11 February, and went straight to bed. They got up in time to catch the fly at 2 p.m. and ate their first meal of the day ("breakfast") at Rochester.

[6] Probably John Stewart of Allanbank, a friend of Hume's, who had been instrumental in securing lodgings for Rousseau in London.

[7] Probably James Macpherson, the "translator" of Ossian.

[8] Boswell perhaps refers to news items in *The Gazetteer and New Daily Adver-*

Temple; embraced most cordially in old style. Wine and bread. Were too dissipated by innumerable ideas. Both cried, "Hope shall not marry these women."[9] You was for revolving all deaths. He said, "No, it makes [one] callous." Sat till four; went home. Up all night.

THURSDAY 13 FEBRUARY. Yesterday morning, after having read a daily all night, went and rung at Dempster's door, but he was not stirring. Then in post-chaise to Dr. Pringle's. He embraced you cordially, [saying,] "Glad to see you on several accounts." Talked to you of letter to Lord Mountstuart. You was a little obstinate; found the Doctor very easy with you.[1] Then went to Mlle. Le Vasseur, with whom was Hume. You breakfasted, and then carried her out to Chiswick.[2] She said Hume had told her you was "mélancholique," which was in your family. You was too high. You was ready to kill any offender. You gave her word of honour you'd not mention *affaire* till after her death or that of the philosopher.[3] Went to Rousseau; de-

---

*tiser*, which would have been copied from *The London Chronicle*. Or he may simply mean the "gazetteer" (that is, journalist) responsible for printing these items.

[9] That is, Zélide and Miss Ann Stow, whom Temple did marry in August 1767.

[1] Sir John Pringle was physician to the King and later President of the Royal Society. A great friend of Lord Auchinleck's, Pringle had persuaded Mountstuart to write to Boswell at the end of December 1765 strongly urging him to return home for his father's sake. Boswell received this letter on 12 January 1766, and three days later replied to Mountstuart complaining of his lack of sympathy. Boswell's letter is missing, but we know its tenor and some of the phrases he used from a letter of Pringle's dated 28 January, in which Pringle reveals his share in Mountstuart's letter and advises Boswell to offer Mountstuart an apology immediately; for, he says, "I never knew any letter require one more."

[2] Where Rousseau was lodged in the house of a grocer.

[3] Boswell seems to have kept his promise, and even to have deceived Temple. On 24 April 1790 Temple wrote to him concerning the second part of Rousseau's *Confessions*, which had just been published: "In what a strange light do those last volumes exhibit him! In his flight to England, I suppose we shall have an account of you and of your dishonourable attempt on his virtuous friend and companion. There was probably as little truth in her accusation of the old gentleman." (Rousseau had accused a one-time friend, a man of about sixty, of having attempted to seduce Thérèse by reading to her from a pornographic book and showing her illustrations in it. The implication of Temple's remarks probably is that Boswell at some time had attributed Rousseau's later falling out

livered her over. *Quanta oscula,*[4] &c.! He seemed so oldish and weak you had no longer your enthusiam for him. Told him all about Corsica, and he cried, "Pardi! I am sorry not to have gone there." He was incited by what he heard. He was to go to Wales.[5] You asked if Scotland had not a claim to him. He said, "I shall act like the kings; I shall put my body in one place, and my heart in another."

Back to London. Immediately to Johnson; received you with open arms. You kneeled, and asked blessing. Miss Williams glad of your return. When she went out, he hugged you to him like a sack, and grumbled, "I hope we shall pass many years of regard."[6] You for some minutes saw him not so immense as before, but it came back. Voltaire's Pope in chaise, and Dryden [in] coach.[7] JOHNSON. "That is very well. But the truth is they ride both in coaches, only Dryden is always either galloping or stumbling; Pope [goes on at an] even trot." You dined at the Cecil Street Coffee-house (Temple's place), and there you met George Redhead, a fat, jolly planter. You and Temple had fine chat. He was much easier than formerly. At eight you met at Mitre Mr. Johnson. Told him how Baretti was corrupted [and had said], "As man dies like dog, let him lie like dog." JOHNSON. "Why, Sir, if he dies like dog, let him lie like dog." BOSWELL. "Baretti says, 'I hate mankind, for I think myself one of the best of 'em, and [I] know how bad I am.' " JOHNSON. "Sir, he must be very singular in his opinion if he thinks himself one of the best of men, for none of Baretti's friends think him one of," &c. He said no honest man could

with him to a charge by Thérèse that he had made advances to her — a charge which he allowed Temple to believe false. See p. 299.) — Lord Marischal innocently wrote to Rousseau in March 1766: "I rejoice with you on the arrival of Mlle. Le Vasseur, and with Mr. Boswell on the pleasure he has received in being able to do you a service; he is a truly honourable man, a perfect gentleman" (*Correspondance générale de J.-J. Rousseau,* xv. 82–83).

[4] Such kissing.

[5] Rousseau changed his mind, and in March he and Thérèse went to Wootton, Staffordshire, where they remained until May 1767.

[6] The following conversations are repeated, with modifications, in *The Life of Johnson* (February 1766).

[7] Voltaire had compared Pope and Dryden for Boswell at Ferney: "Pope drives a chaise with a couple of neat trim nags but Dryden a coach and six, with postilions and all" (*Boswell on the Grand Tour: Germany and Switzerland,* 27 December 1764).

be a deist, for no man could be so after a fair examination of the proofs. BOSWELL. "Hume?"[8] JOHNSON. "No, Sir, Hume owned to a clergyman in the bishopric of Durham that he had never read the New Testament with any attention."

He said, "Now you have five and twenty years, and you have employed 'em well." BOSWELL. "Oh, no! Do I know history, mathematics, law, &c.? No." JOHNSON. "Why, Sir, though you may know no science so well as to be able to teach it, and no profession so well as to be able to follow it, yet your general mass of knowledge of books and men renders you very capable to study any science or follow any profession." (This was enough.) I said Wilkes bid me not be a lawyer as I should be excelled by plodding blockheads. He said, "Sir, in the formal and statutory practice of law, a plodding blockhead may succeed, but in the equitable part of it, a plodding blockhead can never succeed." I said, "I fear I shall not be a good advocate." JOHNSON. "Why, Sir, to be sure you will not be a good advocate at first, and, Sir, no man is a good advocate at first; and perhaps in seven years you will not be so good a lawyer as your father, and perhaps never. But it is better to be a tolerable lawyer than no lawyer, and, Sir, you will always see multitudes below you." You talked of attending great men. "Sir, would you have done it?" JOHNSON. "Sir, I was never near enough to them to court them, but I would have done it. You are never to do what you think wrong, and you are to calculate and not pay too dear for what you get. You must not give a shilling's worth of court for sixpence worth of good; but if you can get a shilling's worth of good for sixpence worth of court, you are a fool not to pay court."

He said,[9] "If convents are allowed at all, they should be numerous. But they should only be retreats for those unable to serve public, or who have served it, and the religious should never be admitted till of a good age. Our first duty is to serve society, and after that we may attend wholly to the salvation of our souls. Youthful passions for abstracted devotion should not be encouraged." You talked of second sight and predictions which may happen by chance. JOHNSON. "Yes,

[8] Hume himself denied being a deist.

[9] The following topics of conversations have to do with Corsica, and Boswell's perplexities about what he had seen and heard there.

Sir; but these have happened so often that mankind have agreed to think it real." He was as great as ever. He maintained that, setting aside the heat of party, the differences among Christians were very small, only about the means to attain the same end. Talking of Corsica and your scheme of publishing some account of it, he said, "You cannot go to bottom [of the subject] but all you tell us is what we don't know. Give us as many anecdotes as you can." You was fine. Home and slept sound.

FRIDAY 14 FEBRUARY. Yesterday morning went and called for Dun,[1] and made him go with you to Pero's Bagnio[2] in St. James's Street. Temple came to you. Found all genteel and noble. Saw Dun a most forward, rude fellow, but as he was obliging and attached to your family, bore with him. Felt by comparison with former days in London how superior you was. Temple joked, how from your being with princes and *literati*, he was afraid to meet you. You replied, "But I make all that easy for you! Don't I?" Dined together at Cecil Street. Home with him. He showed you letters from Miss Stow; insisted on his having her. Then Dr. Pringle's. He and Sir A. Mitchell insisted wrong to Lord Mountstuart. You was outrageous. Clack was at Temple's; felt him low.[3]

SATURDAY 15 FEBRUARY. You had consulted Johnson, who bid you be independent, though prudently attached to great men.[4] You called at Lord Mountstuart's elegant house (would not call [on] Mallet); was made wait. He appeared, and was reserved. You said you was sorry he had been offended, but could not see you was wrong. Asked him freely not to be angry any more. He kept up the prince. Sat down by him and asked him how he got cured; so brought him down. He said, "Thank God, I know you. Your wife will be quite unhappy at first, till she finds you out, and then she'll never mind you, but take her work, or go walk in the garden." You with spirit would

[1] Boswell had dealings with this man, who seems to have been a tailor, in 1763.

[2] A bath house and probably also a brothel.

[3] John Claxton, a Cambridge friend of Temple's, a lawyer and antiquary. Boswell had first met him in London in 1763, when he thought him "a very good sort of a young man, though reserved at first" (*Boswell's London Journal*, 15 May 1763).

[4] Boswell probably refers to their recent conversation, and introduces it here to justify his possible connection with Mountstuart.

have him be no more angry. [He finally said,] "I don't care sixpence about it." Poor. You called on Lord Eglinton. He received [you] with affection. Fine house pleased you, but felt yourself so detached from interest and worldly vanities, was like a Johnson in comparison of former days. He talked of your father, and bid you *affect* gravity. You told him you now *was* grave. Saw honest Crookshanks, just the old rattling man. Called on Lainshaw. He looked very ill.[5] It was not an unpleasing, sad consideration. Mrs. Montgomerie was a good woman. You was quite master of yourself. You found that when now enlarged and enlightened by travel, even worth could not make you often bear uncouth Scots manners, and you are not obliged often to bear them. Dined with Dr. Pringle. Called Clack's. Supped [with Temple at] Cecil Street. German played on sticks. Young Bosville came to you. Was quite easy with him.[6]

SUNDAY 16 FEBRUARY. Yesterday at three went to Mr. Bosville's in Great Russell Street, Bloomsbury, where you was asked to dine, though you had disappointed the Captain yesterday to go thither at one.[7] Mrs. Bosville, stately sensible woman; Godfrey Bosville, Esq., plain-looking man, but a judicious, knowing, worthy gentleman. Down to dinner. Miss Bosville, vastly pretty: black hair, charming complexion, quite modest; Miss Julie, brisk little girl. Fine to see so many Boswells.[8] Miss Annabella Wentworth, sister to Mrs. Bosville, genteel town lady. Miss hardly spoke; [perhaps] better. You was talked to [by] all of Paoli, and was quite well and as you could wish. After dinner Mr. Bosville walked you about and gave you anecdotes

[5] James Montgomerie of Lainshaw, Boswell's first cousin and brother to his future wife. Montgomerie died in December of this year.

[6] William Bosville, an ensign in the Guards, and later well known as a *bon vivant*. He is referred to as "Captain" below. Boswell had met him in London in 1763.

[7] Perhaps Boswell means that the Captain had made an appointment with him which Boswell had broken to go to Godfrey Bosville's house at one o'clock, but he had not actually arrived until three.

[8] This was Boswell's first meeting with the Bosville family. He came to regard Godfrey Bosville of Gunthwaite, Yorkshire, as the chief of the Boswell clan and established with him one of the most pleasant intimacies of his life. Miss Bosville, the "Miss" referred to below, was Elizabeth Diana, the eldest daughter of the family. In 1768 she married Sir Alexander Macdonald, brother and heir to the Sir James Macdonald referred to on p. 189.

of family, and showed two pictures of Cromwell.[9] After dinner Mr. Bosville asked you to come at any time and eat his family dinner. You drank tea and sat by Miss, and she told of Lord Eglinton. . . .[1]

You went to Mitre; had engaged Mr. Johnson. Presented Temple; fine to have *Magnus Apollo*[2] and dearest friend together. Mr. Johnson had been at Cambridge (a great concession).[3] You told him he looked ten years younger, and that Davies had said he now got up at eight. JOHNSON. "Why, Sir, if I were a friend of John James Rousseau then everything that concerned me would be of importance. As it is, Sir, it concerns nobody but myself." You quoted Wilkes for something. JOHNSON. "It seems you have kept very good company abroad — Wilkes and Rousseau!" BOSWELL. "My dear Sir, you don't call Rousseau bad company? Do you really think him a bad man?" JOHNSON. "Sir, if you are to talk jestingly of this, I don't talk with you. If you would be serious, I think him one of the worst of men; a rascal who ought to be hunted out of society as he has been. Three or four nations have expelled him; and it is a shame that he is protected in this country." Temple talked like a very courtier of his Creed.[4] You said, "Sir, I don't deny but his novel may do harm, but I cannot think his intention was bad." JOHNSON. "Sir, that will not do. We cannot prove any man's intention to be bad. You may shoot a man through the head, and say you intended to miss him, but the judge will order you to be hanged. The want of intention, when evil is committed, will not be sustained in a court of justice. If you are no better lawyer than that, Bos., we must send you back to Utrecht. Sir, Rousseau is a very bad man. I would sooner sign a sentence for his transportation than for that of any felon who has gone from the Old Bailey these many years. Yes, I should like to have him work in the plantations." BOSWELL. "Sir, do you think him as bad a man as Voltaire?" JOHNSON. "Why, it is difficult to settle the proportion of iniquity between 'em." (The first day after your arrival he said, "People have nowadays got into a strange opinion that everything should be taught by lectures.

[9] The word could be read "Cromwellian(s)." Godfrey Bosville's great-grandfather was an officer in the Parliamentary army under Cromwell.

[1] One or more illegible words are omitted here.

[2] Horace, *Satires*, II. v. 60.

[3] On a visit in 1765. Johnson had been a student at Pembroke College, Oxford.

[4] "The Creed of a Savoyard Vicar."

Now, I can never see that lectures can do so much good as reading the books from whence the lectures are taken. I know nothing that can be best taught by lectures, except where experiments are shown. You may teach chemistry by lectures. You might teach making of shoes by lectures.")

He talked of subordination, and said, "So far is it from being true that men are naturally equal, that no two people can be half an hour together but the one shall acquire an evident superiority over the other." You mentioned Hume's notion that all were equally happy, who were happy.[5] JOHNSON. "Sir, that all are equally happy is not true. A peasant and a philosopher may be equally satisfied, but not equally happy. Happiness consists in the multiplicity of consciousness. A peasant has not capacity for having equal happiness with the philosopher." You was of his opinion, but to be more fully confirmed you was going on. He thought you was going to push him with contrariety, and called out, "My dear Bozzy, let us have no more of this. It is extremely disagreeable to me. You are making nothing of this argument. I had rather you'd whistle me a Scotch tune." BOSWELL. "But, Sir, philosophers bid us take consolation by thinking of those who are worse than we are. But, Sir, this cannot apply to all, for there must be some who have none worse than them." JOHNSON. "Why, Sir, to be sure there are, &c.; but they don't know it. There is no being so poor and so contemptible who does not think he has somebody below him."

You said that your Swiss said, "I can never believe [the Scriptures], for I can never read the books in the original, nor know but what they're invented." JOHNSON. "Why, foolish fellow, has he any better authority for almost everything that he believes?" BOSWELL. "But, Mr. Johnson, the vulgar never can be sure they're right, but must submit themselves to the learned." JOHNSON. "To be sure, Sir. The vulgar are the children of the state and must be taken care of." BOSWELL. "Then, Sir, a poor Turk must be a Mohammedan just as a poor man in Europe must be a Christian?" JOHNSON. "Why, Sir, and what then? This now is just such stuff as I used to talk to my mother when I first began to think myself a clever fellow, and she ought to have whipped me for it." You took this in perfect good humour, and said, "You ought then to whip me."

[5] Expressed in his essay, "The Sceptic."

He was engaged to go at ten. Temple had said little, but behaved very genteelly. You and he sat on together. He said Mr. Johnson was monstrously overbearing, and, when you disputed with Temple, he would imitate Johnson, and cried, "Come, come, Jamie, let us have no more of it. This is children's play." This was the finest humour I ever felt. Temple had been hurt by reading Hume and Helvétius and other modern philosophers, but you could not be angry, for you thought it a weakness. He was, however, much improved. His implicit veneration for Mr. Gray was lessened, "For," said he, "I like to see a man have some weaknesses as others." He maintained that to lead an agreeable life was the most important plan, and that if he had been born to an estate, he would never have been anything, but enjoyed books and the country one half the year and the town the other, or been in Parliament; and he would not sacrifice his own happiness even to that of father. All this was free and well, but he has done more for his father than any man.[6]

He said, "It is long since I have thought either of happiness or misery. Boswell, you are more of a philosopher than any man I know, really so; but that makes one unhappy." You and he with much good humour laughed at your airy, youthful plans of grandeur, when he was to be a great man in the state, and you a great statesman and a great poet into the bargain. You now formed true, easy, probable plans of happiness: to come one to the other every summer, to be now and then in London, to go and pass a spring and May at Paris and live there *perfectly* well, and come away when money spent. He was happy to find you no longer avaricious, but said he believed you took extravagant fits. You had showed him some leaves of your journal, which he liked much. You said, "Temple, if I was your son, would you be pleased with me?" He replied with real truth, "Entirely pleased." Your delicate sentiments were a little hurt that your friend, who doubted, should subscribe the Thirty-nine Articles. But (as he said) its being just a form ("Like declaring King James has no right," said you) made it of no moment.

MONDAY 17 FEBRUARY. Yesterday morning Temple came to you. He bid you not leave town till you was acquainted with Miss

[6] Temple's father went into bankruptcy in 1762, and Temple satisfied his creditors at the expense of nearly half the estate which his mother had left him two years previously.

Bosville, and bid you try to have her to correspond with you. He had got you a servant (Thomas), a good, clever little lad, though not elegant, but you could not yet fix. You had meantime a Thomas at two shillings a day, a clever, active man. Temple said you wrote in too swelling a style; that he had quoted your letters but was obliged to leave out the rodomontade. Bid you read a page of Burke's *Sublime*[7] before you wrote letter, and so acquire easy simplicity. He and you had consulted on writing to Mr. Pitt, and you threw out many bouncing sallies which Temple repressed. At last you gave him a clean, neat, short letter which pleased, and was sent.[8] You and Temple went to Lincoln's Inn and saw Claxton a little. He went out, and then you looked out your books and papers left in Temple.[9] Had a most curious pleasure in revising old ideas. Read *Erskine's and Boswell's Letters*; could not bear your own except one or two.[1] In general mere forced extravagance and no real humour. Erskine's will please still, though not so greatly as once. You and Temple were now both well. You smiled and said, "Come, our happiest days are to come, when we're settled men with families," and Temple declared he was still determined to be a very learned man.

We adjourned to the Cecil Street and dined and had our bottle of mountain.[2] We both felt that dining at a coffee-house was below us and made us feel awkward, so when both should be really in office (he parson, I counsellor), we should have dinner at home brought from tavern. With great good humour we owned neither of us knew any one science, and Temple said he never could give any account of a book he had read, but maintained that upon the whole we reaped as much advantage as others, for it had an imperceptible effect upon us. After laughing at each other with unlimited freedom, I said, "Temple, if our Scots friends were to hear this!" He said, "I would not

[7] Edmund Burke's *Of the Sublime and Beautiful*, 1757.

[8] The dates of Boswell's letter and Pitt's reply indicate probably that Boswell wrote up this section of the journal some time later and forgot on what day this conversation had taken place.

[9] Boswell had lived in the Inner Temple during part of the summer of 1763 in Temple's rooms, during the latter's absence.

[1] *Letters between the Honourable Andrew Erskine and James Boswell, Esq.*, 1763. It was a youthful bagatelle, full of private references and jokes.

[2] A Malaga wine.

[have it] for a great deal, for they would despise us both." I confessed an unhappy want of decision. He said he had a good deal of it but I had more, and that last night I wanted him to walk past the Turk's Head where he slept in order to have a few minutes more to determine how we should pass the next morning. Our minds were now surprisingly opened, and, what amazed me, Temple had kept pace with me though he had not travelled. He said my father had not the proper value for me as a man of agreeable conversation. In short, we were as well as men could be.

We passed the evening at Claxton's, and his diet loaf[3] was very pleasing to us. At ten I went with Temple in a hackney as far as Fleet Ditch, as he was going to lie at the inn of the Cambridge coach, which he had taken for next day. It is hard that we have met I know not how many times, just to be separated. We bid adieu with the warmest affection. I went, late as it was, to Dempster's, where I had called several times, as he had for me. I found him and Miss Dempster, and got over the awkward ceremony of meeting after my travels. Dempster had a real ministerial look. Our conversation was not at all so free as formerly, and I was not ill pleased at this. But I was still too open, talking how my Swiss had governed me, and in raptures with my beautiful cousin. I gave here well accounts of Corsica.

[Boswell to William Pitt][4]

St. James's Street, Saturday, 15 February 1766

SIR: — I am just arrived from Corsica, where I had several conversations with Signor de Paoli, who wished much that I could see you on my return to Britain.

If you can give me an audience, I shall be very happy to pay you my respects, and to acquaint you with some things which passed between Signor de Paoli and me. If not, I have done my duty in comply-

[3] A large sponge-cake.

[4] From the original, by kind permission of the owner, C. B. Tinker. Boswell's draft is practically identical. Pitt, as he explains in his letter below, held no office at this time except for his nominal position as Privy Councillor, but he was the most powerful man in politics outside the government.

ing with the desire of that great man. I am with the highest esteem, Sir, your most obedient and most humble servant,

JAMES BOSWELL.

TUESDAY 18 FEBRUARY. Yesterday at twelve went to Lord Eglinton's. He had said that men only differed from their parts, for rank had no effect but when you play at representation. The King jumps aside, so, and then my Lord must come so. You maintained, "No, my Lord. You know you are my superior, and I am other people's superior." He carried you to Court and presented you to Lord Denbigh, who presented you to King. HIS MAJESTY. "*Lately come over?*" All he said. Was quite easy and not a bit struck, but liked it. Dined Cecil Street. Then called Mr. Bosville. He alone; were well together. BOSVILLE. "Well, when will you come and dine?" BOSWELL. "When you please." BOSVILLE. "Well, tomorrow and Sunday too. We shall have company in the afternoon." You have from time to time called at honest Lainshaw's. You supped there tonight. He has a most curious life, never reading a word and playing at catch-honours[5] with Graeme, his huntsman, who, as Dr. Pringle says, plays inimitably his various offices — bringing up coals, giving a plate, or sitting down to table. Lord Eglinton was with us, and Stewart-Shaw, who was lively and good-natured but really too rattling. Johnson has raised you above your fellows. Keep to the dignity he has given you.

WEDNESDAY 19 FEBRUARY. Yesterday Major Preston called on me, a jolly, agreeable, pretty man. I run about leaving cards. London had no longer that fascination which formerly blinded me. I dined at Mr. Bosville's, and had nobody there but the family. The Captain was determined to go to America to see that country and to rise in his profession. He said the Americans believed the Highlanders were wild, and that they had been taken by gins. My first night Mrs. Bosville had set me by her daughter, who talked most genteelly of routs, and yet she liked the country, reading and walking. She was as mild as before. Yesterday [she] said she never danced or played cards. This was comfortable. You told her at table how Lord Eglinton said he was afraid to be near her, and you very gallantly praised her extraordinary beauty without direct flattery. Father and mother would

[5] The Ayrshire name for a card game, known elsewhere as catch-the-long-ten.

not seem to encourage this. You have been both times asked to sup, but you went and called [on] Lord Advocate,[6] with whom you was easy. But you could not bear to hear people say, "I suppose you are convinced you judged as well as he." Oh, sad world! Lord Advocate had vague ideas of farming,[7] &c. You resolved to be seldom with Scots. Mr. Johnson was not at home. In Strand you met a Miss Davies. Home with her and performed; good girl, but angry at self.

THURSDAY 20 FEBRUARY. Yesterday run about all day, and dined at Cecil Street. Called Wilkie in St. Paul's Church yard, who would put in [notice of your] arrival *gratis.*[8] Night with Dr. Pringle.

FRIDAY 21 FEBRUARY. You have had answer of three pages from Mr. Pitt. Saw self great man to a certain degree. Called at Mr. Bosville's. Met Clack in Great Russell Street. CLAXTON. "Well, [what about] Temple's marriage?" BOSWELL. "He wants to be off; but he shan't. Do you watch him there, and I'll watch him here, and I warrant you he shall not escape."[9] High whim! Sat hour and half with Mrs. Bosville; talked a great deal of marriage. Her notions were just. Saw it was not proper to have Miss's picture. Dined at Lainshaw's, hearty. Found self most superior man. Lord Eglinton and Dr. Pringle disputed American Stamp Act.

[Pitt to Boswell][10]

Hayes, Sunday, 16 February 1766

SIR: — The honour of your letter reached me here, where I have been some days detained with a fit of the gout. My present situation puts it out of my power to receive the favour you are so good to intend me; when I return to London I shall be very proud to see you. In the mean time allow me, Sir, to suggest some doubts of the propriety of

[6] Thomas Miller, a neighbour of the Boswells at Auchinleck. The Lord Advocate's position in Scotland might be compared roughly to the Solicitor General's in the United States.

[7] A doubtful word.

[8] John Wilkie was the publisher of *The London Chronicle.* Since the notice of Boswell's arrival had already appeared, "would" probably means "insisted on."

[9] The division of these speeches is arbitrary.

[10] First printed in volume seven of Colonel Isham's privately printed *Private Papers of James Boswell.*

a simple individual as I am (in all respects but that of a Privy Councillor, which adds to the difficulty) receiving any communication from an illustrious personage circumstanced as General de Paoli is. Under these considerations, might not a communication to His Majesty's Secretary of State answer better the views of the able Corsican chief?

In the mean time, Sir, I desire to assure you that I shall esteem myself fortunate in the opportunity of being introduced to your acquaintance. I have the honour to be with great esteem and consideration, Sir, your most obedient and most humble servant,

WILLIAM PITT.

[Boswell to Pitt][1]

St. James's Street, 19 February 1766

SIR: — I have had the honour to receive your most obliging letter, and can with difficulty restrain myself from paying you compliments on the very genteel manner in which you are pleased to treat me. But I come from a people among whom even the honest arts of insinuation are unknown. However you may by political circumstances be in one view "a simple individual," yet, Sir, Mr. Pitt will always be the prime minister of the brave, the secretary of freedom and of spirit; and I hope that I may with propriety talk to him of the views of the illustrious Paoli.

Be that as it may, I shall very much value the honour of being admitted to your acquaintance. I am with the highest esteem, Sir, your most obedient and most humble servant,

JAMES BOSWELL.

SATURDAY 22 FEBRUARY. Yesterday I called at Mr. Bosville's at three o'clock, and freely took their family dinner. The Squire had bid me come in at any time, and Mrs. Bosville said, "We shall make no

[1] This letter has been published in *Correspondence of William Pitt, Earl of Chatham*, ed. W. S. Taylor and J. H. Pringle, 1838–1840, ii. 388, and in *Letters of James Boswell*, i. 87–88. Boswell's draft shows only trifling differences from the letter as sent. The dating of this letter is not so paradoxical as it looks, since Boswell is careful in his entry for 21 February to say "You *have had*" a letter from Mr. Pitt.

stranger of you, Sir." Miss was still quite reserved. You stayed all afternoon with the Squire and wrote from his house to Father. He showed you a humorous attack on *Joseph*,[2] and showed you he was no orthodox. You supped and Miss opened you some oysters. You was just as you could wish to be.

SUNDAY 23 FEBRUARY. Yesterday at nine called at Mr. Pitt's in Bond Street.[3] Not up. BOSWELL. "I'll call ten times." Went back at eleven; shown into parlour, and but a very plain one. Another servant came: "My master will be glad to see you, Sir." Carried upstairs; entered room, a very decent one. A gentleman, Mr. Dowdeswell, went away. Lord Shelburne and Lord Cardross[4] were with him. He was tall man in black clothes, with white nightcap and foot all wrapped up in flannel and on gout-stool.[5] He made a genteel reverence, and said, "Mr. Boswell, I came to town only yesterday, and have been engaged with the business of the House; otherwise, I should have sent to you and appointed a time when we might have met." He talked of English gentlemen of good estates living independent in the country with great dignity. He said he was ashamed to say he had never read Rousseau, but would now read him. You told him Rousseau's great admiration of him, and how he'd never forget the gentleman who gave him a print of Mr. Pitt.[6] You told him Voltaire's saying of there being only a king and a half in Europe — King [of] Prussia and King [of] Sardinia. Mr. Pitt was mightily pleased with it, but said, "If it may be allowed to improve upon M. de Voltaire, I would give both to the King of Prussia, and say, 'He is a king and a half,' and let the other kings just be kings." Lord Cardross

[2] Perhaps the story of Joseph in the Bible.

[3] Boswell picked a dramatic moment to call, since the debate on repeal of the Stamp Act had lasted until 1:30 the previous morning, at which time the motion for leave to bring in the repeal bill was carried by a vote of 275 to 167. Pitt had taken a leading part in urging repeal.

[4] David Steuart Erskine, later Earl of Buchan, a distant cousin of Boswell's. An able but ridiculous creature, he is best remembered for his premature plans for the funeral of Sir Walter Scott. In a note on this interview made some time after Boswell's death, he says that Boswell came in Corsican costume and presented a letter from Paoli, both of which statements appear to be false.

[5] The manuscript can perhaps be read "joint-stool."

[6] Symonds told Boswell in Genoa that he had given Pitt's picture to Rousseau.

showed away[7] by being at his ease, leaning on knee, and sticking switch into boot, [saying,] "Mr. Pitt. Eh?"[8] He talked of materialism: (Good now! Metaphysics here!) Mr. Pitt said, "I did not think there would have been so great a majority — 108!"[9] You asked if it would not have been possible to have forced the Americans. Said he: "Abstracting from the equity of the cause, it would not have been possible. They are all united." Lord Shelburne showed a list of 280,000 acting militia that they could spare for war. Mr. Pitt said, "If severe measures were ever to be used, it must be done when they are divided; but let us use them with indulgence, and they'll always find it their interest to be with us."

The lords went away. He then began in form: "Mr. Boswell, I am very happy to make your acquaintance. I had heard of you before. I had seen an account in the foreign papers of your being in Corsica." (He had indeed asked some questions before the company.) "Now, Sir, I will explain to you how I cannot properly receive communications from General de Paoli, for I am a Privy Councillor, and have taken an oath to hear nothing from any foreign power that may concern Great Britain without declaring it to the King and Council. Now, Sir, it is in your breast to judge whether what you have to say is of a nature fit to be told or not. I shall be very happy to hear your accounts of the island as a traveller. Some time hence things may turn about, and I may be at liberty to receive communications from Corsica, and then I shall be very happy to hear all you have to say. I am now just a private member of Parliament. I had once, Mr. Boswell, something to do in the affairs of this nation. But when they had come to me in distress and in perplexity, 'Think for us, act for us, venture for us!' and I had thought, acted, and ventured — for 'em then to come and tell me, 'Now you must think as we choose!' When I had rolled the stone to the top of the hill, then! My Lord Temple and I were the only two in the Council that stood firm. We waited to see if this would last, and, finding a change of measures, and that I could be of no farther use, I resigned;[1] and ever since I have known

[7] That is, showed off.

[8] Or the "Eh" can be read as an exclamation of Pitt's.

[9] See p. 293 *n.* 3.

[1] On 5 October 1761, when the Cabinet refused to support him in his demand for a declaration of war against Spain.

William Pitt, later 1st Earl of Chatham (1708–1778), from a painting by William Hoare of Bath, in the National Portrait Gallery, London.

no more of what has been doing in the Cabinet than the most remote man in the Kingdom. I know not what Genoa has been able to obtain by means of France. I — " BOSWELL. "Sir, that, the General — Paoli — felt severely: to be given into the bargain that poor Corsica should be considered as nothing." PITT. "Mr. Boswell, I own it appears strange that an island of so great consequence to the navigation in the Mediterranean should be neglected. How are their harbours?" BOSWELL. "One or two excellent, with some expense." PITT. "Sir, that is of great consequence to a fleet on some grand enterprise. We have no such place on Italy." BOSWELL. "Sir, General de Paoli said — " PITT. "Sir, you'll remember my situation." BOSWELL. "Pray, Sir, may I ask you if you never received a letter from General de Paoli?" PITT. "Never, Sir." BOSWELL. "Why then, Sir, after the Proclamation,[2] he wrote to you, and, as he has the highest admiration of your character, he was most sensibly hurt to be neglected by Mr. Pitt." PITT. "Sir, I never received his letter. I suppose *those next the King* have taken care it should not be delivered. I could not have answered it — could not have been in correspondence with General de Paoli, but I should have taken care to let him know my regard for him. Sir, I should be sorry that in any corner of the world, however distant or however small, it should be suspected that I could ever be indifferent to the cause of liberty."

Yesterday dined at Dempster's. Talked too much of Miss Bosville. Sandie Duncan, with honest Scots sagacity without sarcasm, said, "What, is she so extremely pretty?" BOSWELL. "Yes." DUNCAN. "Then we shall have no more of Paoli!" Stewart was there who wrote *The North Briton Extraordinary*.[3] You paid him just compliments on it. You felt yourself even at Dempster's *almost* as well as you could wish, but found it prudent to be seldom with old dissipated company.

You met at Mitre Dr. Goldsmith whom you had before called upon. You both went to Mr. Johnson's, who was still bad and would not come out. "Come then," said Goldie, "we will not go to the Mitre tonight, since we can't have the big man with us." But we had sent for Davies, and I insisted on going. Goldsmith said, "I think, Mr.

[2] See p. 146.

[3] This pamphlet, published in 1765, has been attributed both to Boswell and to Smollett. Unfortunately, Boswell does not here completely identify the author. He seems not to be the same as the John Stewart previously mentioned.

Johnson, you don't go near the theatres. You give yourself no more concern about a new play than if you had never had anything to do with the stage." JOHNSON. "Why, Sir, our tastes alter. The lad does not care for the child's rattle, and the old man does not care for the young man's whore." GOLDSMITH. "Nay, but, Sir, your Muse was not a whore." JOHNSON. "Sir, I don't think she was. But as we advance in the journey of life, we drop some of the things which have pleased us; whether it be that we are fatigued and don't choose to carry so many things any farther, or that we find other things which we like better." BOSWELL. "But, Sir, why don't you give us something in some other way?" GOLDSMITH. "Ay, Sir, we have a claim upon you." JOHNSON. "No, Sir, I am not obliged to do any more. No man is obliged to do as much as he can do. A man is to have part of his life to himself. If a soldier has fought a good many campaigns, he is not to be blamed if he retires to ease and tranquillity. Sir, a physician who has long practised in a great city may be excused if he retires to a small town and takes less practice. Sir, the good I can do by my conversation bears the same proportion to the good I can do by my writings that the practice of a physician, retired to a small town, does to his practice in a great city." BOSWELL. "But I wonder, Sir, you have not more pleasure in writing than not." JOHNSON. "Sir, you *may* wonder." In short, Goldsmith and I could make nothing against him.

He talked of making verses. He said, "The great matter is to know when you have made good ones. I generally have 'em in my mind, perhaps fifty at a time, walking in my room; and then write 'em, and often from laziness wrote only the half lines. Sir, I have written a hundred lines a day. I remember I wrote a hundred lines of *The Vanity of Human Wishes* in a day. Doctor, I made one line t'other day, but I made out no more." GOLDSMITH. "Let us hear it, and we'll put a bad one to it." JOHNSON. "No, Sir, I have forgot it."

We left him, and as we were going along Fleet Street, Goldsmith very gravely said, "Don't you think that head's failed — wearing, eh?" O fine! BOSWELL. "No, Sir, I think he is rather more impatient of contradiction than he was." GOLDSMITH. "Sir, no man is proof against continual adulation."

Davies could not come to the Mitre, so Goldsmith carried me to his chambers in the King's Bench Walk, which he has furnished, and is quite magnificent. We talked of writing against authors from envy; I said if I wrote against anything it would be against his chambers. He gave me a repast and we were well. I touched him by the story of "Johnson and Goldsmith and those blockheads," and upon his honour that he would not say anything of it, I told him 'twas Smith.[4] "Well," said he, "by telling me it was he, you have given me a plaster for the sore." Such is human nature.

We talked of French and English. You said the English were like noble standard oaks, which could be alone and well. The French, slender shrubs, that are nothing but in a copsewood. Goldsmith said, "I have passed the summer among the great," and forsooth affected to talk lightly of this. You brought him down with Johnsonian principles and Johnsonian force.

[EDITORIAL NOTE: The journal breaks off at this point, not to be resumed until January 1767, but the story of the decline and conclusion of Boswell's relationship with Rousseau belongs to this volume. Boswell, as we have seen, found Rousseau rather disappointing on their reunion in London, and apparently made no further effort to see him before departing for Scotland, his father, and the law in early March 1766. He wrote to Rousseau, however, from Scotland, and made a copy of part of the letter, which he entitled "Extract to M. Rousseau."]

[Boswell to Rousseau. Original in French]

Auchinleck, 25 March 1766

DEAR AND SINGULAR PHILOSOPHER, — Do not believe that *I have neglected you* (as you have accused me of doing), since your arrival in England. Truly, for the majority of men the presence of those whom they have most admired destroys admiration. If by chance the sun fell to earth, ten days would not pass before it was made into a ball to play ninepins with. But I am not like most men. . . . "[5]

[EDITORIAL NOTE: The specific bases of Rousseau's charge of neglect remain unknown, but he must have been quick to see that Boswell was no longer the enthusiastic disciple he had been at Môtiers. The mixture of awe and amusement with which Boswell regarded

[4] Adam Smith's anecdote here hinted at seems not to have been recorded.

[5] Nothing omitted. The dots are indicated in the original.

him is well illustrated by a paragraph which *The London Chronicle* printed on 8 April:

"The celebrated M. Rousseau, to whom the Corsicans applied to obtain his assistance in forming their laws, has pleaded the weak and uncertain state of his health as an excuse for declining a task which would require the greatest application of mind. He is, however, to employ his pen in honour of the brave islanders by writing their history, for which materials have been collected by the ingenious Abbé Rostini. We may expect great entertainment from seeing the wild philosopher appear in the character of an historian; his extraordinary eloquence could never be more properly exerted than in transmitting to posterity the annals of Corsica."

Whatever were the particular difficulties which occasioned Boswell's defence in his letter of 25 March, they were soon swallowed up in the more important quarrel between Rousseau and his English sponsor, Hume. The trouble began with Horace Walpole's effort to amuse himself. He wrote a letter in French, supposedly from Frederick the Great to Rousseau, making fun of the latter's apparent zeal for martyrdom, which was published in *The St. James's Chronicle* on 3 April 1766. This *jeu d'esprit* gave rise to a number of newspaper squibs which ridiculed Rousseau, including one by Georges Deyverdun, a minor essayist and critic, that Rousseau attributed to his old enemy, D'Alembert. Driven from the Continent and harried in England, Rousseau began to give free play to his paranoid fancies; he accused Hume of plotting against him with Walpole and D'Alembert, although Hume had actually obtained a pension for him from the British government. To what extent Rousseau implicated Boswell in this plot is uncertain, but he knew that Boswell was well acquainted with Hume, and that Boswell's letters were being forwarded through him.

On 10 July 1766 Rousseau wrote Hume a violent letter accusing him, among other treacherous acts, of having opened one of Boswell's letters to him, probably the one from which Boswell made the extract printed above. In his reply of 22 July 1766, Hume mentioned that Boswell had complained to him of Rousseau's silence, and enclosed another letter to Rousseau from Boswell. This letter, now missing, apparently evoked the following reply.]

[Rousseau to Boswell. Original in French][6]

Wootton, 4 August 1766

SIR: — I find your letters hard to understand. However, I thank you for the interest which you are so good as to take in my health and that of Mlle. Le Vasseur. With the exception of an attack of sore eyes, she has been well since her arrival; I wish I could say as much for myself. Allow me in my turn to recommend to you the care of your own health, and especially to get yourself blooded from time to time; I think it might do you good. Please accept, Sir, my most humble greetings.

ROUSSEAU.

P.S. Your letters, both of which have come through Mr. Hume, have been greatly delayed. The first was almost open, and the second, which I did not receive until a month after its date, might easily have been opened, to judge by the condition of the envelope.

[EDITORIAL NOTE: The tone of this letter makes it obvious that Rousseau's suspicions of Boswell had not diminished. He had, of course, excellent grounds for a quarrel, but it is not very likely that he knew of them. It is true that Boswell, though at the time professing innocent bewilderment as to the cause of Rousseau's "peevishness," seems actually to have suspected Thérèse of telling tales. Temple's letter of 24 April 1790, already quoted (see p. 280 *n*. 3), is most easily clarified by such an assumption. But if Thérèse had made such a charge — even without admitting her own frailty — would not Rousseau's letter have been at once more furious and more explicit? It is probably a waste of time, Rousseau's mental condition being what it was, to look for good reasons for any of his actions during this period.

Boswell replied on 11 August with letters to Rousseau and Thérèse (both of which are missing), but the correspondence seems then to have lapsed. A letter in *The St. James's Chronicle* for 18 December

[6] This translation by F. A. Pottle and the French original are printed in volume eighteen of Colonel Isham's privately printed *Private Papers of James Boswell.* A variant version of this letter, dated 2 August, is preserved in the Neuchâtel Library and is printed in the *Correspondance générale de J.-J. Rousseau,* xv. 365. The latter is probably Rousseau's draft.

1766 defending Rousseau and attacking the "boreal Hume" and the "butterfly antiquarian," Horace Walpole, has been tentatively attributed to Boswell,[7] but the next certain statement of Boswell's feelings was made in a letter in French to Deleyre, dated 15 October 1766:

"I have an idea that M. Rousseau would have been willing enough to accept a pension. But he wished to have it on a footing that no man can ever have a pension on. He has ideas of independence that are completely visionary and which are unsuitable for a man in his position. Tell me, I ask you, how Jean Jacques Rousseau *can* live independently, except as regards his mind, the activity of which never depends on anything but the extraordinary vigour granted it by Nature? But as regards his external situation, he must necessarily be dependent. If Jean Jacques were young and robust and hardy, like one of those savages he wishes to make us admire so much, then he could ignore the human race, and running through the woods cry, 'Vivo et regno.' But Jean Jacques is actually a man advancing in years, and a man whose life has not been easy. He is infirm, ill, and delicate to a degree that I would never have believed had I not seen it. He is a man who is fond of his little delicacies even, and who would be very discontented if he were deprived of good food and a soft bed. He can think the thoughts of a Hercules. But behold the man as he is, and tell me if such a man does not need a great deal of attention and a great deal of affection from his fellows — and consequently if he does not depend on them as we all depend on one another?"

In March 1767 Boswell wrote to Temple from Edinburgh: "David Hume, you know, is gone back to be a minister of state, being appointed secretary to Mr. Conway. . . . I was very hearty with him here this winter. . . . His quarrel with Rousseau is a literary tragicomedy. I wrote verses in the character of each of them. I also designed a ludicrous print. They have altered my idea and made a glister be applied to David. But you may have the substance of it from

[7] See F. A. Pottle, "The Part Played by Horace Walpole and James Boswell in the Quarrel between Rousseau and Hume," *Philological Quarterly*, iv (1925). 351–363. For a somewhat different general view of Boswell's relations with Rousseau, see R. A. Leigh, "Boswell and Rousseau," *Modern Language Review*, xlvii (1952). 289–318.

one of the London print shops under the title of The Savage Man. You must know Rousseau quarrelled with me too, and wrote me last summer a peevish letter with strong marks of frenzy in it. For he has never yet told me the cause of his offence."[8]

Boswell's "design" for the ludicrous print was merely verbal; it appeared in *The London Chronicle* for 8 January 1767: "As the public has for some time past been entertained with an exhibition of the quarrels between Rousseau and other modern wise men, we are told that an ingenious engraver in the city is going to publish a most ludicrous print on that subject. Mr. Hume is to be represented as a bluff English farmer, holding a measure of excellent oats, which John James like a hairy savage is tempted to follow. Mr. Walpole is busy putting *papier mâché* horns and a tail to him. Tronchin applies a blister to his back, and Voltaire, in the figure of a schoolboy, is licking his legs with a wet handkerchief." In his marked file of the *Chronicle*, Boswell wrote at the bottom of this page: "N.B. My idea of this ludicrous print was really executed with some alterations and additions. I have a copy of it at Auchinleck." The print is reproduced in C. B. Tinker's *Young Boswell*, opposite p. 60. The odd transformation of a blister for Rousseau into a glister (or clyster) applied to Hume suggests that the unknown artist who made the drawing had not read Boswell's paragraph but had merely been told about it. Boswell, of course, had nothing to do with the affair beyond sending the paragraph to the newspaper.

Except for his remarks on Rousseau in *Corsica*, and some unimportant later references, Boswell's relationship with Rousseau ends here in distrust on Rousseau's part, and in disillusionment on Boswell's.]

[8] *Letters of James Boswell*, i. 103. The originals of this letter and of those to Temple quoted below, pp. 308 *n.* 8 and 310 *n.* 3, are in the Morgan Library, New York.

# APPENDIX A

*Correspondence with Girolama Piccolomini (Moma),*
*1766–1769*

[1. Received 9 March, Girolama Piccolomini to Boswell. Original in Italian]

Siena, 14 February 1766

DEAR, DEAREST BOSWELL, — If you knew how many times I have sent to the post-office to ask if there was a letter from you, you would not repay me by saying that for several weeks you have been unable to write to me. Ah, how well I know that phrase! I know also with certainty that when one cannot express the sentiments of the heart, it is a clear sign that they are not really felt; on the contrary, when one loves one never lacks words. I could write to you from morning to night without ever stopping; and though I did not tell you things that were well expressed, I should still tell you things that were as sincere and loving as though you had never left me. But, alas, you have left me! And when I think of the confession you made in your letter about the lively French girl[1] it makes me feel even more powerfully how far away from me you are — or would make me, if I were capable of greater pain. Lovable Boswell, your remoteness from me would grow ever more unendurable if I did not have the consolation of telling myself that, without possessing you, I love you with passion and with constancy. Passion consumes itself in enjoyment but constancy endures for ever, and will be mine even when I shall have become convinced that you have not a shred of affection left for me. So my entire consolation consists in thinking myself superior to the mass of men, who are directed for the most part only by the impulses of the machine.[2]

[1] Boswell had written to her on 20 January 1766 (Register of Letters). He apparently mentioned Susette, the girl he had met in Marseilles (see p. 241).

[2] In Italian, *per gli impulsi della macchina.* One thinks at once of the lines, "And now I see with eye serene/ The very pulse of the machine" in Words-

If you do not understand the delicacy of such love, is it because you laugh at whatever is not in the range of your immediate understanding? You have made me pay for having been a little coquettish with you; made me realize that you would not be so trifled with, and that any one who wished to try you out would pay dear for the experiment. So it happened to me, and I was content when the price of the trial proved to be my freedom. But just as I acquiesced in its loss, so I shall never give a thought to regaining it. You are and always shall be the absolute master of my heart; and if my hard lot forces me to remain far distant from you, at least the memory of you and the total dependence on your commands that I wish to maintain will always be the sweetest thoughts of my existence. I affect no disguise with you; I should do wrong if I did. I do not tell you *all* I feel, but I shall never tell you anything I do *not* feel.

You ask what I think about your marrying a highly spirited lady.[3] If I consulted my heart and my own interest, I should reply that liberty is a good thing and one ought not to lose it. I should like to write you a treatise on liberty. But I want to divest myself of the interest of a lover, and assume the character of a true friend. Taking a wife I believe to be a loss of good when one does not find a person who is compatible, or when one marries for money; but if two people of good character are joined together, when love prevails over interest, and mutual esteem is the basis of the relationship, I think that the road of matrimony ought to be taken unhesitatingly, especially when one knows that one's temperament is inclined to debauchery. Examine yourself, and if you find the factors I have spoken of are dominant, then marry her; and nothing will remain for me but to envy your lucky bride, and to be vain enough to think that I know your qualities as a lover better than she will be able to know them in the entire course of her fortunate existence. Let me know what you decide to do, and be assured that I am thinking of nothing but your

---

worth's "She was a Phantom of Delight." The closest parallel to Wordsworth hitherto adduced is a passage from Bartram's *Travels* (1791) which certainly does contain the words "pulse" and "machine" in the same sentence. Moma's use of a very similar expression makes one suspect that the real source is to be sought in Italian poetry — in which, by the way, Wordsworth was well read.

[3] Zélide.

welfare without the slightest regard for my own troubled spirit. Do you know how I reply to my poor distracted heart? "Well, why did you conceive so violent an attachment for one whom you ought not to have loved?" But it does not listen to me, and its malady grows more and more chronic. Tell me if I do not deserve compassion, if I have not earned some small sacrifice from you. I am not suggesting that you give up your money, but only your libertinism. Am I not reasonable?

I live with the same crowd of councillors,[4] with the exception of Placido, who has not been willing to come here any more since your departure from Siena. Our carnival was no gayer than the rest of the year; and even if it had offered diversions, lacking you I lack everything. Occasionally I think I should like to enjoy myself, but I think immediately of you, and I find that the actual presence of another man has less effect on me than the mere memory of you. And you — how did *you* pass the carnival? Were plays and balls your only diversions?

Remember that you have promised me your portrait. Although I can see you as though you were present, I want it very much. You can send it with the things I asked you to order for me, if you are willing to take the trouble of speaking to the woman you mentioned.[5]

I have no more room to write, and I have a thousand things to tell you. No, I shall not — because your letter is full of sincerity but not of tenderness. Besides, I do not want to tell you all the crazy things you make dart across my mind, and thus make myself unworthy of your esteem, which I wish to preserve at all cost. Good-bye.

I remain as I was when we were in the darkness in the large room. By the way, do you remember the little room? Do not our transports there come back to your mind? I long to go there now to get away from my guests for a while; besides, I am in the same state as then. Yes, I am going there now, now, and you will be kind enough to meet me and assuage my desires. Oh — Heaven, to how strong a transport have I abandoned myself!

Please, my dear, forgive the outbursts of a spirit shaken by pas-

[4] *Consiglieri.* Perhaps some private joke about Moma's "court" of followers is involved.

[5] See p. 265.

sion, and the thoughts of a heart that loves you endlessly. At least give yourself the pleasure of believing that you will always find in me an unchanging attachment, for my fate, my destiny wills no other.

To tell the truth, I do not know what I am saying, what I want; I can only assure you that solitude is my means of relief, for in solitude, at least nothing interrupts my thoughts, which I devote to you. I beg you now, dear heart, to be grateful to a heart which beats and lives only for you.

It is time now to break off, but first I must tell you that La Porzia has banished all notions of fidelity to my Lord, for she is making conquests right and left at a terrible rate.

In reading over this postscript, I find that physical passion has taken possession of my senses, and that I can no longer truthfully say, as I did above, that I do not love you through impulses of the machine. Confess at least that even at this great distance you do terrible things to me. Oh, *coquin*, if one day you also learn what real passion is!

I have written so much that perhaps you will only be bored; and perhaps you will not understand what this letter is all about. So that I may know that this is not so, give me precise answers to my strong — my too strong — doubts.

You write our language very well; the only fault I find is that you show so little tenderness. Good-bye — really, this time. I love you; that's all. And you, how do you love me? Believe me, I have written this page in a genuine state of distraction, but finally I have recovered a little from my seizure and ask your forgiveness. I am, with all respect, yours to command.

Only one word more: do you still have the ribbon I gave you, worked by my own hands? I always carry your fan, in spite of the terribly cold weather.

[2. Received 11 May, Girolama Piccolomini to Boswell. Original in Italian]

Siena, 23 February 1766

Your letter of the 29th of last month struck me like the fall of a thunderbolt. The news of the loss of your dear mother has truly afflicted me because of the grief it undoubtedly is causing you. I enter only too deeply into everything that can make you unhappy; and as I well know the goodness of your heart and the grief that a mother's death brings, I see your sorrow with perfect clarity. Permit me, dear Boswell, to mingle my tears with yours, and to be the companion of your sorrow.

The other part of your letter which upset me further is the fact that you have returned to Scotland. Although you had written me that you would not come back again to Italy, I still cherished a slight hope of your return as long as you were on your travels. But now that the case is hopeless, I have no other recourse but to abandon myself to despair. It is a relief — a relief that can be understood only by those in my situation.

You did not let me know your address. If by any chance that was to prevent me from writing, you can see that you did not attain your end, for I trust this letter to chance, and implore the justice of my cause to see that it is delivered to you.[6] Tell me if you received another letter addressed to you at Paris, in which I revealed my feelings for you with some liberty.[7] Never think because you have returned to your native land, that I do not wish your portrait. On the contrary, I certainly want it, and you can send it to Signor Crocchi, asking him to deliver it to me with the greatest secrecy.

I dare not risk explaining to you the state of my heart, not knowing what may be the fate of this letter. I only beg you to remember one who loves you sincerely, and who longs for opportunities to pay

[6] Moma's direction is of heroic simplicity: "A Monsieur / Monsieur Giacomo Boswell / Scozia." But there are no postmarks or other proofs to show that the letter, with this cover, went through the mails. Presumably she sent it to Paris inside another wrapper, addressed to Boswell in care of John Waters, his banker there.

[7] The preceding letter.

clearly to your great merit at least that quantity of respect which the shortness of your stay in Siena prevented her from paying while you were here. Be certain that you will always find in me an honourable woman, a true friend, and a constant lover, all united in one. Dear Boswell, accept this declaration of mine, if it gives you any pleasure, and in so doing give me fresh proof that you sincerely reciprocate my affection.

Do me the kindness of believing that, having such feelings, I live for you; and that neither space nor time can make me change from what I am. My feelings for you will be indelible, for the impression of real merit is never lost. I have lived more during one moment with you than in the longest days that I have spent away from you. Hearing from you revives those sweet moments which are the only ones that count in the system of my life. So make things easier for me with your letters, and rest assured that I love and esteem you. I seal this letter and pretend to myself that you will receive it, but who knows, letter, in whose hands you will fall?

[3. Received ?August 1767, Girolama Piccolomini to Boswell. Original in Italian][8]

Siena, 20 March 1767

Sir, — You are the man who swore to me in person and by letters that you would never stop writing to me, and that *twenty years from now I would still be receiving letters from you filled with the same expressions*. Those are your own words. I keep the written record of them, not for my own sake, for I remember in minute detail all you ever said, but to have documentation for my saying and reflecting on the fact that one can count little on a man's friendship, even though he is credited with a good character and a good heart. When the object of love is gone from his eyes, all fades away. And in truth these thoughts are not new, but I am sorry to say that sad experience confirms their truth in regard to you.

[8] The date on which Boswell received this letter is unknown, since his Register of Letters for this period, if he kept one, is missing. It seems likely, however, that it reached him after No. 4, having been sent through Paris, in care of Waters. On 11 August 1767, Boswell wrote to Temple: "I had the other day a letter from my Signora at Siena written with all the warmth of Italian affection" (*Letters of James Boswell*, i. 120).

I received a single letter on your arrival in Scotland, which I did not fail to answer immediately, addressing it according to your instructions, as I shall do with this one; but I am afraid they have not reached you with that address, and I do not understand why you do not give me your address in your own country.

I am well so far as health is concerned, and except for some minor illnesses I always have been well. My councillors are always the same. The only new thing this season has been a German gentleman who has called on me. The *turno grosso* (as you called it)[9] is over, and everyone has gone back home. The country is not very gay, because of the sufferings of the poor and the deaths of many people, but in May our Sovereigns will come, and then there will be great celebrations and many people.[1]

Now, give me news of yourself in detail. What are your love affairs? Do you ever think of me? Do you understand Italian? Are you as inconstant as ever with women? Do you still keep up your friendship with Rousseau and with Signor de Paoli? I beg you to answer all these questions. You may be sure that a letter from you will give me great pleasure, the more so because I have despaired of hearing from you. You promised me your portrait, and I do not intend to release you from your promise. Therefore you must keep it, or I shall appeal to your friend Rousseau; I am sure he will take my side, because of the justice of my claim and because the thing you promised is so valuable.

[9] *Turno grosso* may have been Boswell's rendering of "grand tour" in the days when he was learning Italian. When Moma uses the phrase later, it seems to mean "social round."

[1] Sir Horace Mann wrote to Horace Walpole from Florence on 14 February 1767: "We and all Italy have had a most cruel winter, but some gentle rains have melted the vast quantities of snow that surrounded us, by degrees, and by that means have freed us from the danger of an inundation. But many people in the country have literally died of hunger. There is no want of corn of late, for the great plenty will ruin the merchants that have sent for it, but there is no money to purchase it, I mean for the use of these poor creatures, even at the low price it is fallen to." On 18 April, Mann wrote Walpole from Florence, "The apprehensions on account of a sickness that has reigned for some months at Siena are abated there, but are come hither" (from the unpublished manuscripts, by kind permission of the owner, W. S. Lewis). The "Sovereigns" were the new Grand Duke of Tuscany, Leopold I, and his wife, the Infanta Maria Louisa. See 25 July 1765.

If I can serve you, I expect you to command me. Be assured that neither time nor space will alter my feelings. You will be ashamed to know so faithful a lady without being able to imitate her example, and without being able to say to yourself, "I have no reservations" — which *I* can say, and which I now set my name to, taking my leave of you with this letter. Who knows whether it will come to your hands, and if it does, who knows whether you will be able to read it? But sometimes one must take risks, just as I am now doing.

Your most devoted and most obliged friend,

GIROLAMA NINI PICCOLOMINI.[2]

[4. Received ?June 1767, Girolama Piccolomini to Boswell. Original in Italian][3]

Siena, 3 May 1767

SIR, — This has been the first letter that I have received from you since your return to Scotland. I did not receive any of the others you mention in yours of 25 March. I give you a thousand thanks for assuring me of your friendship which is so dear to me, and for having freed me from a great impatience to hear from you. After having waited for letters from you for a long time, I decided to write to you about a month ago, and addressed the letter to your banker at Paris.

So here we are, both justified in regard to our friendship. I am equally justified in regard to gallantry, for I am living without any tender attachment, and much less do I care for casual encounters. But all this will mean nothing to you while by your own confession you are sunk in vice, transported by sensual pleasure, which keeps you from tasting those feelings of delicacy which accompany good manners and are the spice of all pleasures. But I do not wish to play the preacher, and in any case I could not persuade you, for you think me too interested in the result.

[2] This is the first letter of Moma's to Boswell to bear a signature, and the only one in the series to bear a full signature.

[3] The curious postal history of this letter is too complex to be traced in detail here. It left London, however, on 29 May 1767, and Boswell must have received it at Auchinleck in early June. He wrote to Temple on 12 June: "I must tell you my Italian angel is constant. I had a letter from her but a few days ago, which made me cry" (*Letters of James Boswell*, i. 112).

I can give good reports of myself so far as my health is concerned. As to the company that comes here, it is always the same, except for Placidi, who left me after your departure from Siena. Last winter a German baron, who was visiting here, came to see me all the time, but the gallantry between us did not go beyond the preliminaries. Our *turno grosso* continues on the same footing. Porzia is pregnant; this will surprise you as it surprises everyone, but it is a fact.

Our Sovereigns arrive on Wednesday[4] and will stay until the 18th. During that time we shall have a great many visitors and as splendid festivities as our city can arrange.

Certainly I wish your portrait. One does not promise, as far as I am concerned, without keeping one's word. If only in like manner I could make you keep your promise to love me! But he who is absent is always wrong — and with you perhaps, he who is present is wrong too.

I am greatly surprised to see that you write Italian, and even write it better than when you left. This makes me suspect that you have studied the language further, or that you are carrying on an intrigue with some Italian girl. I beg you to enlighten me on this point.

I sent your address to Abbé Crocchi so that he could write it out for me on a piece of paper, as I was not sure I had done it correctly by myself. He copied it and corrected it where he thought it inaccurate, and asked me to send you his very best regards.

Tiburzio thanks you again for remembering him, and very often we talk of you with Tiburzio, as do all my friends, who remember you with much pleasure. It is impossible to have known you without remembering you vividly.

Your letter came safely to my hands, so you can continue to use the same method for getting future letters delivered to me. But do not recall things so openly, for the letters might get lost, and many other accidents might follow, which I do not mention for lack of space. Remember me, and write, if you wish me to believe that you do.

[4] 6 May.

[5. Received ?December 1767, Girolama Piccolomini to Boswell. Original in Italian][5]

Siena, 16 November 1767

IT HAS BEEN SOME DAYS since I received your dearest letter, but as I was in the country and had not carried your address with me I could not reply immediately, as I should have liked to do. I am ever more and more obliged for the solicitude you continue to show in writing to me; it appears that you take an interest in even the smallest things which concern me.

To give detailed replies to all your questions: my small retinue of servants is completely changed because of a burglary that occurred in our house. The *turno grosso* has begun again, if not every night, at least often. Porzia was safely delivered of twin boys, but they have ruined her, and it would have been better for her to show fewer signs of youth, if that entailed becoming pregnant, than to be so disfigured.[6] The news of myself is good, so far as my health is concerned. My circle of friends remains numerous, but Placidi visited me no more after your departure from Siena. I live very quietly so far as gallantry is concerned, and think I shall continue to do so as long as I live. Why do you not follow my example? Does it seem so fine to you to flit every moment to a new object of passion, amusing your body without nourishing your heart — a kind of sustenance necessary for a man of birth and talent like yourself?

I have no doubt that you are on the point of winning the lady whom you wish to marry[7] (to know you is enough to cause me to believe it); I only fear that when you have a wife some wench will take your fancy. Then it will not merely be you who will pay the penalty, but there will be two to suffer; quarrels will follow, and a peaceful life will be changed into an intolerable one. So I cannot say whether or not a wife will make you happy. I can only tell you that you have all the qualities necessary for being loved and to make another's happiness, but, with all these fine qualities, I fear you also

[5] Postmarked 14 December, which indicates the day it arrived in either London or Edinburgh.

[6] Porzia was then thirty-seven.

[7] Catherine Blair, a rich ward of Lord Auchinleck's.

have the ability to vex a wife. But to whom am I presuming to give reasons? I forgot that I was speaking to a lawyer who will find a thousand ways to turn my argument against me; who will have to allow himself to be swayed by false arguments. Perhaps you will persuade me too, and I shall believe that you are right. So I beg you for the future to be faithful in letting me hear from you, but not to ask me again for my opinion, as I do not have the temerity to argue with a *jurisconsult;* and if I esteemed you before, now I esteem and tremble before you too.

Why do you no longer exchange letters with Rousseau? It seems to me that a correspondence with him is more appropriate for you than one with Paoli.

I await your portrait anxiously. Address it to Signor Crocchi so that he can give it to me privately; but have it painted after you have recovered from your illness. Otherwise you will be too pale.

I am amazed how you can make progress in Italian without speaking it with anyone, but the good in you amazes me as much as the bad.

I intended to write you a letter only one sheet long, and without realizing it I have made it two. But have patience, and give your avarice the boot[8] — you once confessed to me that you were inclined to avarice, which is unbecoming when it exceeds just economy. I, now, am free from this vice, for one must be rich to have it. You see that even from poverty one draws some advantages. But for all that, I should not be comforted by that adage if I did not know that there are those who lack the very necessities of life.

Keep up your friendship for me, and if it gives you pleasure to know that it is returned with interest, rest assured of it, as you must be if you will oblige me by the honour of your commands.

[8] "Date un calcio all' avarizia." Postage on a letter was paid by the recipient, not the sender. For two sheets double postage was charged.

[6. Boswell to Girolama Piccolomini. Original in Italian][9]

Auchinleck, 5 November 1768

My dearest friend, — It is truly difficult for me to know how to begin a letter to you after having let so many months go by without replying to the most affectionate one I last had from you. Yet I assure you that this indolence has caused me great pain. I have looked upon myself as ungrateful to a lady of talent, of beauty, and of goodness, to whom I owe more than I can express. Forgive me, dear Momina. You are accustomed to forgiving me. I am a most sincere penitent; and truly you will not have occasion to forgive me again, for I am resolved to show my affection by the regularity with which I shall answer your sweetest letters.

I have been some months at London, where I enjoyed again those sensual pleasures against which your delicacy of feeling has protested so strongly. But I hope in the future to be more moderate, and more worthy of your friendship.

I am at the moment deeply in love with a *belle irlandaise* who is only seventeen years old. She is sweet and lovable, and has a handsome fortune.[1] But I am too changeable where women are concerned. I ought to be a Turk; I believe I should make a very good sultan.

I am obliged to pass the entire winter in our capital city, Edinburgh, but in the month of March I shall go to Ireland to see my dear Mariana. I beg you, dearest friend, to write to me at once and tell me if Mariana is not a beautiful name.

You see that I remain the same man whom you knew. I have the same spirit, and rest assured, dear friend, that I have still the same heart. You must not think that I have forgotten my promise to send you my portrait. I really did have it done, but it is not as like as I wish it to be. For that reason I am having it done by another painter, and you shall have it this spring without fail.[2]

[9] This letter was sent by mistake to the Rev. Robert Richardson, chaplain to the English Ambassador at The Hague, who returned it. Boswell never seems to have redirected it to Moma. As will appear, Moma got the letter intended for Richardson through the same error.

[1] Mary Ann Boyd, whom he went to visit in Ireland in the spring of 1769. On the trip Boswell was accompanied by his cousin, Margaret Montgomerie, who became his wife on 25 November 1769.

[2] Nothing is known of these two portraits (which were probably miniatures).

I thank you for your Sienese news. Porzia's feat filled me with amazement. Two boys! It is truly heroic. Oh, if it were possible for me to visit sweet Siena again! It is not impossible, for surely I shall go again to visit Corsica. Dear friend, tell me if you do not feel a lively compassion for that brave people, who are doing so much for liberty. Please send me all the news about yourself. Your friendship consoles me in this cold country. Believe me always your most affectionate friend,

JAMES BOSWELL.

Address me, "All' Illmo. Sigre., Sigre. Prone. Colmo., Il Signor Giaccomo Boswell di Auchinleck, Par Londra, Edimburgo."

[7. Received ?January 1769, Girolama Piccolomini to Boswell. Original in Italian][3]

[Siena, ?December 1768]

SIR, — From what seems a blunder, I flatter myself that you still remember me. The blunder is this. I received a letter from you this week clearly addressed to me. But when I saw that it was written in English, I hesitated long whether I could risk having it read by any one who understood English, because of the chance of putting him in possession of some passage intended only for ourselves. But I concluded that since you knew very well that I did not understand your language, you would have written only generalities. So I found the courage to have it read by a gentleman who knows a little English, and we gathered that you were writing to some gentleman, a friend of yours, and that perhaps you had written also to me and had mistaken the covers and sent my letter to your friend. Tell me if my inference is correct, or whether my hope that you still remember me makes me read matters too much to my own advantage. I have only too certain and too varied proofs that much time has passed since you last favoured me with news of yourself, though I have always desired such news eagerly, and neither time nor distance shall diminish in the slightest the esteem which I have ever felt for you since your stay in Siena.

As to news of myself (if that still interests you) I can report that my health is good. As for amusements, you know how few they are in

[3] Postmarked 2 January.

this city, but I always take advantage of the assemblies here and the small diversions which the country offers. As to my heart, I find that only with difficulty can I keep it engaged since I came to know you. I live calmly so far as love is concerned, preferring the company of friends to that of a lover. Can you say as much? Speak frankly, without using the circumlocutions of a lawyer.

I shall not tell you the news of the city, because after so long a time it must have ceased to be of interest to you. I am afraid that you have forgotten Italian. If so, our correspondence would be a fine thing: I shall not understand your letters and you will not understand mine. Tell me if you love debauchery as you once did; tell me if you are to be married; tell me too if you still correspond with the illustrious Paoli, who merits that designation more every day. Apropos of Paoli, I understand that in your *Account of Corsica* you show great partiality in the epithet you give our city, calling it a *dolce soggiorno*[4] — which shows how much you are given to praising everything.

I return your letter for you to dispose of as you please. I do not know whether I ought to address it to Auchinleck[5] (the place of writing of the misdirected letter), or whether I ought to send it to Edinburgh, but I shall ask a Scotsman who happens to be here.[6] Send me through Crocchi the portrait that I have desired for so long. I want an opportunity to be able to obey you; and if you wish to do justice to my constancy, you ought not to forget me, who am entirely yours. Your most devoted and most obedient friend,

G.P.

[4] A sweet resting-place. See p. 149.

[5] Her actual spelling, Anchirleck, illustrates one of the serious difficulties in reading Boswell's hand. His *n*'s and *r*'s, *u*'s and *v*'s are ordinarily identical.

[6] The letter is addressed to Edinburgh.

# APPENDIX B

## *Letters of Rousseau to Thérèse Le Vasseur*

[EDITORIAL NOTE: The following two letters of Rousseau to Thérèse from the Boswell papers are given in the original as well as translation since they have never been printed before. As well as providing direct evidence of the stable and easy domestic relationship of the pair, these letters are significant because of their rarity: only two letters from Rousseau to Thérèse and one from her to him are to be found in the twenty-volume *Correspondance générale de J.-J. Rousseau.* Boswell left no indication as to how he obtained them; he may have fished them out of a waste-paper basket, but more probably he begged them from Thérèse as a souvenir of the great man. Rousseau's French is printed without normalization except for his capitalization of the letter "s," which has been handled arbitrarily.]

### [1. Rousseau to Thérèse Le Vasseur]

A Basle le 30. 8$^{bre}$ 1765.

J'arrive aujourdui Mercredi dans cette Ville sans grand accident, mais avec un mal de gorge, la fiévre, et la mort dans le cœur. A peine mon voyage est-il commencé et je sens déja l'impossibilité totale de l'achever, sur tout dans cette saison. Je vais pour sortir tout à fait de la Suisse me rendre à Strasbourg d'où je vous instruirai du parti que j'aurai pris. En vérité je ne sais que devenir. De tous les partis qui me restent à prendre je préfererai celui qui nous rejoindra le plustot. Voila, quant à présent tout ce que je vous puis dire. Je vous en apprendrai davantage de Strasbourg où je partirai pour me rendre le plustot que je pourrai. Si M-. de Luze, qui sort d'ici, peut me procurer une voiture, je partirai dès demain. Conservez-vous, tenez vous gaye, ayez soin de vous pour l'amour de moi, et faites mille amitiés de ma part à tous les habitans de l'Isle. J'ai amené Sultan, et il est à présent couché sur mon manteau sous la table où j'écris. Il va devant la voiture comme un coureur; il a fait hier dix lieues au galop. C'est un chien unique, mais qui ne laisse pas de m'embarrasser beaucoup. Adieu, chére Tante, je vous embrasse mille fois.

[1. Rousseau to Thérèse Le Vasseur. Translation]

Bâle, 30 October 1765

I ARRIVED TODAY, Wednesday, in this city without any great mishaps, but with a sore throat, a fever, and death in my heart. My journey is scarcely begun and I feel already the utter impossibility of completing it, especially at this season of the year. In order to leave Switzerland entirely, I am going to go on to Strasbourg, and from there I shall let you know what course I shall then have adopted. In truth, I do not know where to turn. Of all the choices which are open to me I shall prefer that which will bring us together most quickly. That is all I can say to you at the moment. I shall tell you more from Strasbourg, for which I shall depart in order to arrive there as soon as possible. If M. de Luze,[1] who is also leaving Bâle, can procure me a carriage, I shall leave as early as tomorrow.

Watch your health, remain cheerful, take care of yourself for love of me, and give my best regards to all the people on the Island.[2] I have brought Sultan along, and he is at present lying on my coat under the table where I am writing. He runs before the carriage like a courier; yesterday he covered ten leagues at a gallop. He is an invaluable dog, but a great deal of bother all the same. Good-bye, *chère Tante*, all my love.

[2. Rousseau to Thérèse Le Vasseur][3]

A Strasbourg le quatre Novembre 1765

Je vous ai écrit de Bienne, et puis de Basle; je vous écris maintenant de Strasbourg; vous devez être contente de moi. Je viens de faire le plus pénible et le plus desagréable voyage que j'aye fait de mes jours, et sans les bons soins de M. de Luze ç'auroit été pis encore. Aussi je n'en puis plus, je m'arrête, et n'étant plus en Suisse je vais me reposer dans cette Ville, d'où j'espére qu'on ne me chassera pas dans

[1] Rousseau travelled to Strasbourg and Paris with Jean Jacques de Luze, who also accompanied him and Hume to England.

[2] The letter is addressed: "A Mademoiselle / Mademoiselle le Vasseur, / A *L'Isle St. Pierre*."

[3] Addressed: "A Madame / Madame le Veuve Heuer / pour l'Isle St. Pierre / *a Nidau* canton de / Berne."

cette saison et dans l'état où je suis. Ainsi si vous voulez me donner de vos nouvelles ici j'aurai le tems de les y recevoir et je les attends avec tout l'empressement de la plus tendre amitié; n'oubliez pas de m'en donner aussi de l'Isle dont je salue cordialement les bons et heureux hâbitans.

Cette Ville est grande et belle, bien peuplée; il y a beaucoup de trouppes, mais je ne sais pas s'il y a des officiers de ma connoissance: car je ne suis point encore sorti, et je mange tout seul dans ma chambre avec Sultan qui me tient fidelle compagnie, surtout à table, et qui mange comme il marche; c'est tout dire. Je tâcherai de me tirer un peu de prison en m'allant promener sur les remparts à l'heure où il n'y aura personne, et dans mes promenades solitaires je penserai souvent à l'Isle St. Pierre et à ce que j'y ai laissé. Je n'ose pas me promener dans les rues de peur qu'on ne me reconnoisse et que ma chambre ne desemplisse pas. Cependant M. le Commandant n'ignore pas que j'y suis; car il a fallu lui envoyer mon nom en arrivant, ce qui me fait craindre que ce ne soit pas un secret longtems.

Adieu, chére Tante; il faut pour me consoler de vivre sans vous, que j'espére bientot nous rejoindre. J'y ferai tout de mon mieux, je vous assure. En attendant, prenez patience; vous étes plus heureuse que moi.

mon addresse / A Monsieur Rousseau chez M. Kamm à l'enseigne de la Fleur *A Strasbourg*.

Priez quelqu'un de mettre l'addresse, car si elle n'est écrite très correctement et très lisiblement, la lettre ne me parviendra pas.

[2. Rousseau to Thérèse Le Vasseur. Translation]

Strasbourg, 4 November 1765

I WROTE YOU FROM BIENNE, and again from Bâle; now I write to you from Strasbourg. You ought to be pleased with me. I have just finished the most painful and most disagreeable trip of my life, and without the kind attentions of M. de Luze it would have been even worse. So I can go no farther. I am stopping here, and being out of Switzerland, I am going to rest in this city, from which I hope they will not chase me at this time of year and in my present state of health. So if you care to write to me here, I shall have time to receive your letter, which I await eagerly and with the most tender feelings. Do not forget to send news also of the Island, whose good and happy people I cordially greet.

This city is large, beautiful, and populous. There are a good many soldiers here, but I do not know if there are any officers of my acquaintance, for I have not gone out at all yet. I eat all alone in my room with Sultan, who keeps me faithful company, especially at meals, and who eats as he runs — which tells the whole story.[4] I shall try to escape a little from my prison by going to walk on the ramparts at a time when no one will be there, and in my solitary walks I shall think often of the Isle St. Pierre and of what I left there. I dare not walk in the streets for fear that I shall be recognized and that my room will be constantly full of people. However, the Commandant knows I am here, because I had to send him my name on arrival, which makes me fear that it will not long be a secret.[5]

Good-bye, *chère Tante*. To console myself for living without you, I must hope soon to arrange matters so that we can be together. I shall do my very best to see to that, I assure you. In the mean time, be patient. You are happier than I am.

My address: Monsieur Rousseau, *chez* M. Kamm, at the sign of the Flower, Strasbourg.

Ask some one to write the address for you, for unless it is written very accurately and legibly, the letter will not reach me.

[4] Rousseau had demonstrated his fondness for Sultan before Boswell at Môtiers. His extraordinary attachment for the dog was shown again at Chiswick, according to an anecdote told by Samuel Rogers: "Rousseau had lost a favourite dog, and Hume, having exerted himself to recover it, now brought it back to its master, who thanked him with expressions of the most fervent gratitude and shed tears of joy over the animal" (*Recollections of the Table-Talk of Samuel Rogers,* ed. Alexander Dyce, 1856, pp. 106–107). For another incident concerning Sultan, see *Boswell on the Grand Tour: Germany and Switzerland,* 15 December 1764.

[5] Rousseau's forebodings were fulfilled: he received a very cordial welcome in Strasbourg, and his operetta, *Le Devin du village,* was performed in his honour.

# APPENDIX C

## *Discarded Portion of Letter from Boswell to Rousseau*

[Boswell to Rousseau. Original in French][1]

Lucca, 3 October 1765

... A FEW DAYS LATER I set out for Naples, where I found a mild climate which infused my mind with its mildness. Assuredly climate colours our existence. Its effects are as certain as the influence of the sun upon matter. Saint-Preux experienced this when he dwelt in the lovely mountains of Switzerland; and it astonishes me that Jean Jacques Rousseau, who is no longer a citizen of Geneva but a citizen of the world[2] — it astonishes me that this great philosopher remains in a northern country, exposed to rough changes of weather and obliged to spend many of his precious moments warming himself at a vile stove. I should like to have him bring out a complete edition of his works, and leaving to that ungrateful corner of the earth a monument of his celestial genius and to mankind in general a body of precepts to make them happy when their minds shall have been purified of gross prejudices — I should then like him to go to the delightful East, to live the rest of his days in the sweet tranquillity of a paradisial retreat, to draw his last breath under a benignant sky, and pass to a better world from those plains whence the pious and respectable shepherd-patriarchs passed to the God of Abraham.

But Jean Jacques Rousseau is not so great a philosopher as one would wish him to be. Jean Jacques Rousseau was born and reared in a corrupt society, and cannot free himself from certain propensities unworthy of him. He frets over what men, beings whom he scorns, think of him. He renounces civilized society and subscribes himself orang-outang, but he is like a boy who, in order to avenge himself on those who have caused him some displeasure, hides behind the window curtains and exclaims to himself, "Well, Sirs, I have left you all. You shall see me no more." Jean Jacques Rousseau on the mountain,

[1] See p. 5 *n.* 4.

[2] Rousseau had renounced his Genevan citizenship on 12 May 1763 as a consequence of the furor over his *Lettre à M. de Beaumont.*

where one would have thought him above the petty quarrels of petty states, occupies himself night and day in writing against the magistrates of Geneva, and involves himself in squabbles with Calvinist ministers! Heavens! To see in print a dispute between J. J. Rousseau and Pastor Vernes![3] *Risum teneatis, amici?*[4] Or rather, *Quis talia fando . . . temperet a lacrimis?*[5] Illustrious philosopher, go to the East. We shall take care to write to you each time a statue is erected to you. And Deleyre and I will come to visit you, will venerate you, will love you, and through our feeling for you partake of your happiness.

## APPENDIX D

*Paragraphs from "The London Chronicle" concerning Corsica and Boswell, sent in to the "Chronicle" by Boswell himself from Marseilles and Paris*[1]

TUESDAY 7 JANUARY. The island of Corsica is now become an important object in Europe, General de Paoli having acted with so much wisdom and spirit that the brave Corsicans are actually in possession of the whole island except the five fortified towns on the seacoast, which are still under the dominion of the Genoese. The command which Corsica can have of the navigation in the Mediterranean must render those islanders very considerable now that they have thrown off a foreign yoke, and are at last formed into a nation; having for many years been so divided into opposite parties that they were looked upon by foreign powers as so many tribes of savages or troops of banditti. I am, yours, &c.

[3] See p. 259.

[4] "Could you restrain your laughter, friends?" (Horace, *Ars poetica*, l. 5).

[5] "Who, in telling such things, would keep himself from tears?" (Virgil, *Aeneid*, ii. 6, 8).

[1] See the Editorial Note, p. 244.

THURSDAY 9 JANUARY. Extract of a letter from Rome, 5 December 1765: "You have been amused with reports of Britain's sending an embassy to the island of Corsica. Your newspapers were once very positive that the Duke of York was determined to visit that island, and of late we were assured of Mr. Stanley's being to go over. I can, however, inform you for certain that a British subject has actually been there. About the middle of October Mr. Boswell, a Scots gentleman upon his travels over Europe, sailed from the port of Leghorn for the island of Corsica, with a very ample and particular passport from Commodore Harrison. He landed on Capo Corso, and went above a hundred miles into the territories of the malcontents, as they were formerly called, but must now have the title of the nation. He found Signor de Paoli in one of the provinces on the other side of the great range of mountains which divides the island. He, no doubt, presented to that chief very sufficient recommendations, for he was received by him with every mark of distinction, was lodged in a palace of the noble family of Colonna, and whenever he chose to make a little tour, was attended by a detachment of guards. He passed ten or twelve days with General de Paoli, dined and supped with him constantly, and was every day in private conference with him for some hours. Mr. Boswell gave it out at Leghorn that he went to Corsica merely for curiosity, but the politicians of Italy think they can see more important reasons for his visiting that island. The Genoese have been not a little alarmed by it, and having received very early intimation of Mr. Boswell's having sailed from Leghorn, they procured constant intelligence of his motions during the whole time of his stay in the island; but all the intelligence sent them has only served to throw them into greater perplexity. What appears most difficult to be explained is Mr. Boswell's having sailed almost before anybody knew of his intention. He carried all the appearance of a gentleman travelling for his amusement, passed some time with the Count de Marbeuf, Commander-in-Chief of the French troops in Corsica; and afterwards went to Genoa, where he stayed above a week, and seemed free and unconcerned as if he had nothing to do with state disputes. People in this part of the world are curious to know what will really be the consequence of Mr. Boswell's tour to Corsica."

SATURDAY 11 JANUARY. When Mr. Boswell was presented to

the General de Paoli, he paid this compliment to the Corsicans: "Sir, I am upon my travels, and have lately visited Rome. I am come from seeing the ruins of one brave and free people; I now see the rise of another."

TUESDAY 14 JANUARY. Signor Pascal de Paoli has the title of his Excellency the General of the Kingdom of Corsica. He is absolute commander in the military affairs, and in a civil capacity is head of the Supreme Council. He is a man about forty, tall, well made, and of a noble countenance. He speaks his own language remarkably well, and is very much master both of French and English. He is, without doubt, one of the illustrious men of the present age.

When Mr. Boswell took leave of the General de Paoli, his Excellency made him a present of a gun and a pair of pistols of excellent workmanship made in Corsica, and of one of the large mountain dogs so famous in that island for their hunting the wild boar, and for their guarding their master.

THURSDAY 16 JANUARY. All hopes of accommodation between Corsica and Genoa are now at an end, all the inhabitants of the island having a most inveterate hatred against their former oppressors. Nine and twenty years of war cannot fail to have fixed this hatred very strongly. . . .

THURSDAY 23 JANUARY. Florence, 16 December. We think we are now in possession of the true motives for a late expedition into Corsica which had greatly engaged the attention of some politicians of this place. The story is this: a gentleman who had for some time resided here, all on a sudden went off in a vessel for Corsica. Various were the conjectures which followed him, being a person of some distinction; but the conversation on the subject in a little time subsided, and no more was said about it till very lately from Genoa we had the following account, *viz.* that the above-mentioned gentleman with some of his friends, being sensibly touched with the misfortunes of the young Chevalier Charles Stuart, and impatient at the thoughts of his languishing away the remainder of his days in a tedious and starving obscurity, formed a project of beating the pulse of Signor Paoli, in order, if possible, to procure some kind of establishment of sovereignty for their high-born Prince in that island. Mr. B., we are assured, arrived safe in the quarters of the Corsican chief, and was received and treated by him with great civility and politeness; but whatever intimations or insinuations Mr. B. might hint or drop to the Corsican General with regard to the pretended project, they have not yet transpired, nor perhaps never may. But this is certain, that Mr. B. was sent off under a very honourable and distinguishing escort into the French quarters, where waiting on M. Marbeuf, with whom he had a short conference, he stayed a day or two, and from thence made the best of his way to Genoa.

To this remarkable anecdote must be added another, which is told with the greatest assurance at the same time, which is that the young Chevalier himself had not the least knowledge of or participation in this notable scheme, but that it was purely the effects of the warm but unauthorized (and, as is common in such cases, ill-judged) zeal in a few of his banished partisans.

THURSDAY 6 FEBRUARY. Extract of a letter from Genoa, dated 2 January: "The Sieur Boswell, who has given such inquietude to our rulers by his visit to our enemies in Corsica, upon his return from that expedition was forced, by tempestuous weather, to take refuge in the island of Capraja. Colonel Matra and Captain Grimaldi found themselves in the same situation, and although they strongly suspected the Scotchman's attachment to Paoli, they treated him with so great politeness that he accompanied them to this city. These officers, who have distinguished themselves so much for the Republic, were under great apprehensions of being taken by Paoli's corsairs. They declare that, during several days' conversation with Mr. Boswell, they could not certainly discover whether his motives for having been in Corsica were of a public or private nature. They could only observe that he had a good many papers, about which he seemed very anxious; and that he avoided talking freely of what he had seen in his singular tours."

TUESDAY 11 FEBRUARY. Extract of a letter from Leghorn, dated 3 January: "Nothing can be a greater proof of the weak and desponding spirit of the Genoese than the apprehensions which Mr. Boswell's tour to Corsica has occasioned. Is not the curiosity of an observing traveller a sufficient reason for such a tour, without imagining that the British nation have any serious political designs with regard to the island? It is said that a gentleman lately come from Corsica diverted himself with the strange fears of the Genoese, who, from long trying to persuade others, are at last come to believe themselves that the Corsicans are like the anthropophagi — the most terrible of barbarians. To a Genoese gentleman who asked, with much earnestness, what Paoli was like, he replied that he was like the astonishing beast in the Revelations, with seven heads and ten horns, full of eyes before and behind, and taking no rest day nor night."

THURSDAY 13 FEBRUARY. Extract of a letter from Turin, 6 January: "We are exceedingly happy here at the flourishing state of affairs in Corsica. Our gracious and benevolent Sovereign has always been a protector of the brave islanders, and his subjects are sincerely animated with the same sentiments. Sardinia and Corsica are separated by a narrow channel of no more than ten miles, so that it is much the interest of both to maintain a good understanding. We remember to have seen in this city, in the year 1746, two nobles of Corsica who were charged with some secret negotiations with the Earl of Bristol, at that time His Britannic Majesty's Ambassador to our Court, the result of which has never yet been known; for although some English ships of war did actually bombard Bastia, they acted only as allied forces of the Empress and of our Sovereign. The British, who glory in their freedom, and would represent the others of us on the Continent as little better than slaves, have never yet done anything of themselves for the spirited and firm little nation, which for these thirty years has been making the noblest struggles against oppression. On the contrary, when they had concluded the last peace with France, they published a proclamation declaring it high treason for any British subject to assist the Corsicans — the rebellious Corsicans — and for this proclamation, the then Prime Minister of England was severely censured by the daring Sieur Wilkes, whose *North Briton* made such an uproar.

"The gazettes of late have talked a great deal of a certain Mr. Boswell, a Scots gentleman, who has been in Corsica. It was at first rumoured that he was a desperate adventurer, whose real name was M'Donald, and who had served during the last war in North America; but it has since appeared that he is a gentleman of fortune upon his travels, a friend of the celebrated John James Rousseau, who is an enthusiast for the Corsicans, and has been honoured with the title of their legislator. We do not give credit to the reports of Mr. Boswell's having had instructions from his Court to treat with Signor de Paoli, but we are in great hopes that from what he has seen, he will be able to undeceive his countrymen with regard to the Corsican nation."

SATURDAY 15 FEBRUARY. Yesterday James Boswell, Esquire, arrived in town from his travels.

A MAP OF ITALY
at the time of Boswell's tour
locating many of the places mentioned
REDRAWN BY HAROLD K. FAYE
FROM A MAP BY ROBERT DE VAUGONDY, 1756
SWITZERLAND
FRANCE
ITALY
DALMATIA
ADRIATIC SEA
LIGURIAN SEA
MEDITERRANEAN SEA
TYRRHENIAN SEA
CORSICA
SARDINIA
CAPRAJA
Geneva
Lyons
Pont St.-Esprit
Avignon
Aix
Marseilles
Cuges
Toulon
Le Luc
Fréjus
Antibes
Nice
Mentone
Monaco
San Remo
Ventimiglia
Porto Maurizio
Pietra
Finale
Noli
Vado
Savona
Genoa
Mt. Cenis
Turin
Milan
Piacenza
Parma
Reggio
Modena
Bologna
Ferrara
Brescia
Castelnuovo
Verona
Mantua
Padua
Rovigo
Venice
Lucca
Pisa
Leghorn
Florence
Siena
San Marino
Rimini
Ancona
Loretto
Foligno
Terni
Tivoli
Rome
Frascati
Naples
English Miles
0
25
50
75
100
125
150

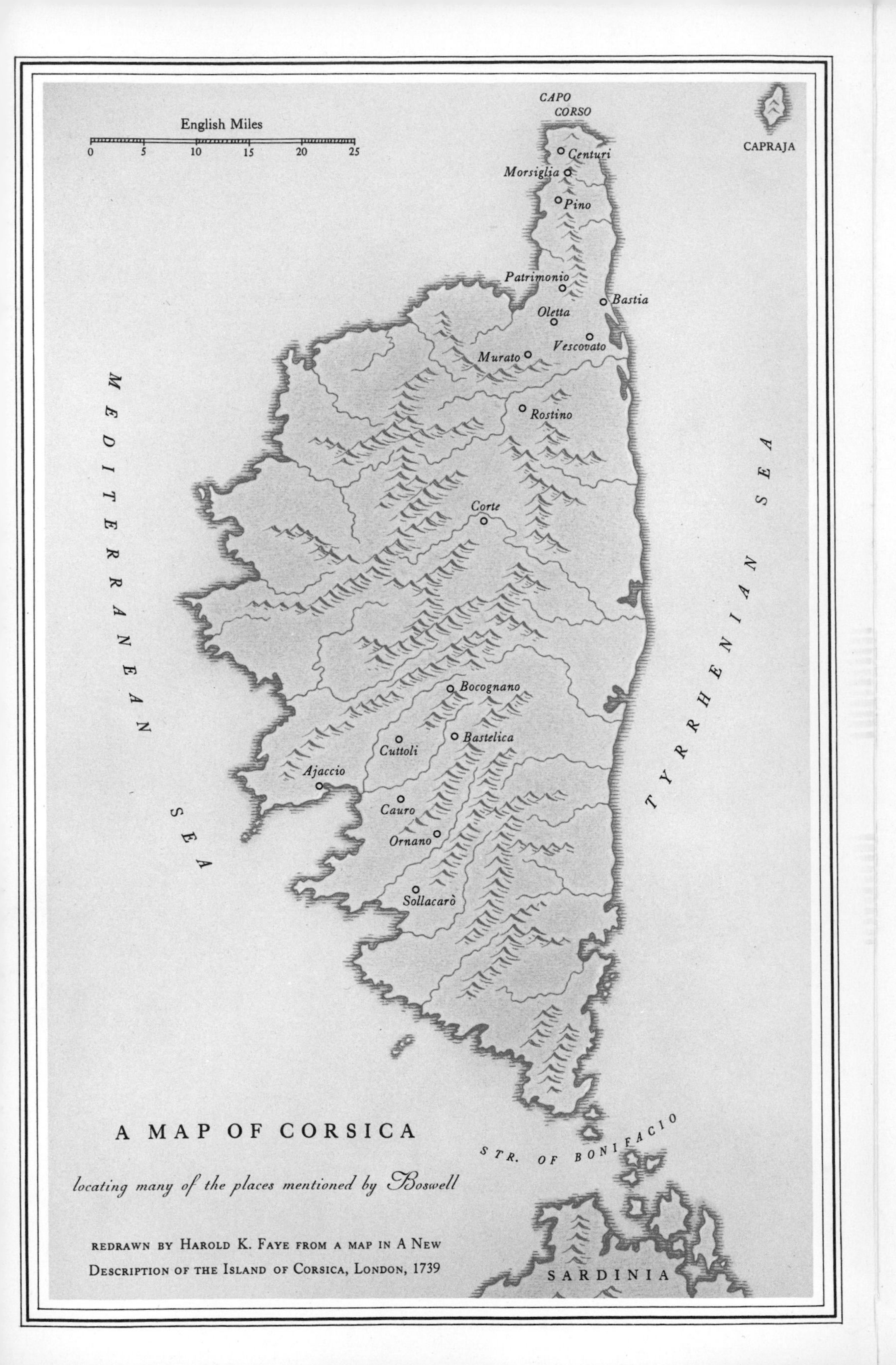
English Miles
0 5 10 15 20 25
CAPO CORSO
CAPRAJA
Centuri
Morsiglia
Pino
Patrimonio
Bastia
Oletta
Vescovato
Murato
Rostino
MEDITERRANEAN SEA
TYRRHENIAN SEA
Corte
Bocognano
Bastelica
Cuttoli
Ajaccio
Cauro
Ornano
Sollacarò
STR. OF BONIFACIO
SARDINIA
A MAP OF CORSICA
locating many of the places mentioned by Boswell
REDRAWN BY HAROLD K. FAYE FROM A MAP IN A NEW DESCRIPTION OF THE ISLAND OF CORSICA, LONDON, 1739

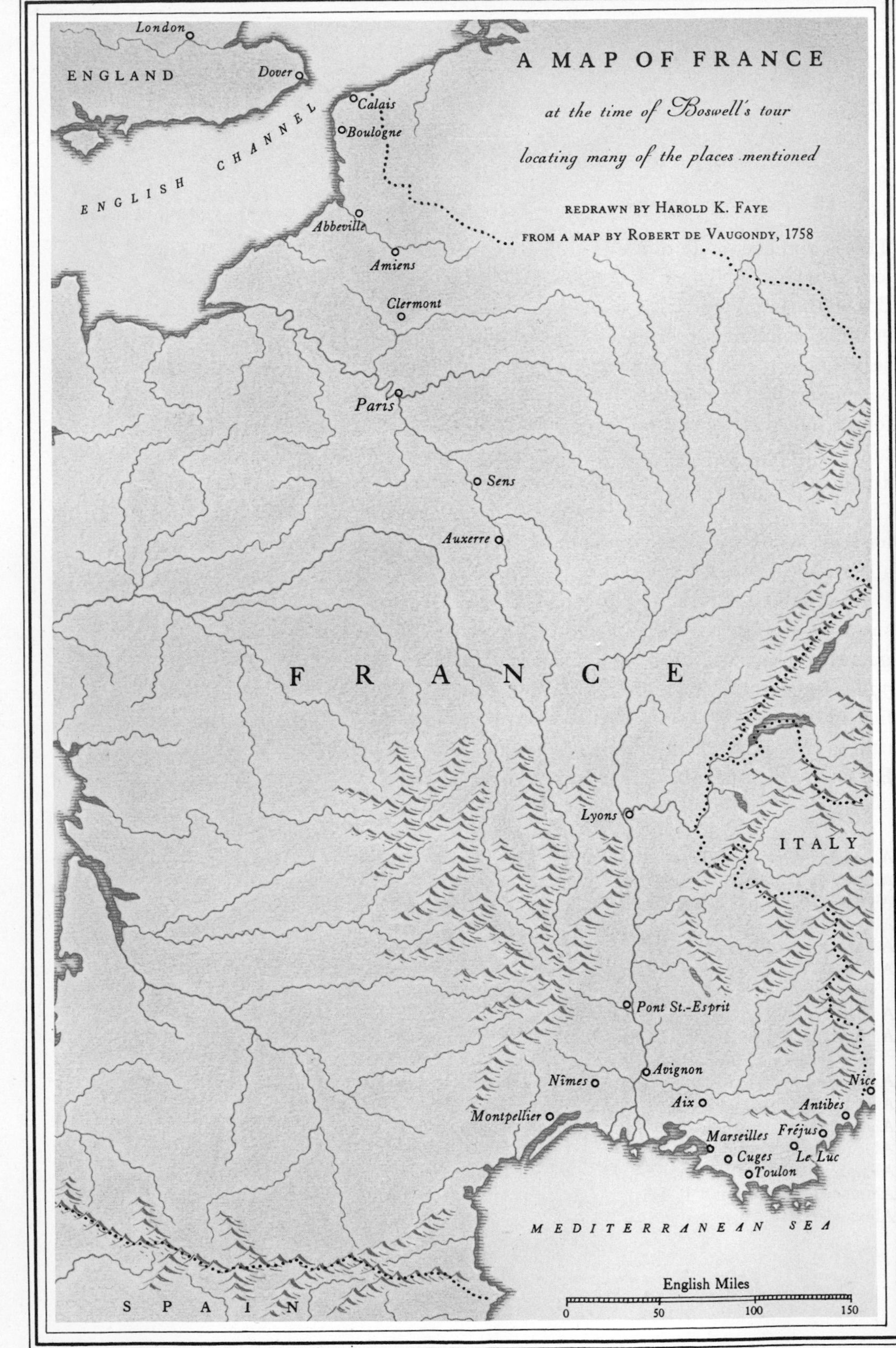
London
ENGLAND
Dover
Calais
Boulogne
ENGLISH CHANNEL
A MAP OF FRANCE
at the time of Boswell's tour
locating many of the places mentioned
REDRAWN BY HAROLD K. FAYE
FROM A MAP BY ROBERT DE VAUGONDY, 1758
Abbeville
Amiens
Clermont
Paris
Sens
Auxerre
FRANCE
Lyons
ITALY
Pont St.-Esprit
Avignon
Nîmes
Aix
Nice
Antibes
Montpellier
Marseilles
Fréjus
Cuges
Le Luc
Toulon
MEDITERRANEAN SEA
SPAIN
English Miles
0 50 100 150

# INDEX

This is in the main an index of proper names, with a certain number of subject articles, but Part I of the article BOSWELL, JAMES collects and digests Boswell's references to his states of mind, traits of character, opinions, general observations, experiences with unnamed persons and places, &c. Observations on specified persons and places are ordinarily entered under the person or place in question; for example, Boswell's opinions of Paoli will be found under Paoli and not under Boswell. Churches, inns, streets, mountains, &c. are given separate articles in the main alphabet. Popes, emperors, kings, Italian rulers, and British princes of the blood are entered under their Christian names; other princes (even when sovereign), noblemen, and lords of session and their wives, under their titles. The styles chosen are usually those proper to 1765–1766. Well-known names (e.g., Rome, Philip of Parma) have been anglicized in cases where it was thought that English-speaking readers would be more accustomed to the English forms. Maiden names of married women are given in parentheses. Titles of books are listed under the name of the author, except where the author has not been identified in the text or notes, in which case a cross reference is given from the title to the author. The following abbreviations are employed: D. (Duke), E. (Earl), M. (Marquess), V. (Viscount), JB (James Boswell).

Semedei, Ruggero, ship captain, 209

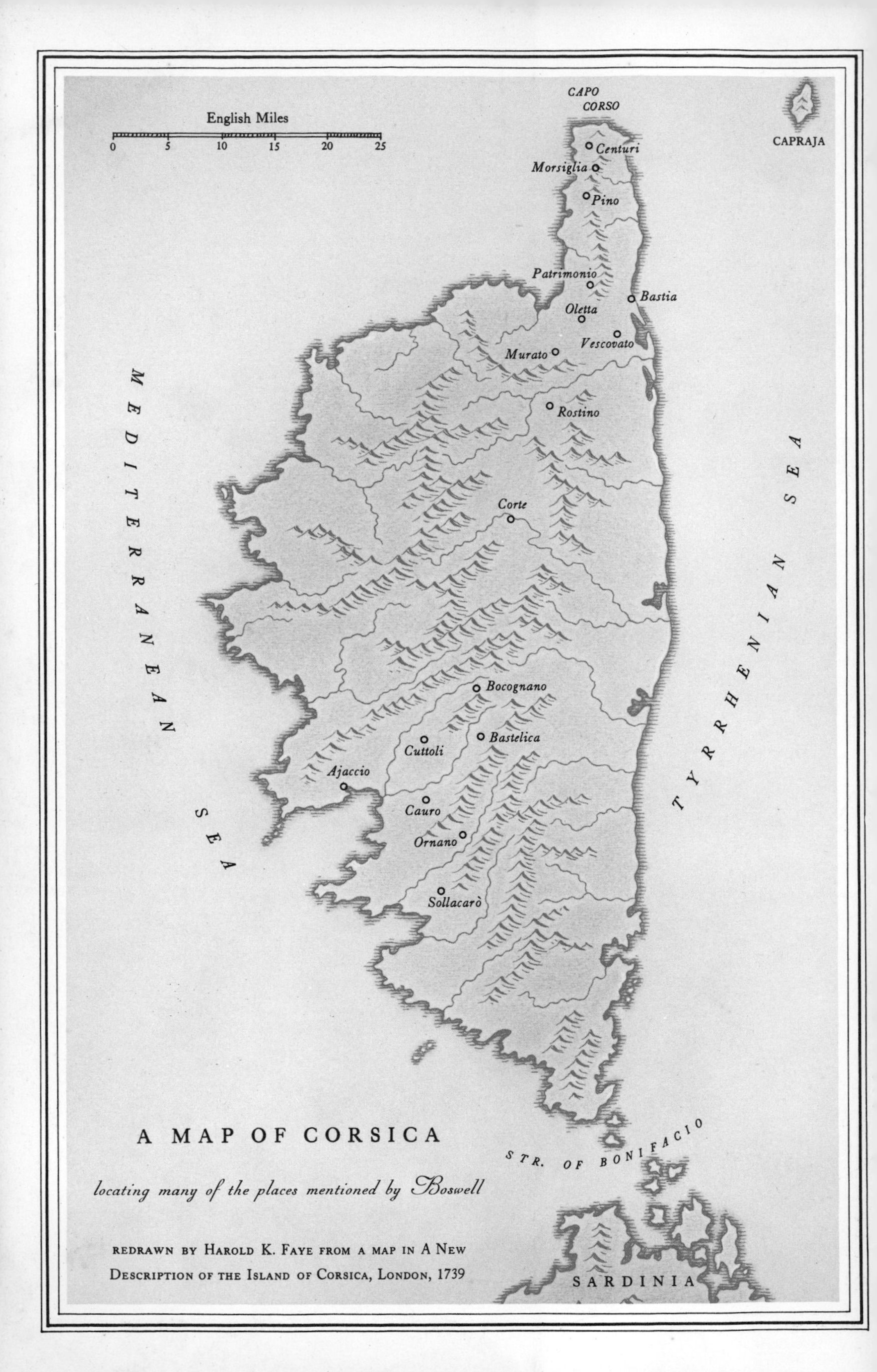


A MAP OF CORSICA

*locating many of the places mentioned by Boswell*

REDRAWN BY HAROLD K. FAYE FROM A MAP IN A NEW DESCRIPTION OF THE ISLAND OF CORSICA, LONDON, 1739